Jerome Gratian

St Teresa of Avila's Friend

Carlos Ros

Translated by
John McGowan OCD

First published in Great Britain in 2016
by ST PAULS PUBLISHING
ST PAULS by Westminster Cathedral
Morpeth Terrace, Victoria
London SW1P 1EP
Ph: +44 (0)207978 4300
www.stpauls.org.uk

ST PAULS PUBLISHING
Moyglare Road, Maynooth
Co. Kildare, Ireland
Ph: +353 (1) 628 5933
www.stpauls.ie

First published in Spanish as *Jerónimo Gracián*
El amigo de Teresa de Jesús in 2006

ISBN 978-1-910365-15-1

A CIP catalogue record for this book is available from the British

Layout by Pagewise
Printed by Ashford Print & Publishing Services, Hampshire, UK.

ST PAULS is an activity of the priests and brothers of the Society of St Paul
who proclaim the Gospel through the media of social communication

To my mother, who will read this book in heaven.
To the Carmelite Nuns in Seville,
with gratitude and affection.

Contents

TRANSLATOR'S PREFACE

In 2009 I asked the Postulator for the Causes of our Carmelite Saints, Fr Ildefonso Moriones, how far had the cause of Jerome Gratian got – the process for his beatification began in Brussels in 1999. He told me it was going nowhere until the man was better known. The problem is that Gratian was expelled from his Order four hundred years ago, and since that time very little has been written about him; indeed, as the title of this book suggests, he has been forgotten. I translated this biography by Carlos Ros in the hope that it will be one small step in making Gratian better known. He deserves to be better known as he did so much to establish the Discalced Carmelite Order.

I am grateful to the author, Carlos Ros, for his permission to translate the book. To date I know of no other substantial biography on Gratian. The entire Carmelite family owes him a huge debt of gratitude. The Order also owes a huge debt to the Carmelite, Fr Juan Luis Astigarraga OCD. He spent seven years researching in archives and libraries in Spain, Belgium and Italy, including those of the Vatican and the Spanish Embassy in Rome. I was present in the Eternal City when he presented his findings (cf. *Monumenta Historica Carmeli Teresiani*, Vol. XIX). Listening to him I was convinced of the grave injustice inflicted on Gratian by his own Order. It is late but it is not too late to tell the whole story and why he should never have been expelled.

I have added the occasional footnotes for those not familiar with Spanish history and culture. I would like to thank the following for their help: Fathers Stephen Watson OCD, Antonio Fortes OCD, Sean Conlon OCD and Philip McParland. Also, Sr Margarita Salinas, Mgr Aidan Turner, Mrs Françoise Forster, Vivienne Hamilton, Letty Wicks, Angela Rogerson and Margaret McNulty, and especially Monica Bratt for her kindness and professionalism in preparing this book for publication.

John McGowan OCD

15th December 2015; 16th Anniversary of Gratian's restoration to the Order
Tabor Retreat Centre,
Preston, England

CHAPTER ONE

The Unknown Man

'Jerome Gratian the man in St Teresa of Avila's life.' This is the way I entitled this biography about the great but unknown person of the (Carmelite) Reform. Gratian was Teresa of Jesus' man, 'her man' according to those who knew Teresa well. Historically, the outstanding figure of St John of the Cross has been associated with St Teresa and with good reason. However, many people will be surprised to learn that not only did she have many more dealings with Jerome Gratian but, that she had a much deeper relationship with him than with St John of the Cross. It was to him, not to St John of the Cross, that Teresa confided how she understood the Reform she had begun. She depended on Gratian. She promised obedience to him. He was the man she had been looking for; Jerome Gratian was her man.

I suspect this might surprise some or seem novel but it is true. I hope this will become clearer as you go through these pages in which I shall try to make this man better known; a man who has not only been forgotten, but humiliated and vilified.

When Teresa met Gratian it was as if she were wounded by some kind of arrow. In her *Spiritual Testimonies* (36.2) she described this friendship as divinely inspired; she even had a vivid image of Christ as a 'matchmaker'. 'The Lord took our right hands,' she said, 'and with our hands joined He told me that He wanted Fr Jerome Gratian to be in His place for the rest of my life and that both of us should conform ourselves to one another in everything.'

Teresa described Gratian to Rossi, the General of the Carmelite Order as 'an angel', who made her happy in her old age. To King Philip II she confessed, 'Truly he seems to me to be a man sent by God and by His Blessed Mother... to help me, because for more than seventeen years I have suffered alone from these Fathers of the Cloth and I can bear it no longer; my own weak efforts were insufficient'.

Jerome Gratian of the Mother of God
An oil portrait on copper.
Discalced Carmelite Nuns, Seville.

The 'Fathers of the Cloth' are the Calced Carmelites with whom Teresa struggled in the first years of the Reform. In spite of his youth, Jerome was to be her support and shield in undertaking to develop the Reform. She was twice his age: Teresa was sixty, Jerome thirty.

I do not wish to compare the figures of Jerome Gratian and John of the Cross, nor give a distorted picture. Teresa's heart was large and generous; it overflowed with affection and emotions. In her feminine heart there was enough room for John of the Cross, Gratian and many others who had helped her with her desired Reform. St John of the Cross was her *little Seneca* because of his small stature. He was a saint in Teresa's eyes, 'a heavenly and divine man,' she told Anne of Jesus, another of Teresa's favourites. She will admit, 'I have not found anyone like him in the whole of Castile, or so much fervour on the way to heaven.' In a letter to the nuns in Beas she writes, 'My Father, John of the Cross, for in truth he is the father of my soul.' However *my Paul*, the code name she gave Gratian, is clearly her favourite. In her *Book of Foundations* she dedicated the whole of chapter 23 to him, in which she says, 'He is a man of great learning, understanding and modesty. He has been virtuous all his life.'

What can I say? this is how I see Teresa's relationship with Gratian. I know that many Carmelites in the past and still today will agree. What I have written in this biography is based on documentary evidence. Today Gratian is esteemed in his Carmelite Order as a saint, even a great saint. I have written about his life with great fervour because his life was a series of adventures which did not finish when he was expelled from the Discalced Carmelite Order, but continued with his journey to Rome, his capture in Tunis and his exile in Belgium, where he was welcomed, interestingly by the Calced Carmelites in Brussels, where he died. Jerome was gifted by nature, which he inherited from both his father and mother. He had a gentle demeanour and was kind-hearted, which was sometimes mistaken for naïvety. As Bishop Palafox said of him: *Speculum mirabile adversitatum et afflicionum, (he was an admirable mirror of adversity and afflictions).* During his life his adversaries 'roughed him up a little' to use a modern expression. In spite of this he maintained his integrity and did not write about the terrible lies and abuses he suffered at the hands of his fellow friars, even when he wrote his autobiography, *The Pilgrimage of Anastasius*, published at the end of his life.

St Teresa of Jesus
Detail of an oil painting by John of the Miserere. Discalced Carmelite Nuns, Seville.

Teresa of Avila, who never came to know the way Jerome was persecuted, had already warned him, 'Be tougher and don't be so naïve!' Again she wrote elsewhere, 'In time you will lose a little of your naivety, which I understand is because you are holy.' However, he did not know how to change even though on one occasion he confessed to a friendly friar that 'I have been maligned now for years and my face has become hardened.' However, neither the wickedness of certain friars nor personal misfortune changed the attitude of this 'noble gentleman of faith' (Fr Silverio), 'this modern day Job' (Carmelite Chronicles). He always forgave people; he never repaid in kind those who slapped him in the face. In the words of Donazar, 'nothing distracted his soul from those high ideals that converted him into an angel.'

It was Anselm Donazar who awoke in me a desire to delve into the life of this outstanding figure. Donazar's book *Principio y fin de una Reforma*[1] came into my possession some time ago. It was published almost secretly in Bogota (Colombia) in 1968, with a meagre printing of just five hundred copies. I was struck by the courage of the author who, forty years ago, drew people's attention to the secrets of the Reform. Donazar's book challenged the official account of the Carmelite Chronicles and gave me a great interest in the person of Jerome Gratian. I decided to dedicate my time to write his biography, to extol such a fascinating yet unknown character from the sixteenth century.

Donazar states in his book, 'To write a biography of this person would be a tempting task for a writer.' And so Fr Donazar, I have fallen into this temptation. I was determined to write this book or die in the process. I say this because it was not easy to delve into the life of such a highly complex character, whose lengthy life had so many loose ends and who was so emotionally close to Teresa of Jesus, a woman who broke the mould of her day in becoming the archetypal woman, mystic, writer, poet, in fact every thing.

Gratian writes in his *Pilgrimage of Anastasius*:

> You know that she loved me tenderly and I loved her more than any other person on this earth... However, this great love I had for Mother Teresa and she for me, is very much of another kind than the love that can only be had in this world, because that kind of love is dangerous, disturbing and gives rise to thoughts and temptations that are not good. It is a love that distresses and disheartens the spirit, and arouses one's sensuality. However, the love I had for Mother Teresa and she for me helped me to be pure, spiritual and to love God. For her part, as she told me often, she found consolation and support for her work. I would not want even my own mother to love me more than she did.

1 The beginning and end of a Reform.

Mother Teresa had died twenty years before Gratian put these words into the mouth of Anastasius.[2] He referred to the suspicions they both had endured due to gossip, even vicious slander from some friars.

> Blessed be God, Jerome continued, who has given me such a great friend. I wonder if her love has abated now that she is in heaven. I am sure that she will be a blessing for me. However, look at what some malicious people are saying, about the way Teresa and I communicated in such a familiar way, that it was not a holy love. When they did not criticize her who was so saintly, as indeed she was, they criticized me; I was considered the worst in the world. They should not suspect such bad things from a sixty-year-old woman, so enclosed and hidden away. It was because of all this malicious gossip that we concealed our intimate friendship, so that they would not have interpreted our relationship badly.

Gratian's enemies had, in fact, interpreted his relationship with Teresa badly, as they did with his relationship with another of St Teresa's favourite daughters, Mary of St Joseph, Prioress of the Carmelite convents in Seville and Lisbon. Mary was an admirable woman, a writer and poet, whom Teresa called 'my scribe'; she was also one of the main pillars of the Teresian Reform. The slandering that Gratian and Mary of St Joseph had to endure was of much cruder kind than that directed at St Teresa.

What Teresa said to Gratian on one occasion is well known when he reprimanded her severely for her terms of endearment, 'Don't you know that every soul, no matter how perfect it may be, still needs some kind of outlet?'

The Carmelite Reform was different from the reform of other Religious Orders, in so far as it was begun by a woman who had urged men to join. Teresa was the Reformer in the first place of women and then of men. In the sixteenth century this was new, almost revolutionary, when it had always been considered proper that any reformer of men and, at the same time, women, would be male. Yet here was Teresa a woman, leading a reform of women first and then of men.

In order to be a reformer of both sexes she needed a male co-reformer, so

2 He entitled his autobiography *The Pilgrimage of Anastasius*. He uses a literary technique, popular at the time, of question and answer between two friends: he takes the name Anastasius, his friend, Cyril.

to speak, who would help her with this undertaking. This was to be Gratian and not John of the Cross, even though John came into the Reform first. 'Jerome Gratian, together with Teresa of Jesus,' wrote Donazar 'is a perfect example of someone who has a reverence for the Church but, at the same time, thinks like a reformer.' They were both collaborators in the Teresian Reform.

In a society where men had power and where women kept quiet Teresa, for reasons of her own, promised obedience to him in a hermitage in Ecija, while on the way to Seville. It was a curious episode in her life which we shall recount in detail. However, it was done with such feminine reservations and guile that she always did what she wanted. Fr Bartholomew of Medina said, 'She would never do anything the priest had not told her to do, but the priest would not ask her to do anything she did not want to do.' Jerome, her Confessor, knew this well and discussed with Teresa, as he related in his autobiography. He would order Teresa to do something but she would raise an objection, then they would argue until an agreement was reached. This is how it always was.

Gratian had total confidence in Teresa and confided with her about some of the deepest aspects of his being. He would send her his notebooks in which he had expressed his spiritual ideas. He wrote in the *Pilgrimage of Anastasius*, 'I gave her an account of all that was happening in my soul and often I sent her something I had written in a notebook that she kept.' Unfortunately we do not have these notebooks nor the numerous letters that he wrote to Teresa. On the other hand, a hundred and ten letters from Teresa to Gratian have come down to us, thanks to his concern to keep them. These letters are an extraordinary source of information,which enable us to evaluate both their spirits. After her death, St Teresa's legacy fell once more on Fr Gratian's shoulders. Donazar makes the following observation:

> Those who today contemplate this canonized woman often forget this truth [that Gratian inherited Teresa's legacy]. However, if they believe that an innocent man can be hoodwinked and abandoned to his fate, in order to secure the eternal glory of another saint, they fall into a theological absurdity. Had Father not remained inflexible before the tribunal that condemned him, Teresa of Jesus would not have been honoured as a saint. The canonization of Teresa of Jesus came about because Fr Gratian remained resolute in [the priory of] Saint Hermenegildo in Madrid and because, later, he went to Rome where he refused to be cowed by the threats of those who

> had sentenced him in Madrid. Also because years later in Belgium, where he lived a holy and, at the same time, upright life, he, together with those who knew Teresa well, endorsed her holy life. In a word, because he acted from beginning to end *coram faciem Ecclesiae.*[3]

If the Roman tribunal to which he had appealed had not passed a resolution confirming his innocence, which it did after a lot of suffering and turmoil for the poor friar, the figure of Teresa would have fallen under suspicion and her canonization would have been called into question.

> Today there can be no shadow of doubt that had Fr Gratian accepted a penance as a form of punishment, no matter how small, it would have been tantamount to acknowledging his culpability of those things he had been accused of, it would have totally changed history's assessment of the woman, Teresa of Jesus. (Donazar)

However, in the Order's Chronicles it was Jerome who paid the price; Teresa was canonized, Gratian was ostracized. Yet, in a way, St Teresa was also abused by the Order's history; by emphasizing her it hid the figure of Gratian.

'A difficult history to recount' was the title of a chapter in a book by Fr Moriones, *The Teresian Carmel.* I believe this book was also subject to pressure before it could appear in 1978.

> It was never easy for an author of the XVII century [recounts Moriones] to write about the first years of the life of the Teresian Carmel. The author had to satisfy those within the Order and 'edify' those outside. Not only was it difficult to be objective and shed light on what actually happened but it was also difficult to recount the history to the liking of the superiors who were then governing the Order, as they felt almost directly implicated in the events being narrated.

To write about Jerome Gratian (the Order) would have to put to one side the official Chronicles in order to concentrate on the many papers and documents that have come to light. To the credit of the Discalced Carmelite Order these papers and documents have been made known in recent years in books and

3 In accord with the Church.

reviews written by the Order.[4] Today almost all of Gratian's papers and documents have been published. I applaud the Discalced Carmelite Order's *mea culpa* and its purification which culminated at Christmas 1999 with a solemn declaration from the General of the Order, Camilo Maccise and his General Definitory:

> On 15 December 1999, the General Definitory at its 47th session, following the example of the Holy Father in this Jubilee Year judged it fitting to make an official declaration that REVOKES THE SENTENCE OF EXPULSION FROM THE ORDER passed against Fr Jerome Gratian, beloved son and disciple of our Mother Saint Teresa of Jesus, as an official gesture of rehabilitation and reparation for the injustice he suffered.

The declaration went on to state:

> We feel a profound sorrow for these events of our history, especially the expulsion from the Order of Fr Jerome Gratian and his secretary Fr Bartholomew of Jesus, as well as the grave afflictions imposed on Mothers Anne of Jesus and Mary of St Joseph, people who had the highest trust of our Holy Mother and who gave the very best example as founding members of the new Order. It is also regrettable that to the injustices suffered during their lifetimes we must add their unjust treatment throughout our Carmelite history, where their names have sometimes been erased from the places where they have been or defects have been attributed to them which in fact they did not possess.

A year later, Christmas 2000, the General Definitory met in Rome to formally begin the Cause of Fr Gratian's beatification: the path to his canonization has begun, four hundred years after his expulsion from the Order.

Will this book I have written be about someone who failed? Gratian had wanted to implant Teresa's charism, her Reform, as it was handed down to him by St Teresa. However, he was cut down by the astute and cunning hand of Nicholas Doria, a vengeful, ambitious and clever Italian who entered the Discalced Carmelite Order in the priory of Los Remedios in Seville and who was to become a powerful figure.

4 Mention should be made of the monumental work on by Fr Juan Luis Astigarraga OCD, 'Expulsión del P. Gracián, Documentos de un Processo 1587-1601', Rome, 2004, in *Monumenta Historica Carmelitanum Teresiani*, Vol. 21.

Was it Gratian's fault that he let himself be walked on by this man? Fr Hippolitus of the Holy Family thought that Gratian must have tried his utmost to create schools and foster disciples to carry on his work and not let himself be suppressed by his troublesome adversary. However, Donazar contests this:

> This is to think like his adversary [Doria]. If he created disciples it would have been to favour them with perks as Fr Doria did, but this was neither evangelical nor ethical. We should understand that what he tried to do was to set them an example by the way he lived and, by his rational arguments, for all this was there for everyone to see. Moreover, no one who supported him was capable of converting his lessons into a programme. St Teresa did not form disciples or successors in secret; what she did was there for all to see. When she and her principal associates disappeared from the scene the Teresian institution continued to persevere not by a hierarchical succession but by her own influence. Why didn't Gratian's charism inspire the male Reform? Because, while still a young plant it was torn up by a malicious hand. If the authorities had taken away Teresa's licences, after she had just founded her first convent in Avila, or if she had been imprisoned, then the contrary ideas of Mother Mary of Jesus [Estrella convent, Alcala] or of Mother Catalina de Cardona, would have prevailed among the nuns.[5] Fr Gratian did not lack good friends and good disciples but they could do nothing to help, and many abandoned him. Similarly, many of the friends of St John of the Cross also abandoned him and some complained about him on his death-bed. It is not always the best who prevail in history but the most powerful. The ruination of Fr Gratian has created an enigma for succeeding generations, to which as yet they have not known how to respond.

It is said ingenuously about the life of Sr Frances of the Blessed Sacrament, a venerable Discalced Carmelite nun from St Joseph's convent, Pamplona, that one day St Teresa of Jesus appeared to her together with St John of the Cross and Jerome Gratian, following an argument in the convent about which of the two (friars) had to suffer greater trials. Teresa told her in the vision:

5 Mary of Jesus and Catalina de Cardona were contempories of St Teresa. The former had founded her own convent as a Carmelite but she was never of the same mind as St Teresa. The other, Catalina, never lived in a community but as a hermit; she was supported and esteemed by some of the friars, especially Fr Mariano, who opposed Gratian.

> Daughter, do not concern yourself with this, both of them suffered a lot and enjoy great glory.

On another occasion Sister Frances was upset that Fr Gratian, whom Teresa had loved, had been expelled from the Order. Again in a vision the Saint said to her: 'Who has asked you to be God's judge? In His providence His Majesty allowed this for His own superior ends, and I love him … more than you do.'

In God's providence Teresa and John of the Cross attained the highest honours in the Church. They were both canonized but, the third member of the Teresian triangle, has been passed over in silence. However, it has to be said that if St John of the Cross was saved from the plots that also surrounded him until the last moments of his life and was not expelled from the Discalced Carmelite Order, it was because he died in time, otherwise he would have come to the same unfortunate end as Gratian.

The subject of this book was treated in the worst possible way. His adversaries humiliated him, they slandered him, they expelled him. It is a shameful page in Carmel's history. In God's providence I do not happen to be a Carmelite, neither Calced nor Discalced. I have made no vow of obedience to either. There are historical records and documents that reveal what happened to Gratian. It is my desire to write about it objectively. His life, as the reader will discover, arouses passion. I acknowledge that my book is full of passion. I will recount his life and let God be my judge.

Chapter Two

Johann Dantisco, Grandfather and Bishop

Jerome Dantisco was born in Valladolid, 'in a small room in Don Alonso's house' on 6 June 1545. He was baptized in the parish church in Santiago on 13 June. As Jerome recounted, 'My Godparents were a nobleman known as Adan Costilla and Catalina de Reinoso, the wife of the moneylender Hernando de Somonte.' Gratian's father, Diego de Alderete, 'latin Secretary to his Majesty,' was about fifty years old. Jerome's mother, Joanna Dantisco, was a young eighteen-year-old, who had already given birth to three children: Joanna, who died in infancy, Anthony and Luke; the latter would succeed his father as a secretary to the King. Then one child arrived after another until there were twenty in all; several of them died in infancy. The name Jerome, with which he was baptized, already existed in the family. A brother of his father was called Jerome, a Captain Jerome Alderete, who served the Emperor in Peru and made his mark in the discovery of Chile.

Charles V was outside of Spain, fighting battles in Europe. He lived in Worms, Germany, where the Assembly of the Spanish Empire had gathered. In Spain, Philip, the Prince Regent, dealt with affairs of the State with the help of a council. Exactly one month after Jerome's birth on 8 July, the first of Prince Philip's children, Charles, was born in Valladolid. He was to have a sad end. Charles' mother, Mary of Portugal, had a long and complicated labour. Ruy Gomez, a friend and advisor to the Prince and protagonist in some outstanding events in Spanish history, hurried to Worms to give the good news to the Emperor. Philip wrote to his father Charles V, 'At midnight yesterday it pleased Our Lord to deliver me the good news that a son had been born, and even though the birth had been exhausting because it went on for about two days, she [the Empress] is now well; may it please God that all will continue to go well.'

The Emperor ordered that a *Te Deum* be sung. However, four days after the protracted birth the young princess died. The bloodletting practised by the ignorant doctors left the poor pregnant woman very weak just at the time when she was giving birth. Prince Philip, widowed at eighteen years of age, fell into depression. For a month he left everything and retired to a monastery in Abrojo. In the meantime, in Don Alonso's house, the Dantisco family was overjoyed by the first cries of their son, Jerome.

Let us go back in time to place the figure of Jerome within the context of his family, and in particular look at his maternal grandfather, Johann Dantisco, as well as his father, Diego de Alderete; they were both important humanists and there is a lot to tell about both of them.

When Jerome was born his grandfather, Johann Dantisco, was Bishop of Warmia, a diocese in northern Poland. At the time the bishop had no contact with his family in Spain. His correspondence with his daughter Joanna and his son-in-law Diego had ceased years before, as the family relationship had broken down.

After the birth of his son, on 11 July, Diego presented the following petition to the lawyer Ronquillo, who was responsible for the House and Court of the Emperor's Council. It was the day before the death of Princess Maria of Portugal (Philip II's wife). The Court in Valladolid was delighted on the one hand that a son and heir for the Prince had been born, but worried on the other hand for the fate that awaited his mother. Diego requested that Johann Dantisco be recognized as the father of his wife, Joanna Dantisco, 'so that I can take advantage of this when I need to.'

The reason for the request was the following: Isabel Delgada, the mother of Joanna Dantisco, was close to death in the house of her son-in-law (Diego). By this stage she was unable to resolve the paternity question because she could not testify according to the laws of the Kingdom as, according to the testimony of witnesses, Isabel was considered incapable of testifying that Joanna Dantisco was her and Johann Dantisco's natural daughter. Diego therefore presented a list of witnesses who had known Johann Dantisco in Valladolid; Johann had gone there, to the Court of Charles V, as the King of Poland's Ambassador.

The witnesses responded to a set of questions. There were nine witnesses; all responded in the same way. Suffice to quote from the testimony of Maria Gonzalez, a neighbour in Valladolid, widow of Pedro de Huerta. Maria was Joanna Dantisco's wet-nurse 'until she was two years old.' She testified that at that time 'the said Ambassador went around in secular dress and she heard him say that he was not a cleric, nor married nor engaged and that Isabel Delgada (the mother of the child) was young and unmarried. For these reasons she knew that Dona Joanna was the illegitimate daughter of the Ambassador and Isabel Delgada.'

Johann Dantisco was born in Danzig on 1 November 1485 in the bosom of a well-to-do German family. His father, Johann Flashbinder von Höfen, was a merchant. His mother was Christina Schulze. Johann Danstisco was an outstanding humanist and Latin poet; he called himself in Latin *Joannes Dantiscus de Curii*: 'Dantiscus' because of his native city, Danzig, then in Germany. Today Danzig is known as Gdansk in Poland and is one of the most attractive cities in that country, rivalling Cracow in beauty known as 'The Pearl of the Baltic.' Danzig is a spa-town with the charming atmosphere of a mediaeval city. It sits on the banks of the river Vistulla and is close to the sea. *De Curii*, (Von Höfen, in German) means court. Sometimes Jerome's grandfather used his other paternal name 'Flashbinder', a cord or ropemaker, in Greek, *Linodesmon*.

Johann Dantisco studied at the Cracow Academy where in 1504 he obtained the title of Bachelor. He also received a royal scholarship to study abroad. He went to Italy where he visited Venice, but instead of matriculating at the University of Padua he set sail for the Holy Land, disembarking on the way at Crete, Rhodes and Cyprus. After his tour of Palestine he returned to Poland passing through Sicily and Italy.

In 1507 after travelling through Asia and Europe Johann returned to Cracow. He became familiar with the intelligentia of the city. Cracow's culture and learning was enhanced by the support of the Royal Court of the Jagellones' dynasty. Johann distinguished himself as a poet. At the same time he fully participated in the 'drinkers and diners club', which ate and drank without moderation under the patronage of Bacchus and Venus. This hedonistic renaissance reached the frozen terrain of Poland in the kingdom of Segismund the Elder, sovereign of the Polish-Lithuanian confederation. Johann Dantisco transformed himself into a royal secretary, dealing with the affairs of Prussia. Later, he was appointed as a diplomat to the court of the Emperor Maximilian I, who granted him the title of *comes palatinus*,[1] and a shield with the name *poeta laureatus*.

As an Ambassador for Segismund I he attended the Spanish court on

1 Imperial companion.

Johann Dantisco was received in audience by Charles I of Spain, on 21 February 1519

three successive occasions: 1518-1519, 1522-1523 and 1524-1532. The first of these was a secret mission, whereby he disguised himself as a pilgrim on his way to Compostello. Dantisco was received in audience by Charles I of Spain, not yet Emperor, on 21 February 1519. He explained to the Emperor the attempts of Isabel of Aragon, the mother of Queen Bona Sforza, wife of Segismund of Poland, to obtain the inheritance of Joanna IV, Queen of Naples. Johann did not achieve a great deal on this his first trip but he remained fascinated and stunned by his experience of the great Spanish Court, so very different from Poland's. It was a real school of diplomacy where he learnt to be patient, skeptical and insincere.

The second visit was official (June 1522 to July 1523). On the way he stopped off in England where he had an audience with Henry VIII and met Thomas More. He later arrived in Asturias. On 4 January 1523 he wrote to the Polish Vice-Chancellor, Tomicki, from Valladolid where the court was established:

> They *gave* me a better, more dignified lodging than on my first visit. His Imperial Majesty has sent me, through the master of his court and Señor Hannard, four large silver pitchers of wine, as is the custom here. He asked

> me to order always from his Majesty's shop where I can have all the wine I want. I do not know if he gives anything else to the Ambassadors here. I would prefer he sent me firewood instead of wine, which in this wretched Spain is very expensive to buy in the market as indeed is everything else.

Halfway through the year Johann Dantisco returned to Poland without having achieved much of his diplomatic mission. However, he was successful in terms of a friendship he formed with the Chancellor, Gattinara, and the latter's associates, which would serve him well in the future. On his return journey to Poland he passed through Wittemberg where he got to know Luther. According to a friend, Dantisco got the impression that Luther was like a man 'possessed and very alike in appearance and in manner to Christian, the expelled King of Denmark.'

For the purpose of this biography I am particularly interested in Dantisco's last visit as an Ambassador. He was sent to the court of Charles V in 1524 in order to defend the rights of Queen Bona's inheritance in Bari. She was the wife of Segismundo and a daughter of Isabel of Aragon, Duchess of Milan and Bari, and Princess of Rosano, of the House of Sforza. Dantisco was Ambassador to the Court of Charles V for eight years, five of which he spent in Spain.

He reached the Court of Valladolid on October 1524. He had a choice of where to live, either in the house of a priest without a kitchen or living room, or another two houses with courtesan women, which lacked any facilities for servants and horses. He accepted one of the latter for three ducats a week. However, some days later, Charles V ordered his 'chief administrator', Juan de Ayala to tell the Polish Ambassador that the house was not for rent. He, the steward, should look for good lodging for Dantisco so that he would have no reason to complain. On 12 November, Dantisco wrote to King Segismund, 'They have given me a place to stay that is quite comfortable and next to my colleague but just as we had got used to living there we had to leave once again. We had to look for somewhere else in Madrid, but we already know what will happen...'

Then the Court transferred to Madrid. As Charles V was convalescing, the Polish Ambassador had still not been able to present his respects to him. Johann complained to his King:

> Most people believe that we live here in great luxury... It is one thing to be an Ambassador in the Court of Your Sovereign Majesty it is another to be

> one here. In Poland the Ambassadors are housed, have servants and are respected by everyone. There is nothing they want that they don't have. Here you have to run, beg, wait and remain in a reception room and then go away again without having been received, especially in the irritating affairs which are my fate. This Court is worse than the one we saw before.

In Madrid Dantisco renewed his friendship with the Chancellor, Gattinara, who promised to help him. Finally on 3 December he was formally received by the Emperor. Charles V was seated on his throne surrounded by the Grand Chancellor and other Court officials. After the meal the Emperor 'left to one side a book of the gospels and a cross, he called us Ambassadors to kneel down before him. We took an oath of homage to him; others present also did the same. When we actually came to do him homage in person, the Emperor put forward both his hands, his fingers intertwined like a comb. Each of us separately put our hands in those of the Emperor also with our fingers intertwined.'

When the ceremony was over the courtesans thronged around the Monarch. Only by forcing his way through was Dantisco able to greet briefly Charles V. However, he did not have the chance to explain the reason for his visit. The Emperor was in a hurry: he was off hunting. He sent Dantisco to the Chancellor. Such waiting was to be Johann Dantisco's destiny. Following his Court appearance he received repeatedly encouraging news concerning the matter of Bari, which was the reason he had come before the great lord of Europe. It was a very important matter for Queen Bona. However, Dantisco received nothing more than words of encouragement.

His letters to King Segismund and to the Polish Court reveal a shrewd observer and analyst of the European politics discussed in the court of Charles V. Dantisco wrote on 7 February 1525:

> I have never seen the Court so poor as it is now. Money is accumulated by unknown means and everything is sent to the army in Italy.

Life in Valladolid was less expensive than in Madrid, in which you needed one hundred ducats just to maintain servants, a house, furniture, horses, etc.

> None of the servants I brought from Poland wants to remain with such a salary and they ask for an increase in ducats a month if they are to remain here in Madrid where everything is more expensive and double the price it

> used to be in Valladolid. Last summer and this one it is not just hot, it's an inferno. My butler spent ten ducats in three days. This autumn, with more abundance of everything and with the help of the sale of some horses, I have the same amount of money but only for four days. I have no idea how long it will last.

The news of the victory against the French in Pavia (24 February 1525), and the capture of Francis I, arrived at the Court of Madrid on 10 March. Dantisco together with the English Ambassador presented themselves at the Palace to celebrate with the Emperor. Dantisco gave a short speech in German, congratulating the monarch for establishing peace among the Christian princes. Johann Dantisco hoped that the Emperor's armies would now tackle the infidels, i.e. the Turks. The latter had just invaded Hungary, becoming a threat in the East.

The Court spent the summer in Toledo. The Inquisition made it a difficult period for Dantisco:

> The Inquisition took two of my servants. These marranos [non-Christians] were held for five months in prison, in spite of the Emperor's promises to free them. In the end my persistent efforts were successful. They were released on 4 December. The Emperor insisted that one of the Inquisitors be made bishop.

On 10 March 1526, Dantisco attended the wedding of Charles V, who married Isabel of Portugal, at the royal palace in Seville. 'The celebration of the Emperor's wedding was not in the grand style and the Ambassadors were not invited. This was because it was both Lent and, at the same time, they were still mourning the death of the Queen of Denmark, the Emperor's sister.' Charles V spent his honeymoon in the cool of the elegant gardens of the Royal Palace. It was around this time that Dantisco first began to show off the woman he loved. She had come with him from Valladolid. Her name was Isabel Delgada. Later, during that florid spring in Seville, he made her pregnant. Nine months later, in January 1527, when the court returned to Valladolid, a baby girl was born. She was given the name Joanna, the illegitimate child of Isabel and the Polish Ambassador.

Dantisco lived in Spain for about three more years, but never completed his task. He begged Tomicki, the Vice-Chancellor of the Kingdom and Bishop of Cracow, 'I am a captive here. In your kindness do not forget me in this exile.' Dantisco wanted to return to Poland and felt imprisoned in the Court of the Emperor. His beard and hair had turned grey. He wrote, 'I look like a Dominican.' In the winter, on a tiring journey from Granada to Valladolid, with a furious gale blowing, on a road covered in mud and with incessant rain and snow, he passed the entire journey with an acute pain in his head as well as suffering from gout, which affected his feet and his right hand. 'I cannot tell you what I suffered,' he complained to Tomicki. At the end of February he could not write because of gout: he even felt tempted to cut off his hand.

Dantisco lodged in the house of Maluenda, a university lecturer, in Teresagil Street, Valladolid. Isabel Delgada gave birth, not in the Dantisco's lodging, but in the house of Maria Nunez, who was to testify years later that, 'The ambassador asked her to look after Isabel when she gave birth and paid her generously. He also paid a lady, Maria Gonzalez, to be Joanna's wet-nurse which she was very happy to do. Dantisco called the baby girl his daughter and treated her accordingly.' Maria Gonzalez was Dantisco's neighbour in Valladolid, and wet-nursed the baby until it was two years old. Dantisco paid for all the expenses.

The child was baptized in the parish church of San Salvador by Fr Peter Andres de Anguiano. The godfather was Garcia Cocon, who lived next door to Professor Maluenda's house, which was also where Dantisco was living. The latter asked Garcia Cocon to find another godparent, who turned out to be Anton Alvarez. Dantisco boasted about his daughter saying that she looked liked him. The curate who baptized the baby testified years later that he had witnessed touching scenes; 'I saw the Ambassador holding Joanna in his arms, and making a great fuss of her, calling her his daughter, and this is the way he treated her. Joanna was often in the company of the Ambassador, Johann Dantisco, who often said, speaking with this witness [Fr Peter] in Latin, that Joanna was his daughter; he was clearly very happy.' Joahnn would take the baby girl in his arms and proudly show her to his friends when they called at his lodgings. He called her 'Juanica.' As a good Latin scholar he used to repeat the Latin phrase: *Optimum naturale generare similem sibi;*[2] which meant that his daughter looked exactly like him.

2 The natural offspring is the best likeness to the man himself.

Dantisco's right leg was badly swollen by gout. His right hand too was affected, causing him great pain. He put ointment on his hand and bandaged it. 'It burns me so badly that I thought about amputating it. I haven't been able to write anything for some time.' It was May 1527, and he complained about the fees he had to pay to the doctors, apothecaries and alchemists. He also complained about the continuous use of boiling water which damaged his stomach. However, he consoled himself with the thought that anyone suffering from gout was in the same boat. 'These are the rewards and the blessings for the things we have been negotiating for such a long time in Spain, besides I am not the only one suffering from this problem, there is also Count Nassau, the Prefect of Waldkyrschen, Vice-Chancellor of the Empire, and many others.'

The Emperor's principal doctor, the old Doctor Liberal, was trying to heal his hand, but died on 29 July. Dantisco felt duty bound to attend the funeral. The Nuncio, Baltasar de Castiglione, was also present as were the various Ambassadors from Venice, Milan and Florence. As at every funeral where they speak about everything except the dead person, the current topic was the sacking of Rome and the brutal pillaging of the Eternal City by the imperial army on 6 May that year. 'The Nuncio told me,' Dantisco reported to his King, 'how the Emperor excused himself from what had happened in Rome – that it was not his fault.' However, the cruelty with which the troops went about sacking the Eternal City has not been seen since the time of (the barbarian) Alarico. It was a violent and sacrilegious orgy that spread fear and death in Rome and shocked the Christian world.

Before the Court transferred to Valladolid, the King was called a *ridiculus mus*, a ridiculous mouse. It was Dantisco who made up these words: 'They [the Ambassadors] all agreed not to give anything to the Emperor.' Dantisco, a shrewd observer, implied by this phrase the lack of financial income obtained by Charles V for his undertakings against the Protestants. The Court went on until 14 April and they [the Ambassadors] unanimously refused to give money to the Emperor, 'since the money was not used against Turks but against Christians.'

Eventually Dantisco overcame the pains in his hand and leg. His lodgings became a centre where intellectuals from the Court liked to gather, in particular those members who supported Erasmus. Erasmus of Rotterdam was a well-known figure at that time and in the gatherings in Dantisco's dining room they discussed his works and his thoughts while drinking to their hearts' content.

Philip II, the Emperor's first child, who would become famous, was born in Valladolid on 21 May and was baptized in St Paul's Cathedral by the Archbishop of Toledo. His mother was Isabel of Portugal, daughter of King Manuel. She was Empress of Germany and Queen of Spain. Years later the heir to the throne was disturbed when news arrived that Pope Clement VII had been imprisoned in the Castel Sant' Angelo and that the Duke of Bourbon had died during the sacking of Rome. Charles V ordered the festivities to be suspended and asked for prayers for the prompt release of his own prisoner; this seemed ironic, as indeed it was. The Duke's funeral was celebrated in the Church of St Benedict in Valladolid and his imperial Majesty sent dispatches, *in continenti,*[3] to Rome for the Pope to be freed.

A devastating plague had ravaged Valladolid since June. Charles V, stubbornly refused to move, but two months later, in August and without warning he left in search of a safer place. The reason for this sudden change Dantisco suggested in his letters:

> On August 6 the Emperor's butler, Meteneus, died within twenty-four hours. He had served the Emperor at his dinner table only the previous evening. It was then that the Emperor decided immediately to go. Many also stayed away from the Court, but because so many people were dying these people were hardly noticed. How frightened the people are of death!

Before the Emperor left, Dantisco together with the Marquis of Brandenburg, searched for him in the palace. He managed to catch him as he was leaving his room and beseeched him once more to look into the Bari affair. 'I will deal with it as soon as I possibly can,' was Carlos V's reply. 'Which was always the reply he gave,' Dantisco wrote in his diary.

The plague caused the court to scatter; on 19 August the Emperor with the Empress and the Prince departed for Palencia. Dantisco said to himself: 'I don't know where to go.' However, in October he was to be found in Burgos. He wrote to his King on 1 November:

3 continuously.

> Burgos is the coldest town in Spain, for this reason I am attacked by terrible pains in my left knee. In six days I have only been able to sleep for one hour due to these [painful] nights. I have to walk around with the aid of a stick. They say that afterwards we shall go to Palencia at the end of the month. With the weather so bad, the condition of the Emperor is peculiar...

In Valladolid Dantisco abandoned Isabel Delgada and his daughter Joanna Dantisco. Isabel was again pregnant. Early in 1528 she gave birth to a son, about whom we have little information, only that he was given the name John and died aged two.

Chapter Three

Jerome's Father, Diego de Alderete

JEROME GRATIAN'S FATHER, Diego de Alderete, was one of those followers of Erasmus who used to frequent Johann Dantisco's literary circle. He was twelve years younger than the Polish Ambassador. He must have been born about 1499 in Tordesillas or perhaps in a place called Fresno, in Valladolid. He completed his studies in Paris and Louvain where he stayed eight years. 'I had a lot of expenses,' he recalled, 'but with no one to support me.' In Louvain he studied under Juan Luis Vives, an eminent humanist from Valencia and a friend of Erasmus. Diego lived in the same house as his professor, together with a fellow student, Honorato Juan; the two became great friends. Honorato was a committed humanist and was later to become Bishop of Osma.

The two students must have lived in Juan Luis Vives' house between 1519 and 1521. Bataillon states that it's possible Diego had been a disciple of Juan del Castillo from 1522-1524. In order to support himself, Diego later served in the palace of Princess Margarita, the daughter of the Emperor Maximilian, who married Prince Don Juan, son of the Catholic Monarchs, following an ardent romance which ended when the Prince fell seriously ill. Afterwards Diego took refuge with Maximilian Transilvano in the latter's castle in Houthem, near Maastricht. Maximilian was one of Charles V's Secretaries, whose book, *Relacion*, became well known. It was written in Valladolid in 1522, about Magellan's expedition and his circumnavigation of the world which Elcano[1] completed.

Of those who frequented Dantisco's house Diego was one of the most strident supporters of Erasmus. As I have said already these young intellectuals from the Court would meet there and drink to their heart's content. The friars never stopped mocking this intellectual circle. Erasmus'

1 A famous Spanish sailor and navigator, was Magellan's second in command.

phrase in his *Enchiridion militis christiani, 'Monachatus non est pietas'*[2] is famous and emblematic. The *Enchridion* was read in the Court of Valladolid, with the *imprimatur* of Alonso Manrique, Archbishop of Seville who was also the Inquisitor General.

Alonso Manrique was considered by contemporary humanists as a magnanimous man. He was also a politician and a courtesan, a man caught up in the spirit of the Renaissance. He suffered from gout but alleviated his pain by laughing heartily at the tales of the friars which Erasmus described in his book, *Elogio de la locura.* And so when a small book on the errors of Erasmus, just seventeen chapters, edited by the friars, was denounced to the Inquisition, it fell into good hands.

Dominicans and Franciscans were well known especially for accusing Erasmus of heresy before the Dutch Imperial Court; Erasmus was born in the Netherlands. In this said country the preachers and secretaries of State were steeped in the ideas of Erasmus, as indeed was the monarch. In the *Enchiridion, or Manual of the Christian Knight*, Erasmus attempts to offer a method that would lead to holiness, converting the fighter into a Christian and the Christian into a soldier for the sake of Christ. According to Bataillon this book was the 'spiritual nourishment for many generations in Spain at that time', and prepared the way for the Reformation in Germany.

Ignatius of Loyola read Erasmus' book during the time of his conversion. According to the Saint's biographer, Ribadeneyra, 'He threw it into a corner because he felt that while reading it, his enthusiasm waned and his piety cooled, so that by the time he finished reading the book it seemed that his fire had gone out and his spirit vanished. However, there can be no doubt that it influenced St Ignatius, who was converted into a Christian soldier and founded the Company of Jesus, based on Erasmus' idea of *Militia Christi.*'

The Court of Valladolid was infested with the supporters of Erasmus, so that the friars put pressure on the Emperor. Charles V was to some extent also a supporter (of Erasmus). In 1516, when Erasmus was appointed Councillor to the then Duke of Burgundy, he wrote for the Emperor the treatise *Institutio principis christiani*, where he taught that a prince must love virtue above all and hate wickedness, in obvious constrast to the *Principe* by Machiavelli and, to a certain extent, to *El Cortesano* by Baltasar de Castiglione, who at the time was the Papal Nuncio in Valladolid.

Alonso Manrique (the Inquisitor General) accepted a file on behalf

2 It is not the right behaviour for a monk.

of the Holy Office, which accused Erasmus of heresy. He made copies of the accusations and sent them to thirty theologians to study. Later Alonso invited these theologians to Valladolid in order to address the matter at an Assembly. Known as the 'Congregation of Valladolid', this Assembly opened its sessions on 27 June 1527 with a Mass of the Holy Spirit. The theologians from Alcala defended Erasmus, while the Dominicans and Franciscans attacked him, almost forming a single block. Frances de Vitoria had the task of exposing the suspect texts. However, after sixteen sessions with opinions both for and against, Manrique suspended the Assembly, using the epidemic that was ravaging Valladolid as an excuse and sending the Congregations away before they had reached any conclusion.

Dantisco wrote a letter to Queen Bona in which he spoke about the meeting of the theologians:

> I fear greatly that the scourge from Germany will end up here and that we shall be here when it occurs. The works of Erasmus are being discussed by everyone. There are fifteen Doctors of theology here, called together to decide whether the works of Erasmus of Rotterdam should be read or not in Spain. The *Enchiridion*... translated into Spanish without any objection from the Bishops, is being read by everyone throughout Spain. In this book there are many things against Church ceremonials. Little by little this book is gaining ground.

When Erasmus was informed of the Assembly of Theologians by his friends in Spain he reacted bitterly. He wrote a pamphlet entitled *Apologia adversus articulas aliquot per monachos quosdam in Hispania exhibitos.*[3] He had it printed in Basle and sent a copy to the General Inquisitor, Manrique.

Erasmus' friends were also sent his *Apologia* against the friars. 'It is,' wrote Diego to the Archdeacon of Alcor, 'what we should expect from a man like Erasmus, or better still, it is as much as the friars deserve. Our Valdes, whom you esteem greatly, would have sent you a copy, only certain scruples prevented him from so doing. However, he will send you one soon with a letter from the Emperor to Erasmus.'

The regular gatherings in Dantisco's lodgings, which were a festive counterpoint to the Congregation of Valladolid, were also curtailed by the epidemic. However, the echo of the jokes and taunts against the friars in the

3 A defence against articles written by some monks that appeared in Spain.

correspondence that Diego kept up with Erasmus and others including the brothers Alfonso and Juan de Valdes, Maximilian Transilvano, has reached us. Diego wrote the following funny story of a friar to Juan de Valdes on 1 January 1528:

> Some days ago a certain friar of the Order of Saint… [unreadable] asked alms from a Canon in Palencia. The latter believed this would be used for some pious purpose and so gave the friar a silver coin. The friar went off but the Canon asked one of his faithful servants to follow him. The friar made straight for the fish-mongers and, taking out another silver coin which he had acquired under similar circumstances, bought a fine big eel for two silver coins which he then prepared in a pastry shop. The faithful servant returned to the Canon and recounted all he had seen. The Canon ordered him to go back and not lose sight of the friar until he found out what he was up to. The friar took the eel and entered the house of a very beautiful widow, leaving the door ajar so that anyone who entered would not suspect anything. The servant returned once more to recount what he had witnessed. Then the Canon, guided by his servant, strode quickly to the house which he immediately entered, and saw the friar and the widow tucking into the eel with the greatest delight. The Canon, being the funny and amiable man he was, took a chair and sat down at the table and said: 'If you do not want to get into trouble, you'll let me join in this feast, after all I paid for it.' This funny story was told to me by someone irreproachable.

These 'funny stories', as Diego called them, were frequently exchanged between the friends. On one occasion, being in Toledo, 1 April 1529, Diego wrote to Juan de Valdes: 'It must seem strange that I am writing you a letter without including any funny story. But don't be surprised, because I must tell you that after my meal I confessed to a Franciscan friar, and I fear that if I say something against the friars, they will make me recant.'

Paz y Melia, who studied the figure of Diego Gracian at the beginning of the last century, recalled the testimony of Marmol and Nicholas Antonio, and confirmed that 'Diego was very grateful to Saint Teresa for the virtues he acquired.' Paz y Melia asked if these virtues 'were such that they obscured the principles he professed, or perhaps the Saint did not know of his correspondence with Erasmus, and the brothers Valdes, Maximilian Transilvano and others, because the correspondence, besides proselytizing Erasmus' ideas, shows a constant hostility towards the friars. Here and there he wrote phrases of such marked *voltarian* taste, that Teresa could not have heard them without being scandalized.'

I do not believe Teresa of Jesus would have been scandalized. 'Human weakness does not frighten me,' the Saint often repeated. However, it is quite clear that in the letters of Diego de Alderete, preserved in the archives of the Duke of Alba's house and unfortunately damaged by fire, there appears a young non-conformist, someone who knew Erasmus in Belgium, who breathed deeply the air of renewal that had spread through Europe. However, it is also quite clear that when he grew older he became a very different person, who gave seven children to the Church and for whom St Teresa had a particular affection.

Some days later, while in Burgos, Diego wrote to Juan de Valdes:

> I believe you know the name of the Archdeacon of Alcor, who translated Erasmus' *Enchiridion* into Spanish. The ill-will that this work provoked against the author and translator is known even by children, and I am sure that if the friars could they would swallow up both of them. One of them, a Franciscan, a preacher in a small town near Palencia, during his homily began to fume at Erasmus [not a novelty among the friars], straining himself with such horrible comments so as to instill fear in those listeners who might have read Erasmus' works. 'What do they expect, he cried out, those who always carry with them the chirrion or the chicharron of Erasmus, and read it assiduously at their meetings or even in the streets? Have they forgotten that days before, the earth opened suddenly and swallowed up the archdeacon of Alcor, who translated the Enchiridion of Erasmus?'
>
> Nobody should doubt that such a thing could have occurred. However, on the following day when the Collector of the Crusade was passing by he explained to us the text of the Franciscan's sermon in this way, 'It is very certain that the earth, suddenly opened up and swallowed up the Archdeacon of Alcor, to separate him from the wretched bunch of friars; but in the end it spewed him out in Palencia, where I saw him yesterday safe and sound.' So you see what is happening. Write to me, my dear Juan, about things that are not so serious.

The Archdeacon of Alcor (based in Palencia cathedral), Alonso Fernandez, from Madrid (1475-1559), in the summer of 1526 published in Alcala a Spanish translation of Erasmus' *Enchiridion*. The book was passed around in the Court, as we have seen, and enjoyed much success.

We heard about a prank by Diego Gratian on the Archdeacon of Alcor, when he wrote a long letter to Erasmus. The letter was handed to Alfonso de Valdes who was to deliver it. However, Diego summarized the said letter before it was sent to Rotterdam, 'because this man, [Erasmus] who is so busy with such holy matters, would be offended by its long-windedness, and would tire of reading it.' Diego, who had excellent handwriting, copied the Archdeacon's handwriting and abbreviated the letter before sending it to Erasmus, justifying himself before the Archdeacon of Alcor in a letter from Palencia, dated 13 November 1527:

> I copied your hand-writing and the way you write as best I could. If you could have seen both letters, you would say: By Jupiter, even Titus would have to accept the false letter.

Then he added,

> Valdes would not have believed that I had written it, not having seen the letter from the Archdeacon. I take no credit for this, because in doctrine and knowledge I admit that he is a thousand times superior to me. Regarding the letter I wrote, it is elegant, varied, embellished and non-repetitive, which is what I learnt to do during much of my adolescence. I think I have reason to praise myself. If our Valdes asks me to write something for you, I will do it with pleasure as it will be for you.

Two letters have survived from Diego Gratian to Erasmus and one from Erasmus to Diego. In one of the latter's letters he recalled how when he went to Belgium he found the Emperor's palace had become a battleground between the followers of Erasmus and those who opposed him. However, Diego met Alfonso de Valdes in the Court, who told Erasmus that he found Alfonso to be a courageous defender of his dignity and name. In the same way Diego found Maximilian Transilvania to be a similar defender (of Erasmus) in Belgium, in the Court of Princess Margarita.

> After I left my Lord Maximilian of Transylvania, I sent you two letters, most learned Erasmus, in which I informed you of all the efforts I have been making to preserve your good name with Princess Margarita. There was no shortage of warnings that she should not develop a keen interest in you. Afterwards, I went to Spain where in the Court of Cesar [Charles V]

> a debate was stirred up against you, not unlike what happened in Belgium. Also, another Maximilian was also here, I mean to say, Alfonso Valdes, Cesar's secretary, who faithfully defended your cause. Do not let men's malice discourage you too much, my dear Erasmus. It is nothing new for good people to be hounded by tribulations. On this precise point, from the very beginning of this spiteful world there has been a persecution of goodness.

Alfonso de Valdes, Latin Secretary to the Emperor, was like an older brother to Diego whom he held in such great respect that on one particular occasion he waited six months before writing to him so as not to interrupt his studies 'with silly letters from such an ignorant person as he.' Diego was also close to Juan de Valdes, Alfonso's twin brother, famous for his book *Dialogo de la Lengua*, and wrote many letters to Juan exchanging amusing anecdotes and funny stories, at the expense, as we now know, of the friars. The Valdes brothers were the most highly esteemed representatives of Erasmus in Spain. When they left Spain it was Diego Gratian who took up their mantle.

It is not easy to track Diego Gratian's life from its very beginnings and later as a young man. Even Jerome Gratian did not know his family properly; he confused his paternal grandfather with his great grandfather. Perhaps the dates were changed? Henry Llamas, who has spent a long time tracing our Carmelite's family tree, believes that 'part of his genealogical lineage on his father's side was falsified.'

On other occasions, Jerome Gratian was not consistent when writing about the family tree, as we can see from the following example, taken from a legal statement he made:

> I am the legitimate son of the Secretary, Diego Gratian Alderete and of Joanna de Antisco. My father was the legitimate son of Diego Garcia, armourer of the Catholic King, from Medina del Campo and of Isabel de Hermosilla Alderete, from Tordesillas. My mother was the illegitimate daughter of Johann of Danzig, Ambassador of the King of Poland to the Emperor Charles V. My grandfather, a cousin of Cardenal Stanislaus Osio, became her [Joanna's] father while a layman. Later he became the Bishop of

> Vernia and Culmas in Poland. My grandmother was Isabel Delgado, from Salamanca, a widow, who had been married to Miguel Navarro Azpirqueta, brother of Doctor Martin Navarro Azpirqueta.

Jerome Gratian's paternal grandfather, was called Pedro de Torres, not Diego Garcia, who was in fact his great-grandfather. This fact is verified by Henry Llamas from witnesses and from documentary evidence. Diego Garcia, Armourer to the Catholic King, was married to Ines Garcia ('of an old christian family who was known for her goodness') and lived in the centre of Valladolid, 'under the arcade of the chairmaker.' They had four children, among them Pedro de Torres, Jerome Gratian's grandfather, from Valladolid, and also an armourer like his father. Diego Garcia, the great-grandfather, was a member of an aristocratic family, 'a nobleman'. He must have died around 1485 and was buried in the priory church of St Francis in Valladolid, where years later Christopher Columbus would be buried.

Pedro de Torres, Jerome's paternal grandfather, was a nobleman like his father before him and held the same office: armourer. He married Isabel de Hermosilla in Medina del Campo who was the daughter of Pedro de Monzon, the 'Court Financier'. In the war with Navare, Pedro de Torres was wounded in the foot and could not continue to supply the army of the Catholic King. It was his wife, Isabel de Hermosilla, who took over his work. Being the strong woman she was, she persuaded her husband to resist the heads of the Provinces and to align himself on the side of the Emperor in the War of the Provinces (1521). Pedro de Torres must have died shortly after, in Medina del Campo. Isabel de Hermosilla married again, to Francisco Xerex de Godoy, also a nobleman. She died in 1566. From the marriage of Pedro de Torres and Isabel de Hermosilla was born Diego Gratian, father of the subject of our biography, at the end of the 15th century, (some suggest it was in 1494).

Regarding Jerome Gratian's error about his paternal grandfather, Henry Llamas asks, 'Was it deliberate or simply ignorance?' However, he does not venture to answer his question. We cannot figure out the causes of this error, except to say that it is an error and that is clear and obvious. With the greatest respect to our admirable Fr Jerome, the most eminent Discalced Carmelite since St John of the Cross in the 16th and 17th century, we shall hold a veil over this last problem and keep silent about the motive and reason for his mistake. The fact is that I do not know the reason for his error or oversight.

Regarding the surname Garcia converted into Gracian (Gratian), Andrew de Marmol offers an explanation, which is confirmed by Nicholas Antonio in his *Bibliotheca Hispana Nova*:

> The use of Gratian and not Garcia began with his [Jerome's] father, who studied in Louvain in the house of the scholar Luis Vives. The Belgian used the name Gratian instead of Garcia (the Belgians call people by their surname: Garcias, es), and later when he returned to Spain he retained the name of Gratian.

Diego Gratian was fluent in many languages, especially Latin and Greek. He became a secretary of languages in the Court of Charles V and Philip II. He also became a professional translator, translating important works by Plutarch, Thucydides, Xenophon, etc., which were published from 1533 onwards. Diego later admitted that he had to do this to keep bread on the table. In a document written in 1553 he described himself as 'His Majesty's Latin Secretary.' Bataillon, in his book *Erasmus & Spain*, considered Diego Gratian to be the most typical representative of the great humanist translators.

There is an important series of letters that reveal the character of Diego Gratian, written in Latin to Johann Dantisco, the Polish Ambassador and his future father-in-law. The letters are preserved in archives in Upsal University, Poland.

Diego Gratian arrived in Spain by boat after his studies in Belgium in 1527. The vessel he sailed on was shipwrecked and he lost all his possessions; he specially felt the loss of his books. He arrived in Valladolid, his mother's town, where he came across the Court of Charles V. He was employed by the Marquis of Elche, who did not pay him one cent in salary, 'I was paid in food for my services.' Diego was upset to be treated like a poor servant and quickly left the Marquis. Thanks to a recommendation by Alfonso de Valdes, he became a Secretary in the service of Juan Manuel, a nobleman from Belmonte de Campos. Juan Manuel was an able and intelligent politician who knew how to endear himself to the Emperor.

By now Manuel was old. He was the favourite of Philip of Mermoso, and had experienced mixed fortune while Cisneros was Regent, becoming Ambassador in Rome from 1520 to 1522, and a member of the Council of State under Charles V. 'With this old man, full of experience, a young man like myself can learn much,' wrote Diego. He worked for Juan from September 1527 to May 1528. He then went into the service of the Bishop of Zamora, Francisco de Mendoza. I do not know the reasons why he left Juan Manuel, perhaps the latter went abroad on a diplomatic mission. Diego remained with the Bishop until the latter died in 1536 and received a regular salary from him and food for his servant and horse.

Francisco de Mendoza had replaced the famous Bishop Antonio de Acuna of Zamora, who had been executed by the populace in Simancas on 23 March 1523. However, as President of the Empress's Council, Francisco was in the Court and therefore did not step into his diocese until the year 1531. Diego Gratian, his Secretary, has left us a detailed account of the occasion when the Bishop eventually took charge, in a letter written to Doctor Juan de Vergara, a Professor at Alcala University. Juan de Vergara was one of the most important followers of Erasmus, but his career was ruined when he fell foul of the Inquisition.

'I am going to tell you about our journey, because I know it will amuse you,' Diego told Vergara in the said letter. He described the journey the episcopal entourage made from Toledo to Zamora. It was Lent in 1531 when the Bishop and his party processed into Medina del Campo. There they stopped for three days before continuing their journey. The Bishop used this time to reconcile Diego Gratian with his family, with whom he had been on bad terms, including his mother, Isabel de Hermosilla; Diego claimed that he had been treated badly by the family during his absence in Belgium.

> Francisco de Cordoba, the husband of my aunt, [Diego wrote to a Dr. Fabrizio], and richer than Croesus, had maintained a good relationship with my father. However, as a Curator of our patrimony he acted like a wolf among sheep. It was such a shame to find our meagre inheritance destroyed and reduced to nothing by the treachery and neglect of the person who should have saved and enhanced it!

Diego complained in a similar way to the same Dr. Fabrizio about his stepfather, Francisco Xerez de Godoy:

> I am not so naïve to believe a leopard can change its spots, but, as God is my judge, they [Francisco Xerez] and my mother cannot say that they

> made any great efforts to help me. Believe me, it is better I go to live between Sarmantas and Getas[4] than at my mother's house. Sed his satis.[5]

In spite of Diego Gratian's grievances following his time in Belgium he was reconciled with his mother and relatives. The (Episcopal) entourage then proceeded to Rueda where the Bishop went to confession. He did this 'because his conscience told him not to take charge of his diocese without first going to confession.' At supper time they reached Villalar, 'a small town, made famous by the deaths of those leaders who incited the Castillians to civil war.'

Now, take note of this: 'The following day we entered our town, Fresno, on the river Duero, a pleasant and cheerful place.' What is to be understood by 'our town'? Diego wrote in the Latin original, '*Fresnum nostrum*'. Paz y Melia sees this as a reference to his birthplace. When they reached Toro many of the noblemen turned out to greet the Bishop. Three days later, the procession left for Zamora.

> Everyone was dressed up, led by our Bishop who was dressed in purple and wearing a broad rimmed hat. The mule he was riding was also dressed in purple. A mile before the city the City Council came out to meet us, which, after greeting the Bishop, gave way for the Prior of St John's, the Count of Alba de Liste and other dignitaries from Zamora, some of whom pranced about on their horses, and raced in nearby fields. Next came the aldermen, the mayor and those who held public office, once they had greeted the Bishop they marched off. It was then time for the fiesta to begin. [The noise] caused such a fright to our camel that it pulled down the post to which it was tied, his driver fell off, and all this in sight of the Bishop.
>
> The games followed: groups of young maidens, others dressed in Egyptian dress, who danced to the rhythm of the music. Interspersed with them were clowns, jesters, pantomime figures and others, with lots of masks like fierce demons. Among the revellers, and led by the organizers of the games, were children wearing elegant head dresses. The townsfolk raised banners, on many of which was written, Here is the Pastor whom heaven has sent us. May you live for many years so that you will be a faithful servant of heavenly gifts until your old age. Bringing up the rear of the procession

4 Two small towns near Valladolid that were always fighting each other.

5 Enough is enough.

> was a large troop of young men showing their skills in the use of swords and spears. There were also groups of silversmiths, carpenters, blacksmiths, masons, indeed anyone in the city who exercised some kind of public office. We entered the city accompanied by all this pomp and made our way to the church. The townsfolk stood gazing at us from their windows. Some threw flowers and perfumed rose-petals in the Bishop's path; it was like a shower of leaves falling in the woods during the first winds of autumn. The delighted prelate responded by blessing the people, because in this he was generous. He swore the customary oath in the atrium of the church. He then entered and the ceremonies came to an end. He again blessed the people and walked to his lodging…

Diego Gratian was now in Zamora. He distracted himself by reading books. However, all good things come to an end, and 'he had to leave those holy duties to return to the annoying affairs of the Court.' He found life boring in Zamora. There was no one he could talk to about his literary interests. The people he considered ignorant: *barbaros*, in the original Latin. Why didn't his friend, Alfonso de Valdes, he bemoaned, who was employed as Secretary of languges in the Court of Charles V, try to find work for him, even if it meant guarding sheep or treading grapes? In a letter from Zamora to Valdes, dated 13 August 1531, written when the Royal Court was about to move to Germany, he poured out his heart to his friend, listing reasons why he wanted to return to Belgium:

> Firstly, because in Spain I have hardly ever enjoyed good health, which is of more benefit to me that any treasure; secondly, when I see that for a miserable stipend my brain is dying with such ignorant companions, among whom I can't find one with whom I can speak about my interest in Greek and Latin; finally, and most importantly, because in the Court of the Emperor I will be able to use my secretarial skills, a role in which I have made enough progress, and perhaps in this area I have surpassed every other employee. Since you have been away I have rendered good service to the Empress, translating Latin, French and Italian letters, as there was no one in the Palace who could do this work as well as I.
>
> Nowhere else have I done so much work as in Spain, without having gained a cent more in fortune, I am beginning to believe that I shall search for happiness outside my country. Therefore, I beg you, earnestly, if you know of some worthwhile job there write me at once. I shall look for means

> for the journey. I shall go immediately and be reunited with the Emperor in Germany, where, I shall so enjoy your company and amiable manner and get away from these ignorant companions; I would happily watch over sheep or tread grapes.

Diego Gratian de Alderete continued to work for his Bishop, within the courtly circle of the Empress. Fate would ensure that years later he would run into his old friend who formed the Erasmus' circle, Johann Dantisco. Diego experienced many vicissitudes in his life.

Chapter Four

Jerome's Mother, Joanna Dantisco

JOHANN DANTISCO LEFT VALLADOLID before there was any danger from the plague and took refuge in Paredes de Monte, near Palencia where Charles V had taken up residence. When the Emperor went to Burgos, Dantisco settled in the town of El Cid, where he spent the winter. In the service of Queen Bona he considered himself a martyr for the hardships he endured 'because of the cold that penetrates one's bones, it's worse than in Poland.' For this reason Dantisco felt a strong desire to return to his native land. His role as Ambassador had become like a millstone around his neck. However, for now he was obliged to follow the Court, taking with him the few possessions he owned. The Emperor had shut down the Court on 20 February and moved to Madrid on 7 March . Charles V chose this city so that Prince Philip could be invested in the chapel of St Jerome. Isabel Delgada, her daughter Joanna and the new offspring, Juanico, as they called him in Burgos, returned to Valladolid. There Isabel received financial help occasionally from the Polish Ambassador.

In May Johann Dantisco was in Valencia, as this was where Charles V had moved to. Next the Emperor moved from Valencia to Monzon, where he presided at the Aragonese Court. However, Johann delayed leaving Valencia. Alfonso de Valdes, who travelled in the Emperor's retinue, wrote to him from Sagunto, 'I wanted to say goodbye to you, but you were sleeping soundly. Take care and do not delay getting back to your duties, don't be seduced by the songs of the young maidens in Valencia.'

Once again the Court transferred from Monzon, via Zaragoza and Calatayud, to Madrid again. It was there that Dantisco met Hernan Cortes, a Conquistador, who had arrived from Mexico. The Ambassador and Cortes formed a close friendship as evidenced from letters sent to Johann from Mexico. They must have gone out on the town, revelling together on several occasions. We know this from a letter that Hernan Cortes wrote from Santo Domingo, in which he alluded to their shared, sinful adventures in Madrid.

On 29 August, Johann Dantisco received the news of the termination of his ambassadorial role and the arrival of his replacement, Jan Lewicki. He was received at a farewell audience by Charles V on 20 November and given a royal patent with orders to the border guards and inn-keepers wherever he went to treat him well and supply him with his needs for the journey. Johann and his servants were to be put up in good lodgings, his animals fed, and he was to be given money to cover the usual expenses. He returned to Valladolid to take leave of his family and to spend the winter there.

What happened then? Charles V regretted the decision and ordered Dantisco, who by this time was in Vitoria (northern Spain) on his way to Poland, to accompany him on his trip to Italy. Thus we see Dantisco once again following the Emperor, who in July 1529 set sail from Barcelona to Italy in a ship belonging to Andrea Doria.

The Empress Isabel remained in Madrid as Regent of the Kingdom. Diego Gratian de Alderete was in her service, as her linguist. Dantisco was accompanied by the Bishop of Zamora, Francisco de Mendoza, who had been appointed President of the Council of the Empress. Our Ambassador then followed Charles V to Italy and Germany, leaving us this epitaph, *Hispania mihi relingqunda est.*[1] Spain remained in his heart, yes, but he would never return to walk its streets.

At the beginning of the year 1530, the Emperor was in Bologna (Italy) where he was crowned by Pope Clement VII. After the painful episode of the sacking of Rome, reconciliation was reached between Cesar and the Pope. Charles V would have preferred to be crowned Emperor in the Eternal City, but Rome still showed signs of the damage caused by his imperial army. Johann Dantisco was in Bologna, as an invited guest, when on 22 February Clement VII crowned Charles V King of the Lombards. Two days later, on 24 February, the thirtieth anniversary of the Emperor and the fifth of his victory over Pavia, the Pope placed the crown on his head as the Holy Roman Emperor.

Dantisco must have been in Bologna when he received a letter from Isabel Delgada; the first of her letters to him that has been preserved. It was dated 31 December 1529 in Valladolid. She had not yet begun to complain

1 Spain is to be left to me (or, is mine).

about the cold and the distance from her forgetful lover. He had only recently begun his trip. He sent Isabel a letter, twelve gold coins and a portrait of himself. She told him how she had problems with one of her hands, and that she and the children had been through unfortunate times, especially with regards to their maintenance, but she always trusted in whatever decisions Dantisco made. 'Your children are very well. There is no doctor who knows more than Juanica: she is the most talkative and wittiest child in the world.'

On 21 April, when the Emperor travelled to Germany, Isabel Delgada wrote to Dantisco again, informing him that she and the children had been ill, but they had already made a recovery. They had little money so she asked for more, and knowing what a womanizer the Ambassador could be she reproached him gently:

> Seeing that you know how to have children, do not forsake the ones you have here for the others you have had. You ought to know that no one is as truly yours as those you leave here... Your Lordship, do not stop writing to me because I am not very happy in Valladolid. If the baby did not still need breast-feeding I would not have delayed in being with you, even though you are far away...

It is not clear whether the Ambassador had left other children behind, though Dantisco did regret in his old age the frivolous years of his youth.

The further Dantisco moved away from Spain the more he forgot the family left behind in Valladolid. In June, he was in Hamburg where the Imperial Court had arrived. There he received news of his elevation to the episcopate. The Bishop of Chelmno (or Culm in German), Johann Canopetizki, had died in Poland, and King Segismund wanted to give Dantisco the position. Dantisco gratefully accepted. As a layman he had to be ordained a priest and pledge himself before a bishop; this could not take place until he arrived back in Poland. There were still two long years left to fulfil in the Imperial Court in Germany and the Netherlands. However, by now he was already a most Reverend in Christ. On 1 June 1530, Luis Aliphius, who knew already of the Ambassador's new role, wrote to him from Cracow: '*Reverendissimo*

in Xto Patri et Domino Johanni Dantisco E. Episcop Culmensi...et fratri honorantissimo.'[2]

The news had not yet reached Isabel Delgada in Valladolid. She had begun to get anxious at the lack of correspondence from her lover. She wrote another letter to him on 2 June 1530, which Johann Dantisco received in Augsburg on 29 July, in which she complained that he had not replied to any of her letters.

> This letter is to let your lordship know that I have written to you often but never received a reply. I do not know if you have forgotten your children as well as me. You have no reason to do this. Remember how much I once meant to you as did your children. Do not forget them. You know I cannot earn money to feed them nor myself. I never wanted to marry anyone else so as not to give my children a step-father. Nor will I do so until I have put them under your control. Afterwards I would be at your Lordship's disposition to go wherever you sent me. In other letters I have informed your Lordship how we have been placed in dire need, due to the times we are living in. I also told you that my infirmities and those of my children have greatly spoiled the joys your Lordship left me... The children are very good; the boy is already walking and is the most beautiful child that I could have wished for. Likewise the girl is so healthy that it does me good just to look at them. If you will not agree to send for them and for me I shall sell what you left me and keep the money...

For Dantisco it was a question of out of sight out of mind. He was also short of money, in fact, though appointed Bishop, he did not have the money to pay for the papal Bulls from Rome. His friend, Alfonso de Valdes, interceded with the Emperor asking him to order Rome to reduce the cost. And so, an official letter from Charles V was sent, via the Imperial Chancellery, with recommendations from Valdes to the Spanish Ambassador in Rome. Valdes explained that 'because of the great expenses the Polish Ambassador has incurred in our Court, he finds himself penniless, and has nothing left with which to pay for the Bulls.' He begs the Pope 'to be so kind as to dispatch the Brief to Danstisco and in the least expensive way.'

Dantisco received some bad news: his young son, Juanico, had died.

2 Most Reverend in Christ, Father and Lord, John Dantisco E. Bishop of Culmens... and most honoured brother.

However, there is no record of his reaction. Unfortunately, among the numerous papers and letters from Johann Danstico, there is no allusion to this son. In a letter of 16 January 1531 Isabel Delgada informed him of the tragic event, which he received in Brussels on 7 March.

> Sir, you will know from my other letters of the great efforts I have made for your son and how God has wanted to take him away from me. Your Lordship can imagine what a terrible experience his death has been for me… I beg your Lordship not to forget Juanica who, I believe, is the sweetest child that exists between Valladolid and where you are located. She and I want to leave Valladolid to join you where you are. We beg you to make up your mind to send for us, as soon as possible. Your Lordship must know of the dangers a young unmarried woman like me faces, without father or mother and without relatives or friends. I have only your Lordship to turn to who has always been kind to me. Juanica never stops asking me to beg your Lordship not to forget her, so, do not forget her from now on…

We know from Isabel Delgada's letters to Johann Dantisco that it snowed a lot that spring in Valladolid. Dantisco was very busy with his work in the Imperial Court in Brussels. However, apart from the snow we know that nothing else had changed: Isabel continued to write complaining about her terrible misfortunes while he remained as silent as the grave. She told him on 7 May that Joanna had begun to read, and that she wanted to go to Poland to be with her father; one wonders why she doesn't ask that both she and her daughter go to join Johann Dantisco, not least because she found life in Valladolid so very boring? However, the Bishop-elect kept silent. Isabel Delgada begged him:

> I beg Your Lordship, I who have endured two years of being on my own, that I don't want to remain in Spain any longer. And I beg your Lordship not to forget me and what I meant to you when I was still with you and the many favours you granted me and still receive…

There was a new lamentation on 11 July. Now that her son Juanico had died she wanted another one by Dantisco, even though he might have married. It appears that Isabel did not yet know that Johann Dantisco had been appointed a Bishop-elect a year ago for a Polish diocese.

> Little Joanna is a real gift, but that is no reason why I should look after her on my own. She is a really good and fine young lady. She keeps asking all the time where is her father… and now that God has taken away Juanico, I have not given up hope of having another, even though you may be remarried.

Eventually, the Ambassador did show signs of life. On 16 August Isabel Delgada received a letter from him. She was happy and optimistic, even though she also felt anxious because she thought he had forgotten them. She quickly replied to him the following day:

> Little Joanna is going to school but says she does not want to go there anymore until I give her a silk dress. I have gone to ask Alberto for ten gold coins to dress Joanna and to help with expenses... Joanna is pretty and what she says is beyond her years, in fact when she speaks she uses full sentences, and is witty, like that of a woman of twenty-five, not like a child. I am sure, if your Lordship knew what she was like, you would not let her remain here one hour longer. As for myself, I must tell you that I remain very sick. I cannot eat much and when I do I bring it up. I pray to God not to die until I have set eyes on you again. Then He can do with me as He pleases…

All that Dantisco wanted to do was return to his country. 'When will it be my turn?' he complained. Other Ambassadors were allowed a successor, so why not him. He asked his King to be merciful, to allow him to return to his country. Besides, what was the purpose of his being in Brussels, where the Court was established at that time? 'Here we do nothing else but attend banquets, and obtain money in a thousand ways. No one is concerned about the Turkish problem, everyone is concerned only for their own affairs. I, like many others, am dying slowly here.'

Three years had passed since Dantisco left Spain. Isabel continued to play the same tune, constantly complaining about Dantisco's forgetfulness. That winter in Valladolid was very cold, which was nothing new. Isabel recalled it in a letter of 7 February 1532; she spoke of the cold and that she had no means of income that would have allowed her to support her daughter; a daughter who was so proud of her father, and who behaved just like any five-year-old:

> I want your Lordship to know that she reads very well, and whatever they show her she understands it well. She is quite crazy as she does not want to

> go to school if she cannot take a servant with her and if they put the servant next to her she orders her to take herself elsewhere, since she is the daughter of a great Lord and wants to be treated accordingly.

On 23 April Isabel wrote the last of her many letters to Dantisco, which he received in Ratisbonne on 13 May. Joanna had been ill for a month with a heavy cold, but she was now better. Isabel wrote, 'I want to tell your Lordship that she is the most beautiful girl that there is in the whole of Valladolid and the most intelligent. She is big for her age and everyone who sees her takes her for an eight- or nine-year-old.'

On Maundy Thursday, which that year fell on 28 March, they were robbed of everything, both the daughter's things as well as Isabel's. 'I have apprehended one of my female servants as I cannot imagine who else could have done this if not her.' Isabel continued to complain about Johann's silence and that he did not take them with him:

> I promise your Lordship, whom, thank God, I think well of, that if you make up your mind to send for us, that kind of encouragement is all the child and I need and we will soon pack our bags. I cannot bear any more unhappiness in Valladolid. Well I, who must die one day, want to die in the service of your Lordship, whom I beg, for the love of God, not to forget the time that we had together in Valladolid. I want to tell your Lordship something that is beyond doubt; that I do not have any other Lord nor father, neither I nor your daughter, only you and God. Therefore, I beg you, do not forget us. Your Lordship knows well that I feed many other people who are not relatives or children as is Joanna Dantisca.

It is the last letter to Johann Dantisco… for the time being.

Johann Dantisco left Ratisbonne, where Charles V had been holding Court. After eight years of absence Johann now returned to Poland. He arrived in Cracow on 18 July 1532. Before leaving Ratisbonne, Alfonso de Valdes had left him a note that reveals something of their frivolous life; our Ambassador is about to leave for his country where he will be consecrated Bishop and take control of his diocese. Alfonso de Valdes told him:

> Sometime in the past I sent you some gloves so that with them you could win over some young lady. Now I am sending you a cotta, made in Spain by a very beautiful lady. If the gloves have little value for you, you should have more success with the cotta.

By October he was already living in his Palace in Lubawa, a city in the north of Poland, belonging to the bishops of Chelmno. Dantisco, being Bishop of the diocese, resided in this city. He was consecrated at a Mass on 20 April 1533, Low Sunday, and invited to the ceremony the Bishop and Canons from the neighbouring Diocese of Warmia, that he aspired to and one day obtained. However, Copernicus, a canon of Warmia diocese, did not attend the ceremony.

Chelmno is a picturesque Polish city perched on nine hills, with mediaeval walls and a Gothic municipality building. A relic of St Valentine was kept for several centuries in the parish. Because of this they celebrated St Valentine's on 14 February in Chelmno, as the 'city of lovers'. I don't think they celebrated this feast when Dantisco was there as Bishop. In any case, his life had changed, which we sense from his later writings and letters. The way he treated the family he left behind in Spain did not change much. Isabel knew that there was no place for her beside a Bishop; that she was not going to be called to Poland; in any case she did not want to be together with him. However, she wanted her daughter to have a proper education either in Belgium or in Poland.

In order to deal with the mother, the Bishop entrusted the matter to two diplomats called Schepper and Wajanowsky; both of them were based in Spain. The negotiations became painstakingly long because Isabel was not going to comply willingly. She told the negotiators that she had placed her daughter in a convent, though this did not appear to be certain. She asked for two hundred gold coins (ducats) for Joanna, 'or failing that, a sum which would allow Joanna an annual interest of twenty-five ducats until her death.' Otherwise, Isabel would take her daughter with her so that Joanna could look after her when she got old. The negotiators promised to give her twenty-five ducats annually, by banker's draft. However, Isabel wanted the two hundred to be placed in a bank straight away, 'because we are all mortal' the negotiators wrote, 'and she wants something tangible, i.e. in her hand, before taking leave of her young girl.'

There was no resolution. Moreover, the two negotiators informed Dantsico that 'on market days the mother goes around with her daughter using your name among the merchants. She exaggerates her poor circumstances. She even threatens that because she has no money, she would soon have to prostitute her daughter.' It was during these difficult negotiations, when for long periods nothing was happening, that Diego Gratian de Alderete appeared in Valladolid in June 1536; he would add a new twist to the drama.

Chapter Five

A Special Marriage

Diego Gratian, a polyglot and professional translator, as he usually called himself, returned once again to his hometown of Valladolid in June 1536. He was part of the Imperial Court that had come to the city on the banks of the river Pisuerga, with the Empress Isabel, regent of the Kingdom. Diego's Bishop, Francisco de Mendoza, whom he had served faithfully since 1528, had died some months earlier. Charles V was in Italy and would not be back until the end of the year. Diego was a translator of the daily dispatches that arrived at the Court of the Empress, especially those in Latin, the diplomatic language of Europe. As documents in Greek did not often appear in the Court, he made use of his free time to translate some classical writings. He began with the *Morals* by Plutarch in 1533, followed by Thucydides, Xenophon, etc. In the afternoons, he would spend a couple of hours with the Cardinal of Toledo, Juan de Tavera, discussing matters in Latin or read a book in Latin. He wrote that because the Cardinal 'had such a facility in speaking Latin, this was a portent that perhaps he was destined to reach the top of the pontifical ladder.'

Diego Gratian found accommodation in Isabel Delgada's house. He noticed how her child, Joanna Dantisco, deserved a certain sympathy… in contrast to her mother, 'whose customary ways are not really appropriate, and for whom nothing gives her pleasure except money.' Indeed, Isabel did not appear to be a very honest person.

Joanna, at nine years of age, was already showing signs of being a little lady. When Diego saw the girl, she looked so much the living image of her father that he was reminded of former times ('seven years ago and more') when he enjoyed a close friendship with Johann Dantisco and Alfonso de Valdes. Diego made up his mind to marry little Joanna. It was a decision that from our perspective several centuries later appears astonishing. After all he was almost forty years old and the girl had not yet reached her tenth birthday. Diego wrote to Dantisco, as her father, on 13 September and asked permission for her hand:

> The Empress reached Valladolid, on 1 June, thanks to a certain favourable Mercury or, better, thanks to the good and great God who directs our steps. Unaware of the situation, I immediately took lodgings in the house of Senora Isabel, who by chance, is the mother of Joanne Dantisco, your daughter. Every time I look at her, and I see her every day, it is as if I am looking at you. What more can one say? I remember you, and my opinion has not changed concerning your singular virtue and erudition. The girl deserves to be pitied and, for the same reason, to be loved. These reasons have prompted me, with an honest and pure love, to ask to marry her. I request your consent for this.

This appears to be a handwritten request, and evidently it was. As it had been a long time since they last saw each other Diego told his (future) father-in-law about what he was doing at that time, and assured him that his daughter would be in good hands:

> You may want to know what I am doing with my life. I am now with her Serene Empress, doing the same work that our friend, Valdes, performed in the past with the Emperor. It is certainly an honourable employment, but there is a lot to do. Besides the many questions I must deal with every day. I am particularly busy with regards to foreign languages, having to translate French, Italian and Latin documents. When I have finished my work I use my free time almost exclusively in literary pursuits, especially Greek and Latin. There is never a moment when I am not translating, almost every day, for one or other friend. I also give lessons, two in all, one Latin on Cicero's discourses and, the other Greek, on Socrates' or Demosthenes' discourses.

At the end of the year on 29 December, the Emperor arrived in Valladolid. The city had prepared great celebrations but Charles V hardly took part due to an attack of gout from which he suffered badly. There was a war with France and the Emperor, needing money, called together the Castillian Courts. They met in Valladolid in April 1537. Later, he summoned the Courts of Aragon, which met in August in Monzon. In the midst of this meeting Diego Gratian went ahead with his hastily arranged marriage. We don't know if Dantisco replied to Diego's letter; perhaps he received a response from Dantisco's German friends, who were negotiating on his behalf in Spain. On 15 March, two letters were sent to Poland, both in Latin: one from Isabel Delgada, naturally written by Diego, and the other by Diego on his own behalf.

Isabel Delgada complained once again about Dantisco's silence and begged him insistently to write to her. 'Many days ago,' she had notified him about Joanna's matrimonial situation and about the dowry he should give her as a father, but she had not received a reply. Joanna was already mature enough for marriage. 'It is not strange,' she said, 'as she is already ten years old.' It can't be strange if this is what her mother says!

> I hope that the anger you have for me does not redound upon this unfortunate young girl, since she does not deserve it. It is unjust that, while you are living in such luxury, we are dying of hunger. I beg you to write to me before the Emperor leaves here. Please send the letters to my lodger, the Secretary, who has been very kind to us, thanks to you. He has given us money recently. Joanna Dantisca, your daughter, sends you her greetings. Her talent and character are admired by everyone; she is as skilful with a needle as with a pen; she writes well and clearly and does the domestic duties promptly. These duties she is obliged to do due to our need. Both of us are working in order to avoid living a life of destitution. I hope you are well.
>
> Your Isabel Delgada.
>
> Little Joanna is writing this bit with her own hand, Juanita Dantisca.

In his own letter Diego told Dantisco that his daughter would be brought up well and virtuously by his (Gratian's) mother. He told Dantisco that his mother was in Valladolid at that time 'fulfilling the duties of her late husband, who had been the Emperor's chief armourer', and that if he declined to send a dowry to his daughter, at least he should be given an annual salary from the King of Poland for services he could fulfil in the Court of Spain better than anybody. 'There is no one else (I say this in all humility) in the Court of the Empress who could do this better.' It appears that Dantisco did not reply. Isabel Delgada went on the attack again on 23 May:

> It is not right for mortals to continue to hate forever. If, in spite of everything, Your Most Reverend Lord has this hatred for me, it would also redound upon this unfortunate girl, who is already a young lady and

> who now needs help more than ever. In the same way I beg Your Most Reverend Lord to deign to write me before the Emperor's Court leaves, as afterwards it will not be so easy for letters to come here. Send the letters to the Secretary, Gratian, my lodger, who, thanks to you, has been very kind to us. I hope you are in good health Your Most Reverend Lord, to whom I humbly commend myself.

The betrothal, that is, the mutual promise of marriage that a man and woman make, took place on 30 June 1537 in the house of the Fugger family, in Valladolid. For this special occasion Diego obtained for the girl, Joanna, a silk dress, golden earrings and necklaces, and adornments for her head, as if she were a wealthy bride. The guest of honour was the Bishop of Palencia, Luis Vaca. Also attending was Alfonso Polo, Master of Sacred Theology, Preacher to His Imperial Majesty and Canon of Cuenca Cathedral. It was the latter who united 'in the bonds of marriage the dear Diego Gratian de Alderete, Secretary to the Emperor, son of the late Peter de Torres and Isabel Hermosilla, to the no less dear Joanna de Curiis Dantisco, daughter of the Rev. and very illustrious Lord, Bishop of Chelmo, Ambassador and Councillor of his most Serene Majesty, King of Poland, and Isabel Delgada, Spinster.' Attending the bethrothal were, Gaspar Wayler, of the Fugger Company, Christobel Peutinguer, of the of the Welters Company, Albert Cuon and John of Obenburg, Secretary to the Emperor, Gonzalo Perez and Juan Antonio de Taxis and many others. The marriage certificate, duly signed and sealed by a notary, was sent to Johann Dantisco so that he would be informed.

A series of letters from Dantisco's friends arrived in Poland, singing the praises of Gratian and approving of the marriage with Johann's daughter. Reinald Strozi, a merchant, told him that Diego Gratian 'knowing that she was the daughter of your Lordship, did not want to wait for a decision or the obligatory recompense, but acted like the virtuous man he is and left everything in the hands of your Lordship; in whose debt I remain, in all humility, of your Lordship's great generosity and kindness.'

Gonzalo Perez, Secretary to Charles V and Philip II and father of the infamous Antonio Perez,[1] esteemed Diego as a man of great virtue. He reminded Dantisco of his 'esteem and affection for Gratian and for all his

1 Antonio Perez (1539-1611) was famous for his principal role in the murder of Don Juan of Austria's Secretary, in 1578. He was later arrested for this, as was the Princess of Eboli.

friends studying humanities.' It is with affection and respect for you that 'he is marrying your natural daughter, who was abandoned, without a dowry. You had left her without support, from you or from anyone else.' Yes, Gratian married Joanna. It was not 'in expectation of a reward (that is what people now value more than anything all over the world), but only because she is your daughter.' Therefore, Gonzalo pleaded, 'in view of your dignity and my affection for your daughter and son-in-law, you would do well, in keeping with your piety, to care for your daughter and, in your kindness look after your son-in-law. If you agree then it will be seen that you will have done something worthy and you will have helped both of them in a singular way. As for me, I am so much in your debt that there is no one in Spain who appreciates you more than I.'

Alphonse Polo, a Canon at Cuenca cathedral, suggested that this union was divinely inspired, and told Dantisco as much. 'During the feast of St Peter, having brought our friends together in the Fugger's house, by the grace of God, Diego happily and joyfully, and in the presence of the Bishop of Palencia and in mine, took Joanna for his bride. No expense was spared at the ceremony. Dantisco did this not only without a dowry, but also dressed Joanna at his own expense with gold, precious stones and silk, until she looked like a very wealthy woman. He holds you in great esteem and recalls your friendship of former days!' The Bishop of Palencia wrote of his involvement in the very elaborate engagement ceremony, 'the girl reminds me so much of you. I could recognize you in her.'

Diego also wrote to his father-in-law. He had married Joanna in haste and without paternal consent, because, it seems, he was under so much pressure. The Emperor was going to Aragon and he had to accompany him. He could not leave Dantisco's daughter in the rather delicate situation in which she found herself. By celebrating a betrothal he managed to save Joanna from her mother and bring her to his own home, so that Joanna could be educated by his (own) mother, until such time as she grew into a woman. Diego wrote to Dantisco:

> I have been waiting every day, or better every hour, for your letter in response to the one I sent you, with many copies. However, seeing that time was passing and the Emperor had prepared his journey to Aragon, on which I was to accompany him, the first thing I had to do was to get your daughter, Joanna Dantisca, away from her mother. With all respect, to take her as my wife was something I had to do, even though afterwards I had to

> go away. Thus on 30 June, a group of friends of the highest authority, whose dignified presence honoured my betrothal, came together in the house of the Fugger family, as it was a convenient place. It was with much optimism that I took your daughter as my wife. The following day, with great dignity, I sent her with my mother, who is a very respectable and honest woman, to a villa near Medina del Campo. My mother has a house and land there, so Joanna will live with her and learn good customs and manners as well as the duties of an upright woman. She would not have learned these things with her mother, Isabel.
>
> Meanwhile, I shall endeavour to ensure that the same Isabel will become a good woman by a change of lifestyle, which she fully promises to do when she gets your support and generosity, of which we assured her.
>
> Goodbye, Reverend Bishop.

The young girl was taken to Pozaldez, near Medina del Campo, where she lived with Diego's mother and another girl who was the same age. Joanna wrote from Pozaldez to greet her father and tell him of her new situation as someone engaged to be married.

> Since the Secretary, my Lord and husband, writes a lot to your most Reverend Lord, I shall be brief and just ask that you remember me... Right now I am in Pozaldez with my mother-in-law who is the widow of an armourer, and a very respectable lady. She keeps me busy in serving the Lord and with other offices of an honourable woman. She makes me spend hours in prayer each day like a nun and takes me to Mass with her. She also teaches me to embroider and sew and spin. Though I am held in as much honour and respect as could be, nonetheless I would be even more so if your Most Reverend Lord would acknowledge me, which is not an unreasonable request. I hope and beg your most Reverend Lord to write me and remember my mother by helping her. She is already very withdrawn, as she waits upon the kindness of your Lordship to make use of her person in the service of God, and so honour her and me... Joanna de Curiis Dantisca.

All the letters that reached Bishop Dantisco, including those from his German friends, were in praise of Diego and what he did by taking in the abandoned daughter. There was however one exception; Peter de Montroy who was Dantisco's Administrator and Secretary and who later worked for the Chancellery of Nicholas Perrenot de Granvela. He wrote to the Bishop on 12 September, from Monzon, where the Court was established. Peter de Montroy told Dantisco that he had not been to the ceremony because he had not been invited, 'but those who did go told me about the tragedy and Isabel herself told me about it.' He launched into an insidious attack:

> What did Gratian hope to gain by taking Joanna? Did he hope for a reward or to have her as a prisoner of love? The girl is certainly graceful and has a kind of beauty that you do not often find in Valladolid. However, I am telling you what some people are saying, that I myself do not agree with, that he suffers from 'bad french,' or, to be more precise, 'Hispanic', as Gratian himself is Spanish.

When Diego learnt about this slander he was hurt. He wrote an angry letter to Dantisco: 'bad french' meant syphilis. Diego protested that he did not have syphilis; as in fact his long marriage would confirm. However at the time…

Charles V left Valladolid on 22 July for Aragon where he held Court in Monzon. In the end Diego did not travel with the entourage as he had planned. Instead, he remained in Valladolid at the service of the Empress. He lived there as a lodger in the house of his mother-in-law. Her daughter had already left for Pozaldez, where she was living with Diego's mother. Diego managed to get his mother-in-law, who was still young and beautiful, to restrain her inclinations by mixing in better company. In a letter to Dantisco he wrote that he had tried to draw her into the company of respectable ladies who 'willingly strive to bring her to church and accompany her afterwards to her home, inspiring in her a fear of God, a sense of her own dignity and other things of this kind.'

Isabel did change her ways. 'I can see, Diego wrote, that her previously depraved spirit has been corrected, and, in a certain way, it has been cleansed.' He proposed that she choose between two honest states: either get established in the Court with some Countess, Duchess or person of dignity or, get married to an honest and suitable husband.

Isabel found the second proposition more attractive. She was aware of her beauty and was full of life. She did not like the idea of being in a circle of women in the abode of some Countess. And so Diego Gratian, aided in his match-making fervour by John de Tavera, a cousin of the Cardinal of Toledo, found her a husband. He was called Martin Navarro, a native of Navare, who had recently returned from Italy. He was the first cousin of Doctor Navarro, the Professor of Pontifical Law at Salamanca University, where he occupied the most important chair, 'which was tantamount to saying that he was held in the highest esteem and that he was paid more than the other professors.' Martin Navarro was the principal groomsman of Diego de Acevedo, the son of the late Archbishop of Toledo, Alonso de Fonseca, whom Dantisco knew when he was in Spain. Martin was, therefore, a very respectable man.

Martin Navarro agreed to marry Isabel. He resided in Salamanca but the engagement ceremony was held in Pozaldez, on 13 November 1537. The actual wedding was celebrated some days later in Salamanca, where Isabel Delgada had been conveyed 'with full honours, in company with her husband.' 'From that time,' Diego recounted to his father-in-law, 'she has lived in Salamanca together with her husband, who loves and admires her as if she had lived a more chaste life than Penelope.'

Dantisco's situation changed yet again; from Chemno he went to the Diocese of Warmia, in northern Poland, with an income that was three times greater. On 20 September 1537, the Canons of the Chapter in Warmia, among whom was the famous astronomer Nicholas Copernicus, elected Johann Dantisco their Bishop. The proposal was taken to Rome, where the Bulls were dated 1 January 1538. Johann would reside in Warnia until his death in 1548.

While waiting for his translation to the new diocese, Johann Dantisco finally wrote to Diego, his son-in-law. The letter is dated 16 November 1537 from his palace at Lubawa. It is a long letter. He described Isabel Delgada as stupid (*imprudens mulier*, in Latin), because she had wanted to sell something 'that belonged to someone else and for cash when previously she had confirmed it belonged to both of us.' She was still haggling over two hundred gold coins she needed before letting her daughter go to Poland. 'Who can be so stupid and dense as to buy something knowing that it is hers?' he grumbled to Dantisco. He hoped that Diego would be happy with his new wife. 'Endeavour, he says, to educate her and instruct her in accordance with her age, in ways that are upright, as is fitting to the honour of her father and your own.'

Dantisco did not yet know that the 'stupid' Isabel had married. He told Gratian that 'even though he had no hope that she was capable of abandoning her licentious ways, he would let him have twenty gold pieces if he could change her. If, with your refinement, you can encourage her to return to an honest life, you can expect some money every year. However, I fear that she will be like the leopard when it reaches maturity, it changes its spots but does not change its ways.' The postscript is almost as long as the letter itself:

> So that in the future you will have no reason to complain about me I have decided, my dear Gratian, that the time is right to make you also aware of the following: that I will give you nothing in terms of a dowry, of which, perhaps you have great expectations, principally because of the mother. I asked her to send me the girl, and offered good and favourable conditions. She was always opposed to this, unless I gave her a hundred ducats in cash. I considered it very contemptible that she used her daughter to earn money. This put me at a great distance from her and her daughter. If she had wanted to serve God, I would always have advised her to embrace a life in God's service, and I would have done what was necessary for her maintenance; she would not have needed to sell her body which she has abused shamefully. There would have been no shortage of suitors for your wife. Although she is far from me and there is no hope of seeing her again, as if she were already among the dead, I shall continue to love her. It is a love that is my due as her father but you have taken it for yourself and, since it has appeared right to the gods that this should be, do have her for yourself. It is not against my will. If I had to send her a dowry I would lose twofold, whereas you would gain twofold. It is enough for you to have gained one factor, because I shall be gaining nothing. However, in spite of everything, I shall not fail to do all I can to support you both, and I shall be generous, but only after you have consumed the marriage. You may already have done so ahead of time since, in spite of the difference in ages, you are both subject to human passions.

The actual church wedding (of Diego and Joanna) was celebrated in St Mary's Church in Pozaldez, on 19 May 1538. 'I Alfonso Martin Palomo, Rector and Incumbent of this Church, unite in solemn matrimony before the congregation of this Church the nobleman, Diego Gratian de Alderete, son of the deceased Peter de Torres and Isabel de Hermosilla, to Joanna de Curiss Dantisco, natural daughter of His Most Reverend John de Curiis

Dantisco, Bishop of Chelmno, and Isabel Delgada, an unmarried woman…'

It was good that Isabel Delgada was now no longer an 'unmarried woman', since she married the groomsman, Martin Navarro. She then travelled from Salamanca to the wedding of her daughter. The witnesses were Sebastian Curz, a German, and Ines de Torres, sister of the groom. The Church was full of local people and friends of Diego. The Germans, who rode there on horse from Medina del Campo and Valladolid, brought colour to the streets of that small town. After the nuptial ceremony, the groom returned to the Court in Valladolid and his wife, who was only eleven years old, remained in Pozaldez with her mother-in-law until she matured into womanhood.

Some days later, Diego wrote to his father-in-law, 'Most Reverend and Illustrious Lord John de Curiis Dantisco, Bishop of Culm and appointed to the Church in Warmia.' Diego thought the time was right to respond fittingly to Johann Dantisco's malicious insinuations. He wrote a long letter in which he went through them one by one. He obviously felt the need to express his feelings, which he did.

> In the first place, he told Dantisco, you accuse my mother-in-law, Isabel, of ignoring your letters, of wanting to sell her daughter and of many other things. None of these awful facts you attribute to her have anything to do with me. I have always acted with respect in your regard, and with a pure and sincere spirit, and not – as you believe – by mutual agreement with Isabel. I assure you for the love of God that I would never even have dreamt of, let alone have agreed to, persuading the mother not to let her daughter return to you as you wanted, and other such things.
>
> At the same time I would like to inform you that until now I have never seen any of your letters, except the last, which was handed to me by my mother-in-law three days before my engagement. In this you wrote, perhaps with guile, that your daughter was someone else's. My mother-in-law was indignant when she read this insinuation and was hurt by the unseemliness of this matter. She cried when she opened her heart to me. I told her not to worry, that I would not be convinced by such a lie. I told her I would be ready to admit that I was not Gratian, nor she Isabel, than that the child was not yours.

> In the judgment of everyone who knows you, she (Joanna) is the image of you; she has your mannerisms, your movements and other physical features. Above all she is like you in the way she speaks.

If Dantisco did not believe what Diego had written he only had to ask his German friends, who were at the wedding and who encouraged Diego to take responsibility for the child by marrying her. Diego Gratian continued:

> Don't tell me that I should have waited for your consent in this whole affair. If we had had to wait until you received our letter and your written consent, your daughter, being so young and vulnerable, would already have been affected by her perverse mother [*mater perditissima filiam perdidisset*], not least by acquiring her mother's depraved ways. Instead she could develop virtues by living with a very good mother-in- law, which indeed she is.

Diego was not moved to marry Joanna out of love, nor out of sensuality, nor for her beauty but, rather, out of compassion, Christian piety and his friendship for her father.

> By marrying her, I have not taken account of the cost to redeem her, when in a more ignoble way I could have bought her as a concubine from a perverse, destitute and avaricious mother. Even though I do not find this at all easy to say, I am telling you what you no doubt already know from other sources. From the day when I first entered as a lodger in the house of my mother-in-law, Isabel, I have myself spent almost one thousand ducats to support them: to pay for the wedding expenses, and to look after my mother-in-law. She depended on me alone to buy her clothes, furniture, utensils and other necessary things, not counting other expenses that had to be met. I did this in order to honour your name as well as mine.

Isabel Delgada also wrote to Johann Dantisco, her old lover, 'I have married your daughter and mine to this gentleman, because he is a very good man who endeavours to serve God and your Lordship… I did this because the Emperor's Court was being held in Valladolid and I truly believed that your Lordship would have time enough (to give permission). Moreover Valladolid is full of bad women, so I had to do what I did.' Then, getting something off her chest, she said: 'Do not consider me, your Lordship, to be such a bad mother!'

Chapter Six

A Large Family

Isabel de Hermosilla, Diego Gratian's mother, accompanied by Joanna Dantisco, had walked 52 kilometers (c. 32 miles), from Pozaldez to Valladolid in order to register her daughter at a convent. Joanna now remained alone with her mother-in-law, without the company of her sister-in-law with whom she had studied and played. As the Court was on the point of leaving for Toledo and Diego did not want to be far away from his wife, he decided, for the honour of the little girl, to ask her mother to accompany them both to Toledo. 'Even though I am well on in years,' Isabel wrote, 'I had decided that I would leave my house, property and land as well as all the peace and tranquility in order to follow them and keep them company. To this day I have looked after Joanna and run her household. By doing this I think I am serving God and they think it is a good thing to do as will please your Lordship.'

'Your Lordship' is Bishop Dantisco, to whom Isabel de Hermosilla, the Bishop's daughter's mother-in-law, had written a letter. A certain John of Weze, Bishop of Lund and Imperial Councillor, who was about to leave for Valladolid in order to return to his own country, had agreed to deliver her (Isabel's) letter. John of Weze had been Secretary to King Christian II of Denmark, whom he had accompanied into exile. However, Weze separated himself from the King when he began to support the politics of Charles V, for whom he became an Imperial Councillor. In October 1538, Diego Gratian, Joanna Dantisco and Isabel de Hermosilla visited Weze at his residence in Valladolid. They had come to ask the Bishop to help and support them in their dealings with his friend, Dantisco, with whom he was still in contact. John of Weze saw that the family was finding it difficult to live with any kind of dignity: the husband could hardly support himself in his post as Secretary to the Empress.

When John of Weze arrived in Vienna on 6 February 1539, he wrote to Dantisco about his daughter and his son-in-law. He attached a painting of

Joanna that he had commissioned from a German artist in Valladolid, one of the guardians in the Court of his Imperial Majesty.

> I pray earnestly that you duly consider them (Diego, Isabella and Joanna) and do not allow them to live in such great need. If you wish to give them some help or send them sustenance, do it through the Fugger Bank, so that your daughter, Dantisca, will be given an annual allowance the amount of which you could stipulate. When the husband dies she will have something to live on in her old age, on the other hand, while the husband is alive, given the nature of the Spanish, he will take everything and keep it for his own advantage or will spend it.
>
> Dantisca is really beautiful and elegant, as will be clear from the painting that is a good likeness. So I consider that she deserves whatever you favour her with. Do not deprive her, because she will deviate from the established rules if forced by poverty.

However, the hoped-for help from the episcopal grandfather never materialized. The intermittent, one-way correspondence was the only link between the grandfather and his family, but by now it had completely dried up. The Bishop remained in Poland, in the cold part of Europe. In the meantime, in Toledo, the married life of a mature humanist and expert in classical languages began with a teenage girl who from now on would live the life of an adult woman.

When did Diego and Joanna begin to live together? When was the marriage consumed? I think that Diego did not respect the period of time he had promised to wait until 'little Joanna' reached her fourteenth birthday. In fact, it is clear that he didn't, because she had already given birth to a baby girl by the age of fourteen, in January 1541. The baby's name was Joanna, but she died prematurely. Anthony, the eldest child in the Gratian family, came into the world in the same year, 1541; Luke, was born in Valladolid in 1543 and baptized on 23 October in St James' parish; Jerome was born on 6 May 1545, also in Valladolid.

On 1 May 1539 the beautiful, thirty-six-year-old Empress Isabel died while giving birth in the Fuensalida Palace, Toledo; she was holding a rosary with marble beads in her hands. Charles V was present at the time and, in his

Charles V and his wife, the Empress Isabel.
A painting by Rubens, copied from a work by Titian. Liria Palace, Madrid.

grief, retired to pray with the Jeronomite monks in that city. He wrote from there to his brother, 'I am inconsolable, save when I think of her good and Catholic life and her saintly and pious end.'

Her remains were escorted to Granada by the young Francis Borgia, Marquis of Lombay and Duke of Gandia. It was there that the Catholic Kings were interred. When they opened her coffin to certify that it was the body of the Empress, there was a stench from the body of someone who had been the most beautiful sovereign in Europe. Francis Borgia's words are now legendary: 'I shall never again serve a Lord who can die!'

We know from his (Francis Borgia's) later life that he was a disciple of St Ignatius of Loyola that he became the third General of the Jesuits and was canonized with the name of St Francis Borgia.

Diego Gratian was also badly affected by this sad event. In a manuscript he wrote in later life, entitled *Speravi*, i.e. on true and false hope, he described the main characters he had come across in life that had saddened and disillusioned him. *Speravi: I hoped in vain...* However, his recollections of the Empress were not bitter; on the contrary, they were pleasant:

> I placed my hope in the Empress, whom I had served in the absence of her husband with no less diligence than if she had been the Emperor himself. Often when on my knees, I would read letters that I had translated into Spanish, some of which referred to the Emperor's travels and victories,

> others to his triumphs and pageantry. She was full of fitting admiration and clapped her hands, her heart filled with joy at the achievements of her husband.
>
> When I was about to leave and took her hand to kiss it, on more than one occasion I heard these words from her mouth: *I shall reward you*. I was certain she would have done so had that woman of incomparable virtue lived any longer. She was born to do good for everyone. However, I did not receive any kind of reward, nor do I hold out any hope of receiving it now because of her untimely death. She deserves to be mourned by everyone.

Diego did at least obtain one recompense from the Emperor before the Empress died. On 10 February 1539, he was given an official letter, written on fine parchment and with a seal of approval, raising him to the ranks of the nobility, with permission to bear a coat of arms. Henceforth he was to be a Knight, and his children and descendants were to be declared truly noble. However, such honours were not of much use in the house of a poor man. I have the impression that he never used or brandished his coat of arms. The shield (on the coat of arms) was divided into four quarters: in the upper right and lower left there were silver or white crosses on a red background, surrounded by lilies. In the other two quarters there were black round towers on a golden or yellow background. A blue-coloured border with eight golden lilies surrounded the shield, which was crowned by a crest of golden or yellow and with a red scroll, over which was a black eagle with its beak open and wings outstretched.

Diego Gratian was now a Knight and had a shield like his father-in-law, the Bishop Dantisco. However, his anxieties could not have been more different. His home had begun to fill up with children but his work as a translator offered insufficient income. Out of dire need he wrote again to Poland.

June 1546: Diego was in Madrid with the Court. Jerome, still a babe in arms, grew up in Olivares de Duero, at that time a small walled town some 25 km (15 miles) from Valladolid, in the house of Joanna de Olivares and Diego Sastre. He was to live there for the first three years of his life.

Diego had told his father-in-law that he would never write to him again. However, he was forced to change his mind when his needs became acute. He had met in the Court a 'suitable and reliable' messenger who offered to take his letter as quickly as possible. Diego wanted to respond to the lies and calumnies he had heard against himself. The first malicious lie was that he had been ill for a long time, and was always in bed. 'From the time I married Joanna I have not had syphilis or "bad French", *morbus gallicus*, or any other kind of illness. On the contrary, I, with my wife and children, have been and continue to be in good health, thanks to our good and great God who with this and other favours has rewarded me in a way that only He can.'

The second lie was that he had sexual relations with his mother-in-law. Those who said this 'are deceitful men, atheists and Lutherans who hate the Spanish... They are suspicious of the Spanish because we stay up late at night.' From the time Isabel Delgada had become a widow she had lived in the Diego's household, as did Diego's mother, Isabel de Hermosilla. Diego was hurt, and denied he had such relations with his mother-in-law, as his father-in-law had nastily insinuated.

> I married Dantisca [Joanna], who was poor, needy, helpless and sadly neglected. I lent money to her mother at a time when the virtue of her daughter had been put in jeopardy and the mother would have suffered dishonour. If I had not come to her rescue it was certain that they would either have died of hunger or have shamefully used the child's body to make money. By marrying her I scorned any dowry that I could have had by marrying someone else.
>
> These events do not weigh heavily upon me or distress me because we did something truly spiritual and pleasing in the eyes of God. He watches over us; He never sleeps and before Him everything is revealed and open. Our treasure will remain untouched, our compensation entire and the experience gratifying. Further, I am not upset because the same Joanna has a magnificent dowry: her virtue, her honesty and her constantly good and unblemished manners which only the gods surpass. She is clearly unaffected, shy and modest.

The third slanderous lie was that Joanna was not Johann Dantisco's daughter, but rather one of her mother's servants and that her education was due to Dantisco's generosity. All these lies made Diego angry.

> There are letters in existence you have written not only to me and to others, but also to Joanna's mother, Isabel, which she has kept. In addition, there is no shortage of witnesses who know you both (which adds up to a lot of people), and it is clear to them from her face and her physical appearance that she is your daughter. Unless you want proof of the existence of the sun,

> there is proof of this from many credible and reliable witnesses, some of whom, due to these circumstances, have met recently to swear this on oath.

A meeting was arranged to obtain official recognition that Dantisco was the father of Diego's wife. It was held in Valladolid in the presence of the lawyer Ronquillo, who was the main Councillor of the House and Court of the Council of His Majesty. At the meeting new witnesses swore on oath that Johann was the father of Joanna. There is no need to keep on about this point! As the popular expression goes, 'Where human help fails the divine quickly appears.' Diego's wife said that she would place her trust in God alone, who never fails us.

> This [official recognition] is to spare you any more anxiety and to leave you in peace, so that you do not have to strive any more, or force yourself so much to deny your daughter, whom any good and noble man would be proud of and want as a daughter.
>
> Very distinguished men hold her in high regard, and the most upright ladies of this Court like to be seen with her, whether that be in church or in the salons. These ladies come to visit her and are happy to be in her company because of the integrity of her life, the innocence of her ways, and the dignity of her husband. Regarding the latter point, I would like to respond briefly to a certain irony: when you say, 'she would not be short of persons of dignity to marry her,' as if I were a pleb, from the lowest of the low and that she is worthy of a better husband. Either you are referring to my country or my lineage, or to my birth or status in life; whatever you intended, I am not inferior to anyone for any of these reasons.

Diego signed off his letter to Dantisco, 'I hope you are well and will be happy.'

The honourable salary that Diego received from the Emperor was enough to live on. He also hoped to inherit from his mother, 'a woman who is as noble as she is rich, who for some time now has been left a widow.'

Johann Dantisco was not present at the Council of Trent which began on 13 December 1545. The Bishop of Upsala informed him about what had happened at the opening. Dantisco's health was not good, and not long after Trent began he died. Having a premonition of his death he encapsulated the moment in an epitaph, originally written in Latin:

> If God disposes that for me it be the year of passage
> I have here in a few words who I have been:
> For a long time I was in the Royal Court,
> I was sent to the Lords of the world;
> Afterwards, two mitres were fitted.
> In the end the body returns to the earth: in which it sleeps,
> the spirit to heaven for unending happiness.
> You that walk, whoever you are, pray for me.
> So that those who come afterwards shall pray for you.

Dantisco died on 17 October 1548, aged 63. He was a brilliant and talented man, but restless and fickle in character. His considerable correspondence can be found today in different archives and libraries in Poland, Spain, Sweden and Belgium.

In 1548 the Court returned to Valladolid. Diego Gratian and his family were to remain there, except for some short trips to Madrid, until 1559. Then they went with the Court to Toledo and the following year to Madrid. The children were beginning to arrive in clusters. Jerome expressed this graphically, 'My mother gave birth twenty times, counting the miscarriages.'

On 13 September 1548 the Infanta, Maria, sister of Philip II, contracted a marriage with her cousin Maximillian of Austria. They remained in Valladolid as Regents of the Kingdom, before the imminent departure of Prince Philip for his journey to Europe, at the request of his father, the Emperor. In the absence of Charles V and Philip II, Diego served Maria and Maximillian with the same commitment as translator. However, fortune did not smile on him, for he had a meagre salary and a large family. He educated his children as well as his wife in Humanities, Latin and Greek; he found Joanna to be '*plane rudis omnium*';[1] he also taught her how to cultivate the arts.

Diego knew he was highly qualified, but was wearied by the lack of due recompense for all the service he had given. He vented his frustration in a treatise addressed to the Inquisitor, Fernando de Valdes, whom he must have

1 Clearly the backbone of everything.

known from his time in Belgium. Then Valdes was not only the Inquisitor General, a severe man whom people feared, but also the Archbishop of Seville. Diego recounted all his disappointments and frustrations in his treatise (mentioned above) entitled, Speravi. He began with the most important person, the Emperor, whom he had served for twenty-four years, the first nine without pay, in deciphering, translating, interpreting and even editing very difficult and classified letters of a political nature. When Diego dared to raise the question of his salary with Charles V which he was owed for the nine years he had worked without payment, this was the response: 'We shall see to this when we deal with similar business.'

Diego then put his hopes in the Empress, but she died prematurely, as we've already said. He also put his hope in Prince Philip, 'to whom he had given his services no less willingly than to the Prince's parents.' And the response was: 'I shall do whatever I can for you.'

Then he placed his hope in the Prince of Saboya, 'who, alive or dead, I never ceased to give him my solicitous assistance.' He taught him Greek and graphology but the following words were all he received: – '*Il me subviendra bien de vous pour vous faire du bien.*'

He also had hoped in Doctor Diego de Guevara, a gentleman-in-waiting to the King, to whom he had given good service. In his capacity as the Emperor's Armourer, he could have helped the secretary, Gratian. However, the latter only heard the following joke from Doctor Diego's mouth: 'Gratian the Emperor, Gratian the friend: what little money you have!'

Again he placed his hope in the Grand Knight, Francisco de los Cobos, Secretary to Charles V and later to the Councils of Castile, the Ministry of Finance and Mexico. 'Even children know what has been done for them day and night,' Diego lamented. The Grand Knight said to him: 'Gratian, I am in your debt.' However, he never paid him anything.

He hoped too in Francis de Erasso, the Imperial Secretary. He hoped in the Honorable John, his fellow student in Louvain. He had hoped in the Bishop of Palencia, previously of Zamora, Francisco de Mendoza, 'at whose side he spent nine long years as Secretary.' De Mendoza was also Commissioner General of the Crusades, 'but it was I, his servant, who really carried the Commissariat.' At least the Bishop supported Diego in his will, 'To Diego Gratian, because he served me so well, and throughout my life did not give me any problems, six thousand *maravedies.*[2]'

2 A small and not very valuable Spanish coin.

Again, he had placed his hope in Johann Dantisco, Bishop of Culm and Warmia, his father-in-law. In the said treatise he explained why the hurt continued to be such an open wound. 'He acted without fear of God or respect for others.' Johann did accept that he had a daughter when alive but at his death he ignored her in his will, using as an excuse the hatred he still professed for her mother. I think he had not read Falaris, who, distressed by his condition as a tyrant, said, 'Well, since we are mortal, it is not good to keep an immortal hatred.'

He hoped too in Cardinal Tavera, 'who, for eighteen years while Regent in Spain, had very close dealings with me almost every day.' He received from him this repeated promise: 'Wait until Cesar comes and then you will see what will be done for you.' But the Emperor never came; he was always elsewhere in Europe. And Cardinal Taverna, who had been 'venerable in his Christian conduct' died.

He hoped in Cardinal Loaysa, Archbishop of Seville, who succeeded the Bishop of Palencia as Commissioner General of the Crusades. He told him, as if it were a fait accompli: 'I have decided to use you in my service as my Lord Bishop did, and to improve our relationship.' Diego placed himself at the service of the Emperor, who preferred him to Loaysa after the death of his Bishop, Mendoza. Loaysa then withdrew Diego's honours from the Crusades.

He placed his hope in Fernando de Valdes, Archbishop of Seville and Inquisitor General, to whom he had addressed the present treatise. Diego had known him since he was a teenager. What did the Archbishop say in reply? 'Whenever I have had the chance I have always tried to help you.' However, the truth is that Diego did not obtain anything from his letters of introduction.

He had hoped in… enough of this litany of names! Diego ended his treatise (*Speravi*) stating that the words of men are empty, of no use, confused and are not always to be trusted. He concluded by saying, 'I will hope in the Lord, who will not leave me disillusioned.' He put his trust in God alone, 'His creator, who protected him when he was young, supported him in his old age, cared for his children, who does not deceive and is not deceived…'

The tomb of Fernando de Valdés, Archbishop of Seville and General Inquisitor, in the Church of his native village, Salas (Asturias). *By Pomeyo Leoni.*

Yes, in the *Speravi* Diego felt free to express himself. He had done this years before, in a letter he wrote to Archbishop Valdes from Valladolid, dated 1 January 1550. He had sent Valdes a small book that he had been encouraged to translate on the advice of some friars.

> Perhaps you will say, 'Where does so much mania come from for writing and translating books?... From the various reasons people will attribute to me for doing this, you can dismiss the desire for vainglory, or a wish to distance myself from the bad luck, work and regrets that I've never been short of and am still not lacking. I write, it is with shame that I confess this, because like the parrot and the magpie say words in order to obtain some morsel, so out of cruel necessity do I; for the master of all knowledge and the inspiration for all genius is the stomach. In this way you will understand the truth of the Greek adage: knowledge is born out of poverty. To be more precise, so that you will better understand, I can afford to maintain my family, which is no small undertaking with the meagre income such books allow me. If I cannot keep them in luxury, at least I can give them an honest and modest living.

In order to convince the Archbishop (of his impoverished circumstances), Diego recounts what had happened to him a few days previously, 'It is absolutely true and will make you laugh':

> Gaona, the Royal Accountant, advised me to request the governorship from a certain person who, according to the courier specially sent to obtain news, was dying. I went to see the Emperor and Juan Vazquez; both of them agreed to this, without any problems. You could never guess what happened? Well, it was discovered that the Governor, who had been breathing his last, began to improve from the very moment I requested his position, to the extent that today he is fine and healthy. I have been transformed from Councillor to a Pseudo-Councillor. My friends, who had already congratulated me, when they heard that all had broken down, took it very badly, and were upset by my misfortune, adding that it was a pity that the ill person had improved.

This is how Diego's life turned out to be in such financial straits and why he sought refuge through his studies and translations of the classics. When his friends asked him: 'What use has philosophy been to you and your literary studies?', he answered like Dionysius the Younger when they expelled him from the kingdom: 'They helped me to endure so many grave changes of fortune that had pushed me from pillar to post, and impelled me to stupidity, or rather to madness, until I was reduced to throwing stones.' However, Diego Gratian placed his trust in God. He declared that he did not want to offend or malign anyone by what he wrote.

Chapter Seven

To Raise the Flag in the Service of God

It is time to focus on Jerome Gratian, the main character of our story and begin to tell about his adventurous life. I should forewarn you that it will end up as exciting as the lives of his forebears. Even though as a child he had a 'meek and gentle disposition and was a friend of silence and suffering', according to his memoirs, these traits were to be the norm of his life.

Jerome was to become the cleverest in his class, i.e. in the litter of his brothers and sisters, who were also very bright. Devotion and study were in the very air that they breathed at home. He first studied under the teachers Medina and Gaona in Valladolid, and when he was ten he began to study grammar under the direction of the tutor Torres de Cazorla.

Jerome recounts how he was laid low by an illness and was taken to Astorga by a family friend called Roque de Huerta, 'known to the family for having been raised with my father, his mother had been wet-nurse to my mother.' The young Jerome spent eight months in Astorga in the house of the Professor Juan Galan and made such progress 'that in a short time he progressed to the study of grammar at a higher level.'

In Astorga something happened to Jerome that I must tell you about. In his life as a friar, visions and revelations were foreign to him. He tells us himself that his spirit was never guided along the way of 'visible or audible revelations, ecstasies, raptures, miracles or other external phenomena which people are in the custom of esteeming highly.' However, there were two exceptions in his life. The first occurred in Astorga, when he was an eleven-year-old child, and the second, some months after the death of Teresa of Jesus, when he had a vision of the Saint. In his autobiography, *The Pilgrimage of Anastasius*, written at the end of his life, he uses the literary technique of a dialogue between two people called Cyril and Anastasius. When Cyril asks Anastasius the question whether he had had visions, the latter responded:

> Don't ask me this question. Don't you know I dislike revelations and visible phenomena? I used to believe that most of them were ghosts or images caused by fear and that one should not have anything to do with them. Then something happened to me in Astorga, when I was eleven years old; I was walking down a quiet lane around midnight and was still a good distance from the crossroads when I had a shock. The hairs on the back of my neck stood up, even the velvet cap I was wearing on my head rose up. I had no idea what made me frightened until I reached the entrance of the main street. There I saw a shape like a donkey a short distance away, it was like the devil. It was speckled in colour, with fiery black skin, and its large eyes like burning coals were staring at me. I did not look away, but rather I stepped backwards, without taking my eyes off this creature. I entered into an empty house that was under construction and there I blessed myself and recited the Creed. I searched with my feet till I found two stones that I wanted. I wrapped my cape over my left arm and I held one stone in this hand and the other in my right hand. I went out in such a rage and desire to attack this ghost and to hit it between the eyes with a stone. It seemed to me that never in my life did I have such an urge to do such a thing, but when I went outside it had disappeared. I ran as fast as I could to my house without any fear. I was impressed at having so much courage – where did I get it at my age?

Jerome returned to Valladolid. His parents placed him in a school run by two teachers, Tejeda and de Carbonero, 'because my handwriting was very good.' His father wrote well and wanted his children to write well too, in order to guarantee them a secure future in the Court. Jerome continued to study Grammar with a teacher called Torres, and later with the teachers Gutierrez and Salinas. Later on there were studies in Rhetoric and Greek, with a teacher named Bustos. He continued to maintain his fine handwriting. When he was fifteen, having completed grammar, Rhetoric and Greek, he began to study the arts.

Mastery of Greek must have been important because he recounted in his memoirs how his father used to read 'to me and my brother, Anthony, in Greek. Among other things, he read the *Batracomiomachia* by Homer, which could be called 'The war between the mice and the frogs', a humorous poem by the author of the *Iliad* and the *Odyssey*. This detail alone gives us an idea of the kind of classical education that formed part of the atmosphere in that house, and of the lessons that Diego taught his children.

With Jerome's gentle nature that defined his childhood, he recalls a detail of his spiritual life: he began to confess with the Jesuits, 'even though I do not believe I received Holy Communion often.' He tells us nothing about his First Holy Communion that should have taken place when he was twelve, during the course of his studies in Grammar and Rhetoric.

In 1556, Charles V abdicated the throne of Spain in favour of his son, Philip II, and placed the Empire in the hands of his brother, Ferdinand I. The Emperor retired to a monastery in Yuste, in the rugged mountain ranges of the Extremadura, where he died on 21 September 1558. Philip II had been absent in Europe for five years, returning to Spain after signing the Cateau-Cambresis Treaty (3 April 1559). The Treaty ended the long conflict between Spain and France, which began in 1521 with Charles V and Francis I, and was ratified by the marriage of Philip II, widower of Mary Tudor of England, to Isabel de Vallois, daughter of Henry II of France and Catherine Medici. The future Queen of Spain, who lived in Fontainebleau, was only twelve years old and, according to contemporary accounts, played with dolls and other games that children play with; she was to become known as 'Isabel of Peace'.

The Duke of Alba travelled from Brussels to Paris, where he gave Isabel a small chest with precious jewels and a medallion with the portrait of Philip II. The Duke, in mourning for Mary Tudor and dressed in black, surprised the French by his rather somber appearance. The reading of the marriage settlement took place on 20 June in the great hall in the Louvre castle. It was signed on one side by the Duke of Alba and on the other by the Kings of France. Two days later, the wedding was celebrated by proxy in the Notre Dame Cathedral, Paris, officiated by the Bourbon Cardinal, with the Duke of Alba representing the bridegroom. After the festivities and the dancing came the moment for the traditional ceremony in the French Court of putting to bed the two newly-weds. The Duke of Alba, a courteous and pious Spaniard, took symbolic possession of the regal marriage-bed by placing his arm and leg on the bed, before leaving immediately.

A great tournament was celebrated in Paris as part of the wedding festivities, during which the French King was badly injured in a tragic accident. He died some days later, on 10 July. Philip II, who was still in Ghent (Belgium), sent Ruy Gomez to Paris to present his condolences to the widowed Queen and to offer precious jewels to his fiancée, Isabel de Valois, and the promise that he was ready to go to Spain in order to celebrate the marriage.

After five years of continuous absence, Philip II was required to return to Spain. The governing Princess, Joanna of Austria, Philip II's sister, told him of the alarming Lutheran circles that had been discovered in Valladolid and Seville. He returned to Spain by sea and disembarked at Laredo on 8 September. Six days later he entered Valladolid, the city adorned with triumphal arches. The next day his sister, Princess Joanna, handed over the government of the Kingdom, before retiring to a convent in Abrojo, a short distance away. On 8 October, Philip II presided over a ceremony of the Inquisition in the main square, in which thirty people were accused of 'Lutheranism.' The ceremony concluded with the celebration of a Mass. Philip II then departed and the people dispersed. Twelve of the accused, including four nuns, were led to the stake outside the city, two were burnt alive; it was an awful sight.

There had already been another such trial on 21 May, presided over by the Princess, as Governess, as well as the Prince Charles. At this trial a Doctor (of Divinity), Augustine Cazalla, had been condemned. Philip II had often heard Cazalla's sermons, as he was Preacher to his Majesty. In a square, crammed with people, the eyes of a fourteen-year-old Jerome watched this macabre entertainment; he even drew near to the stake. In his *Pilgrimage of Anastasius*, alluding to Doctor Cazalla, he recalled, 'I saw him burnt in Valladolid.'

Philip II moved the Court to Toledo. The Gratian family also went there. When Queen Isabel de Valois arrived on 12 February 1560, two betrothal ceremonies were held in Guadalajara, where the King went to meet her; Guadalajara was the Imperial City, a quiet and attractive place. As the Emperor was there a huge mass of people gathered from every corner of Europe: Spain, France, Belgium, Germany, Florence, Genoa, Portugal, Lombardy… Though Guadalajara was a diverse and multi-cultural city there was no room for so many foreigners, and so the local residents protested.

Days later, on 22 February, the ceremony of the oath-taking by Prince Charles, as inheritor of the throne, took place in the Cathedral. The Queen kept to her bed due to an illness and could not attend. The Princess Joanna, in a sedan chair, took part in a cortège led by the Barons of the Kingdom. The Prince, Charles, was on a white horse, escorted by John of Austria and Alexander Farnesio, son of Margaret of Parma, the illegitimate daughter of Charles V and Governess of the Low Countries. The Courts of Castile that had been meeting in Toledo since 9 December declared that they recognized Prince Charles as their natural and legitimate Lord following the death of his father (Charles V). When it was his time, the Prince swore on oath, 'To guard the rights and laws of these Kingdoms, keeping them in peace and justice and to defend the Catholic faith with his person and property, and with all his might.' When the oath had been taken the Court returned to the Real Alcazar to the sound of minstrels, trumpets and drums.

Jerome continued his studies in Toledo. He studied Greek with the teacher, Alvargomez, and his first steps in art with Doctor Perea. When his studies in humanities came to an end he was fifteen years old and had to make a decision. His father wanted him to follow in the family tradition and train to fulfil the office of secretary in the Court of the King. 'However, I greatly desired for myself a life of study, he wrote, and I kept on insisting with tears that they send me to study, and in the end my parents gave in.' He subsequently contracted a dangerous fever that left him with an extremely upset stomach, 'due to eating some dried apricots while convalescing.' His father proposed that he study law, but he insisted on studying theology.

Jerome's university studies would entail a significant financial burden on the family. The Jesuit, Fr Martinez, who was Jerome's confessor in Toledo, encouraged him to continue his studies in Alcala, hoping that such a bright student might enter the Company of Jesus. In October 1560 Jerome began his studies of Arts and Philosophy in the University of Alcala, a populous walled town. It had nine gates, each one with a tower. It was a small town of one thousand inhabitants but with a fluid student population of another thousand. Gaspar Barreiros, an erudite Portuguese traveller who appeared in Alcala in the middle of the 16th century, described the place as a small oval-shaped town, 'whose houses are better in general than the boroughs of Madrid… It is ennobled by its illustrious University and numerous colleges, and also by the monasteries and churches and magnificent houses that the Archbishops of Toledo built in the past'

The Gratian-Dantisco family continued to grow. We can only surmise at the financial balancing acts the family had to go through. In 1559 they moved from Valladolid to Toledo and then in 1561 from Toledo to Madrid, when the latter became the capital of the Kingdom. The family now had a small but ever-increasing number of children. Added to these were the two widowed grandmothers, Isabel de Hermosilla and Isabel Delgada. After the birth of Anthony, Luke and Jerome, came Adriana, Justina, Thomas and Joanna, besides two others who died in infancy. In later years the family would be completed by the siblings, Maria, Isabel, Peter, Luis, Laurence and Juliana.

In October 1560, at fifteen years of age, Jerome matriculated in his first course in Arts, the course of the so-called *terministae or summalistae.* On the list of those who matriculated he was 29th. These facts I gleaned from the good work by Fr Enrique Llamas, who researched Jerome's studies at Alcala University. Jerome recounted in his *Autobiography,* after Alcala, 'the secretary Zayas recommended that I be looked after by Ambrosio de Morales, who found me lodging in the house of the Lecturer Cosilla. I was given Doctor Andrew de Uzquiano for my Master of Arts course. I also had lessons from the Lecturer Ibarra, who was blind, so that I wouldn't lose the Greek I already knew.' In other words, Jerome had to have a recommendation from Gabriel de Zayas, the King's secretary, to study with Ambrosio de Morales, the famous archaeologist and Spanish historian, who occupied the chair of Rhetoric at Alcala.

Morales had to look for accommodation or lodging (for Jerome) at the house of the Lecturer Cosilla; Jerome did not get a scholarship to reside in one of the colleges at the University until well into the course. A letter from Philip II to the Rector, dated 15 February 1561, indicates that it was the King's will, 'to encourage and benefit him.' 'We have been informed,' wrote the King, 'that he has done some rudimentary study, and to ensure that he is given every chance to continue, I want him to be provided with his university fees from the College.'

We do not know the College in question, perhaps St Philip and St James', named by the King, and founded by Philip II in 1550 for sons of the palace's staff. 'We beg you that if there is presently a vacant university burse for the said faculty that you provide him with it, and if not then when the first one becomes vacant,' concluded the King's letter.

In November 1561, Jerome matriculated from his second course of Arts; and had risen up to number six on the list of students, called *logici seu dailectici.* It was during this course, when he was sixteen years old, that he hinted at entering the Jesuits. However, he put it off for another couple of years, until he obtained his Bachelor of Arts degree.

About this time three students from the aristocracy arrived in Alcala. They stayed in the Palace of the Archbishop of Toledo. They were the Prince Charles, who had a sad end, Don John of Austria and Alexander Farnesio;

View of Alcala de Henares.
By Anton van den Wyngaerde, 1565. National Library, Vienna.

they were respectively the son, brother and nephew of Philip II; all three were exactly the same age as Jerome.

Did they study together? Did they meet in the halls? I don't think so. Master John, who studied in Louvain with Diego Gratian, was the private tutor of Prince Charles. His two companions received private lessons from the most prestigious professors in Alcala University. A terrible accident occurred on 19 April 1562, which ended Prince Charles' studies. He fell down some stairs, fracturing his skull. He came close to the point of passing to the next world, due more to the inexperience of the doctors than to the blow itself.

All the while Jerome continued his studies. In November 1562, he matriculated at the end of his third year of arts: among the *physici seu philosophi naturales*; he was twelfth on the list. At the end of the course, he obtained his Bachelor of Arts degree. By this time his decision to enter into the Jesuits had grown. However, he confessed that when 'examined for his Bachelor's degree, his ardour for that vocation had cooled, even though his desire to serve God had not cooled, in fact it continued to grow.' He had conflicting emotions, not unusual in a young man of his age who had a healthy future. He knew that he had to study, that whatever direction his life would take in the future depended on it; he himself described the dilemma he found himself in:

> He had worked out that for whatever rank he wished to attain, it would be useful to study the Arts, and so he really applied himself to his studies. With the incentive to aspire to the grades of a lofty Arts degree, he experienced mixed desires. On the one hand, it would appear a good thing, to become a Bachelor of Arts or obtain a Licentiate, which he did not deserve, but on the other hand, he considered it of little importance to be Archbishop of Toledo; he did not have any earthly aspirations.

In the last Arts course (1563-1564), he came twenty-second on the list of those who matriculated, among the *metaphysici*. When this course finished, in October 1564, he obtained his Licentiate in Arts.

> He was examined for his Licentiate by Doctor Cantero, Doctor John Gomez, Doctor Albiz, Doctor Munoz and Doctor Mathew Rodriguez. There had been great competition from the other students, which had spurred him on, but he was given first place among the forty-eight Licentiates.

A month later, November 1564, he obtained the grade of Master in Arts, coming first among many other students; some were so old 'that they could have been his father.' His brother, Thomas, recalled this years later to Philip II in a *Discurso* on his brother Jerome:

> When almost twenty years old, Jerome obtained the highest grade among Licentiates in the public examination that is customarily held in order to graduate as a Master of Arts or Philosophy. He came top over all the other Masters listed according to ability, and some of them were old enough to be his father. All the Masters present and many others noticed this, especially Mathew Vazquez, Secretary to His Majesty, who was present at all the exams and also the graduation...

There is a little confusion here, Mathew Vazquez was not Secretary to Philip II at the time Jerome underwent his examinations in Alcala, nor was Vazquez there in a role as Visitator of the University. Born in 1542, he was three years older than Jerome and a mere student. It is true he was Royal Secretary when Thomas Gratian wrote the memoir for the King, reminding him that Mathew Vazquez, whom the King had employed as his 'Principal-Secretary', could testify to the masterly capacity of his brother Jerome. After the exam Jerome suffered a long illness that he attributed to 'exhaustion from his studies for the Licentiate.' For this reason, he did not matriculate in Theology until February 1565.

Jerome changed faculty and also changed college. He moved to the Mater Dei College for which he had obtained a scholarship. The College was founded by (Cardinal) Cisneros in 1513, at first to accommodate eighteen theology students and six students of medicine. It had a bleak appearance, with two towers on either side of the main doorway, typical of the architecture of Alcala de Henares. Throughout the history of the college it had been a residence for forty bishops and a score of royal doctors, 'the cream of all the students who were in the university,' according to our own Gratian. Today the college is a centre for those studying law. Jerome lived here while he followed his four courses in Theology and Sacred Scripture, at the same time he kept up his Greek and Hebrew. This is what he recounted in his book *Fundaciones*:

> The Lecturers for his Masters in Ecclesial Theology were Father Deza, of the Company of Jesus, Doctor Fernando de Balbas, who had a Chair in Alcala University, the same Doctor Uzquiano, who was his Art's Lecturer, and Doctor Juan Garcia. In Sacred Scripture he had Doctor Mendez, who was Archbishop of Granada, and Doctor Alonso de Mendoza. His Lecturer for Hebrew was Doctor Hernando Diaz, a medical Doctor.

When the professors were away, Jerome taught (or read, as they said at the time) certain courses in public, 'therefore they did not look upon him as just one among others, but rather as one of a few outstanding students.'

> When he began to study Theology, Father Deza of the Company of Jesus read the material on Grace, and, as he said so many excellent things about it, Jerome had a great longing to acquire it. From that time he began to confess to Deza and, with the latter's encouragement, to spend an hour each day in mental prayer. He taught himself with books from Luis de Granada. He had some work to do in the college, because, other than the three courses he was studying in Theology, he also had to attend three other Art courses, to give an account of himself to the Lecturer Ocariz and others, without counting the two hours he did in preparation. He spent four years, listening

> and reading, which seemed to go by quickly. His desire to serve God grew. Although the study distracted his soul from a life of innocence, his spirit was satisfied by prayer and by his frequenting the sacraments.

Jerome Gratian spent his holidays with the Count of Chinchon and his son, Andrew de Bobadilla; Jerome acted as tutor for the boy. The Count of Chinchon esteemed Jerome as a 'gentleman, who was and is a saint.' The Count was worried about his son's lack of inclination to study; Jerome proved to be the antidote. It came to pass that Andrew took a liking to books, and benefitted from them to the extent that in time he was to become Bishop of Segovia and Archbishop of Zaragoza. At the end of his theology course Jerome's fees ended. He changed residence from the Mater Dei College to the Count's house, 'where he remained until he entered religious life,' i.e., until he became a friar.

Jerome completed his Licentiate in Theology in 1568, when he began his doctorate. He succeeded brilliantly in all four stages for his doctorate. 'One should know: the first stage, second stage and third stage (*Magna ordinaria, Parva ordinaria and Alfonsina*), but to graduate as a Doctor one needed *Quodlibetos*. These public events, each one lasting at least five hours, except the *Alfonsina* that went on for the whole day, lasted from eight in the morning until well into the night. He was blessed by the Lord who gave him the grace to succeed, which pleased the Doctors and the entire University.'

In Jerome's third year of theology he entered the clerical state. He received the tonsure and minor orders on 30 December 1566. In the second year of his doctorate he was ordained sub-deacon on 25 September 1569. Three months later, 17 December, he was ordained a deacon. On 1 January 1570 he began 'to exercise the office of preacher, as a scripture scholar and a Bachelor of Theology, even though it wasn't at Mass.' He preached his first sermon in Canaleja, near Alcala. Finally, on 25 March 1570, Holy Saturday, he was ordained a priest. That same year he began to fulfil the duties of a confessor in the church of Santa Maria de Alcala. He celebrated his first Mass in the church of the Discalced Reales in Madrid. Princess Joanna of Austria, who had founded the convent and lived in it, was in the congregation.

When serving as a curate something happened to Jerome which was to become an omen for his future. He was involved in a scandal, the first of many he was to endure in his life. He wrote about it in the *Pilgrimage of Anastasius*:

> It happened that a great servant of God, a holy lady, Maria de Medina [she and another woman, the wife of a silversmith, discovered Lutheranism when in the town of Cazalla] rescued a young woman from the control of a cleric with whom she was living. She brought her to my place, where the young woman confessed, and then began to walk along the path of salvation. This holy lady hid the young woman from the man with whom she had sinned. The cleric sparked off a rumour that I was living with this young woman and that Maria Medina had arranged all this. The rumour spread quickly throughout the university; I was left half dead because it was the first time that I had been accused in this way. As my preaching had born fruit and I had become known, I thought my world had come to an end. The cleric came to see me with two daggers in his belt. He wanted to provoke me into saying something so that he could stab me but the Lord came to my help. I went to complain to Maria de Medina for introducing me into this seedy business. With a smile on her face she told me prophetically, 'Are you complaining about this? The time will come when you will suffer so many insults that you will consider this to be nothing.'

Maria de Medina's words were to prove prophetic. This experience was a trifle compared to the slanders he would have to endure years later.

What happened next was not a calumny, but rather an offence on the part of his companions. They called him 'Judas', because (they believed) he had voted for the (political) faction that was opposed to the supporters of the Old Castile party. A companion even approached him with a hidden dagger, intending to stab him.

Jerome's Professor had entered into a public debate for the Chair of *Prima* in Theology. Everyone voted, including Jerome. There were two factions, one from Old Castile and one from New Castile. Our man belonged to the New Castile faction, at least in theory, but kept on good terms with some from the opposing faction. It appeared to some of his companions that he had betrayed them by his vote but it was not clear. He had voted for his Professor. In his naivety, he did not realize there were those who remained friends only with people of the same opinion. Being branded a 'Judas' hurt Jerome. However, he did not try to justify himself with his companions. He confided only in his confessor. The latter told him with a smile, in just the same way as Maria de Medina: 'What are you complaining about? The time will come when you shall see greater and even more scandalous deeds, this is nothing.' Thus he resolved not to try to obtain a chair at the University, or to stand for election.

> The Lord freed me from this danger and gave me, as a reward, an abhorrance for all pretentiousness about scholarship. He made me determined never to seek a University Chair, so as to avoid the crisis of conscience into which many candidates fall, even religious ones. In this way I had nothing to do with that University status with which so many are inebriated. Fortunately, even though they tempted me in Salamanca with an important post at the main College in Cuenca, I did not want to accept it. Even if it brought me a certain degree of honour I considered it to be more important not to break the thread of what I was doing; to become a Doctor of Theology at Alcala, which required nine years and is a very difficult career. Although I declined University Chairs the Lord did not spare me from lecturing, because I substituted Dr. Ocariz for almost his whole course in Arts, and taught Metaphysics to all the pupils of Ocariz and Laxa. There were great men on that course who today hold my writings in great esteem. For some weeks I studied Sacred Scripture with Dr. Alonso de Mendoza, who holds the Chair in Biblical Theology at Alcala.

Jerome Gratian spent the years working on his doctorate in the house of the Count of Chinchon. He now ate meals on a regular basis and even had a servant at his disposal. However, his spirit was restless. Nothing satisfied him except 'to love God and serve Him fully.' It was a desire that grew and grew to the point where 'he could not bear it and detested the comfortable life he had in the house of Don Andrew; it was like being a slave in a galley-ship.'

Jerome usually celebrated Mass in the Jesuit College. However, one day, it was 4 November 1571, he decided to celebrate Mass with the Franciscan nuns in the chapel of St John of the Penitence, where his sister, Maria of St Joseph, had been living for seven years. He found the door closed and the sacristan already gone home, so he decided to go to the nearby convent of the Immaculate Conception, where the nuns had not yet celebrated Mass that day. It was a feast day and therefore it should have been a sung Mass. However, when the nuns invited him to celebrate the Mass he excused himself because he couldn't sing. He preached to the sisters about St Francis of Asissi, as it was his feast day, thinking that they were Discalced

Franciscans. The Prioress, Mary of Jesus, said to him after the Mass: 'We are not Franciscans. We are followers of our Mother, Teresa of Jesus.'

It was the first time that Jerome had heard the name of Teresa of Jesus. He asked the Sisters for their Rule so that he could study it, which he did, making notes in the margins. He wanted to know the origins of the Carmelite Order better. He visited the Discalced Carmelite priory in Alcala, which had been founded shortly before, in 1567. There he read the *Speculum Ordinis*, published in Valencia in 1507. This book helped him to have a better awareness of the Order's history, from the prophet Elijah to the present day. Afterwards he delved into Sacred Scripture and drew out some points regarding the life of the prophets of this Order which he then sent to Teresa of Jesus, whom, as yet, he had no particular desire to know.

Teresa wrote to thank him. Jerome suspected that he owed his vocation to the prayers of St Teresa. He was now resolutely attracted to the Discalced Carmelites, something 'so contrary to all human reasoning.'

At a certain point (in the autobiography) Cyril asks Anastasius: 'One usually has to struggle a great deal before choosing a vocation. Tell me more about how and why you decided?'

And I would like to ask the same question to Anastasius, sorry, I mean Jerome: 'Why did you join this fledgling Order that was not well known and was truly penitential?' Jerome answers: 'It was a struggle that lasted almost a year and a half.'

He explained his motivations not only in the *Pilgrimage of Anastasius*, but also in other places; in sum, he overcame the many obstacles that delayed his vocation. His first motivation was his 'burning desire to serve God with all his heart.' He wanted to do this in an Order like this one, that was 'strict and prayerful, that had only just begun. This, he saw, was all part of God's will for him, to be the most forgotten of all.'

His second was his devotion to the Blessed Virgin Mary. At his ordination they (the Carmelite nuns) had given him an image of the Blessed Virgin that he always kept with him. In his struggle at that time, he would sometimes cover it with a veil, in order not to hear the voice of the image that seemed to speaking to his heart: 'My son, serve me in my Order, it needs you.'

His third motivation was his 'great desire to suffer insults and to work hard for Christ.' He wanted to endure troubles and resentments in order to turn upside down what the world considers valuable, such as having servants in the house of the Count de Chinchon, 'who was very fond of me, and was very pleased that I whetted his son's appetite for study.'

Jerome felt called to hide himself in 'a corner where he could be forgotten by everyone … in the company of the servants of God who encourage me to penance, prayer and the spiritual life.' He believed his sermons would be more fruitful if he was seen in an 'austere habit and with bare feet, like Christ.'

His final motivation was his belief that it was God who kept calling him insistently. However, the difficulties that hindered his vocation were not minor.

The biggest one of all was his family. He owed them a debt of gratitude, having received so much to enable him to finish his studies. At the time, his many brothers and sisters 'had no other means of support apart from their elder siblings, because those who worked in the Court had no income to help their sons and daughters, who had to help each other. Some were better off than others. My parents had spent a lot of money on my education, so I was clearly bound in justice not to abandon them.'

Diego Gratian, the patriarch, was now in his seventies. Antonio, the eldest brother, had replaced his father as Secretary to the King on 1 January 1571. 'The family found itself,' wrote Jerome, 'without any other income other than what they might expect from the support of my brother who had been made Secretary to the King.' When he (Jerome) was at the point of finishing his brilliant university career, he could easily have obtained an ecclesiastical income that would have alleviated the anxieties of the family. The King himself, Philip II, took an interest in the young Gratian and waited for him to complete his doctorate in order to offer him a chaplaincy.

On top of everything Jerome was not well. He knew 'from his complexion that he was weak and ill, and totally worn out from his studies.' How was he going to put up with the rigours and the penitential life of the Discalced Carmelites? It was a bitter struggle that, he admitted, he fought alone, because he feared that if he confided in anyone they might prevent his vocation. In the end he did confide in his confessor, who said to him: 'In twenty days' time you will make a public defence of your treatise in Theology. Before deciding anything, go defend your thesis, as the whole university is expecting you to, otherwise it will look like you refused to sit it out of fear.'

Jerome sat the exam and, afterwards, returned to his confessor, who told him, 'as you have to go to Madrid, consult with Father X, of the Augustinian Order, who is very austere and very saintly.' This Augustinian, who knew Jerome's parents, advised him: 'You should not abandon your parents and brothers and sisters.'

'I returned very sad at this negative response,' confessed the young man. His confessor suggested: 'Do the Spiritual Exercises of St Ignatius.'

However, he did not do them. He called to mind what had happened in the past. This time he did not want others to change his mind and encourage him to join the Jesuits. In 1571 he spent the summer months in the village of Odon, not far from Madrid. It was during this time that he was convinced that he should become a Discalced Carmelite:

> A great desire came over me one day, to become a Discalced Carmelite and to know what that fruit tasted like. My soul so longed for this that I took off my shoes and socks and, as discreetly as possible, my clerical clothes. I went half a league from where I was to a little place to say Mass. On the way the gravel and the thistles I walked over cut my feet, but this seemed a very great gift to my soul, and my heart melted.

Jerome arrived at the Hermitage, celebrated Mass on 5 August, the feast of Our Lady of the Snows. An old lady approached him, she must have been more than seventy, and hidden in her lap was a rope. 'Bless it father.' 'What for?' he asked. 'In order to tie it around my body and do penance,' replied the old lady. Jerome said he did not know such a blessing but sprinkled the rope with holy water.

Some days later, he went to her house. They began to talk to each other. She sat down on an old half-empty sack, he on a seat with a broken back. The lady had a fever and he scolded her for wearing a rope around her body while being ill, 'Oh Father, this is our greatest delusion, that with the pretence of safeguarding our health the devil brings many souls to hell!'

The example of the little old lady, who spoke of suffering and of the wound in Christ's side, etc., left an indelible impression on Jerome Gratian who struggled with the temptation of safeguarding his health. He asked her about mental prayer. 'I don't understand what that means,' she confessed, 'here in my house half my time I read, the other half I pray.' 'And what is prayer?' asked Jerome. 'Don't ask me,' she said, 'as I am rather ignorant in this matter and so I couldn't answer correctly.' However, he recounted that she began to speak of prayer, 'more inflamed than a fire', and in such a way that even 'if I had completed my studies on St Denis and his book about *The Celestial Hierarchy*, I could not have answered better'. He was astonished at what he heard.

> Listening to this saintly old lady was a special grace, and it motivated me to an austere form of religious life and, in my opinion, considering the great blessing my soul received, it was as if God was speaking to me through her words.

In the end Jerome did decide to enter religious life. The 'two obstacles' that had blocked his way had been removed. His parents and siblings were not in extreme need, and he did not have, under pain of mortal sin, to remain in the world to support them. God had called him, also the Blessed Virgin Mary. The second obstacle, his health, he overcame with 'a determination to die very willingly out of love of Our Blessed Lady.'

He abandoned unexpectedly his brilliant university career to become a friar. He had been in the fourth year of his Doctorate, with just one exam remaining, the '*quodlibetos*', to become a Doctor of Theology. On 25 April, 1572, on the feast of St Mark, he put on the habit of Our Lady of Mt. Carmel in the Priory of St Peter in Pastrana. The cloth for his habit he bought with the money he had been given when he supplied for Alonso de Mendoza, the Professor of Sacred Scripture at the University of Alcala.

Chapter Eight

Kicking Against the Goad

THE PICTURESQUE VILLAGE OF PASTRANA lies close to Alcala, in the Province of Guadalajara. In this town there was a villa that once belonged to the Calatrava Order but now was owned by the Prince of Eboli, Ruy Gomez de Silva, someone well known in the Court of Philip II. The Prince's wife was the infamous Anne of Mendoza y la Cerda, who was blind in one eye.

Ruy Gomez was a Portuguese knight. He had a stocky build and was of medium height; he had a fine beard and his hair was dark and curly. By now he was well on in years and renowned for his exquisite manners. He was a child when his parents and grandfather, Ruy Tellez de Meneses, brought him to Spain. His grandfather was head steward to the Empress Isabel when she arrived in Seville to marry Charles V. Ruy Gomez was twelve at the time.

He became an inseparable companion to Prince Philip, his closest and most valuable friend, becoming the royal favourite, if I may use that expression. Such was the intimacy between them that Ruy was called *King Gomez* instead of Ruy Gomez. 'No one was so favoured by a Prince, nor so highly esteemed by his master, as Ruy Gomez was by his Catholic Majesty,' according to Federick Badoaro, the Venetian Ambassador. Thanks to Philip II he ascended to the most respectable places: Head of the Army, Secretary of State for War, Chief Steward and Accountant to Prince Charles, Prince of Eboli in the Kingdom of Naples, Duke of Pastrana, Grandee and Knight of Calatrava.

In 1553 Ruy Gomez married Anne of Mendoza, the daughter of Diego of Mendoza, Duke of Francavilla and Prince of Melito. Anne was only twelve years old, still a child. According to the laws governing marriage he would have to wait two years before the marriage could be consummated. However, his departure from Spain with Prince Philip, who went to England and the Netherlands, meant it would be five years before he returned.

The Prince and Princess of Eboli, Rui Gomez de Silva and Anne de Mendoza.

In 1558, when their first son, Diego, was born, Anne of Mendoza was eighteen years old, Ruy Gomez was forty-two. She concealed her right eye under an enigmatic patch. Was it a pretence? Did she just have one eye? This has remained a historical enigma. She combined a radiant beauty with a seductive air that led her to fall from grace. However, for now she only had time to bring children into the world.

When in 1569 she called on Teresa of Avila, who was in her foundation in Toledo from where she would make a foundation in Pastrana, Anne was pregnant with her ninth child, her son Peter Gonzalez of Mendoza who would later become Archbishop of Granada and Zaragoza and, finally Bishop of Siguenza, in which diocese a century and a half before was the See of his great great grandfather, Cardinal Mendoza.

Anne's character was as disconcerting as her beauty. Compared with the refined and amiable courtesy of her husband, Ruy Gomez, the Princess of Eboli had a manner that was deplorable. She had many character defects: she was proud, selfish, authoritarian, manipulative, ambitious…

Teresa of Avila got to know Anne quickly when the Princess summoned her to come and visit. Before Teresa met her she was unsure what to do, nonetheless she went to Pastrana. I believe she went very reluctantly. It was June 1569 when the Princess sent a luxury coach to collect her. Teresa was to be her guest in a wing of the castle. Curiously, two Carmelite communities were established (in Pastrana) at the same time: one for the friars, St Peter's, on the crest of a hill looking down on the town, and one for nuns, St Joseph's, located within the city walls.

Pastrana was the sixth foundation Teresa made for her nuns. After St Joseph's, Avila (1562), where she began her Reform of the Order, there was a quick succession of foundations: Malagon (1567), Medina del Campo (1567), Valladolid (1568) and Toledo (1569). Pastrana was also her second foundation for the friars following the recent one in Duruelo, on 28 November 1568, as Teresa noted, with a 'friar and a half.' This is a graphic description of her first two male vocations: Fr Anthony of Jesus, who had been a member of the Calced Carmelites and Fr John of the Cross, a young Calced, quite small in stature, the 'half friar'.

The foundation in Duruelo was rugged and remote. As a result, in 1570 it was transferred to the nearby town of Mancera. However, it was the foundation of St Peter's, on the hillside in Pastrana that became the new beacon for the Reform of the Carmelite friars. The success of this foundation was not to be duplicated by the nuns, due to the eccentricities of the Princess of Eboli. A few years after the nuns' foundation, St Teresa was forced to order her nuns to take their belongings and flee from Pastrana under the cover of darkness.

During this period Teresa was still making foundations. On 23 June, she and her nuns left the Eboli Palace to go to the new convent of St Joseph's, accompanied by the Prince and Princess, as well as all the clergy and the curious people of Pastrana, who were keen to catch sight of the distinguised group.

The foundation of the new priory for the friars, St Peter's, was made on 13 July. They took possession and placed the Blessed Sacrament in the chapel. Who were these friars? There were two Italian novices, Mariano Azzaro and Giovanni Narduch, and a Calced Carmelite, Baltasar Nieto, who was placed in charge of the new community.

Some days earlier, on Saturday 9 July, in the chapel of the Palace in Pastrana, two postulants were clothed in the habit, given them by Teresa herself. One of them was called Ambrose Mariano of St Benedict, a grandiloquent, bombastic man and, the other, John of the Misery, a name that signified his simplicity and humility. These two characters were straight out of a novel. I must introduce them, albeit briefly, because they are to figure relatively frequently in our story, especially the former.

Fr Mariano had been a soldier; having fought in the famous battle of St Quentin.He was something of an engineer. Born in 1510, he was by now no longer a young man; in fact he was almost sixty. 'He came to Spain,' recounts Anastasius, 'to work for the Prince of Sulmona. Ambrose had become very disillusioned with his own worldliness and in order to save his soul gave away all his possessions and went to Tardon (Andalucia) together with a certain Fr Matthew, who was in charge of those hermitages.'

Fr Matthew de la Fuente (1524-1575) was born in Almiruete (Guadalajara). He studied in Salamanca and then felt called to the eremitical life, together with some other companions among them, Diego Vidal, a servant of St John of Avila, who had been a monk at the monastery of St Basil, in Tardon, next to the Hornacheulos (Cordoba). St Teresa thought highly of Matthew de la Fuente and mentioned him in the *Book of Her Foundations*. He was the Spiritual Director of St John of Avila and Fr Luis de Granada. Ambrose Mariano and John of the Misery became his disciples.

John of the Misery was born in Naples in 1526. He first tried his vocation with the Franciscans, but they would not accept him. He then came to Spain, walking from Italy to Compostella, where before the famous shrine of St James, he vowed his life to God. He wrote, 'I walked barefoot and on my own from Italy to Santiago, Compostella, without cutting my hair.' Afterwards, he wandered around visiting different places living the life of a hermit, until he arrived in Tardon, where he got to know Mariano, to whom he made a vow of obedience. Brother John of the Misery was quite an accomplished artist as well as a sculptor. His portrait of St Teresa is the only one painted during her lifetime.

Teresa had met both of them in Madrid: she had been in Toledo and was on her way to make a foundation in Pastrana. She had to apply to Rome in order to request an indult to allow these two former hermits to join her Reform. This was obtained with the Bull *Cogit muneris* (1577) by Pope Gregory XIII, who reduced the Basilian monasteries in Spain and cut the provinces to just one. The two future Carmelites were guests in the same house as St Teresa (in Madrid), which belonged to Leonora de Mascarenas, a Portuguese aristocrat, and former Governess of Philip II and Prince Charles. The two ex-hermits had wanted to meet Teresa and she had wanted to meet them.

Mariano told St Teresa about the struggles in his life and how he had come to be a hermit. 'It seemed to me,' recounted Teresa, 'that when I listened to him I could almost see our holy fathers of old.' The conversation switched on a light inside Teresa's head, 'As I have only two friars [Frs John of the Cross and Anthony of Jesus], I thought to myself that if he [Mariano] could be a friar, why not let him be one, that it would be a great thing? I showed them Carmel's primitive Rule and told them how they could serve God with this habit. Mariano responded: "I am surprised to see how my mind has been changed so quickly and especially as it was a woman who did it."'

Teresa of Avila recounted this meeting in the *Book of Her Foundations*. The scholar Maranon wrote how Teresa, 'in her own charming way, and with her innocent feminine vanity, had won over Fr Mariano, who was fair and chaste and not inclined to dealing with women, but nonetheless was won over by a woman.'

Mariano told Teresa that Ruy Gomez had let him have a hermitage on land owned by Gomez in Pastrana, who wanted this hermitage to belong to the Order of St Teresa. Mariano then asked Teresa for a habit. 'I will come myself to make a foundation for our nuns,' replied Teresa. Mariano gave her his word that he would come to Pastrana once the licences (from Rome) had been granted. St Teresa had obtained a licence from the General of the Carmelite Order, Fr John Baptist Rossi, when he visited Avila in 1567, to make foundations in the Kingdom of Castile.

These new foundations were to conform to the Primitive Rule and to the clothing and practices that were observed in St Joseph's, Avila. Teresa was not, however, allowed to make any foundations in Andalucia, from where Rossi had departed after some bad experiences. He was in Valencia at the time Teresa made her request (for the foundations in Pastrana). Before embarking for Italy Rossi agreed that another two foundations of contemplative priories could be made in Castile. These would be subject to the jurisdiction of the Carmelite Provincial of Castile. This meant that no permission was given to make new foundations in the Province of Andalucia.

After the foundations of Duruelo and Pastrana Fr Rossi's quota had already been reached for those priories of the Carmelite Reform that followed the Primitive Rule. Once permission for the foundation had been obtained in Pastrana Mariano and John Narduch went there to begin their life in the Order reformed by St Teresa.

As St Teresa made her way slowly by wagon to Pastrana, she was joined by a strange (Carmelite) friar. She noticed 'he wasn't very old, nor was he young.' This is the way Teresa described Fr Balthasar of Jesus. I would like to warn the reader about this person: he was a sly old fox! He had first been a secular priest, then a Franciscan and now he was a Carmelite. He and his two brothers, Melchior and Gaspar, of the Nieto clan, were from Andalucia. All three belonged to the (Calced) Carmelite Order, and all three lived irregular lives. It was their parent's idea to give them the baptismal names of the three Wise Men.

Fr Melchior Nieto, a violent and irascible man, gave the General Visitator, Master Desiderio Mazzapica of St Martin, a slap in the face when the latter visited the Ecija priory in 1565. Melchior was put in the priory's prison but managed to escape. In later life he became a friar of the Third Order of St Francis. Fr Gaspar, his brother, was Provincial of Andalucia, residing in Ecija, where he maintained a 'morally dubious relationship with the Mother Prioress.'

Fr Balthasar, a brilliant preacher, was received into Carmel by his brother, Gaspar. And just like his brothers he was argumentative and a womanizer. He took part in the rebellion against the General, Fr Rossi, when the latter made a Visitation to the Carmel in Seville in 1566. For helping his brother, Melchior, escape from prison Balthasar was himself imprisoned for eighteen days, his feet clamped in irons. He was also deprived of active and passive voice, and banished to Castile, but not before being whipped in front of all the community by Rossi himself.

Exiled to Castile, Balthazar appeared in Madrid, where he showed signs of repentance. Consequently, on 18 May 1567, the General, Rossi, removed the sanctions against him, so that he was given back active and passive voice. This great preacher was also a man of refined manners; he was a man of the world with contacts in the Court of the King. He asked St Teresa if he could join her Reform, seeing it as a safe refuge. Teresa later wrote, 'as he knew that this convent (Pastrana) had been established, he visited the nuns with the intention of becoming a Discalced Carmelite friar; this he did for which I praised God.'

Did Teresa know of the irregular life Fr Balthazar Jesus Nieto had lived? I am inclined to believe she was far too naïve; also, she was in a hurry. Donazar, on the other hand, thinks that she knew about his bad past but 'was very tolerant':

> Why did Teresa of Avila admit him into her Reform? Perhaps it was because he was an important person who knew Ruy Gomez and had great influence

> in various Curias. He also knew members of the aristocracy. Teresa badly needed influential people and began to realize that she needed to be worldly-wise if she were to achieve her goals. Although this might suggest Teresa forfeited some of her simplicity and greatness, what she did was quite human, because Fr Balthazar was a great preacher and Teresa loved preachers.

Balthasar Nieto eventually became Prior of the second foundation (Pastrana), that initially consisted of two novices: Ambrose Mariano and John of the Misery.

The foundations established, Teresa now returned to Toledo in the Prince and Princess of Eboli's luxurious coach. She had become tired of the Princess's histrionics, which would have been worse but for the good sense of her husband, Ruy Gomez. When she arrived in the Imperial City, an unbalanced cleric cried out to her, 'You are the saint who fools the world and goes around in a coach?' Teresa humbly confessed: 'No one has ever told me my faults like this man.' From then on she refused to travel in a coach, preferring to go in a wagon.

The Prioress of Toledo, Isabel of St Dominic, returned to Pastrana in the same coach. Teresa had appointed her Prioress in that place where she had to struggle with the capricious nature of the Princess of Eboli.

The Carmelite friars in St Peter's, Pastrana, developed spectacularly, in contrast to Duruelo. Three years after the foundation, in April 1572, Jerome Gratian made his profession. He tells us that there were thirty novices, many of whom had been students at the nearby University of Alcala.

When he arrived Fr Peter of the Apostles, from Seville, was the Master of Novices. He had been a Calced Carmelite from the Andalucian Province. He was later replaced by Angel of St Gabriel who introduced alarming and grotesque penances, creating an absurd climate of fervor and rigorism, and yet attracting a lot of vocations.

Jerome denounced these penitential methods and this kind of spirituality. The Prior, Fr Balthasar of Jesus, was almost always away preaching or doing God only knows what, consequently Jerome sometimes found himself having to substitute for the Prior.

Like all beginners Jerome was very happy because 'he had found in the

Order what his spirit desired, which was prayer, charity, simplicity, sincerity and humility, to which he was by nature inclined.' On the same day he received the habit, and was given the name 'Jerome of the Mother of God', he wrote to his mother, Joanna Dantisco, to tell her that she should not blame herself for his entry into the Carmelite Order but the Blessed Virgin Mary, who had hounded him for more than a year. 'It wasn't possible to swim against the current any more,' he confided, 'I believe that my conversion must be for a purpose: to serve God in a great way; and believe me, noble mother, I have not been moved by others persuading me, or by passion, or any kind of bad experience, but by God alone, who knows and does what He wills.'

Thomas Gratian, Jerome's brother, comforted his mother in a letter written from Aranjuez, on 29 April. Though 'the Master's' decision had hurt her (the family called Jerome 'the Master'), he begged his mother, 'consider that the Master is a man of such sound judgment and gifted by God that He must have picked the best, and when we least expect it our Lord gives us the grace to have another Lobo or, perhaps someone even better.'

By 'another Lobo' Thomas was alluding to Alonso Lobo de Medina Sidonia, a famous Franciscan and a good preacher at the time. Thomas was not upset about the temporal problem, i.e. finances; he told his mother that God would provide. 'I am certain that this is the beginning of many and infinite blessings that you will receive from the Master through the mediation of our good Mistress (Our Lady). The good Lady has taken this son for Herself and therefore there is no reason why you, Noble Lady, should be unhappy, quite the reverse, you should have greater confidence in asking God for blessings since you have access to God's Mother through the Master who is Her servant.'

It is fascinating when you realize that Thomas was only fourteen when he wrote this letter. He became a great writer, winning praise from Cervantes and Lope de Vega. We do not know what Thomas was doing in Aranjuez, but his consoling words to his mother reflect the family's anxiety at the decision taken by Jerome.

Joanna Danstisco replied to Thomas, expressing the family's conformity with God's will; we do not have her letter. We do know, however, that Jerome wrote to her a few days later, on 6 May. He told her that he was in 'good form and well fed' in Pastrana. His headache, that had never left him due to the pressure of studies, had now disappeared, as well as the pain in his back. He was happy.

Anastasius and Cyril engage each other in conversation:

> ANASTASIUS: I received the habit. I had thought I would die of the cold and the harsh conditions, but the regular daily pains in my back, head and stomach disappeared. Incredibly, when I took off my ordinary footwear I had such robust health that I could walk without shoes in the snow, which for me was like treading on roses. I do not know how to express what had happened except as they do in books on chivalry written about knights, that when they were badly wounded fairies would take them off to enchanting springs at which they would come out healed and more courageous; they could not be wounded again as happened to Orlando.[1]
>
> CYRIL: It was a fairy, none less than the Blessed Virgin Mary who had done this.
>
> ANASTASIUS: Nor can I explain how I coped with the food, and how the turnips, cabbage and the broth from the refectory table built me up, which in the past would have upset my stomach and killed me.
>
> CYRIL: This seems to have been a great miracle.
>
> ANASTASIUS: It's not a miracle, but it's only natural that when the spirit is in its centre, the body, in harmony, redounds with health and feels good. When the Spirit isn't, the chicken and pheasant become poisonous, and the sugar and jelly and syrup become very bitter, as happened to me when I was in the house of Andrew de Bobadilla [the Count of Chinchon's son], struggling with my vocation.

However, it won't seem to Jerome such a bed of roses when time passes and he settles down to life in the priory.

Balthazar Nieto, the Prior, was always away in Madrid, and because they were all novices and lay brothers it fell to Jerome, even though he too was a novice, to be in charge of the house. 'I was not short of work that year,' Jerome acknowledged. One important challenge came when Teresa decided that her nuns in Pastrana were to be subject to him.

> What put most pressure on me that year and was the start of a lot of work, was when Mother Teresa of Jesus, seeing me in her Order, told the

1 Orlando was a chivalrous knight, like Don Quijote.

> Discalced Carmelite nuns in Pastrana to obey me as they would her. Until then she had not allowed any friar, either Calced or Discalced, to have such authority. Later she broke down in tears when she told me how the friars normally oppressed [the nuns] under the guise of obedience. They took away from them that holy freedom to choose good confessors, which had given the nuns the kind of solace that Teresa esteemed so highly but they [the friars] abhorred in the same measure. The confidence that Mother Teresa placed in me [because of it she transferred obedience from the bishops to the friars] rankled in the hearts of many of the friars, and later grew until it became a great fire. That fire caused much damage in the souls of some of the professed, as they began to spread rumours and some of the friars in the Priory of Pastrana began to persecute (me) and not only in that Priory. This happened because, although only a novice, I had the responsibility of a professed friar and even of a superior; they knew there were not many who could do these things.

I would like to point out here, something that I shall return to later, that when, in 1575, Teresa of Avila got to know Jerome Gratian well, she put herself under obedience to him. What prompted Teresa to put him in charge of her nuns in Pastrana? At the time he was just a simple novice; a young man who had only just entered the Order. At the appropriate time we shall ask the same question: what prompted her to do the same with herself when she got to know him personally?

Jerome was worn out by the temptations and the fear he felt inside of being in charge. His heart was greatly distressed; 'you left the world for fear of governing others', he said to himself. Did he have to tie himself down with new precepts, obligations, constitutions and rules?

It was when he was feeling like this that the young novice with responsibilities of a Prior, went to Mother Isabel of St Dominic, the Prioress of Pastrana, and poured out his doubts and fears to her.

Jerome had to go to Madrid on a matter of conscience; he discovered in confession that Prince Ruy Gomez was dying; that his doctors were slowly poisoning him with some kind of medication: a red-coloured syrup, composed of arsenic and sulphur. However, the doctors were warned that it was known, and changed the Prince's medication, giving him the appropriate antidote. They 'replaced the medication with rhubarb treacle and this saved his life,' recounted Jerome; that is, they gave Gomez a purgative, rhubarb treacle, a medicine made up of many ingredients which was used at that time as a cure for poisonous bites.

'If I had not made that visit and if the medication had not been changed then Prince Ruy Gomez would have died, instead his life was saved.' The event that Jerome refers to was not, to my knowledge, acknowledged in the biographies of the Prince of Eboli. However, we should not be taken aback because Ruy Gomez died the following year; though it was not due to the illness referred to by Jerome; only God knows why he died.

The young Gratian used the trip to Madrid to visit his family. His mother was seven months pregnant and, due to a virus, was at the point of death. However, she eventually gave birth to a baby girl, Juliana, her twentieth and last child. It was the year 1574; many years later Juliana would become a Discalced Carmelite nun in Seville.

When Jerome visited his mother, Fr Balthazar Nieto accompanied him. Jerome assured her that 'he had not taken the habit because he was unhappy but to serve our Blessed Lady.' Joanna turned her head to look at a picture of the Blessed Virgin and exclaimed out loud, in the hearing of Fr Balthazar: 'O Holy Mary, I have been very foolish to be upset that you took my son away for your service, now I give him to you and I do so very willingly.'

People were stopping Joanna in the street and telling her: 'Console yourself, Lady Joanna, you have given a son to our Lady.' To which she replied: 'I haven't given him, she has taken him.'

And so we learn that, in the hearing of the Prior, she had now accepted the will of the Blessed Virgin, our Lady of Mount Carmel.

Jerome's visit to Madrid caused some to talk about him breaking the rules of the novitiate. He later wrote: 'God, who knows all secrets, understands well that often for God's law people have to break man-made laws.'

Some friars also complained that even though he was a novice he had the authority of a professed religious, and even of a prior; that he went out to preach and to hear the nuns' confessions. However, Jerome was the only priest (in the novitiate); the others were novices or lay brothers. It was thanks to his efforts that the priory had enough income to afford food. 'If I had not gone out the novices would have gone hungry and would have left,' he wrote.

Balthasar Nieto was in Madrid at the priory of the Calced Carmelites, which opened in 1573. Mariano, who was the eldest, was not ordained nor did he wish to be. Instead he wanted to be a lay brother. Other recently professed friars were not well educated, nor did they have experience or prudence. The rest looked to Jerome Gratian to improve the conditions in the house, even though he was a novice. They also looked to him to moderate the 'holy but crude' practices that often destroyed the spirit and the credibility of their lives as religious.

So terrible was the storm that arose against Jerome that he had been on the verge of leaving. It was Mother Isabel de St Dominic who allayed his fears and calmed the storm in his spirit.

There were things that were disturbing in the Pastrana house. One example concerned a priest who wanted to teach a novice how to be perfect. To this end he sent the young man off to set fire to some wet wood without using a match, using only prayer as the prophet Elijah had done on Mt. Carmel. The priest kept flogging the young man on his bare back until he lit the fire.

The novices were to seek to recollect themselves in the hills before returning to the priory carrying a load of heavy wood on their shoulders. One day Mariano accompanied Jerome. A neighbour of theirs in Pastrana asked Jerome: 'Why are you carrying the wood on your back? Mariano replied sarcastically: 'Because this way we warm ourselves twice over.'

These ridiculous exaggerations were due to the Sub-Prior, who was Master of Novices, Angel of St Gabriel; in all charity, let's just say he was eccentric.

> It was very cold at the time and I walked about in the snow without shoes. As I went into the towns and small villages to preach, my feet became swollen like aubergines, so much so that the [town] Council asked the Superiors to tell me to put on shoes. However, this was not possible as the Discalced Carmelites, at the beginning, were very rigorous. Sometime later they introduced shoes and sandals. We lacked food, because the Superiors couldn't attend to everything, to the extent that months went by and especially one Lent, when we did not eat anything except turnips and broth. When at Easter someone gave us a little fish that was off, it seemed to us we were eating like kings.

The (Royal) Court heard about the rigid penances in Pastrana. The members wanted to see for themselves and to this end sent a representative, a Fr Hernando del Castillo, to visit the priory. When Fr Hernando returned to the Court, Prince Ruy Gomez asked him what he thought about his friars. Hernando replied: 'In the eyes of the world, crazy; to those with faith, angels and ministers on fire in spiritual bodies, so that we who are weak can see something of the spirit glowing in them.'

Faced with such foolish behaviour Jerome was tempted to think he had taken the wrong path. However, he was the only one with sense who could rectify all this. Donazar is clear that 'without the input of Fr Gratian, Teresa of Avila's plans for the friars would have ended up going awry.' St Teresa confirmed this opinion in her capacity as the Foundress, 'It seems that our Lady listened to him for the good of this new Order. He came at the right time. There were times when I regretted starting this work. It was not bad; but it started to fall apart very quickly.'

The foolish mortifications were introduced from the beginning by Frs Peter of the Apostles and Angel of St Gabriel, the first Novice-Masters. Teresa described the latter as, 'a very young friar who lacked education, had little ability or the necessary prudence to govern.' She was astonished at the mortifications the novices were obliged to undergo.

Much of the blame for these exaggerated penances in Pastrana was due to the influence of a woman named Catalina de Cardona, whom people called 'the good woman'. She was given this title when, in 1571, during a visit to Pastrana, which was on the road to the Court, she became a Carmelite, not a nun but a friar! Surprisingly, she was supported in this by none other than the Princess of Eboli.

Catalina was born in Naples, the illegitimate child of Ramon de Cardona, a captain from Aragon. She came to Spain with the Princess of Salerno, but when the Princess returned to Italy Catalina remained in Spain in the service of the Princess of Eboli. She became Governess of Prince Charles and Don John of Austria. However, led by the Spirit to be a hermit, she disappeared from the Court and took refuge in a cave, near the town of La Roda. Anastasius described the place where she lived:

> She left Ruy Gomez's house, and led by Fr Pina, her Spiritual Director, came

> to a deserted place near La Roda, a village in the La Mancha Province, where she lived in a cave. She had a bed made of stone with a small rock for a pillow. She wore sack-cloth next to her skin. She disciplined herself harshly each day, not eating more than a piece of stale bread that she prepared with a little flour given her every three days by the local people. She drank water from the River Jucar, on whose banks her cave was located. She spent most of the day and night in prayer. Hers was one of the harshest and most mysterious lives that there has ever been seen in Spain at this time. The people admired her and called her 'the good woman'.

Catalina lived in that cave for eight years and was admired by all around for her extreme penances. St Teresa described her in the *Book of Her Foundations*: 'Her clothes were made of coarse material and her tunic sack-cloth, and designed in such a way that people thought she was a man.' Catalina was not very feminine in appearance, having a small body, her face lined and her skin dark. By now she was well on in years and thought of perpetuating her cave with a monastery, not of women but of men. She contacted the Prince and Princess of Eboli. On one fine day in the spring of 1571 she appeared in Pastrana. Fr Angel of St Gabriel, who became greatly devoted to her, said, 'Her appearance was more like that of a strong but emaciated friar, than the delicate and beautiful woman she had once been. Now she was small, and bent over, her skin weather-beaten.'

The Princess of Eboli wanted to bring her straight away to the Carmelite sisters, but Catalina preferred to go to the Palace. The (Discalced Carmelite) Chronicler wrote that 'there was little of the feminine about her, nor did she tolerate anyone touching her head.' The friars did not hesitate to give her one of their habits. Fr Balthazar presided at the (clothing) ceremony. Also present was her sponsor, her former Mistress, the Princess of Eboli. Catalina de Cardona put on the rough Carmelite habit, over which there was a white mantle and capuche. She did not wear sandals but remained barefoot, as she had always been.

Accompanied by Ambrose Mariano she went to Madrid to collect alms for her foundation called La Roda. When in Madrid it was found out that the friar was not a friar but a woman it caused quite a stir at the Court. A large crowd of people wanted to see this female hermit and as a result she collected a large sum for her new priory, which she put in 'a box made of walnut until it was filled with enough money, silver and gold, that it weighed a bushel.' The Prince of Eboli asked Brother John of the Misery to paint a portrait of Catalina 'in the same clothes she was wearing, to satisfy the appetite of the people.' However, no such portrait has come down to us. The Nuncio was horrified to learn that Catalina was going round Madrid dressed as a friar and that she was welcomed by King Philip II into the Escorial Palace.

Catalina called into Pastrana on her return to La Roda. It was March 1572, a month before Jerome received his habit. Frs Ambrose, Mariano and Brother John of the Misery remained with her at La Roda. Catalina de Cardona died five years later on 11 May 1577 and was buried in the chapel of La Roda priory.

The community at Pastrana had fallen under this woman's spell. It is curious that Catalina, who travelled to the Court (in Madrid), and passed through Toledo, where she visited the Carmelite nuns recently established by Teresa of Avila, showed no interest in meeting Teresa. In the early days of the (Discalced Carmelite) friars the waters seemed to flow along channels of such strident rigorism that it would have been difficult for them to have survived. Catalina had become the model, who, with her friar's habit, brought into question the future of Teresa's Reform of the friars. It was Jerome Gratian, whom Teresa saw as sent by God, who took on the challenge of putting order and sanity back into so much nonsense. However, in doing this he would endure wounds that never healed, and became the object of lies that never seemed to end. Thirty years later, after the death of St Teresa and Jerome's exile, Fr Angel of St Gabriel, the Sub-Prior and Novice-Master in Pastrana, wrote the following important words:

> Even though I am going against the current by saying that Mother Teresa of Jesus is the Foundress of the Discalced Carmelite nuns and friars, I was impressed by Mother Cardona. The Discalced friars would be better to imitate more the hermit Cardona than the nun Teresa.

And just to underline what he said above and remove any possible doubt, the same friar added:

> It is a bold statement to make that Mother Cardona was no less Foundress of the Discalced friars than Mother Teresa of Jesus. Thanks to the Pastrana priory, founded by Fr Mariano and John of the Misery, this is even more the case. The Order has multiplied more than it did in Mancera, founded by the two Calced friars [John of the Cross and Anthony] whom Mother

> Teresa turned into Discalced. That house in Mancera has already closed [it transferred to Avila in 1600], thus the Pastrana house is now the first and, consequently the womb and yardstick of our life.

However, this is another matter that we can return to later. St John of the Cross, apparently, made a brief visit to Pastrana before Jerome arrived there, in order to bring a little harmony and common sense to the place. He had been sent there by Teresa. When Jerome arrived the eccentricities were still commonplace, as Catalina de Cardona had only recently died. The motto of the Priory of St Peter at Pastrana, according to Donazar, could well have been, 'get ill in order to die, and by dying you will be able to see God.' This was not what St Teresa wanted. Her motto could have been what she wrote on a certain occasion to Mary of St Joseph, Prioress of Seville, 'It is better to be self-indulgent than to be ill.'

Jerome Gratian made profession in Pastrana after his twelve-month novitiate. 'We were ten novices,' he recounted, 'Fr John of Jesus Roca, Fr Alonso of the Angels, Brother Peter of the Purification, Brother Simon Stock and many others. That novitiate year ended on the feast day of St Anastasius, 1573, which was when I made my profession.'

The feast day of St Anastasius of Sinai, a bishop, was, according to the Roman martyrology, on 21 April. Perhaps this was why he used the pseudonym Anastasius in his autobiography, *The Pilgrimage of Anastasius.*

Days later, on Saturday 25 April, the feast of St Mark, the 'Master, Jerome de Antisco, made his profession; son of the Secretary, Diego Gratian and Joanna de Antisco, from Madrid, in the Toledo diocese.'

Jerome used the following formula that I translated from the Latin original: 'I Brother Jerome of the Mother of God… make profession and promise obedience, poverty and chastity to God and to the Blessed Virgin Mary of Mt. Carmel, and to Fr John Baptist Rossi de Ravenna, Prior General of the friars of the Carmelite Order and to his successors, according to the Primitive Rule of the said Order, that is, without mitigation, until death.'

The name he chose, Brother Jerome of the Mother of God, was no doubt in memory of his college in Alcala, where he had studied, and because of his devotion to the Blessed Virgin. His swimming against the current had been to no avail.

Chapter Nine

Apostolic Visitator and Vicar Provincial

RUY GOMEZ DIED IN MADRID ON 29 JULY 1573. Before the funeral cortege left for Pastrana the widowed Princess enacted yet another theatrical gesture: she asked Ambrose Mariano for a friar's habit and, dressed in this, went to Pastrana with the intention of becoming a nun. What a *prima donna*.

Anthony Perez, the King's Secretary, who became the Princess' lover, sent a letter to Philip II informing him of the widow's surprising resolution: 'When her husband died she put on a habit of the Discalced Carmelite nuns and left tonight for her convent in Pastrana with courage and an extraordinary resolve.'

In observance of mourning protocol, the Princess travelled in a cart instead of her luxurious coach. Balthasar Nieto went on ahead to St Joseph's convent, arriving after nightfall. He told the Prioress, Isabel of St Dominic, the incredible news that the Princess of Eboli was coming to join the convent. 'The Princess is to become a nun?' exclaimed the astounded Prioress, 'she will destroy this household.'

The Carmelite nuns had a custom of picking at random a small piece of paper with a virtue written on it; the idea was to put that virtue into practice. At the draw the day before the arrival of the Princess, Mother Isabel drew the virtue of patience. Not knowing what was about to happen she asked, 'Why do I need to practise the virtue of patience?' But it was not long before she found out; she would soon have to deal with the Princess.

The Princess duly arrived at the convent the following morning and gave the Prioress a brief explanation: 'With the death of my husband I am no longer in the world.' The nuns, who had prepared rooms for the Princess and her mother, who had accompanied her, altered her habit as it was neither appropriate nor clean. She took 'Sr Anne of the Mother of God' as her religious name.

In her megalomania the Princess also asked two of her maids to put on the habit. Astonished by this the Prioress told her, in all humility, that it would be necessary to obtain a licence from the (male) Superiors. The Princess exclaimed angrily: 'What have the friars to do with my convent?'

The following day, Ruy Gomez was buried in the collegiate church and the Princess received condolences in the convent. 'Many servants entered with their masters,' recalled the Chronicle, 'brushing aside the Council's decrees, the orders of holy Mother, the peace and silence of the nuns, and all good government.'

This intrusion made the community's life quite impossible. Indeed, the Bishop of Segorbe came to offer his condolences and left appalled by what he saw.

By October the Princess had been in the convent for five months. On 10 October, Fr Anthony of Jesus told the Duchess of Alba, 'We have some surprising news of our novice, the Princess, she is five months pregnant! Also she is acting as if she was the Prioress: she insists that the sisters speak to her on their knees and treat her as a great lady. Will Your Excellency please inform our Mother about this, if she does not already know.'

The Prioress wrote to St Teresa in tears, asking their Foundress to send them to another convent where they could observe the Rule of the Order in peace. Teresa sighed: 'I have great esteem for our nuns in Pastrana, who are like captives.'

The Princess, annoyed by the Prioress' entreaties and threats that Teresa would transfer the nuns if she did not moderate her impertinent behaviour, decided to go and live with her mother and her maids in a hermitage in the convent garden, which had a small window through which she could climb down into the street.

King Philip II himself and the Council of Castile had to intervene to persuade the Princess of Eboli to desist from her crazy ways and dedicate herself to the care of her children and the administration of her estate.

After six months with the nuns, an angry and vindictive Princess returned to her palace. The community of sixteen then left the convent in April 1574 under cover of darkness. Climbing into five covered wagons that were waiting for them on the outskirts of the town, they arrived in Segovia days later to a new foundation established by St Teresa. However, the furious Princess of Eboli thought up a diabolical way to punish the nuns. She handed Teresa's manuscript of the *Book of her Life* to the Inquisition and denounced the foundress as a visionary. A Franciscan community (Conceptionists) took over the convent in Pastrana, receiving new donations from the Princess, and is still there to this day.

Gratian was facing a dilemma which he shared with Mariano, who had arrived in Pastrana with the funeral cortege:

> If the two of them remained in Pastrana they could either take the side of the Prioress and the Order but, in doing so, be out of favour with the Princess and consequently the entire Order, or, take the side of the Princess, in which case they would badly affect the perfection and observance [of the Reformed Order].

They decided to take themselves away from this situation by leaving Pastrana for Andalucía, while 'commending to God the negotiations between the Princess and the nuns, which seemed impossible to resolve satisfactorily.' It was August 1573.

Cyril asks Anastasius: 'Tell me, how many difficulties did you have to overcome after making your profession?' Anastasius replies: 'I don't want to waste time talking about every detail of my past. I will tell you just two things about all the time I was a Discalced Carmelite. Firstly, I suffered from the Calced until the (Discalced) Order was set up and the foundations and Provinces were established and, secondly, I suffered from the Discalced.'

This would be the pattern for the rest of his life. If what Jerome suffered with the Calced Carmelites was humiliating, it was no less so with the Discalced Carmelites.

Some years before the saga of the Princess in 1574, the Carmelite General, John Baptist Rossi, was travelling throughout Spain to visit the various Provinces. Unbeknown to him, Philip II (who supported the Reform) had obtained a Brief from Rome to appoint Apostolic Visitators for Castile and Andalucía. It was only on Rossi's return to Italy a year later, that he discovered this and immediately asked that the Brief be revoked. However, two Dominican priests had already been appointed in August 1569: Peter Fernandez for the Castile province and Francis de Vargas for Andalucia.

The Carmelite priories in Castile lived in relative harmony and Peter Fernandez, a prudent and capable man, completed his task peacefully, and together with the Carmelite Provincial he completed all he needed to do.

For example, in 1571, he made Anthony of Jesus Prior of Toledo; a Discalced in charge of Calced Carmelites. He also made Teresa return as Prioress to reform her old convent of the Incarnation in Avila.

However, Andalucia was an entirely different matter; it was a wasps' nest. After visiting the priories in that Province, General Rossi had left chastened by his experiences.

The Dominican, Vargas, wearied by the rebelliousness of the Andalucians, took a different approach from his counterpart in Castile. He decided to create priories for Reformed Carmelites only, against General Rossi's express ruling. Jerome tells us, 'Vargas said that there was no better way to reform the Calced Carmelites than by closing those of the Calced and increasing the number of Discalced priories.' Thus, in 1572, the priory of St John del Puerto (Huelva) was handed over to those Calced friars who wanted to be Discalced.

Vargas also promoted foundations of Discalced Carmelite nuns in Andalucía. For example, he established convents in La Penuela and Granada, and in May 1573, with the support of the Count of Tendilla, he founded the priory of Los Martires.

The priory of St John del Puerto 'had from the beginning only known dissensions among the Calced Carmelites of Andalucia.' Jerome could see that this was dangerous:

> As they [the Calced Carmelites] were not entering by the narrow door of perfection, they were convinced that if they were to grow, they had to uproot the new plant sown by the newly founded Discalced friars before it began to spread. They saw that all the customs they had built up in Castile would come crashing down if the Discalced Carmelites grew, so they decided to uproot the seedlings. Therefore, when Jerome and Ambrose fled from the Princess, they decided to visit Andalucia to establish priories of authentic Discalced Carmelites and put right the Congregation that was just beginning at that time.

Jerome's motive for beating a hasty retreat from Pastrana with Ambrose Mariano was to uproot the Calced Carmelite trees and create authentic Discalced Carmelite communities in the fertile land of Andalucia. They had also been summoned by Vargas (the Apostolic Visitator), who had written to Mariano in Pastrana to come 'with some Discalced Carmelites from the Order, because previous Calced friars who have become Discalced are not credible, so that they would never have been accepted as Discalced friars.' This was what led to a fracas in St John del Puerto.

It was August 1572 when Mariano and Jerome left Pastrana for Granada, to meet Vargas. In April the latter had ceded his authority to act as Apostolic Visitator to Balthazar Nieto. This was due to either laziness, or tiredness, or some other reason, while he should have made foundations in Granada. However, Balthazar, who from Granada had gone to Madrid and then Pastrana to accompany the body of the Prince of Eboli, knew he was unable to fulfill the requirements of this Bull in a worthy manner in Andalucía, where his deceitful ways were well known. He therefore entrusted the task to Jerome. The patent was signed in Pastrana on 4 August 1573 naming Jerome Gratian 'Apostolic Commissioner and Visitator of the Carmelite Order for the Province of Andalucia'.

'Just after my profession I was burdened with the task of Visitator and Reformer of the Calced Carmelites in Andalucia,' laments Anastasius.

Jerome and Mariano escaped quietly (from Pastrana) to Madrid (before going to Granada) without alerting the Provincial of Castile, Angel de Salazar, who would not have let them go. There, Jerome visited his mother, who encouraged them both to keep going. (It is interesting to note that he speaks a lot about his mother in his writings, but says hardly anything about his father). In Toledo, Mariano received the ministry of reader before they made their way to a recently founded Discalced Carmelite priory at La Penuela. Next, they visited Baeza before reaching Granada, where they met up with the Dominican Provincial and Visitator, Francis de Vargas.

Jerome was now twenty-eight years old, a newly professed friar who has been given the difficult task of Apostolic Visitator to the Calced Carmelites in Andalucia. He had the original Papal Bull and also a Patent giving him faculties to take charge of the Discalced friars. These had three houses (in Andalucia): Penuela, Granada and St John del Puerto, all founded, as we have seen, against the express wish of the Carmelite General.

No small task! Did he know what he was letting himself in for? It seems that he did not seek this office, but nor did he turn it down, even though he should have foreseen that he would fall flat on his face in these impossible circumstances. He headed for Seville with Mariano, his credentials in his pouch, where his first task would be to close the Priory of St John del Puerto.

In Seville, Jerome and Mariano were warmly welcomed by the Calced friars when told that the principal purpose of their visit was to dissolve the Discalced Carmelite priory of St John del Puerto and get rid of those Discalced Carmelites who were there against his [the General's] will. The newly appointed Visitator recalled how they were treated with kindness and fraternal charity. However, he noted that there were still voices of discontent: 'The Discalced are now going to dissolve this Discalced priory, but we shall dissolve all that they have founded, so that we never hear of them again.'

The two Reformers, with the Provincial and other Calced Carmelites, reached St John del Puerto on 17 October 1573, just in time for Vespers. Jerome read out the official document that appointed him Apostolic Visitator and called the friars together for a Chapter meeting, during which he handed the priory back to the Calced. He took the habit away from all the novices except that of Brother Angel of the Presentation, who was only one month from profession. Finally, with a theatrical gesture, he gave his sandals to the Calced Carmelites.

The next day, Jerome visited the nearby priory of Gibraleon: founded in 1332, it was the Carmelite Order's first foundation in Spain.

To prevent St John del Puerto being closed, some Discalced friars went to the local Lord, the Duke of Medina Sidonia, to plead for his support. Jerome therefore sent Mariano to exert his authority.

Gratian returned to St John del Puerto. Early the next morning, while the friars were getting up for morning prayer, he took the novices and walked with them to Seville, a distance of about fifteen leagues. Singing the *miserere* with them, he encouraged the novices, who were upset and afraid. On arrival in Seville,

> Fr Gratian had no choice but to call a halt to what he was doing. Here he was alone in a strange land with eight or nine fragile and poor companions, without shoes. The only place he knew to take them was the Carmelite priory, to the same Calced fathers whom he most feared. However, he commended himself to God and to our Blessed Lady, to whom he offered this new foundation. When the group arrived in Seville the local people, on seeing our habit, were filled with devotion and praise. The friars had kept to a certain routine on the journey: in the morning they walked two or three leagues, and when they arrived at a village, went directly to the church where they said their office and celebrated sung Mass as if they were in their own priory.

There were no beds available for the novices at the Seville Carmel, but Jerome insisted that 'they did not want to go elsewhere, the hallway between the chapel and the Prior's cell would do.' So there they stayed, using straw mats on the floor for beds, their habits as mattresses and their mantles as blankets.

It was November and already cold in Seville. The novices and Gratian arose for Matins with the resident friars, and then remained for an hour of private prayer. As in Pastrana, they took the discipline three times a week. During the day, according to Jerome, 'they split into groups; some helped in the kitchen, others cleaned the house and others helped in the sacristy and assisted at Mass, always maintaining silence, modesty and composure.'

Many of the Calced Carmelites admired the simplicity and modesty of Fr Gratian's young friars. Even in the city the people spoke about them. The Archbishop, members of the Inquisition and their Assistant took an interest in them and many people gathered to hear Gratian when he preached.

> However, the harmony within the community broke down when Gratian denounced a Carmelite professor who preached against indulgences, stating that two of this man's proposals were heretical. The denunciation coincided with the arrival in Seville of two [Calced] Fathers from Castile, who spoke badly of Jerome and Mariano and complained that the Discalced priories were gaining in reputation as in Castile.

One evening, when it was really dark, an unknown assailant stabbed a Calced novice in the thigh as he was leaving the chapel with the Discalced friars.

> This novice was the same size and shape as Gratian; in fact he looked so much like him they could have been taken for twins. He [the novice] was so loved by everyone that 'no one could imagine who could have done this, unless, that is, the knife was meant for Fr Gratian who had not gone to the chapel that night as he was feeling unwell.

In addition, the novice's father was a benefactor of the Priory. 'Many of the friars said that the attacker made a mistake, that it was me he meant to stab,' explained Jerome.

Faced with this threat it was time to look for another priory. Jerome did not dare leave at the same time as Mariano, 'because if some misfortune should occur to one of us, the other could inform the Archbishop what had happened'.

Mariano was certain that the friars would kill Jerome. As they were walking together through the streets of Seville, he pleaded with him not to return to the priory, but, Jerome said he was not afraid and would not be put off. The two friars soon arrived at the convent of the Recollects of the Name of Jesus, where Jerome had previously preached and heard confessions. Mother Juliana of Jesus, the Abbess, approached Jerome after Mass and told him that there was no doubt he would be in danger if he returned to the Carmelites. She insisted that it was not Mariano who had alarmed her, as he presumed, but that at the moment he raised the Host during Mass she had sensed the danger they were in.

To obtain a property for the Discalced friars, Mariano visited the Bishop of Esquilache, but left empty handed. Nor did he manage to acquire the Bethlehem Hermitage on Alameda de Hercules Street. When they explained to Archbishop Christopher de Rojas the danger they were in he provided a solution; he offered them an ancient hermitage on the banks of the river, in Triana.

Years before, a hermit called Fr Rodrigo had cultivated crops at this hermitage of Our Lady of Perpetual Succour, to supply visiting seamen. It was not far from the Franciscan priory of La Vittoria, whose friars, not wanting any competition, had several times pulled down the new hermitage. When advised by the Carthusians of Santa Maria de las Cuevas to find a place elsewhere, Fr Rodrigo confided in them his premonition that some very holy religious would come to live there, who would bring forth abundant fruit for the town.

After Fr Rodrigo's death, the hermitage came under the jurisdiction of the Chief Inquisitor, Andrew Gasco, who turned it into a house where Inquisitors could come and relax. Sadly, Gasco was kicked by a horse and died in 1566, so the hermitage then became the property of the Curia, who in turn gave it to Jerome Gratian for the Discalced friars, who gave it the name Los Remedios Priory.

After two and a half months in Seville, Jerome and Mariano and their eight or nine novices secretly left the Carmelite priory on 5 January 1574, 'on foot and two by two'. Crossing the Guadalquivir River on a bridge made of barges they reached the Hermitage, where the Archbishop's Secretary gave the legal documents they would need to claim possession. Jerome celebrated Mass and reserved the Blessed Sacrament on the following day, the feast of the Epiphany.

The Calced friars were incensed and sent a venerable old Carmelite, Fr

Diego of Leon, to head a delegation to demand of Jerome by what authority he had removed the Discalced friars from their priory and founded another one in Triana. Fr Diego, a scholar of Greek and Hebrew, was the retired Bishop of Columbria and had taken part in the Council of Trent. Jerome explained that the papers giving him authority over the Discalced were with the Archbishop. When the Archbishop was asked he confirmed this.

Life was not easy at the Los Remedios Priory. A long way from the town, the only food they ate was, 'sardines that at the time did not cost much and slices of bread which served as plates. We had but eighteen *reales* when we arrived, all that was left from two gold coins (*doubloons*). I gave one coin to a poor traveller who was going to South America, telling myself that to make a foundation we had enough with one or two coins.'

In founding and establishing Los Remedios Priory, Jerome had gone beyond the commission given him by Fr Vargas.

Los Remedios Priory near Seville was the first Discalced house founded by Jerome. However, many hurdles had first to be overcome: Gasco's house attached to the hermitage was too small; alms were scarce, and the town was far away. In addition, the Franciscans in los Victorios served them lawsuits as they presumed the new foundation was on their property, and a local priest served another lawsuit, saying he owned some of the trees in the garden (which provided him with an income). With mediation by the Inquisitors, a perpetual obligation to celebrate a sung Mass with a sermon on the feast of the Immaculate Conception and on its Octave settled the second dispute.

In spite of these difficulties the number of novices began to increase. In spring 1574, Brother Louis of St Jerome, who would become Provincial of Catalonia priory, received the habit; also, a Brother Peter of the Mother of God became a good theologian and preacher.

The burgeoning community was joined by Frs John of the Miserere and Alonso of the Mother of God from Pastrana, and Fr Soto, a school administrator from Seville. He lived with them in Los Remedios until his death from a worldwide epidemic in 1580.

Brother Angel of the Presentation, who had been professed in the Seville Carmelite Priory on 21 November 1573, described the difficult circumstances that surrounded the origins of the foundation:

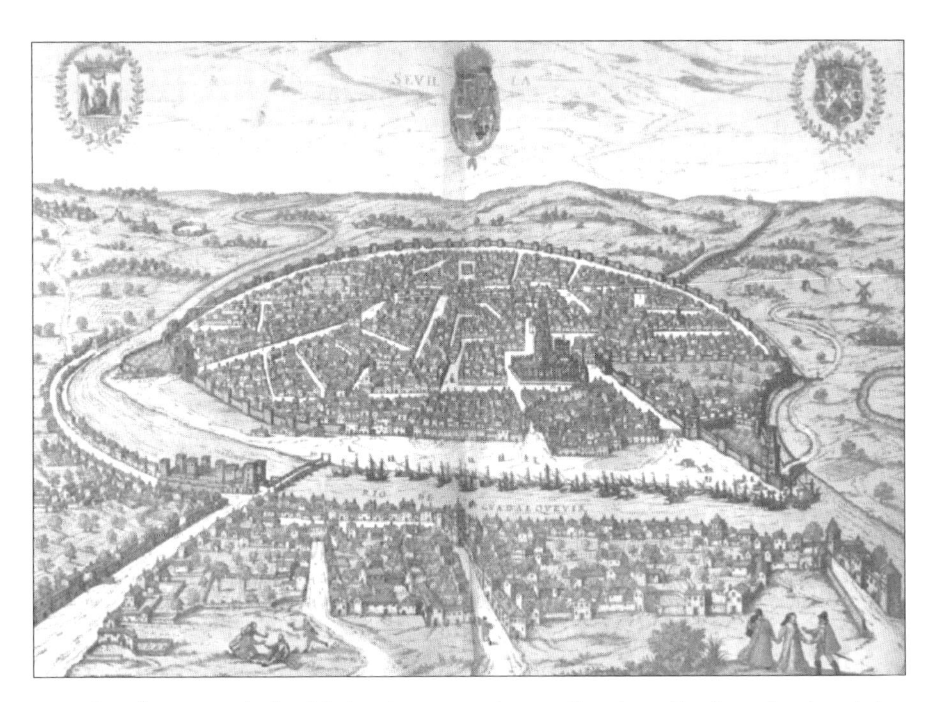

View of Seville, 1588. In the far right hand corner can be seen the priory of los Remedios, founded by Jerome in 1574.

It is hard to believe that in such a rich and devout city as Seville there could be such meanness… For some months we did not have a cooked meal, nor did we have wood for a fire, save for a few twigs and dried-up aubergine plants that were in the garden. Our food consisted of bread, not always enough, and small sardines grilled on gathered wood, or a few smoked snappers, the toughest and thinnest fish in the sea. We only ate on days when we had a little money with which to buy food, or were given alms. Nor did we even have plates on which to eat our sardines or snappers, except two or three old and broken ones left in the house… The lack of clothing and covering was terrible… Everyone slept on mats, our habits and mantles served as coverings to keep us warm. We were similarly short of all other necessities. However, each disregarded his own needs as if they didn't matter. Such was our fervor for observance, our perseverance in vigils and prayer, our great devotion to the praises of God and to our choral office that we seemed to be more like angels from heaven than men clothed in the weakness of human flesh.

Jerome Gratian was the Superior of Los Remedios and Mariano, recently ordained deacon in 1573 and priest in 1574, was the Master of Novices. Unfortunately, after being overcome by the music in the chapel, Mariano tripped and fell down the stairs. He passed out and broke his teeth so that when he came to his senses his mouth was crooked and his eyes crossed. The doctor diagnosed a stroke but Mariano recovered and lived long enough to become a difficult old man.

The Priory was supported both by the Archbishop, Christopher de Rojas, and the Inquisitors next door. When the Archbishop found himself in debt to the tune of ninety thousand *ducados*, Mariano managed to restore his finances, helped by an Italian named Nicholas Doria, a merchant who had done well from trade with Latin America. Not only did Doria help restore the Archbishop's income but he also paid off the latter's debts. This financial wizard who now enters our story will in time become Jerome's cruel tormentor.

The Priory made headway when wheat and food for the infirm was donated by the Archbishop. Jerome made his name through preaching and was offered the Chair of Sacred Scripture at Seville Cathedral.

To the poor who knocked on the door, the friars gave vegetables from the garden and shared the little bread they had been given. Asked by friends why he was giving away food when there was not enough for the friars, Jerome responded, 'I made a contract with God. I said to Him, "Lord, it is to you I give food when I give to the poor; give me and my friars yourself to eat, who also are poor and on the day the poor stop knocking at our door we shall die of hunger."'

There were occasions of generosity; a woman called at the door wrapped in a patched up shawl whom Jerome thought had come to ask for alms, but she handed him a banker's draft for one thousand *ducados*. Peter Cerezo Pardo, one of the merchants who supported the friars, sent enough money for them to create additional rooms to the priory.

The contents of Jerome Gratian's letter to Rossi, the General of the Order, can be inferred from the latter's reply on 26 April 1574, when he praised Jerome for his astuteness in defending the integrity of the Order and its antiquity against an Augustinian. This may be just a story but he recommended to Jerome not to respond to such ignorance, because there is so much that could be said in favour of the Order. There is no shortage of historical material to use. However, we can see the General's displeasure when he considers Jerome is acting 'contrary to obedience and so incurs punishment and censures', which, to the General, did not seem 'to be done in the service of God.' In the Reform of the Andalucian (Calced) Carmelites, the General advised Jerome to proceed with caution, since he was still not much more than a Novice and feared 'he would be led down paths and tracks that were not right.'

Jerome also made contact with St Teresa. He amazed her by what he had done since leaving Castile. Teresa wrote to her niece, Maria Bautista, from Segovia (where she had made a foundation) about the disturbance that Jerome and Mariano had caused in Seville.

> Oh, if you could see the uproar that is taking place, even though in secret, in favour of the Discalced! It is something for which we should give praise to God. Gratian and Mariano, who were in Andalucia, are responsible for this. The pleasure I get from this is tempered by the trouble that this must give to our Father General, whom I am very fond of. On the other hand, I see the precarious state we are in. I shall entrust this to God.

The General, Rossi, took offence because the house was founded in Andalucia without his authorization, and he had been inundated with complaints from the Calced Carmelites. The latter knew they would not be listened to in Madrid so they turned to Rome. The Provincials of Castile, Aragon, Catalonia and Andalucia, plus Portugal, came together and wrote a letter that the Portuguese Carmelite, Jerome Tostado, was entrusted to give to Rossi. In the letter they asked the Roman Curia to revoke the provocative Bull given to the (Dominican) Commissioners, so they would not be allowed to visit those houses in Spain already visited by the General of the Order nor those houses that had already been visited by the Commissioners. In August 1574, Rossi was told by Pope Gregory XIII that the appointment of Apostolic Commissioners would revert to the members of the Order.

The Archbishop of Seville, Cristobal de Rojas, informed the Nuncio, Ormaneto, that the Visitator, Vargas, did not want to continue with the Visitation of the Carmelites, under the pretext of having been elected Provincial of his Order; it seems Vargas had 'caught a cold on the Visitation.' Furthermore, Vargas was a man with a gentle disposition. 'In order to tame those wild men,' explained the same Nuncio, someone more robust was required for the Visitation.

The latest scandals at the Carmelite priory in Seville prompted the Archbishop to inform the Nuncio of the situation. On New Year's Eve, the local authorities arrested a friar who went around dressed as a layman and day and night gravely insulted people. The Archbishop's Secretary asked that the authorities keep the man in a prison 'until such time as he would be condemned to the galleys.'

On another occasion, the same secular authority found the Subprior in the house of a dishonest woman. The Provincial deprived the Subprior of his office and expelled him from Seville. However, the Subprior went to see the General in Rome and, instead of punishing him, the General gave him permission to return to the Seville Carmel, which, according to the Archbishop was 'a very scandalous thing to do.'

We already know about the dagger plunged into the leg of a novice, mistaken for Jerome. Another friar, about the same time, punched a theology lecturer in the face because the latter had criticized his work. Instead of being punished the Carmelites sent him off for further studies. And all this is not to mention the 'tough and scandalous' factions in the Carmelite priory, which should only be found among the secular and lost souls.

Vargas (the Dominican Commissioner) had come to Seville in March, 1574. Faced with the situation there he wrote to King Philip II, advising him that he preferred the new foundation by the Discalced Carmelites in Los Remedios, and that the Calced were reforming their lives. 'In this city of Seville there are Frs Mariano and Jerome Gratian, and other Fathers who, with their life and teaching edify many in this city, even though some of the Calced continue to oppress them.'

Vargas mentioned all of this as well in a letter to the Nuncio, Ormaneto, who doubted if his (Vargas') authority extended beyond the four years stipulated in the Bull. The said Bull stated that his appointment as Apostolic Visitator was for four years, now completed, after which it was up to the Holy See.

Vargas asked the Nuncio if his faculties had expired. For this reason, he admits that 'I am quite willing to carry out the Visitation in the hope that these Fathers would keep the Acts and Constitutions that I had left them to uphold, under pain of excommunication and grave penalties.' However, Vargas realized that he had been duped by them since his last visit in 1571. Those whom Vargas had banished from the Province *in perpetuum* had returned 'and what is worse, had celebrated Mass and continue to do so and recite the Divine Office and offer the sacrifice of the Mass, even though they have been excommunicated, and accept more candidates into the Order.' Those whom, because of their dishonesty and scandalous behavior, Vargas had deprived of active voice and office, the General, Rossi, absolved and reinstated, stating that false witnesses had come forward; when in truth, they were caught 'red-handed by the same secular justice in dishonest and infamous houses.'

Ornamento wrote to Vargas on 8 May, that his faculties as Visitator had not expired, even though the period of four years stated in the Bull had expired, and that the Pope who had issued the Bull, Pius V, had died. Thereby, he could continue with his Visitation. On 13 June, Vargas, whose authority had been reestablished by the Nuncio, wrote a formal letter from Cordoba appointing Jerome Gratian Vicar Provincial of the Carmelites in Andalucia. 'It seemed right to me that Your Paternity be Vicar Provincial, as you will see from the Patent.' I pray that you accept this 'because there is so much work that all of us have to do what we can.' Jerome exercised his responsibility as Vicar Provincial with the support of the Archbishop, who asked him:

> To order all those Carmelite friars who had not been professed in the Province of Andalucia to leave. And the same for all the friars that Your Paternity, should find who, following the Visitation, were sent away from the Province, that they do not return to it under penalty of excommunication if they returned; and they have returned without my written permission and have celebrated Mass even though they were under censure and in great contempt of His Holiness and of God. Ask them to take off the Carmelite habit and make them wear the clothes of the secular clergy.
>
> I give you faculties to absolve them from apostasy, just as I myself have this faculty from his Holiness the Pope.
>
> Moreover, can Your Paternity expel all those friars who have entered the Carmelite Order from other religious Orders, even though they did so with permission from some Superior of the Order. Will you please keep me informed as to what is happening so that we do everything for the good of this holy Order, which is my wish, and which is as important to me as my own salvation.

What a small task they have yet again given to Gratian! Now he is Vicar Provincial of the Calced and Discalced Carmelites in Andalucia. He is asked to use a stick, in other words, 'to appoint and expel ministers and prelates in the said Order.' However, as the Calced Chronicler wrote, 'Fr Gratian did not exercise his authority as he was ill.' It was a 'serious illness,' Jerome stressed, 'and for this reason I begged Fr Vargas not to compel me to obey what he had asked.'

If Jerome accepted this uncomfortable responsibility it was for the sake of the Order. 'Writing to Teresa (*La Madre*) about this it seemed to her and to all our friends that it was better I accept this cross, so that the Calced did not bring an end to the priories of the Discalced.'

On 22 September, the Nuncio tightened the screws a little more on the Carmelite Reform. He appointed Francis de Vargas and Jerome together, '*in solidum*', as Reformers of Carmel in Andalucia: 'if one was obstructed on his Visitation the other could proceed'. At the time Vargas had been made Provincial of the Dominicans and so he was often obstructed and absent from the city of Seville.

What Ormaneto did not know was that days before (13 August), the General of the Order, Rossi had obtained a Brief from Pope Gregory XIII terminating the faculties of the Dominican Visitators and their Delegates; faculties that had been given by Pope Pius V. The Nuncio found out about the Brief from the Carmelites of Andalucia. He was surprised at this news and wrote to Cardinal Tolomeo Galli, the Papal Secretary, on 10 October, asking him if the Brief (the Calced called it a counterbrief) limited his own faculties as Nuncio in Spain, and was this the Holy Father's will?

On 17 October, the Royal Council wrote to the King's Representative in Seville, Francis Zapata, Count of Barajas, that he take hold of 'the Brief that the Carmelite friars had brought [from Rome] in order to raise the subject of the Visitation' and deliver it to Madrid; since all Papal Bulls or documents that had not been previously presented to the King were invalid. The King's agreement was required.

Philip II, who was living in the El Escorial Palace, was informed by the Count of Barajas that the Brief brought from Rome for the Carmelite friars could only be given to them if Fr Francis deVargas, the Apostolic Commissioner, visited the said friars. The King ordered Vargas to do this and informed the Archbishop of Seville to support the Visitator in mutual agreement with his Royal Assistant: if needs be the sword would be used in the service of the Cross.

Cardinal Galli wrote to the Nuncio, Ormaneto, from Rome on 16 December, pointing out that the Nuncio's faculties for the reform of the

Religious had not been revoked by Pope Gregory XIII's Brief, which only referred to the revocation of the Dominican Visitators.

Jerome was wise not to take the Brief to the King, even though he had papers and letters that entitled him to do so, because it 'smacked of secular affairs.' Instead, he stayed in the priory of Los Remedios and, while the storm abated, limited his Visitations to the houses of the Discalced.

Gratian was summoned by the Nuncio to Madrid. However, due to a commitment to preach during Lent in the Cathedral, he was prevented from leaving Seville until Easter: 3 April 1575. He knew that Teresa of Avila was at the foundation in Beas and so, before crossing into La Mancha, he made his way to Beas in order to make her acquaintance. It was to be a providential meeting for the Teresian Reform!

Chapter Ten

An Angel Called Jerome Gratian

Jerome and Teresa of Avila had never met before; they had only communicated by letter. It was in mid-April 1575 and in Beas de Segura that they got to know one another. From the very beginning there was a mutual attraction. Teresa of Jesus had reached her sixtieth year, which would have been considered old in those days. She, a 'restless vagabond', had attained the upper echelons of the spiritual life. Jerome, on the other hand, was not even thirty years old, an inexperienced but very intelligent friar.

When they met they both experienced a special chemistry; in Teresa, a maternal affection, in Jerome a filial love. Teresa had been looking for a man for her Reform, and realized that this man standing before her was the one. Her prayers had been answered; in fact, God gave her more than she could have imagined. Jerome Gratian was the man, her man. In her *Book of the Foundations* she wrote:

> Our Lord truly saw the great need there was for a person like this to carry on the work that He had begun. I often praise Him for the favour He granted us in this matter. Had I very much desired to ask His Majesty for a person to organize all the things pertaining to the Order in these initial stages I could not have succeeded in asking for all that He in fact gave me in Father. May the Lord be blessed forever.

The meeting in Beas was to be decisive for Teresa's fledgling Reform, in fact, all the Teresian scholars considered it to have been providential. Jerome remained in Beas about a month. It was in that small town, in the spring of 1575, that Teresa had just made her tenth foundation for the nuns. Jerome later wrote:

> She revealed her soul to me, keeping nothing back, and in the same spirit I did the same with her. It was there we agreed to be always in conformity in

> all our dealings. Later, following a special revelation, she made a particular life-long vow of religious obedience to me.

Teresa recorded this special revelation in her *Spiritual Testimonies*. She was seated at a table having something to eat, when all of a sudden and without warning she was overcome by a rapture and in the flash of lightning, she had a vision:

> It seemed to me our Lord Jesus Christ was next to me in the form in which He usually appears. At His right side stood Master Gratian himself, and I at His left. The Lord took our right hands and joined them and told me He desired that I take this Master to represent Him as long as I live, and that we both agree to everything because it was thus fitting.

This extraordinary experience happened in Beas on 24 April. I point out this date because, one month later, on 23 May, on the second day of the Easter Octave, while on her way to Seville, in a hermitage in Ecija, Teresa of Jesus made a vow of obedience to Fr Gratian. She noted: 'It must have been about a month after my resolution.'

It was in Ecija that Teresa wrote her vow of obedience. Recollected and alone in the hermitage's small sacristy, she formulated her submission to this young friar:

> The Lord gave me great confidence so that it seemed that it was the Holy Spirit who made me make this promise, and that the Spirit was obliged to give you light so that you in turn might give it to me. It also seemed, I recalled, that it was our Lord Jesus Christ who had enlightened me. And at this point I knelt down and promised that for the rest of my life I would do everything he asked me, as long as it was not in opposition to God or my Superiors to whom I was obliged.

What had happened that she should surrender herself in this way to Fr Gratian? Doesn't it seem an unusually bold thing to do?

Recalling this time Teresa said: 'Blessed be He who raises up persons who please me to the extent that I dare do this.' She wrote to her Sisters, 'he is perfect in my eyes… I have never seen such perfection combined with such gentleness.' To the General Rossi, who had been outraged by what he had read about Jerome and the Discalced Carmelite nuns in Andalucia, she wrote in a letter, 'Gratian is an angel.'

Teresa's spontaneity sometimes embarrassed Jerome. More than once he felt he had to reprimand her over familiarity; because some people could twist things, and misinterpret them and begin to gossip. In Pastrana, Jerome recalled, she ordered her nuns to obey him. 'This trust that the Mother had in me… was a trigger in the hearts of many… who began to gossip.'

Sure enough, soon, in Seville, people began to say slanderous and indecent things. Teresa laughed at the wickedness of some people, but these wounds would leave scars. On one occasion Jerome asked her why she used such terms of endearment. Teresa laughed and replied: 'Don't you know that anyone, no matter how perfect they are, needs some outlet. Let me have this one, for however much you tell me, I am not going to change the way I am.' What a pity we don't have a detailed account of all they said during their conversations that month!

It was in Beas that the friars had been altering the features of the reform of the nuns. Clear as Teresa was in her mind of how her Reform should be, the friars, on the other hand, did not share her clarity. It was for this reason that she had placed her nuns under the authority of the local bishops rather than under the friars, until, that is, she met Jerome. Here was a man who combined the spirit of the Discalced Carmelite Order with a knowledge of philosophy and theology, and a man who knew how to steer the friars towards reform. He was a Discalced Carmelite and a man of learning, who did not believe in damaging people through the imposition of excessive penances like the disciples of Peter of Alcantara.

Teresa could have gone ahead with her reform of the nuns without recourse to a parallel reform of the friars. However, this would not have been possible at the time. However, she found the right man to help her with her reform: a man with the heart of a Discalced Carmelite and a scholar from the University of Alcala. She found in this man someone who would be going to the Court, and she encouraged him to accept from the Nuncio the faculties he had been offered. These would allow him to establish the Discalced Carmelites with a separate Province and thus free them from the oppression of the Calced.

He was not the first friar, acknowledged Teresa, this was Anthony of Jesus and John of the Cross, but 'he came at the right time' to put a little order into the men, who were without Constitutions and 'in each house did what they liked… seemingly making up rules as they went along.' 'Sometimes they made life so difficult for me!' she complained.

Teresa of Jesus had been give permission by the General of the Carmelite Order, Rossi, to make foundations in Castile. She made one foundation (Beas) right on the edge of the said territory; for she had understood that Beas, under the patronage of St James, was in Castile. However, the foundation was in fact in the territory of Andalucia. (It was here in Beas that Teresa was 'continually importuned by the foundress, Lady Catalina Godinez de Sandoval', who put on the (Carmelite) habit and took the name Catalina of Jesus). It is understandable why the Saint, having passed Despenaperros after a great deal of difficulty, and seeing those fertile olives groves, should have thought the semi-desert of La Mancha was behind her.

However, she was naïve, and did not know, nor did she think of asking. 'If she had known that Beas was in Andalucia she would not have made that foundation,' wrote Jerome. He was the one who had to pay the price. He spoke with his travelling companion, a Franciscan lay brother, Sebastian of St Mark, from Seville, who had already been to Beas when he accompanied his Franciscan Provincial on a visit to his Order's priory there. Jerome asked him: 'Is your Provincial the Provincial of Andalucia?' 'Yes' replied the lay brother.

Now Beas, realized Jerome, was part of the district of Andalucia, and Teresa did not have a Patent from General Rossi, to make a foundation outside Castile. He consulted with experts in Beas as well as the Franciscan friars, and found out 'that according to the law makers from the Chancery it was a district within the district of Castile, but according to the Religious Orders it was in the district of Andalucia.'

Gratian had a Patent as Visitator of the Carmelite Order in Andalucia, given him by Francis de Vargas (the Dominican Apostolic Commissioner). He informed Teresa that she was under his jurisdiction, and subject to his authority.

> I renewed her permission to found a convent in Beas. My relationship with her became that of a Superior and Confessor. She did not appear to be upset by her mistake because it had given her an opportunity to establish Discalced Carmelite nuns in Andalucia, which she knew was such a great service to God.

Teresa had arrived in Beas with two groups of nuns; one for the foundation in Beas, with Anne of Jesus as Prioress, the other for Caravaca, in the Kingdom of Murcia, with Mary of St Joseph as Prioress. As the licence from the Council of Religious Orders for the foundation of Caravaca had not arrived, Teresa thought of making a foundation in Madrid, but Gratian said no, that she should make a foundation in Seville.

He told Teresa: 'Ask the Lord to enlighten you as to what is best: to make a foundation in Madrid, where there is a possibility, or in Seville, where they need a convent of reformed nuns?' After praying about this Teresa told him: 'It is better to make a foundation in Madrid, because having a house of nuns there it will be better for dealing with matters concerning the Order.' However, Jerome's response was: 'It will be better if they go to Seville.' Teresa did not utter one word of complaint; on the contrary, she got ready to go with her nuns to Seville.

Some days later, Jerome asked her why she had not opted for the Madrid foundation suggested to her by the Lord, given that his own decision that she should go to Seville was human and therefore fallible. She replied: 'All the revelations that I have had do not give me certainty that they are from God but when my Superior orders me I accept in faith that it is certainly a command from God.'

With this evidence Jerome was convinced that 'someone who respects obedience need not have any great fear of revelations when one gives them little credit.' He asked her, however, to ask the Lord again. Teresa responded: 'He told me that I did well to obey before making the foundation in Seville, but it will cost us much labour.'

Jerome justified his reasons for wanting to make a foundation in Seville in his book *Scholias*, which was not made on a whim. The most important and powerful people in the Christian world were to be found in Madrid, thought Jerome, and he did not want the Order to be located among the world of business people nor have other distractions which could destroy the spirit of prayer and trust in God, as was clear from the Rule they professed: *in silentio et spes erit fortitudo vestra*, 'in silence and hope will be your strength'. In Seville, furthermore, one of his desires would be fulfilled: Teresa would be subject to him.

Jerome made his way to the Royal Court. Teresa set out some days later with her nuns for Seville. She took with her Mary of St Joseph, who would be Prioress, and another five nuns 'with such great gifts, and the one who would be Prioress, particularly gifted for this task.' 'They were such great souls,' remarked Teresa 'that it seems to me I would have dared to go with them to the land of the Turks.' She did not go to the land of the Turks, but Seville, where the Lord had already told her in prayer that it would cost her a great deal.

The General Chapter of the Carmelite Order, convoked by Fr Rossi, began in Piacenza, Italy, on 21 May 1575. Present at the Chapter were Calced and Discalced Carmelite friars and nuns. Only those from Catalonia, Spain, were there from the start. The friars from Aragon did not come. The Definitor from Castile signed the Acts, even though he arrived only when the Chapter had closed. The Provincial of Andalucia and his Socius arrived late, on 8 June, when the matters concerning Spain, which were particularly relevant to the Andalucian Province, had been finalized by the Chapter.

These decisions concerning Andalucia were particularly forceful. Pope Gregory XIII's Brief of 2 August 1574, revoked the Dominican Visitators and another Brief, dated 15 April 1575, and granted the Chapter apostolic authority in all its deliberations. The reports and protests from the Calced Carmelites in Andalucia achieved their goal. The Discalced, whom they called 'rebellious Carmelites,' were told that they were not to be represented in Piacenza, and a number of arrangements that left them breathless were approved; it was nothing less than a war of attrition to have them wiped out.

The priories in Andalucia of Granada, La Penuela and Seville, founded against the will of the General, had to be closed within three days. (An order as quick as it was naïve.) The Discalced were still forbidden to form a separate Province: they should always belong to the Province of Castile. They were to be addressed as 'Contemplatives' or 'Primitives', but not Discalced, and there was to be no division in the Order by calling one 'Discalced' and the other 'of the Cloth'.

The friars and nuns of the Primitive Rule were to follow the liturgy of the Order with their own hymns, offices and masses. They were not to go around without shoes; they had to wear what the people called '*alpargatas*' (rope-soled sandals). The 'Contemplative Carmelites' were not to use staffs except on long journeys or in case of infirmity: (Can anyone explain this rule to me?). Each 'Contemplative' house was to elect its Prior, who would be confirmed by the Provincial, who had the right to make a Visitation; and many other resolutions along these lines...

One resolution that does not appear in the Acts was the order to confine St Teresa to a convent of her choice. It was the Saint herself who revealed this when she wrote from Seville, on 30 December: '...they have notified me of the mandate of our most Reverend Father; that is, I must choose a house and remain there permanently and make no more foundations, for I can no longer go out, because of the Council. Clearly this is due to their annoyance that I came down here [Andalucia].'

The General, Rossi, had previously written two letters to her, in October 1574 and January 1575, but they had not arrived at their destination until the month of June (1575), when the Saint was already at the foundation in Seville. She had been incriminated by the decisions of the Discalced Carmelite friars. Now she had to stay in a convent and not make any more foundations. However, Jerome, to whom she was subject, ordered her to remain in Seville.

Mary of St Joseph, the Prioress of Seville, recorded these events in her book *Ramillete de Mirra* in which she described the tension at this time and place:

> The Father General was very annoyed with our Mother. No matter how many letters she wrote, nor other means she used, she could not appease him. This was a trial for the saint, which she felt keenly. In the end the matter reached the General Chapter, which was taking place at that time. They declared that all the Discalced Carmelites were apostates and outcasts, and they ordered that all the houses that had been founded without permission from the General were to be closed; only the three that had been founded with permission from the General were to remain open. The Chapter also ordered that the patents and commissions that our Mother had been given to make foundations were to be taken from her and that she remain in one convent without leaving it. The Discalced Carmelite friars and nuns had to put on shoes and sing in the choir a certain way, and other things like this.
>
> Anyone would be scandalized to learn that a man as holy as in truth our Father General is, and many good Fathers and Servants of God, could act so unreasonably, by ordering the houses to be closed that had been founded with apostolic authority. However, when one only listens to one side, and this one biased, as the Fathers from Spain who went to the Chapter were at that particular time, it is understandable how they erred in judgement and took for criminals those who were not [biased]. This error was even more understandable when the demon gets involved, as here he must have done

in order to close the houses of the Discalced Carmelites. Our Lord showed this would happen to our holy Mother, while at prayer, as she had asked Him not to allow the closure of those Discalced houses. He told her: this is what they are after, but will not see it, on the contrary.

Gratian arrived in Madrid on Pentecost Sunday, 22 May. He was accompanied by a young lay brother called Sebastian of St Mark, to whom, on advice of St Teresa, had his head shaved (had a tonsure). 'In order that it would not seem that I was isolated I arranged for a choir brother to accompany me,' Jerome related.

They went to the Carmelite priory in Madrid, as there was no Discalced priory. The Provincial, Fr Angel de Salazar, would not let him stay because he had been excommunicated: 'this was what he (Angel) had been told by his General.' Jerome had therefore to find accommodation with his parents. When the Nuncio heard about this he was upset that they could treat as excommunicated someone who had come to Madrid on his orders. He called on the Provincial and scolded him. And so Jerome was able after all to reside with the Carmelites. He preached in the Royal Court.

The Nuncio, Nicholas Ormaneto, was a good man. He was from Verona, Italy, and the same age as Teresa. He had had a long ecclesiastical career that culminated, in 1572, in his being made Nuncio to Spain. He had been sent to Madrid by Pope Gregory XIII to reform the Orders in that country, having already played an important role in their reform in Italy during the pontificate of Pius V. He had been to England with Cardinal Polo and later had assisted at the Council of Trent. St Charles Borromeo, the great conciliar Reformer, made him Vicar General and later Bishop of Padua. It was not strange that such a man should have shown such an interest in reforming Religious. He was a good and profoundly holy person, and gave so much away to the poor that when he died two years later, in June 1577, Philip II had to pay for his funeral expenses.

Jerome spent three months with the Nuncio in Madrid. In this time the latter was able to discern that this young Carmelite, being 'young and new to Religious life,' was 'prudent, a good listener, gentle and very learned.' On 3 August Ormanento issued a Brief that increased the powers given to Jerome, whom he considered to be a holy and exemplary person. He gave him 'apostolic authority to visit, reform, punish, and do whatever was right and necessary to the Observant (Calced) friars in Andalucia.' He also gave him full authority over the Discalced friars and nuns in Castile and Andalucia. The Nuncio did not want to aggravate the Calced Carmelites in Castile, nor distress Jerome with such a task, so he decided to take on the Visitation himself.

Jerome Gratian, with his Brief to make visitations, went to Pardo (near Madrid) where the King, Philip II, resided. The latter gave him letters and provisions for the Bishops and Ministers of Justice in Andalucia, through his secretary, who was Jerome's brother, the Secretary Anthony Gratian. Jerome asked his brother why he needed these royal provisions. The King knew exactly why and told his Secretary: 'It's obvious he is new and has not dealt with friars. Now he will discover from experience that he will really need them.'

Anthony knew deep down that it would not be good for his brother to take on the visitation of the Calced Carmelites. He made this known to St Teresa and persuaded her not to agree to his brother getting involved in that war. We know this from a letter written by Mary of St Joseph: 'I saw his [Anthony's] letters to our holy Mother.'

Jerome was content to occupy himself with the Discalced Carmelites, who now were 'not subject to the Calced, so that they could not close our priories and I could make foundations.' However, he was afraid of them, even to the extent that they might kill him: 'Calumny and slights I can cope with.' He confided his fear to Gaspar de Quiroga, Bishop of Cuenca and the Inquisitor General, asking him to intercede with the King that he be freed from (visiting) the Calced, but the Inquisitor reprimanded him saying: 'To whom have we entrusted this but to a man of noble blood, who has the right lineage?' Jerome saw that he had no choice but to accept. 'Thus,' he later wrote, 'I resolved to lose my life. With the Brief from the Nuncio, Ormaneto and letters from the King, I set out to return to Andalucia.'

Ormaneto was convinced that all the Religious Orders in Andalucia needed to be reformed as soon as possible. Many contradictory reports arrived at his desk, but what he didn't have, and wanted, was reliable information. Ormaneto had sent the Jesuit, Melendez de Valdes, on a secret mission: he was Rector of a college in Madrid. This mission was to obtain information in accordance with the letter he had been given by the Nuncio, who also had the support of Philip II.

The Nuncio wrote to Cardinal Galli, the Pope's Secretary: 'He [Melendez] is a good man, fearful of God, and has much experience as Vicar to the

Archbishop of Seville, and has a lot of experience of the ways of Religious.' However, Melendez's mission, 'who did not visit or exercise any jurisdiction that he had not been ordered to', had to be abandoned when the secret mission was discovered in Seville. The friars caused such a commotion that the Royal Council came to hear of it. An order from Philip II to the President of the Council not to speak more about this matter, resolved the problem.

Jerome began his Visitation with the Discalced Carmelite priories and convents in Castile. He spent all of August, September and October doing this. Thanks to the influence of St Teresa he did not have much to do with the nuns. With the friars, on the other hand, he had to use all his talents as a Reformer to regulate the many inequalities and moderate the penitential practices that were to be found in many of them. He ordered that the sick and those convalescing should be given fish and wine on certain days. In Pastrana, he suppressed the penances that Fr Angel of St Gabriel had introduced of parading the novices in front of all the people.

The acceptance of the Visitator's orders remained on a purely superficial level; it did not change minds or hearts. The 'zealots', as the Chronicler called them, whispered together that they wanted Gratian to leave. They saw that his attitude, which was in harmony with that of Teresa, was a relaxation of the primitive spirit.

Jerome met St John of the Cross in Avila. We know what John thought about the Visitator following their meeting, from a letter St Teresa wrote to Jerome, which he received in Toledo while on his way to Andalucia. 'Seneca says (she refers to St John of the Cross in this way) he is very happy, and could not have been happier with his Superior; what great thanks we should give to God.'

In Almodovar del Campo, Jerome met Fr Anthony of Jesus, Prior of Seville, and asked him to join him on his journey to Seville. The Visitator valued his presence, because as an ex-Calced Carmelite, Anthony got on well with the Calced. Jerome also thought that he would be useful in the battle he foresaw in the Carmelite priory in Seville.

They passed through La Penuela. Seventy friars who lived in that wilderness came out to greet him. These ate a diet of grass and many died as a result. Jerome moderated the fasts, suggested they add a little wine to the water to help digestion and use a little oil to pep up their meals; after all that part of Spain produced so much of this precious commodity. He made them plant a garden next to the priory. He also lightened their workload so that they would have more time for prayer. 'Those who were good friars in obedience accepted these practices, though the more zealous felt that changing their rigorous lifestyle would allow moderation to enter into the house. They knew that nature does not like to be kept in check and will always fight to increase its comfort, and if these zealots find Superiors who will endorse their views, they will canonize and adore them,' wrote the Chronicler.

Gratian divided the friars into choir members and lay brothers. He ordered them not to accept any more novices and sent some to other houses to create more room in the priory of La Penuela. When he heard the news, as yet unclear, of the decisions made at the General Chapter in Piacenza, he felt his blood go cold at the thought of having to make a visitation of the Carmelite priory in Seville.

On the journey to Seville he fell ill with a fever at the very thought of the bitter chalice he would have to drink. I am not surprised that the thought of this should make him ill. In the Priory of Los Remedios a Fr Mariano awaited him; an intransigent and ascetical man, who would soon clash with Jerome's gentler and more reasonable approach.

Near to the Priory in Seville, in a street named 'Calle de las Armas', Teresa, who in a letter to Gratian had written, 'I find your absence painful to bear,' was with a group of her nuns in a rented property, experiencing more sorrows than joys.

Jerome and Anthony of Jesus reached Seville in the middle of November 1575.

Chapter Eleven

'This is not for the faint-hearted!'

Teresa of Jesus arrived in Seville on 26 May 1575. She had travelled in a convoy of four covered wagons. The climate there was not good for this middle-aged woman from Castile. The journey under a hot sun had left her very tired… 'You see this sun is not like in Castile, it is much more trying,' she wrote in one of her letters.

She and her small party installed themselves in a rented house that Fr Mariano had found; it was'very small and humid', and located on Armas street. He provided them with some mattresses and their neighbours lent them several items: a table, a mat, a frying pan, one or two oil lamps, a mortar, a cooking pot, some pitchers and plates and other such things. However, 'the neighbours later sent someone for the frying pan, another for the cooking pot and the table; so that nothing was ours, neither the frying pan nor the mortar, not even the rope for the well.'

The beginning of their stay in Seville was difficult. Soon the first novices began to arrive from the locality. The Archbishop, Christopher de Rojas, was initially reluctant to authorize a new convent founded on poverty; i.e. without rent, but fortunately he agreed after a visit from St Teresa. She had also to undergo a visit from the Inquistion following the denouncement of a forty-year-old novice for going out of the convent. The situation was put right and Teresa and her nuns left emboldened by the Inquisition. In her *Spiritual Testimonies* Teresa wrote about her many dreams and desires. We find among them her 'Eliseo', in other words, Jerome Gratian:

> One day I was very recollected, commending Eliseo to God. I heard the words: 'He is my true son, I will always help him,' or words to that effect, but I don't remember this well.

On 9 August, hot and exhausted by the heat of the midsummer sun, she wrote:

> I found myself in spirit in a very delightful garden…I saw my Eliseo there, certainly not any way black, but with a strange beauty. On his head was something that resembled a garland of precious stones, and many maidens went before him with branches in their hands singing songs of praise to God…I seemed to hear music from small birds and angels… I observed how there was no one else in the garden. I heard the words: 'He deserved to be among you, and this whole festival you see will be had on the day when the feast in praise of my Mother will be established,[1] and hurry if you wish to be where it is.' This vision lasted more than an hour and a half and caused me great delight… what I gained from this was more love for Eliseo and a remembrance of him in that beauty. I had feared lest it be a temptation, for it was impossible that it be the work of my imagination.

In November, some days after Jerome arrived in Seville, Teresa tells us:

> One night I was very distressed because it had been a long time since I had heard from my Father, and he had not been well when he last wrote… A light appeared in the interior of my soul, and I beheld him coming along the road, he looked happy and his face serene. This light showed me that he had a white countenance; it seems to me that so do all those who are in Heaven. I wondered if the light and brilliance that comes from our Lord makes them white. I heard: 'Tell him to begin at once without fear, for his is the victory.

Jerome had arrived in Seville mid-November, accompanied by Anthony of Jesus. I do not know if he was happy and with a white countenance, as Teresa had seen him in her *Spiritual Testimonies*, more likely he was pale-faced due to the purgatory that awaited him. While travelling along the road from Toledo to Seville he had heard rumours of the resolutions of the General Chapter in Piacenza. He also heard that the Carmelites in Seville had produced a Counter-Brief so that they could disobey him. Could it be that his faculties as Visitator had ceased? His anxieties got the better of him, so he wrote to the Nuncio, who answered on 11 November.

The Brief that revoked the authority of the Dominican Apostolic

1 According to Jerome Gratian she is referring here to the feast of the Presentation of Our Lady in the Temple.

Commissioners did not affect the authority given to him by the Nuncio. There remained, 'however, the decision of the General Chapter and the apostolic letters given to the Order.' The Nuncio's response dispelled Jerome's scruples. In a postscript the Nuncio added, 'Your Paternity, do everything you can to reform those Carmelites and get rid of all abuse, make them follow and observe all the orders of the Apostolic Visitators, which I oblige you to do in conscience.'

He met up with St Teresa in Seville, and as overall Superior of all the Discalced Carmelites,

> gave her new commissions to make foundations and agreed with her about all that had to be done, so that I did not do anything for the Discalced Carmelites nuns without her orders, so that even though I signed the licences and confirmed the elections as Superior of the nuns, she had first commanded this and so I would never change anything concerning the Discalced Carmelite nuns without her written or verbal opinion; I kept to this approach all the time I was a Superior, which was from this time until the day she died.

It was because of his respect for Teresa that they said he was subject to a woman; others said nastier things. Such words distressed him but only succeeded in making Teresa laugh, who said: 'It did not bother me but it distresses him!'

In Los Remedios Jerome showed the others the Brief and Patents from the Nuncio for the Visitation of the Carmelite Priory in Seville. He discussed with Mariano, Anthony of Jesus and Gregory Nazianceno how he would proceed. Mariano's attitude was particularly intransigent:

> Let them submit themselves to the authority of the Nuncio and the King; after that we can be more lenient with the deserving. If our Father General calls us stubborn and rebellious, we are not the first, nor shall we be the last to suffer such insults. We have still not been notified of the documents they allege are from his Holiness. Even if we are given them, we know already that they do not revoke any of the powers given [you] by the Nuncio. Your Reverence should set a date [for the visitation], inform the Lord Archbishop, his Assistant Bishop and the rest of the Ministers. Tell them that you are the Visitator and Reformer, and in this way let them know that you are in charge, then get on with what you have to do regardless of what they think.

Mariano's attitude prevailed over the others. Jerome would have preferred a gentler approach, in line with his character, and so did Teresa. 'If only they had followed my advice,' the Saint complained, 'there wouldn't have been all this fuss and everything would have been settled amicably as should happen between brothers.'

The date set for the canonical Visitation was 21 November, the feast of the Presentation of the Blessed Virgin Mary.

Gratian, accompanied by Frs Anthony of Jesus and Bartholomew of Jesus, who acted as his Secretary, arrived at the (Seville) Priory 'without a lawyer or lay people, so that the Visitation could be carried out in a spirit of fraternal trust' The Brief from the Nuncio was read out before the assembled community. The (Calced) friars, for their part, claimed the Brief had been revoked and they asked that the document be handed over to them. Jerome refused to do this, and so they, for their part, would not obey him.

As they stubbornly refused to submit to his authority and his colleagues', Jerome decided to postpone the Visitation until a more favourable time. He recalled how he and the others had descended by the main staircase and were in the patio next to the front door, when they were surrounded by about eighty angry friars, shouting at the top of their voices. He later wrote, 'I saw that my life was in great danger.' He recalled what had happened not that long ago in Catalonia: how some friars had attacked a Reformer and his colleagues and had run them through with swords. When he saw himself surrounded 'he thought he would die but was ready for it.'

The word went around that the friars were armed. The doors were closed to prevent law enforcement officers entering the place, as well as officers from the Archbishop whom Mariano had alerted. The closed doors also prevented anyone outside from hearing the racket inside. Nonetheless, word did get out. St Teresa was praying with her nuns when people came to tell her that the doors of the priory were locked and that Fr Gratian had been murdered. While praying Teresa heard a voice and the words: 'Woman of little faith be calm, because all will be well.'

She made a vow that if Fr Gratian got out of this alive she would celebrate annually with all solemnity the feast of the Presentation of the Blessed Virgin Mary in all her convents; and so it happened from that time.

Diego de Leon, an ex-Carmelite bishop, heard all the commotion from his room. He came out and and managed to calm the friars, and opening the front door he allowed Jerome Gratian, Anthony of Jesus and Bartholomew of Jesus to escape unscathed: only one friar, Fr John Evangelista, the Sub Prior, had been ready to submit. Recalling this episode later, Jerome wrote, 'I believe that it was only the prayers of Mother Teresa that saved me.'

When the Nuncio learned of this incident he informed the King. He then dispatched a new Brief to the Carmelites in Seville, ordering them, under pain of excommunication, to obey without exception or appeal. However, the friars sent two representatives to Rome, one by sea the other overland. There they complained that Gratian 'entered the Priory in Seville with secular and ecclesial authorities and caused a commotion and scandal'. All of which was untrue.

On 14 September, King Phillip II wrote to Archbishop Christopher de Rojas asking him to give Gratian 'every favour and help that he asks for.' The Nuncio warned Tolomeo Galli, the Pope's Secretary, that some Carmelite friars were on their way to Rome, and that he, Galli, should teach them how they should obey the Apostolic Commissioners. The Pope's Secretary replied to the Nuncio, 'If the Carmelite friars from Andalucia appear, I shall make them regret they ever left Spain for Rome.'

Faced with the stubborn refusal of the friars Jerome excommunicated them on Christmas Eve. The news of the excommunication was posted on all the noticeboards of the churches in Seville, causing a great scandal in the city.

That Christmas was certainly not a peaceful one. St Teresa was notified by the General of the Order to 'choose a house where she should remain and not make any more foundations.' She wanted to go straight away to Valladolid but Jerome would not let her go before the summer. Teresa confided in a letter to Mother Maria Bautista 'right now he gives me more orders than our most reverend Father General.' She added, 'Let us pray a lot for our Father, for a reliable person told the Archbishop today that they will perhaps kill him.' Teresa cried out: 'This is not for the fainthearted!'

Jerome Gratian was not happy at all with so much such resistance and scandalous behavior. If it had been left up to him all this could have been avoided. However, he was under pressure from the Nuncio in Madrid and from Mariano and Anthony of Jesus in Seville; all of them told him to be stricter and to punish the friars. If he had followed their advice, the Nuncio's Brief would have been revoked and then the Calced Carmelites would have taken them to court. While this was being resolved, he could have quietly got on with his Visitation to the Discalced Carmelites, 'because this had been his principal intention in reforming the friars: to protect those Discalced Carmelites who had not been dissolved, rather than attempting to reform the Calced.'

However, the Lord had given him 'an unbearable cross' that was to obey the Nuncio and follow the advice of Mariano and Anthony of Jesus,

> who made no attempt to adopt a more reasonable approach, nor did they forsee the subsequent scandals that might have arisen as a result of their rigorous attitude. They remained inflexible: to be strict and to threaten punishment. However, the Order could never be reformed in this way. They sought to humiliate the Calced Carmelites in Seville and in other places by getting them to leave their houses to the Discalced, but this would leave the Father [Gratian] and his companions in the greatest danger. On the one hand Gratian struggled with the Calced Carmelites, who constantly raised up false testimonies against him, and even [as indicated in some places] thought to kill him. On the other hand, he had to lessen the demands of his rigorous friends, so different to his own. He needed especially to try and help them understand that with their approach they would do more harm than good. These two conflicting attitudes, from friends and foes alike, was a heavy and continuous cross to bear. He resigned himself to the possibility that while carrying out these Visitations he might be killed. He knew that the Calced were capable of anything; hadn't they murdered another Reformer in Catalonia and for doing far less than he was intending to do. Although they were constantly fabricating lies about him he could live with this; at least it was not as big a sin as murder.

On 15 January 1576, twenty-one days after the excommunications, the Seville Priory pledged obedience to the authority of the Nuncio and to Fr Gratian. Afterwards, the other Priories in Andalucia, to which Anthony of Jesus and John de los Rios had been sent, also pledged obedience. The following day Jerome began his Visitation of the (other) friars and nuns in Andalucia.

He began with the Calced Carmelite nuns in Seville, visiting the convent of the Incarnation, founded in 1513 by Ines Farfan. The General, Rossi, had visited this convent ten years before, on 3 September 1566. However, they had continued with their vices and violations of the Rule. Blanca de Guzman, who during Rossi's Visitation was a Novice, continued to dance and enjoy masquerades as if she were still 'in the outside world.' Blanca, the Prioress's niece, had received the habit without the consent of the other nuns. She called herself 'Doña'[2] and lived in the convent with a servant and a slave. Some days before Jerome's Visitation she had even celebrated a banquet with the local towns folk.

Jerome's Visitation, with his gentle approach, helped these nuns, 'because by guiding them lovingly…he achieved a great deal.' He introduced mental payer: 'a half hour at prime and a half hour at matins.' He consulted with the Nuncio about getting rid of 'the stairs'; this was 'an apparatus that allowed people from outside to enter the convent, so that the nuns could speak to them, that was commonly used in Spanish convents. Ormaneto ordered the nuns to receive visitors only in the convent's parlours, 'that should have double grilles, secured in such a way that not even a finger can get through.'

Jerome asked the female boarders to leave, exempting only those girls who were less than twelve years of age and who kept to the rules. He had to punish a Provincial and two Carmelite Priors due to the grave accusations that had been levelled against them *de rebus quae ad sacrarum virginum castitatem attinent*: when he wanted to be discreet he wrote in Latin. He had written, 'in things referring to the virginity of holy nuns'. The Fathers concerned were: Augustine Suarez, Provincial, Luis Navarrete, Prior of Utrera, and Hernando de Lara, Prior of Gibraleon.

When Augustin Suarez, one of the accused, left the tribunal he had him arrested and ordered him to remain in the Priory in Osuna. This measure frightened the other two: one tried to run away, the other was arrested.

On 21 February, the Visitation of the polemical Carmelite Priory in Seville began. Jerome wrote that he 'endeavoured to introduce the recommendations of the Council of Trent for Religious Orders, which were concerned principally with the vows of poverty and chastity.' He discovered scandalous abuses against poverty: 'Each one kept whatever he wanted, and dressed as he liked and spent as much money as he liked. Everyone prided themselves on having savings of fifty or one hundred *ducados*; plus some income from doing business with South America. When he took away the deeds from one of them, worth 20,000 *ducados* that he had in South America, there was such a protest at the Visitation, as if it were something

2 A formal title.

wicked and scandalous.' There were as many abuses against chastity in the friars' houses as in the nuns'; things happened that it would be better not to mention. Not all the priories, of course, were like this.

This was not the only place with problems. There were about twenty houses in Andalucia, whose Priors had been able, each triennium, to accumulate about 'four or five hundred ducados with which they used to lord it over the poorer Priories.' Jerome found this loathsome and wrote that 'they deserved to be in the galleys.' They were absent from mental prayer and ridiculed manual work, as if it were beneath their dignity. For the Discalced Carmelites (work) was a sign of their identity: the friars and nuns did not ask for alms but lived off what they earned from their work.

Jerome appointed Fr John Evangelista as Prior of the house, as he was the only one who did what was recommended in the Nuncio's Brief. He also ordered Fr Sebastian of St Mark to transfer from the Discalced Carmelites in Los Remedios to help. He put Brother John of the Conception at the door (*portineria*), with orders that these two were to have the keys to the cloister. He appointed two other Discalced Carmelites as Master of Novices and Assistant. He decided to make Seville the only Novitiate in the Province. He forced about fifty of the friars to live according to their means and the alms they were given. He endeavoured to break up the cliques by transferring certain friars to other carmels. He dealt with everyone in such a way that all accepted the (new) legislation willingly.

The Visitation ended on 1 April. Ormaneto congratulated him on having obtained the obedience of 'the Carmelites of the Cloth' in Seville and asked him to carry on with the other houses. 'I need not tell you every detail, because I know your Paternity will know how to complete the task very well.'

Did Jerome complete the task well? He complained about bearing 'the greatest cross' from friends and foes alike. The (Calced) friars shocked him with their threatening behaviour.

However, Fr Padilla and Brother Mariano did not understand his (tolerant) approach; they 'wanted to see these people punished and sent to the galleys.' Juan Calvo de Padilla was a priest who had spent a long time in America. On his return he advised the Nuncio on how to reform the friars and nuns. Teresa of Jesus praised him highly, though Jerome did not hold him in such high esteem. Once the Nuncio, Ormaneto, died, he (Fr Padilla) was arrested by the Inquisition. Mariano, for his part, now began to undermine Jerome's reputation within the Teresian Reform.

The other heavy cross he had to bear came from the false accusations made by the Calced Carmelites:

> Some said he had stolen six thousand ducados from the Seville Priory to pay for his sister's wedding; others, that he told lies about his family history; others, accused him of being dishonest; again, others, that he wore expensive clothes; others said they found a bag containing the bones of hens and sheep he had eaten secretly during his Visitation to the nuns in Seville Carmel. Others made up such similar lies. These things were said very publically and in great detail by the Calced Carmelites. When they heard this the people of Seville and Andalucia were deeply upset; such disturbances had seldom been seen. Some people believed what had been said but others refused to believe and defended Gratian.

Jerome had to be careful not to eat everything he was offered. In one particular Priory he declined to eat a salad they had been given him, but his companion who was not so cautious became quite ill and almost died. Indeed, Jerome was warned by a Discalced Carmelite nun in confession to be careful, because they (the friars) wanted to kill him. On another occasion a lizard appeared out of a jug of water he had in his cell. Throughout his Visitation of the Calced Carmelites he ate with fear and trembling, his stomach full only of anxieties. He never asked for any kind of special diet, 'as by eating whatever the community ate he felt safer.'

However, what upset Jerome the most were the slanders levelled against St Teresa. He recounted in his book *Foundations*:

> What really hurt was the malicious gossip: the dirty and offensive things that were said about the Father and his relationship with Mother Teresa of Jesus, and with some of the Discalced Carmelite nuns. What was said cannot be repeated because it is so disgraceful; the words were both ugly and ignorant. The basis for their anger and this slander were the improper relationships of the Calced friars with her [Teresa's] nuns. It is a long established truth that dishonest people think that everyone behaves as they do. There was also jealousy when they saw the love Mother Teresa of Jesus had for the Father. The latter advised her nuns against talking to any other Calced or Discalced friar or forming a relationship with them.

These malicious lies circulated around the streets of Seville. Jerome wrote that the Archbishop was really upset and fearful, for it was he who had brought the nuns to the city. The Inquisition became involved and Jerome could see that the Order would be ruined and the Discalced Carmelite nuns discredited. 'Where could I look for support?' he asked. He turned to St Teresa, who was clearly unruffled by the slander. She told him: 'Calm down, dear Father, don't be afraid that the holy Inquisition, that takes the place of God in order to protect the faith, will trouble someone like yourself, someone who has deep faith.'

St Teresa and Sr Isabel of St Jerome were denounced to the Inquisition in Seville by a Novice, Maria del Corro, a forty-year-old widow. This Novice had been encouraged to do this by a 'melancholic' priest (as Jerome described him), who accused Teresa and Isabel of practices similar to those known as 'alumbrados'. This same priest harassed the nuns, telling them to 'put on new habits and get ready because within two or three days you will all be going to the Holy Office.'

Jerome admitted that because of these accusations he could neither eat nor sleep. One day he saw many dismounted horses and mules in front of the nuns' convent. At the sight his 'blood ran cold. I could not move, imagining what could have happened.' The men from the Holy Office were there to question the nuns.

In recalling these events Mary of St Joseph in her book, *Libro de las Recreaciones*, reassures us that there had been no need to worry: 'The Inquisitors came to the house and established the truth: and that was that…' However, the investigations by the Inquisitors went on for quite a while, maybe throughout February and March. 'Seeing the Inquisition coming and going left a very bad impression on the people.' Teresa wrote in a letter, 'They began to ask what the Nuns were accused of? They had heard that we tied up our nuns by their hands and feet and whipped them.'

Mary of St Joseph wrote about other improprieties told by Maria del Corro: 'As we were poor and did not have many veils, or in some cases because the sisters neglected to bring their veils when they went to communion, some of them would borrow from others: it was our custom to do this… We had a courtyard that was bathed in sunlight and to be more recollected after communion each one found her own space and turned her face to the wall in order to avoid the heat of the sun. She [Maria del Corro] criticized this practice and spread many lies and testified against our holy Mother.' However, it all ended well in the end.

Jerome noticed that when Teresa arrived in Seville she was, 'as tormented in soul as it was possible to be.' He tells us 'with the arrival of Fr Pantoja, the Prior of las Cuevas, came the first rays of a new dawn after so much darkness and wild storms: Fr Pantoja had a great devotion to St Joseph.' He was also very struck by the holiness of St Teresa of Avila, how she touched 'the hearts of many important people in Seville, and gave them something to take away with them when they came to call on the Sisters. The reputation of the nuns began to grow as did the amount of alms they were given.' In the *Book of Her Foundations* Teresa of Jesus said that Pantoja 'did everything to prevent us losing that Priory.' She usually called him 'my poor Prior' or 'that saintly old man', and referred to him often in her letters.

On 21 April, Holy Saturday, news reached Jerome that his older brother, Anthony, who had been a secretary to King Philip II, had died in Madrid on 6 April. This was a double blow to Jerome, not only because of 'his natural feelings for his own blood', but also, 'for the lack of anyone to deal with the Order's affairs.'

Teresa of Jesus complained to the Lord for taking him so quickly: while praying she heard these words: 'He asked me to take him and so I agreed as it was right.'

Anthony was 'a young, handsome layman; many an important young lady would have liked to have married him.' Jerome thought that God had taken his brother at the age of thirty-five so that he would have avoided any deep involvement in the transactions and favours of the Court, 'with the ambitiousness, gifts and praise of some and the jealous rivalry of others.' He believed his brother was a truly holy man: 'From the time he was nine years old he confessed every week and lived a life that was spiritual, recollected and prayerful. He recited the canonical hours as if there was an obligation, he spent two hours a day in mental prayer, he performed charitable works, he visited hospitals...'

Anthony had a vocation to the Jesuits, but never made it to profession. He was the first to establish and classify the library in the *El Escorial.* He died so very poor that King Philip II ordered his own jeweller to do whatever necessary for Anthony's funeral. Someone called Matthew Vazquez took over Anthony's duties.

With Anthony's death the Discalced Carmelites had lost an important friend in the Court of Philip II. Jerome wrote of his brother:

> All these reforms were accepted because they passed through his hands. He had been informed and was aware of the usual fabrications and lies made by dissolute friars to free themselves from my Visitation, and was able to inform the King when necessary. When we needed a favour it was usually granted. The Calced Carmelites did not dare write shameful letters as they would do later, because they knew that these letters had all to pass through his hands. He felt the criticisms which affected him as much as his own brother.

It was time to leave Seville. Teresa exclaimed: 'Oh, what a year I have had here! ... I confess that the people of this land are too different for me and I already want to be back in the promised land, if this will serve God.' Her 'promised land' was Castile to which, for some time, she had yearned to return.

Teresa of Jesus bought a new house very close to the river. In this she had been helped by her brother, Lorenzo, who had returned from South

In order to make a foundation in Seville St Teresa bought this house at 60 Zaragoza Street with the help of her brother Lorenzo and other donors.

America, as well as by other donors. On 5 April they signed the contract for the house. The signatories were: Mother Teresa, Fr Gratian, Lorenzo de Cepeda, Mary of St Joseph and others.

They spent most of the month of May getting the new building ready as a convent. Brother John of the Miserere started to use his gift of painting. Jerome told him to paint a portrait of St Teresa whom he had put under obedience (to have her portrait done). At first she resisted this idea but then

'God forgive you, Brother John. You have made me look ugly and bleary eyed.'
A portrait of St Teresa *by Brother John of the Miserere, as instructed by Fr Jerome Gratian. Discalced Carmelite nuns, Seville.*

gave in, 'won over by the appeals of the nuns who had endured so much and their affection for her. She did not want to leave for Castile without leaving them some kind of consolation,' Mary of St Joseph recounted later.

The Prioress of Seville thought the painting was a perfect likeness, showing so many features, so that future generations of sisters could see the clothes and veil that the Saint wore. Jerome didn't think it was good, 'because though it was a painted portrait, it wasn't a very good one.' There is a popular anecdote that Teresa stared at the portrait and said to Brother John of the Misery, with great grace but not a little feminine vanity: 'May God forgive you Brother John, you have made me look ugly and bleary eyed.'

The Sisters transferred to this new house on Sunday, 3 June 1576. They had hoped to do this with as little fuss as possible, but the people of the city had other ideas. Fr Fernando had alerted everyone. The Archbishop was the first to join in rendering them honours, then the entire city began to celebrate. 'A huge number of people came to join in, and there was a great deal of solemnity. The streets were covered in decoration. There was much music and many musicians. The nuns had the Blessed Sacrament transferred from a nearby parish. When this was complete and just before St Teresa was about to enter the convent's enclosure, she knelt down and asked the Archbishop for his blessing. However, it was he, Christopher de Rojas y Sandoval, son of the Marquis of Denia, who knelt down before St Teresa and asked her for a blessing. Teresa told the Prioress of Beas of how she had felt:

> Imagine how I felt, when I saw such a great dignitary of the Church kneeling in front of this poor woman. He refused to get up till I had blessed him in front of all the Religious and important people of Seville!

That same night, 4 June, Teresa quietly left Seville, and made her way to a convent in Castile. Where had Fr Gratian gone? He had not been seen since 8 May. Had the nuns kept him hidden in their convent? Rumours spread throughout Seville. The Calced friars said terrible things about him during their sermons: that he had been burned and his ashes had been thrown away...

However, Jerome was in Madrid, at an audience with the Nuncio and the King. What had led to this?

Chapter Twelve

The Tostado Is Coming!

We don't know for certain that they actually cried out: 'The Tostado is coming!'

Teresa complained about the lies that were circulating in Seville. On 9 May, she wrote to Fr Mariano in Madrid: 'Oh, the lies they are telling down here! It's enough to make one faint. Now they have just told me that the Visitator for the friars of the Cloth is in Carmona… and that they have obeyed him in many houses.' Teresa knew the friars were lying when they said that Tostado was at the gates of Seville, but she was afraid of Tostado and what was coming from Rome.

Jerome Tostado had been appointed by Rome as Visitator, Reformer and General Commissioner of the Carmelite Order in Spain. General Rossi, under pressure from the Calced friars, especially from Andalucia, appointed Tostado on 10 December 1575 to reform his Order. The appointment was ratified by a Papal Brief. It had been in Andalucia that they criticized Fr Gratian, that he had acted without the General's authority and had not even had the courtesy to keep the General informed of what he was doing.

'The Tostado,' as St Teresa called him, was Provincial of Catalonia when he received the appointment to be Visitator. His task was to fulfil the resolutions of the General Chapter in Piacenza and oppose the Teresian Reform.

Rossi was upset. The letter that Teresa had sent him at the end of January, when she knew of his order that she retire to a convent and not make more foundations, had no effect. 'Your Reverence, we are your subjects and most humble servants of God.' Teresa said in her letter to Rossi, when giving him an account of the foundations of Beas, Caravaca and Seville.

She explained that Gratian had acted the way he did because he had been commissioned Visitator by the Nuncio. 'He has written to your Reverence and would never want to offend you, because he holds himself to be your obedient son… May Your Reverence's reaction be gentle, and forget those matters that have already passed, even though he [Gratian] was not entirely without blame, and accept him as your son and subject, as in truth he is.'

Teresa's letter made no difference. The General, Rossi, was very upset, as he heard only one side: the voices of the Carmelites sent to Rome. One of them, Peter Cota, had already returned from his visit to Rome. He, together with Louis de Navarete, had gone to the Eternal City with orders from the Seville Carmelite friars to obtain a Brief to revoke the authority given to Jerome by the Nuncio.

This Fr Peter had secretly entered Seville where he lodged in a private house to await the arrival of Augustine Suarez, the deposed Provincial, whom Jerome had sent away to Ecija. They wanted to surprise Jerome and present him with the Brief revoking his powers before it could be withdrawn by the King. However, in Seville it is difficult to do anything without being noticed. Word got round that the messenger (Fr Peter) had arrived with the Brief. Teresa was informed and wrote to Mariano: 'Regarding the news about the Tostado, a friar has just come who left him in Barcelona in March. This friar carries a Patent ...which Tostado signed as Vicar General for all of Spain.'

Christopher de Rojas, the Archbishop, Francis Zapata, his assistant and Francis de Arganda, Director of the Inquisition, advised Jerome that it would be prudent to 'hide from them so that he could not be notified of anything until the orders of the illustrious Nuncio were known.' They all agreed that he should go quickly to the Nuncio to warn him (of Tostado's arrival).

Jerome left the Prior of Seville, Fr John Evangelista, to continue as Vicar Provincial, and on 8 May, secretly left Seville for Madrid, accompanied by Anthony of Jesus and Bartholomew of Jesus. Teresa confided in Mariano, 'I see he is going to Castile without continuing the Visitation and by a different route. This is not the time to be calling on someone, for there is a lot of agitation': 'a different route' meant by a route where there were no Calced Carmelites.

The agitation Teresa spoke of arose when Fr Augustine Suarez, the Provincial whom Jerome had deposed, called a meeting of the friars in Ecija and got rid of all the Superiors appointed by Fr Gratian. He sent Fr John Evangelista, the Prior of Seville Carmel, whom he considered a rebel to the Priory of los Remedios.

The Calced Carmelites held a Chapter in a village near Avila, called La Moraleja. This they did principally to elect friars to positions of responsibility and to apply the resolutions of the General Chapter in Piacenza. It began on 12 May. Three Discalced friars were also due to attend the Chapter: Fr John of Jesus Roca, from Mancera priory, Fr Diego of the Trinity, from Pastrana and, Fr Elias of St Martin, the Rector of the college in Alcala. Until this time they all belonged to the same (Calced Carmelite) family and were under the authority of the same General. However, when the Discalced friars arrived a decision had already been made: basically, that 'the Primitives' and 'the Observants' would wear the same habits and would live together in the same houses. The thinking behind this was not well intentioned, as it would lead to the destruction of the Discalced Carmelites.

When the Discalced friars read the resolutions they were aware that 'even though they [the resolutions] were nuanced and intended to unite and to bring about fraternal charity,' as the Chronicles stated, 'it was not very difficult to see the intention of these new norms which were so opposed to the Discalced.'

From then on it was agreed that the Calced would call themselves 'the Observants' and the Discalced, 'the Contemplatives'. They would live in the same houses, mix with each other, changing at will from Observants to Contemplatives, and vice versa. Each one would keep the Rule he had professed, they would all wear the same habit: a brownish-grey colour, not black, the white mantles were to be shorter, and the Discalced had to wear shoes.

John of Jesus Roca protested that the Discalced, being in the minority, could not accept some of the norms that would lead to the death of the Reform. 'Because as well as merging two very different rules and maintaining peace under the same roof', the Chronicles states, 'they stripped them of their distinctive "discalcedness" [distinct habit and customs] and the observance of their own laws, on which they depended. And also welcoming Calced into Discalced Priories and vice versa would have made it impossible for the Discalced friars to increase, either their houses or their personnel. In a few years or even months everything would be crushed; for in the shade of such big trees the tiny seedlings would perish.'

The Chapter in La Moraleja sounded like the beating of distant drums to the ears of the Discalced Carmelite friars, who understood these measures as a prelude to war. In September, Jerome felt compelled to call his own friars together in Almodovar. He had been in Madrid to explain to the Nuncio and the King the situation they found themselves in. He also wanted to find out if the Calced Carmelites had in fact, as they said, a Brief revoking his Visitation. The Nuncio assured him that the Brief held by the Calced did not revoke the special authority he had been given by the Pope. The King promised to give him, if the Pope deemed it necessary, his own royal approval. The two of them, King and Nuncio, then encouraged Jerome to hurry back to Seville.

Jerome wrote to St Teresa explaining all that had happened. She had sent several letters to Seville, believing he had returned there. She wrote from Malagon on 15 June: 'I am telling your Paternity that the thought of you being already in Seville, sent there in such haste by the Nuncio and King, disturbs me greatly.' She complained, 'I don't know why they want to inflict penalties on you and all the others when the excommunications of Father Mariano and Father Prior were enough. The only thing that will relieve my anxiety is to know that your Paternity has visited Doctor Arganda.'

Doctor Francis de Arganda was no less a figure than the Prosecutor for the Inquisition. Teresa, who had undergone an interrogation by the Holy Office, had been his good friend. She told Jerome, 'Please give him my regards.' She advised him to be on his guard among people who were so hot-tempered.

When Teresa heard that a muleteer had offered to deliver her letters to Seville she wrote to the Prioress, Mary of St Joseph, asking her if Jerome had arrived safely. She also wrote to Sr Francis and asked her, 'to record carefully all that he suffered at the hands of the friars.' Teresa was anxious to be involved in whatever might happen to her blessed Father.

However, Jerome had not left Madrid, as the King had ordered him to go to the President of the Royal Council and to the General Inquisitor.

When Teresa found out that her dear Father was in Madrid she asked her sisters to pray that all would be well. She also asked their prayers for the General, Rossi, 'who has fallen from a mule and broken his leg. I am so upset about this, as he is an old man by now.' Rossi, who was sixty-nine, had not much longer to live. However, he continued to put pressure on the Nuncio, Ormaneto, not to allow the Discalced Carmelites to make a Visitation and to support the Order's Visitator, Jerome Tostado.

The war-front seemed to have broadened. Gratian counted on the support of the Nuncio, but, more fundamentally, of the King. They (the Calced) would not forgive the King for this. On 3 August, while he [Gratian] was making a Visitation in Pastrana, he took what was quite a risky step. He signed a Decree that I consider to be a declaration to separate from the Calced Carmelites. In his capacity as the Apostolic Commissioner for the

Carmelite Order and Visitator to the Andalucian Province as well as to all the Discalced Carmelites, by virtue of an Apostolic Brief from the Papal Nuncio he issued a decree creating a Discalced Carmelite Province. He did this for the friars as well as the nuns from Andalucia and Castile

It was not a definitive break from the Carmelite Order, but it was a split that would leave scars. Jerome did it for Teresa, knowing how badly she wanted to form a separate Province, so that the problems and harassment from the Calced Carmelites would end. It would be a separate Province, consisting of the Discalced houses in Castile and Andalucia: friars and nuns under the same leadership, Constitutions and way of life. They would be directly subject to the Prior General, who could visit them, but always accompanied by a Discalced Carmelite friar. Furthermore, they would not accept orders, patents or visitations by any Calced Carmelite who was inferior to the General of the Order. 'By the Apostolic authority confided in me…' Jerome signed the Decree.

In order to bring about the new Province the Discalced Carmelite Priors were summoned to a Chapter in Almodovar del Campo, 'the Sunday after the Octave of Our Lady of Mount Carmel': that is, the following 26 August. There they elected a Provincial and Definitors for the new Province.

Three days later, on 6 August, Tostado arrived in Madrid to present his Patents. Quite by chance he bumped into Gratian in the street! It would be better to let Gratian tell us what happened:

> He met Fr Tostado in the street who told him very bitterly and angrily that he would go to any lengths to get rid of the Discalced Carmelites. Fr Gratian considered what he could do to stop this man. He went to see the President of the Royal Council, and informed him that Tostado was coming and asked what he should do. The President told him to continue his Visitation, notwithstanding the arrival of Tostado, and gave him a proviso from the Council for Justice of the Kingdom in support of his Visitation. When he spoke to the Nuncio about the same matter, he begged the Nuncio to let him quit the Commission in order to protect the Discalced Carmelites from the intentions of Tostado. The Nuncio replied that even though many letters had been written from Rome about him [Jerome], it was the wish of his Holiness and his Majesty [the King] that he carry on.
>
> After that, he went to the Carmelite priory where Tostado was staying. The latter had talked to the Nuncio, and was not as bad-tempered as he had been before; in fact, he treated the Father with courtesy and spoke

> very charitably. Father Tostado let it be known that after his meeting with the King, he would be given a licence to make Visitations and bring to an end the Visitation authorized by the Nuncio. Thus he and Tostado were together in Madrid: Fr Tostado to negotiate with the King and Nuncio about the necessary documents for his Visitations and Fr Gratian to keep quiet about the fact that he already had the documents that Tostado would need to make Visitations.

Jerome, with letters from the King, a proviso from the Council and a mandate from the Nuncio in his pocket, did not want to leave Madrid without saying goodbye to Tostado. The latter was angry to learn that Jerome was to make a Visitation in Andalucia, and appealed to the Nuncio to stop him. The Nuncio reprimanded Jerome for telling Tostado of his proposed Visitation.

Jerome presided over the Discalced Carmelite Chapter in Almodovar; a town about half way between Madrid and Seville. He called in to greet Teresa when he passed through Toledo. Tostado, unable to count on the King's support, was advised by the Nuncio to go to Portugal where he hoped he would have more success visiting the Carmelites there.

St Teresa shared her relief with Mary of St Joseph, Prioress of Seville: 'God has delivered us from the Tostado.' She wrote to Jerome, who by now was in Almodovar: '*Peralta* left for Portugal on Thursday, the same day as your Paternity came here.' *Peralta* was her nickname for Tostado, which may appear disrespectful but Teresa had to use codified names to protect people's identity. Teresa knew that Tostado had informers, had bribed certain people and had even intercepted her mail. For this reason Teresa used her imagination and ingenuity to devise nicknames. She called the Nuncio, who was old and sick, and soon to die, *Methuselah*. She called her daughters, the Discalced Carmelite nuns, *Butterflies*; she called the Calced Carmelites, *Cats*; the Discalced, *Eagles*; the devil, *brass-neck*; Jesus Christ, *Joseph*; her dear Gratian, *Paul* and *Elisha*; she usually called herself, *Angela* or *Lorencia*.

In Almodovar Jerome presided at a meeting of the priors and assistants of the nine Discalced Carmelite houses. They had come from Castile and Andalucia, including St John of the Cross. Their task was to work out how to form a separate juridical Province. In spite of the fact that they were few in number, anxious and fearful, they pressed ahead with the task in hand. The General Chapter at Piacenza had declared them to be apostates, but at the time they were getting conflicting reports.

The (Almodovar) Chapter was a clear challenge, establishing as it did the independence of the Discalced. The assembled members were anxious to find themselves in this situation, it was only Jerome who kept calm. He convinced them that the Nuncio wanted them to create a new Province. 'They often heard him [Jerome] say this was the only way for the Order to have the values and spirituality that suited it.' He created the Province for that reason: to be separate from the Mitigated or Calced Fathers, and though this meant contradicting orders coming from the General Chapter, his faculties to reform the Order were superior and for this reason

> we made it separate. By means of this Chapter we formally united and brought together all the Discalced friars and nuns in Castile and Andalucia, thus fulfilling the Brief according to which our life is to be unified. This would not be possible unless we were subject to one head and form one Congregation.

The election of the Provincial, however, would not occur straight away, but be delayed,

> because, being Commissioner and Apostolic Visitator, I was obliged to make visitations. It would not have been right to have someone else in charge, to elect another head or Provincial, to command and govern, while I was making visitations; it would have caused concern in the said Congregation and Province.

It was for this reason that Jerome ordered, 'by the apostolic authority conceded in me', that when his Commission as Reformer ceased to be because he had to step down, or by the absence or death of the Nuncio, the first Definitor, who was Anthony of Jesus, should call a meeting to elect a Provincial.

The friars at the (Almodovar) Chapter accepted the Constitutions that St Teresa had drawn up for the nuns. They also accepted the Constitutions for the friars that Jerome had drafted on his journey to Seville; he and Teresa had put together the finishing touches. He expelled certain Calced Carmelite friars who had made themselves Discalced; those who showed no interest in seeking perfection.

He also dealt with Teresa's insistent request to appoint two Discalced Carmelites to go to Rome to defend the Reform's interests. In a letter to him she argued: 'I have been thinking that if the Pope accepts them [the Calced Carmelite's representatives] and the false information they give him, but then there is no one to respond, he will give them as many Briefs against us as they want… I believe that it is very important to be ready for whatever comes.' Jerome appointed John of Jesus Roca and Peter of the Angels to go to the eternal city, but it took a long time before they reached their destination.

At the end of the Chapter everyone was happy and Teresa even more so. She wrote to her Fr Gratian from Toledo, where she had been confined: 'Now that it [the Chapter] has been completed they [the nuns] are very happy and I am even more so. May God be praised.'

St Teresa knew Jerome's mother, Joanna Dantisco. The latter had visited Toledo in July to see her eighteen-year-old daughter, Joanna, who had entered a college for noble young ladies. At the same time she left, Jerome's mother left her youngest daughter, Isabel, just seven years old, with the Carmelite nuns. Accompanying them was her eleven-year-old son, Periquito who, years later, became a novice in Pastrana. He left to become a priest; he died as Rector of the hospital, 'de la Latina', in Madrid. Joanna, (the daughter) whom Teresa described as 'very pretty', married but died within twelve months of the marriage. Little Isabel, whom Teresa called 'my beautiful one', became a Discalced Carmelite nun, taking for her profession-name, 'St Joseph of Jesus'.

The meeting between Teresa and Joanna Dantisco, in September 1576, marked the beginning of a deep friendship. In the three days that Joanna spent in Toledo they spoke at length about Jerome, and both women disputed as to who loved him more. Teresa teased Jerome in a letter he received while in Seville: 'Lady Joanna is absolutely convinced that your Paternity does what I ask him to do.'

She praised the virtues of his mother: 'I am telling your Paternity that God has given her such great talents and a nature, the like of which I've seldom seen, in fact, I have never seen. She has an openness and clarity of thought for which I am lost in admiration. Her son is very blessed. I am greatly consoled to be where I can often consult her. We know each other so well; it's as if we've known each other all our lives…'

Teresa betrayed a little jealousy when, somewhat anxiously she asked if he loved her more than his mother, 'I have been thinking which of the two of us you loved more, given that Lady Joanna has a husband and other children who love her, but poor Lorencia, has no one else in the world except this Father.'

When the Chapter in Almodovar was over, and following the wishes of the Nuncio and King, Jerome travelled to Seville to fulfil his duties as Visitator. Those who went with him were frightened out of their wits; frightened that the Calced Carmelites in Cordoba would come out to meet them on the road, in the middle of the Sierra Morena, and do to them 'something terrible to prevent their arrival with the messages for the Visitation.'

Jerome described what happened in his book, *The Foundations*, when they passed through the Sierra Morena. It was common in that part of Spain for there to be bandits on the road. They met a military Captain walking in their direction. 'They gave him a lift so that he would guard them, but when he realized the danger and saw their fear he charged them double.' They reached a country inn situated about four miles from Almodovar. Jerome saw a man whose appearance and behavior made him nervous. He kept staring at Jerome, so he asked the man: 'What do you want?' The one-eyed man replied: 'Are you Fr Gratian, the Visitator of the Calced Carmelites in Andalucia?' 'Yes,' he replied. The man handed him a document and said, 'I have a letter for you from the Prior of Cordoba.'

The letter 'did not make sense, and the handwriting and signature were not those of the Prior', which made everyone even more anxious. The four friars and the Captain got together to discuss the matter. Following their discussions they were in no doubt that they (the Calced) were waiting to kill them at one of the city gates, the one Jerome usually went through when going to Andalucia. The one-eyed man must have been a spy, sent to establish what route our friar would take.

They had to outfox the blind man. They fed him well and asked him to take a letter to Almodovar where, they said, they would be returning in a couple of days. They paid him well for his services and while the man travelled north, they saddled up their horses and went south, through the Sierra Morena 'with such great haste that one of the horses died as a result. They left there [Almodovar] two young men to see if the messenger returned to tell of their arrival.'

Jerome reached Seville at the end of September – there were no more scares. His authority had been consolidated. However, when the Calced Carmelites found out that the Visitator was in the Priory of Los Remedios, they sent a canon lawyer to inform him that they would only obey him under certain conditions. Jerome pointed out that obedience could not be considered conditional.

Then two Calced friars from the oldest Carmelite priory 'in Seville came to see him. They were afraid to enter Los Remedios for fear of being incarcerated in the priory-jail.' However, Fr Gratian treated them 'with much love and kindness.'

> The two Fathers, who had come as representatives of everyone in their Priory, assured him that they supported him in Carmel and that he could make his Visitation as he wished and that all of them would be subject to him. And so it was. They welcomed him warmly, with much courtesy and love, because even though the Calced Carmelites loathed the Visitation and were very much opposed to some of his companions, they always showed love for the person of Fr Gratian, and knew well what he had suffered and that he had worked hard to protect and defend them; and that if the Commission had fallen into someone else's hands then all would have been lost.

The next day was a Sunday, and as usual many people came to listen to the preacher. Word had got round that Fr Gratian was in town, and so the Carmelite chapel was full of people eager to hear what the preacher would say about the Carmelite friar this time. Great was their surprise when they saw the man himself mount the steps of the pulpit. 'The people were greatly impressed when they saw him. There was quite a din in the chapel and it took a long time for it to become quiet.'

Jerome had to ask the people to keep quiet, which should be the norm in any Carmelite house. Some months previously, from the same pulpit, they had heard that (he had been burnt at the stake and) his ashes thrown away. He preached a sermon that was 'blunt'; the people were not expecting this. However, they saw him and heard him; evidently, he hadn't been burnt nor his ashes thrown away.

With the authority he enjoyed as Apostolic Visitator he restored those Priors who had been removed. The Calced Carmelites were won over at last… from an attitude of resignation they now had one of hope of better times. Fr Peter Cota, who had organized the rebellion, was now confined to the Carmelite Priory in Seville and his habit taken from him.

An ugly situation arose in a Carmelite convent in Paterna del Campo, which meant that Jerome was obliged to go there. In this convent there were twenty-four nuns, four were elderly the rest all under twenty-five. A rumour had gone round that three of the nuns were pregnant. The convent walls were so low 'that any child could get over them like a staircase,' said Jerome.

The accused nuns cried their hearts out in front of the Visitator, begging him to defend them against these lies. Just then, quite spontaneously, they took off their habits, leaving just their undergarments and bodices. Fr Jerome blushed and did not know where to look. One of the nuns said: 'It is seven months since they spread these malicious rumours: can you see anything? In the name of God look and see for yourself.' However, Jerome kept his eyes on the ground and replied: 'My sisters, please believe me when I tell you that I know nothing about these things.' They replied: 'Then send for a midwife from Seville and she will prove it.' To which he replied: 'There's no need, better to send for our nuns.'

It was clear that the rumours were false. They had been spread by a Calced Carmelite called Fr John. To punish him for these lies Jerome made him wear a kind of scapular of tongues. The Constitutions stipulated that for telling lies: twelve tongues of coloured or white cloth were to be stitched to the scapular in front and behind.

Jerome himself would 'not be left immune from such lies'; but by now he was used to all kinds of slander.

> Afterwards, these three nuns whom I had freed from this infamy and some trustworthy Calced friars, with whom I had become very friendly, brought terrible false accusations against me, sending letters to the Nuncio, Sega, to begin a legal case against me. This was to cause me no end of problems.

Jerome tried to bring healing to that house in Paterna, in which they did not even know how to pray. In order to reform it he brought two nuns from the Carmelite convent in Seville. They arrived in October 1576 and remained in Paterna until December 1577, a little over a year.

All did not go well. Teresa called these (Paterna) nuns, 'night birds' and 'night owls', because they got up to all sorts of mischief in order to make life more difficult for them (the new nuns). They didn't even want to feed them. They used offensive language all the time. Mary of St Joseph recalled in her *Book of Recreations* how, one day when the Paterna Sisters were particularly hostile, 'the three nuns locked themselves in a small room, underneath a staircase; where there was hardly room to move. They remained there all night without sleeping or moving, because the entire community remained outside the door attempting to enter and threatening to kill them.'

Some good did come thanks to these Discalced Carmelite nuns. 'At least,' said Mary of St Joseph, 'they managed to establish normal life in the convent; they introduced the community to the choral office and to eat together in the refectory; things the community had not known before; nor did they know anything about the Church.'

Cyril heard the account of this farcical scandal from Anastasius, and exclaimed, 'Oh, may God help us, how right Mother Teresa was to say that you should not trust the Calced Carmelites from Andalucia, or trust the "night owls", who were the Calced Carmelite nuns from Paterna!'

'*The Foundations* is an interesting book,' Teresa told Jerome in a letter. She had begun it in 1573, on the orders of the Jesuit, Fr Repalda, a well-known teacher, and finished it in obedience to Fr Gratian in November 1576, in St Joseph's convent, Toledo.

Teresa was anxious to have news of her Fr Gratian, writing anxious letter after letter to Seville, some addressed to him, others to Mary of St Joseph. To the latter she wrote: 'What our Fr Gratian is doing seems unbelievable. Blessed be he who has been given so many gifts.'

Teresa warned him: 'For God's sake be careful what you eat in those priories and convents.' And to Mary of St Joseph she wrote: 'Stop him from visiting the Province until such time as we can see what is happening.' Again to Fr Gratian she wrote: 'I was praying with Joseph [Teresa's codename for Jesus Christ] who told me to warn you to be careful because you have many enemies, some visible some invisible.' She wrote to Mary of St Joseph, at the beginning of 1577, 'You must have experienced a happy Christmas since you have my Father Gratian there, for I would too, and happy New Year.'

Teresa told Fr Gratian that the Nuncio was ill and that she feared he was dying. The Nuncio, Ormaneto, was suffering from gout and old age was now beginning to tell. 'We have commended Methuselah to God.' She knew that the Nuncio, Ormaneto, was the most important supporter of her Reform. What would happen when he died?

Ormaneto was under pressure from Rome. In September 1576, he had received a letter from Cardinal Galli, the Pope's Secretary, who asked him to proceed cautiously with the reform of the Religious Orders. Pope Gregory XIII had received many formal letters of complaint. 'It is the wish of His Holiness that you proceed less drastically and that you act in such a way that there will be no reason for people to appeal to us with complaints.'

One of these letters came from the Calced Carmelites in Andalucia, asking for Jerome to be removed. It did not contain the gross lies they would bring later to King Philip II's desk when Anthony Gratian was no longer alive. They stressed the youthfulness of the Visitator and his disobedience: 'The Monsignor Nuncio of Spain has made Provincial, Visitator and Reformer of the Province of Andalucia a Discalced Carmelite friar, called Fr Gratian. Our Constitutions state that he should be at least ten years in the Order; but the said Father has only been professed for three years. Then he is always disobedient to the General to whom he has promised obedience, and does not appear to fear excommunication, as his brother is the King's Secretary.'

The Pope's Secretary, Cardinal Galli, explained to Ormaneto on 15 January: 'These Carmelite Fathers… do nothing but cry and complain about the grievances and injustices the Commissioner commits against them.' He insisted that Ormaneto, the Nuncio, suspend Jerome's Visitation and confer it on the General's candidate, i.e. Tostado.

Ormaneto replied to the Pope's Secretary on 5 February: 'Tostado has come here with just one thing in mind: to suppress the Discalced Carmelites, especially in Andalucia.' He went on to say: 'These Discalced Carmelite Fathers live very holy lives… they do not beg, but live from what their own hands have made, therefore they won't affect the alms given to others. When Tostado returns, I shall endeavour to help him see that the Discalced Carmelites are like his sons and that he accepts them and helps them to expand.'

How naïve the Nuncio was! Tostado who was in Portugal, soon returned, but not with the best of intentions. His return rekindled all Teresa's worst fears. On 19 February she told her brother, Lorenzo, in Avila: 'We are still afraid of this Tostado, who has come back to the Court.'

Ormaneto urged Rome to accept the virtues of the Discalced Carmelites and those of Fr Gratian: 'Those who have given you unfavourable news about Fr Gratian are mistaken, as he leads a very good and holy life, he is also very intelligent when it comes to matters concerning Religious life. 'I have supported Tostado in all matters,' the Nuncio continued, seeming to go back on what he said earlier, 'and will support him as much as I can.'

Jerome continued his Visitation in Andalucia unaware of the intrigues going on in Madrid and Rome. At the beginning of the year 1577 he began his Visitation of the houses in the (Andalucian) Province. Archbishop Christopher de Rojas signed a Decree on 7 January, addressed to the clergy of his Archdiocese, reminding them to be obedient. He threatened all the vicars, beneficiaries, parish priests and clergy with canonical penalties if they didn't support Fr Gratian's visitations among the houses of the Carmelites that were located outside the city of Seville.

Jerome set out for Granada. He had been ill during the Christmas period and hoped to find a cure in the spring waters of the Antequera and Loja rivers. Was Tostado in Seville?

Teresa is glad that Jerome was not there. 'I am very happy that our Father is not in Seville.' She doesn't want him to meet with Tostado. And she had heard that the Nuncio was leaving.

She wrote to Mariano, who was in Madrid dealing with the foundation of a Discalced Carmelite priory: 'Why are you worried by the Tostado's Visitation? Leave matters to our Lord, for this is His work and He will draw much good from all of this. And though I see that all our affairs seem to be moving against the current, it doesn't cause me any concern as our affairs are going better than those who swim easily with the current. This is how our Lord shows His power. What seems to cause us most difficulties is that he [Tostado] is arriving just when the Nuncio is leaving; when that happens the Commission of our Father will come to an end.'

The shadow of Tostado was lengthening. He was like a ghost: you didn't see him but you felt his presence. Teresa was in Toledo where she heard a thousand rumours that disturbed her deeply. The illness of the Nuncio and that he might leave Madrid made matters worse. She wrote to Mariano on 15 March: 'They say that the Tostado is coming by way of Andalucia. God be with him whatever may happen. I think it will be better to have to contend with him than with the one we have had to contend with until now. May God give us light and may He watch over you and the Fathers who are with you.'

Tostado, who had arrived in Seville, was determined to visit the priories in Andalucia. He had received news from his assistant, Francis Zapata, that the King had forbidden him to make visitations. This meant he would have to go to the Court to meet the King.

Jerome was in Seville in time to celebrate the feast of St Joseph, 19 March, with the Discalced Carmelite nuns. He preached at a profession Mass for Sr Bernard of St Joseph, who would die a year later. After some days, on 24 March, he gave the habit to Nicholas Doria in the priory of Los Remedios. Doria was forty-eight years old, and would become, as we have already pointed out, Jerome's 'executioner'.

After his Visitation of the houses in Andalucia, Jerome made his way to Beas and Caravaca. While in Jaen, he sent the Nuncio a report of his visits and told him of some decrees he had prepared that would lead to the reform of the Province. He also informed the Nuncio about the celebration of a forthcoming Provincial Chapter. Ormaneto ordered him to visit the Court with the documents recording his Visitation.

Jerome met Teresa in Toledo at the end of May. She noticed that 'he has become plump and is happy, thanks be to God.' Tostado had gone on ahead and was already at the Court. 'He passed through here four or five days ago and was in such a hurry that he didn't stay for more than three or four hours,' the Saint wrote. Tostado reached Madrid by 25 May. He resided at the Carmelite priory, where all the friars kissed his hand and swore obedience to him as the Vicar General. He began to act as such, moving friars about and sitting in the Prior's chair in the choir.

Those two souls, Teresa and Jerome, though tired and anxious, found time for quiet moments to discuss spiritual matters. At a certain point Teresa sighed: 'Oh, how well put is that point in the *Life* that is now with the Inquisition!' Jerome had never had the chance to read the book (*The Book of Her Life*) that the Princess of Eboli had handed to the Inquisition. He said to Teresa: 'Since we cannot have it, remember what you agreed [to obey me] and other things, and write another book.' Thus he ordered her, under obedience, to write about spiritual things and of prayer for the benefit of the nuns. It was to be a different style to *The Book of Her Life*, in which Teresa focused on things from her own personal experience. Jerome wanted this book to be more doctrinal and universal.

The following 2 June, the feast of the most Holy Trinity, Teresa, in obedience to Jerome, began to write the *Interior Castle*. The original of this masterpiece is kept jealously by the Carmelite nuns in Seville.

Jerome arrived in Madrid at the beginning of June. He made a formal visit to the Nuncio to whom he offered his greetings. The Nuncio ordered him to write a report of all he had done. However, when it was written Jerome could not hand it in, as the Nuncio was close to death. On 9 June, suffering from a terrible fever and extremely tired, the Nuncio asked for a papal blessing and a plenary indulgence. A week later, on the night of June 17–18, this old, Veronese Nuncio died.

His replacement, Philip Sega, had already been appointed; he had come from the Nunciature in Flanders. And with him came… a storm.

Chapter Thirteen

Like a Criminal in Hiding

The question now was: did Jerome's authority cease with the death of the Nuncio? Was it the end of his role as Apostolic Visitator? He went to consult with the King, who in turn sought the opinion of the most learned members of the Curia as well as the Doctors of the University of Alcala. They all responded unanimously: what he is doing is not contrary to the law, the Commission he began can continue, *re non integra:*[1] the law does not change for the one who has been granted it.

With this confirmation Jerome received orders to resume his Visitation, though it was limited to the Discalced priories in Castile. He understood clearly that for the Discalced Carmelite friars the opinion of learned men would be enough, but not for the Calced Carmelites of Andalucia; he had no desire to venture down there for the time being.

Teresa wrote to the Prioress of Caravaca in a letter dated 2 July, informing her of all that had happened:

> Our Father is well, thanks be to God, but has a lot of work… [His] commission has not ceased even though the Nuncio has died, and so he is to continue being Visitator as before; I believe he is now in Pastrana… The Tostado, the Vicar General sent by our Very Reverend Father General, is in Madrid…

Teresa returned to Avila in mid-July with the intention of placing St Joseph's convent under the jurisdiction of the Order. The Bishop, Alvaro de Mendoza, a friend of Teresa's, and to whom the nuns of the first Teresian convent had been under obedience, had been transferred to Palencia. In opposition to the Bishop, at least initially, Teresa sought to remove St Joseph's from the authority of the local Bishop, and to place it like all her convents under the

1 The law is not affected.

leadership of the Order, 'because if this isn't done, then relaxation [of our way of life] will quickly follow.'

The Bishop, Alvaro, was persuaded to accept this change. On 2 August, before he left for Palencia, he signed a request declaring that the nuns of St Joseph's of Avila were to be freed from his jurisdiction. Jerome Gratian and John of the Cross (the latter was in Avila as chaplain to the convent of the Incarnation) were present at the time. Several days later, on 31 August, Jerome, using his authority as Apostolic Commissioner of the Order of Our Lady of Mt Carmel in the Province of Andalucia, etc., signed a Patent that years later would have repercussions when Avila and Alba de Tormes became embroiled in a dispute over who should have St Teresa's body.

> By the present and by the Apostolic authority conferred on me, I assign the Reverend Mother Teresa of Jesus, Foundress of the Discalced Carmelite nuns of this Order, as a conventual to the convent of the Discalced Carmelite nuns of St Joseph's, Avila, and when it please Almighty God to bring her to Himself, she be interred in the said convent, mindful that this house was the first house of the foundation…

The new Nuncio, Philip Sega, was installed in Madrid, on 29 August. So great was his hurry that he came directly from Belgium without passing through Rome. He was related to Cardinal Buoncompagne, a nephew of the Pope, which was not a good omen (for the Reform), as Buoncompagne was the Cardinal Protector of the Calced Carmelite Order and, as such, had been told that the Discalced Carmelites in Spain were a 'rebellious and unruly rabble'.

Tostado saw his opportunity. He did not delay, and won over the new Nuncio when he visited on 14 September. Jerome waited expectantly for the Nuncio to call. 'He sent for me,' recounted our man, 'and was happy that I should continue my Visitations. I gave him an account of what I had done.' However, Jerome was not that happy at the termination of the audience, as the Nuncio had asked him to bring to him his credentials and papers. Jerome turned to King Philip II who told him not to do anything until they found out from Rome what powers the new Nuncio had. 'From the very beginning the Nuncio did not endear himself to the Court in Madrid, in great part because he was reluctant to show his credentials,' recounted Jerome.

The Nuncio 'shouted angrily because all had not gone well for him,' added Gratian, who, by now, had retired to Pastrana where, living in a cave, he dedicated himself to prayer. He would need all that prayer and fortitude when he had to confront the assaults soon to come his way from the Nuncio and the Calced Carmelites. But for the time being the shouting was directed at him by the Discalced Carmelites. Well… at least from some Discalced.

Philip II received a letter containing a shocking denunciation of Gratian. It had been signed by Balthasar Nieto and a simple lay brother, Michael de la Columna, who had accompanied Jerome on his travels. Jerome considered this Brother among those who 'was not only illiterate, but is incapable of putting two words together.' Before he became a Brother he had helped to build some of Teresa's convents.

The cave called after St John of the Cross in the hillside above the priory of St Peter in Pastrana. It was possibly in this cave, or one like it, that while the Nuncio 'roared', Jerome prayed.

Jerome had had to confine Balthazar Nieto, the Prior of Almodovar, in Pastrana 'for certain scandals that had given bad example.' Like the goat that is attracted to the mountains, as the refrain goes, Balthazar Nieto, at just over fifty years of age, returned to the less than edifying ways of his life. It was difficult for him to return to Pastrana, where he had been Prior for many years, instead he opted to flee, taking refuge in the home of a friend in Madrid, from where he sent a message to Tostado that he was ready to give him his obedience and to seek his protection.

Tostado's response was immediate: 'I accept your obedience and, as the Vicar General of the Order, I shall protect you. There is no other jurisdiction over the Carmelites in Spain apart from my own. Fr Gratian does not have this nor can he have it, as he and all the Discalced Carmelites have been excommunicated by the General of the Order.' Balthazar Nieto transferred himself to the Carmel in Madrid and swore obedience to Jerome Tostado, in spite of the fact that the latter knew well the reasons why Jerome had punished him.

'Both of them,' Jerome said, referring to Fr Balthazar Nieto and Brother Michael de la Columna, 'left the Discalced and joined the Calced Carmelites to assist them with their lies and malicious gossip and with them there were also others.' A malicious document was drawn up in Madrid Carmel, prompted by Balthazar Nieto and encouraged by Tostado. Jerome saw that such outrageous calumnies presented to the King did not make much of an impression on the latter. This was because the King already 'had experience of this kind of backbiting and did not believe what was written.' However, Jerome suffered great shame when the said calumnies became known among the good people: made known by a Discalced friar who described himself as his travelling companion during his visitations, a lay brother he (Jerome) took Brother Michael with him as he travelled by foot and needed a companion.

I shall summarize here the lies they drew up in this libelous document: Gratian ate meat as if he were a Bishop, and delicious meals of chicken, turkey and partridge. In Seville, he was served these meals while 'some nuns sang, danced and entertained him.' In Beas, 'a young and beautiful nun put on pretty clothes and danced in front of him in a way that seemed more like a prostitute than a nun.' In Caravaca, 'he took the Prioress' veil' and gave it to a novice whom he told to be Prioress from then on. In Toledo, 'he went into the chapel where there was a choir-grille, and making a kind of platform out of the pews he placed a chair on top onto which he climbed in order to have a good look at the nuns who were singing and dancing for him.' He wore fine cotton shirts, the sheets on his bed were of linen, which the Discalced Carmelite nuns had sent him when he was in the Seville priory. Every time he entered a Carmelite convent the nuns greeted him with big hugs and kissed his feet, which he never seemed to disapprove of…

He was also accused of being an 'alumbrado'; Balthazar Nieto had subtly introduced this word in order to attract the attention of the Inquisition.

Thomas Gratian, King Philip II's Secretary, wrote a long letter in which he came to the defence of his brother, Jerome. St Teresa wrote to Philip II on 18 September assuring him of Jerome's innocence as well as that of her nuns; they couldn't have been better defended:

> I am astonished at the intrigues of the devil and these Calced Fathers. They're not satisfied with defaming this servant of God (for he truly is and has so edified us that the monasteries he has visited always write to me about how he has left them with a new spirit), but they are striving now to discredit these monasteries where God is so well served. And to do this they have made use of two Discalced friars. The one had been a servant in these monasteries before becoming a friar and did things that made it obvious he often lacked good judgment. The friars of the cloth have used these Discalced friars and others antagonistic toward Father Gratian – for he is the one who must punish them – and had them sign things that were absurd. I would have laughed at what was said about the Discalced nuns if I didn't fear the harm the devil can do with it, for in our communities such things would be horrendous.
>
> For the love of God I beg your majesty not to allow such infamous testimony to be presented to tribunals…
>
> I feel sorry for all that this servant of God suffers, despite the fact that in everything he does he is upright and seeks to do what is right. I must beg your majesty to favour him or give orders that he be removed from this situation so full of perils. Besides being a man of good character, he is also the son of parents who are in your majesty's service. Truly, I think he is a man sent by God and his Blessed Mother. His devotion to her – and it is great – is what led him to the Order and to helping me. For more than seventeen years I suffered alone from these Fathers of the cloth, and I no longer knew how to bear it; my own weak efforts were insufficient…

The accusations were so exaggerated and full of intrigue that they produced the contrary effect. The signatories confessed their guilt. Balthazar Nieto, with obvious hyprocrisy, not only confessed but justified himself. If he had been motivated by jealousy, he confessed, it had been his understanding that Fr Jerome was jealous of him. 'And because jealousy creates such damage and usually leads to blindness, I did not want your Paternity to be jealous of me nor I of him, but rather, for the glory of our Lord, that we work together united in body and soul.'

The lay brother, Michael de la Columna, naïvely and simply confessed his guilt on 24 September. It was through him that we know how the said document came to be hatched. 'In my presence, Andrew Palmero Ximenez, Public Notary by apostolic authority, approved by the tribunal of the Archbishop's palace in Toledo, residing in the town of Pastrana, and before the illustrious gentlemen, the Treasurer Hernando de la Roxa and the Lawyer, Rodriguez, Canons, and the Canon Juan Gonzalez de Rueda and the Prependary, Sebastian de Balbazie, and the Prebendary Francisco de Olivares, Clerics, Dignitaries, Canons and Prebendaries of the Collegial church in this town of Pastrana…' Brother Michael admitted what had happened before this illustrious body in the College chapel of Pastrana and with the Blessed Sacrament exposed:

> I swear by Our Lord and by the orders I hold, that I did not read the said letter, but rather was compelled, constrained and forced by Fr Tostado, who had just arrived as Vicar General, and by Fr Balthazar Nieto, Fr Cardenas, Brother Hernando de Medina and by other Calced Carmelite Fathers from the Priory of Our Lady of Mt Carmel, Madrid. They were older than me and lead me to do this, sometimes through persuasion, other times by threats. Once I wanted to see the papers they had written, because I was really suspicious of what they had done, but one of the Fathers told me that if I didn't keep quiet, he would beat me with a stick, and that if I made him really angry he would punch me. At the same time he told me that I must be mad not to understand what a good thing it was to be in their company, who had clear consciences, whereas with the Discalced Carmelites I was with bad and excommunicated people…

In the end Brother Michael de la Columna was forced to sign without having read the document, as he was considered 'a stupid young friar and not a priest', though what had been written was all pure and utter fabrication. And oh, as for the word '*alumbrado*', he had no idea what it meant.

It had all been the idea of Balthazar Nieto, who had written the document with the help of Diego de Cardenas, a Calced Carmelite from Andalucia who prowled around Madrid. This man would make Mary of St Joseph, the Prioress of Seville's life a misery when he became Provincial of Andalucia: behind all this but in the shadows lurked Tostado.

When the unfortunate lay brother reported to Tostado that Balthazar and Cardenas were writing words in his name, he asked Tostado not to give his consent. Tostado told him: 'Do not worry, all of this is for the benefit of

The College Chapel in Pastrana.

the Order,' and with these words he silenced the lay brother.

On 8 October, Brother Michael asked for a meeting in St Peter's Priory, Pastrana, to denounce Balthazar Nieto. The Prior, Diego of the Trinity convened a community Chapter that degenerated into an angry confrontation. As a result the point of the meeting was lost much to the delight of Balthazar Nieto. The latter's final declaration stated hypocritically: 'I hold that everything written in the said document was a lie, given that, as I said, I hold Fr Gratian to be a very good Religious, but this other [presumably Brother Michael], regrettably, to be very fickle and ignorant. And hereby I sign in my name...'

Two days later, Balthazar wrote a letter to Jerome, who must have been in Alcala, asking for forgiveness. After those words Balthazar Nieto disappeared from the radar of the Discalced Carmelites, having filled St Teresa with bitterness; she who had naïvely accepted him. He died in Lisbon in 1590. Brother Michael de la Columna apparently died having lost his mind. However, the lies due to stupidity on the part of one, and baseness on the part of the other, spread through the Court, where they would leave their mark: pernicious sewage that would fertilize the weeds again.

The King prevented Tostado from making his Visitation of Castile; nonetheless, he continued to harass the Discalced from Madrid. The object of his next treacherous act was not Jerome but rather Teresa of Jesus and, afterwards, St John of the Cross.

Elections were held in Avila for a new Prioress at the Incarnation convent. They were Calced Carmelite nuns yet they had two Discalced Carmelite friars as confessors: John of the Cross and German of St Matthew. The pre-Chapter meetings seemed to favour Teresa, who had just reached Avila. Teresa sought refuge in her Discalced Carmelite convent of St Joseph's. Tostado tried to prevent the election and ordered the Provincial, Fr John Gutierrez de la Magdalena to preside, instructing the Provincial what was to be expected of him.

It was 7 October 1577. In the convent parlour, after expelling the Confessors, who normally assist at this Act, the Provincial read out a letter from the Vicar General, Tostado. In it he made several recommendations, in particular the following: 'Anyone who votes for a nun outside the convent shall be excommunicated.' When the vote was completed they began to read out the voting slips. The second voting slip was read out and on it was the name of Teresa of Jesus. The Provincial began to curse and in anger crushed the slip of paper in his hand. Each time Teresa's name arose he banged the table with an iron hammer. He made clear his anger towards those nuns who had voted the same way. The final result was: Teresa of Jesus, 54 votes; Joanna del Aguila, 39.

The Provincial told the nuns they were excommunicated then got up and left. The distressed nuns took refuge in the choir where they prayed before the cross. However, they were forced to quit the choir as well when the door was locked. Fr Tostado arrived and confirmed the excommunication of the rebellious nuns.

Teresa observed all this from the nearby convent (St Joseph's) where she was staying. She wrote to Mary of St Joseph, on 22 October, telling her all that had happened. 'They have now been excommunicated for a fortnight. They are without Mass, are not allowed to go into the choir, not even to say the Divine Office, and no one speaks to them, neither the confessors nor their own priests.' And yet, Teresa did not want to deal with this 'Babylon' and remained where she was in St Joseph's convent.

In the midst of this uproar Teresa managed to finish one of her most profound pieces of writing, the *Interior Castle*. She had begun it six months previously in Toledo at the express wish of Fr Gratian, and now she finished it on the eve of St Andrew's feast, 29 November.

Tostado was still alive and active and treacherous. Sometime between the night of 3–4 December, John of the Cross and German of St Matthew were abducted; one was confined to the Calced Carmelite priory, Toledo, the other to the Carmelite priory of La Moraleia. Teresa immediately sought help for her friars from King Philip II. She confided to him, 'It would have been better if they were in the hands of the Moors, because they would be shown more mercy.' We feel 'very ashamed to see them in their hands,' because 'this friar [she is referring to St John of the Cross] is so very thin due to all the suffering he has endured that I fear for his life.'

John of the Cross had disappeared as if by magic. 'I am frightened by this strange disappearance of Fr John,' she wrote. No one knew where he was. Nor did John of the Cross himself know, as he was taken during the night and kept blindfolded. Teresa had an idea he was in the Priory in Toledo, since it was the Prior of that place who had abducted him. However, in order to throw people off the scent, word had gone round that the said Prior was on his way to Rome.

In January 1578, Teresa was deeply upset: 'My pain is that they have taken him away and we do not know where.' John was in fact in Toledo. Tostado together with the Prior, Maldonado, had tried him. The latter together with other senior Fathers from the Toledo priory were the ones who abducted John. They condemned him for being rebellious and disobedient. He remained nine months in a small six-foot-by-ten cell that was dirty and windowless, until eventually he managed to escape. The way he was abused during his detention has been vividly detailed in biographies of the Saint, in which there is an implicit criticism of Jerome. It was only Teresa who tried

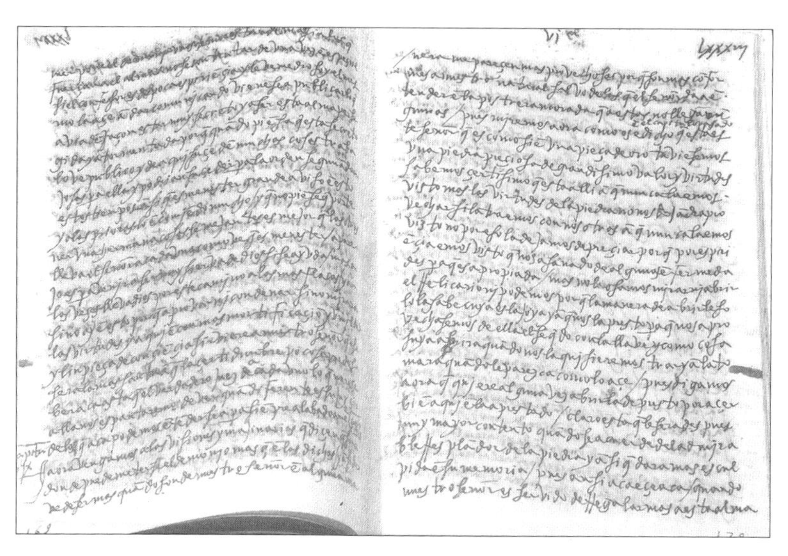

The *Interior Castle*, facsimile edition, from the original preserved in Seville Carmel.

to find John; no one else was interested. Fr Crisogono of Jesus OCD, wrote that Teresa 'was the only voice raised on behalf of the prisoner. The others did not appear to do anything. There is no evidence to show that Jerome Gratian lifted a finger…'

It is clear that there is no evidence; there are no documents to indicate Gratian's attitude towards John of the Cross at this time of crisis. Jerome suffered from the insults of the Nuncio and the malicious deeds of Tostado. He also had to flee to Pastrana, so as to avoid becoming a prisoner himself. 'For more than three months it seems that many armies of demons had joined forces against the Discalced friars and nuns.' Teresa wrote, 'There have been many persecutions. Some people are responsible for stirring up many things against us nuns as well as Fr Gratian. I feel sick to my stomach; all we can do is turn to God.'

These were dark days for the Discalced Carmelites. One bad event followed another; all seemingly linked. Indeed, on Christmas night Teresa fell down some stairs and broke her left arm. This did not heal well and so she was left, effectively, with just one arm. According to her first biographer, Ribera, she could not 'dress nor undress herself, nor put on her veil', for the rest of her life, at least what remained of it.

Teresa had one arm in a sling, Jerome was in a far off cave in Pastrana and John of the Cross was a prisoner… So begins 1578. It was the stormiest of years for the Teresian Reform.

St John of the Cross.

Anonymous portrait, 16th century. Museum de Santa Cruz, Toledo.

The Nuncio was so angry with Jerome that he wanted to hit him. Anastasius confides in Cyril:

> I am stuck in the middle between the King and the Nuncio over the important matter of jurisdiction. The King told me not see the Nuncio until there was a response from Rome. The Nuncio roared with anger because I would not come to him, and imputed that I was impeding his Apostolic Jurisdiction. Then the Pope declared that the Nuncio should not get involved with the friars, except in those matters where the King asks him to. The Nuncio's anger was so great that he said if they did not surrender me to be burnt for having impeded his jurisdiction that he would have to return to Rome. His anger got worse due to the lies and the legal processes against me submitted by the Calced Carmelites; how I had already completed my Visitation even though I had no faculties to do this. He was no less incensed by certain

> letters I had sent to the King in which I told the latter of the great problems that would arise for the Orders in Spain if Nuncios issued Briefs contrary to the orders of their Superiors. The King gave these letters to some influential people in Spain who then showed them to the Nuncio. These two things together upset him to such an extent that I should count myself lucky not to be burned at the stake.

On 28 April the Nuncio had an audience with the King. Sega later wrote to Rome that he had spoken about the Carthusians and the Carmelites. Concerning the latter, the King referred the matter to the President of the Council of Castile, who had not yet been appointed. (Bishop) Diego de Covarrubias (the former President of the Council) had died; he had been a great friend of St Teresa. It was already known that the new appointee would be the Bishop of Patti, in Sicily. In the meantime Tostado had received permission to make a Visitation of the houses in the Kingdom of Aragon. Permission had not been given him for Castile because he had acted first before showing his credentials to the King.

Teresa could not believe it (that Tostado had gone). She wrote to Jerome, who was in Alcala, 'They have written to me from Toledo that the Tostado has already gone; I don't believe it.' And yet it was true, my dear Teresa. However, the Nuncio was in the Royal Court: what an annoying man he was.

The new President of the Council ordered Jerome to begin his Visitation again. Jerome had warned him: 'Look your Lordship, the Nuncio will not agree with this.' However, the President replied: 'It has nothing to do with him, but rather the Lord President.'

Jerome focused on restarting his Visitation, now that he had been ordered to by the President and because Tostado had disappeared. He asked the King to lend him support from the secular arm, as he thought this might be necessary. A Royal Decree, signed on 19 June, ordered all the Justices to support and help Fr Gratian of the Order of Carmel whenever necessary in his Visitations of the houses of the Discalced and Calced Carmelites. Teresa told the nuns in Seville that he would visit them in September.

By mid-July he was in Valladolid, overseeing the foundation of a priory in the gardens of San Alejo. The Nuncio was in Madrid, and there on 23 July, he wrote a Brief, or I should say, a Counter-Brief, dated 23 July, which declared that Jerome was to cease all he was doing as Apostolic Visitator, and that the government of the Discalced Carmelites was to be subject to him (the Nuncio). At the same time he withdrew Jerome's faculties, excommunicated him and ordered him to appear before him in his palace within six days of receiving the decree; our man was to bring with him all the Acts from the Visitations he had already carried out.

News of this Counter-Brief spread like wild-fire throughout all the priories and convents. Teresa of Jesus knew about it on 8 August and uttered the following exclamation: 'God forgive me, I still cannot believe that the Nuncio ordered such a thing.'

Jerome knew about this decree from the first moment. How? I don't know. He was in Valladolid, living in a house outside the city walls with three other friars.

One night some Calced Carmelites came to the house, they were accompanied by a group of armed men and a lawyer to notify Jerome of the decree. Jerome, who had been anxious about what might happen, stayed that night with another companion in the house of a cousin. The Calced Carmelites pounded on the door as if they were going to knock it down. When a neighbour confronted them they drew knives. Inside there were several friars: Fr John of Jesus, Fr Bartholomew of Jesus and Fr Thomas of the Assumption. They climbed out of a window and fled. Then the Bishop of Palencia, Alvaro de Mendoza, arrived with a group of people carrying torches; he took the three friars to his house.

Jerome recalled that the notary had stated officially that he had personally handed over the Nuncio's decree to him. However, he complained: 'This false testimony ended up in the hands of the Nuncio.' Jerome ran away and hid once again. He did not want run into the Calced Carmelites, who were looking to give him the Brief, until he could talk to the King to see what he should do with regard to the Nuncio, Sega. He journeyed between Salamanca and Valladolid, taking refuge in Pennaranda. Teresa wrote to him there, expressing her anxieties and fears at what was happening; but for her, 'my only concern and preoccupation is my Paul's safety.'

He left Madrid and arrived in Avila on 12 August, where he found consolation with St Teresa. Jerome recounted, 'She offered me her condolences for what I had suffered and was moved to see me so harassed.' Teresa told him: 'Do not be upset, my Father, we are not fighting for our own interests but rather for the honour and glory of God and of His Mother, the Blessed Virgin Mary. This persecution will make our Order stronger; do not be in the least afraid.'

Two days later she wrote to Madrid: 'I tell you I was so moved to see your Paternity that all day yesterday, Wednesday, my heart was in anguish not knowing what to do at seeing you so afflicted. Who wouldn't be. You are surrounded by danger on all sides, and you must go around like a criminal in hiding.'

'Like a criminal in hiding': what a most apt metaphor. In Madrid he hid in the house of Diego de Peralta rather than in his parent's house until he could obtain an audience with the King. Philip II referred him to the President of the Council of Castile, but the latter was ill. Teresa advised him that 'it would be foolish to surrender yourself to the Nuncio, until the President sorts things out.' Her advice to him was that, no matter what anyone says, he was under no obligation. She added, 'let no one know you are there.'

Did Jerome hope that the President would be well again before he made a call on the Nuncio? It seems he did, since it was to the President that he submitted the documents and his reports of the Visitations. Later, at the Nuncio's palace, he was warned to submit the documents he no longer had. Jerome took the Nuncio's reprimand in all humility, prostrating himself on the ground. The latter ordered him to confine himself to a priory until his cause was heard. Later, Jerome recorded how the Nuncio spoke to him: 'He said, in front of others, that Luther had not done as much to begin a revolution in Germany as this Father has done in Spain, and that he would return to Rome if he were not suitably punished.'

Jerome went to Pastrana, where he met Fr Mariano. The latter had, on 9 August, obtained a royal provision, which contradicted the Nuncio's Counter-Brief. It ordered the 'Chief Magistrates, Assistants, Governors and other Judges and Justices of the towns and villages and places within our Kingdoms and Estates' to take back the Nuncio's Brief that revoked Fr Jerome's Visitation and submit the same to the Council of Castile. What a confusion of jurisdictions! The Calced Carmelites had the Nuncio's Counter-Brief, the Discalced Carmelites sought protection from the King.

Two Calced Carmelites from Andalucia arrived in Pastrana, Fr Juarez and Fr Coria, to present the Nuncio's Brief. Mariano, with the royal provision in his hands, had arranged for the Justices in Pastrana to take his Brief and send it to the Council. The Calced Carmelites pounded on the door of St Peter's priory. The friars were afraid to open the door. Anthony of Jesus, Mariano and Jerome were inside. Should they open the door? Mariano and Anthony of Jesus did not want to decide without asking Jerome. The latter begged them to leave him in peace because he was fed up with so much trouble; they could do whatever they wanted.

Jerome found himself in this difficult juncture and was on the point of throwing in the towel: did he obey the (Nuncio's) Brief or, with the provision from the Council, override it? He decided to open the door, made the two Calced Carmelites welcome and gave them something to eat. While the friars were eating, the town's Chief Magistrate arrived with the Royal Provision but was asked to leave.

Jerome then did a strange thing. He shut himself up with Brother Benito of Jesus, a small lay brother from Catalunia. This Brother with his white beard and blue eyes was reputed to be a saint but was quite uneducated; he only knew how to spin and to recite the Our Father for the souls in Purgatory. However, Jerome put his trust in him: that God would speak through the mouth of this simple friar.

Brother Benito spoke the following enigmatic words: 'Look, if now you do not obey the little Treasurer, you will lose the great Treasurer, and the Man in black will not be able to do anything. If you obey him [the little Treasurer], until the little Negroes arrive there is a little staircase that will lead to success, and another that will lead to failure. You will see what I mean.'

Jerome understood the meaning of Brother Benito's words. If he did not obey the small Treasurer, i.e. the Nuncio, he would lose the big Treasurer, i.e. the Pope, who is the one who can establish the Order. The little Negro, i.e. the King, can support them but he cannot establish the Order. In other words, in order to climb a further step of the staircase to a final victory, he should not cross the Nuncio and should turn aside from the King. It would be a victory that would be nothing less than a Province independent from the Calced Carmelites, for which Teresa was longing.

The friars came together for a meeting. Sega's Brief was read out and humbly complied with. Jerome submitted the Patents he held from Ormaneto to the two Calced Carmelites. Neither Mariano nor Anthony of Jesus liked the way he had backed down. They felt, in conscience, impelled to convoke a Chapter in Almodovar for 9 October. The King was upset and practically washed his hands of the problem. The Nuncio breathed a sigh of relief. The Calced Carmelites appeared more emboldened each day.

Teresa had come to the following conclusion: those 'of the Cloth' had deceived the Nuncio. 'The sole master of our destiny, for better or for worse, after God, is the Nuncio, and for our sins those "of the Cloth" have given him their version, and he has given them so much credit that I do not know what he will decide to do. They say that I am a vagabond and unsettled, and that the convents I founded were without authority from the Pope or from the General.' She wrote to Roque de Huerta, a friend in the Court, 'I would love to find out for myself about some of the lies that these people tell, because I do not believe what they are saying about our Father.' The Chronicle described these sad times:

> Our Fathers were in a state of great confusion at the time. The King had withdrawn to a cooler climate and was not interested, having been overlooked when he should not have been. The Nuncio was indignant and powerful. The opposition had all the aces and therefore the upper hand. Their friends were sad at not being able to do anything to help. The people made up their own minds about those whom they saw persecuted and imprisoned. Our holy Mother was very afflicted. The priories were disturbed and divided. What happened to the victor, did not leave the vanquished untouched. It was heartbreaking to see the Discalced Carmelites knocked down. The lawsuits attacking them were not any less cruel than the cruel knife that takes someone's life. In order to avoid such harm, our Fathers reminded themselves of what was said at the first Chapter in Almodovar: that they would keep their leadership separate from whoever governs them, and live in conformity to the Primitive Rule and Constitutions…

The Chapter in Almodovar took place on 9 October. There were representatives from the nine Discalced Carmelite priories plus John of the Cross, who had escaped from his prison in Toledo. As Jerome was not there, having given himself up to the Nuncio, they recalled the agreement reached at the first Chapter in Almodovar celebrated two years previously: if the Provincial retires for whatever reason, the first Councilor must call a Chapter and proceed to the election of a new Provincial. Anthony of Jesus, the first Councillor, was elected Provincial of the Discalced. At last the old friar was pleased to savour being in charge of the Reform. However, the sweet taste of power did not last long.

Representatives from the Chapter travelled to Madrid to notify the Nuncio of the resolutions reached at Almodovar. However, the Nuncio blew his top. He shouted insults against Teresa and all her family. The Chronicler recorded this in more discreet terms: 'He called them names that were unworthy of them.' The actual words spoken can be left to your imagination.

We know that he called Teresa, whether now or at another time, 'an anxious and restless, disobedient and incorrigible female.'

The Nuncio excommunicated the friars who attended the Chapter and placed Anthony of Jesus in a prison cell in St Bernard's priory, Madrid. He issued a Decree, dated 16 October, annulling the decisions of the Almodovar Chapter and placed the Discalced Carmelite friars and nuns under the authority of the Calced Carmelite Provincials.

Mariano and Jerome, who were still in Pastrana, decided to go secretly to Madrid. They were fearful of incurring the Nuncio's anger and unsure what to do, but in Madrid they would be able to find out what was happening. It was dark, snowing and bitterly cold by the time they reached Alcala. Fr John of Jesus Roca came to meet them and brought them up to date with the news. It was decided that Mariano should go to Madrid, to try to get the Court to intercede with the Nuncio; Jerome meanwhile returned to Pastrana.

The Nuncio persuaded the King to understand that his castigation of the Discalced Carmelites, regarding Jerome Gratian, Mariano and Anthony of Jesus, was not motivated by anger. In order to be more objective he asked the King to appoint Judges to assist him in the process just begun. Those appointed were: Luis Manrique, the King's principle Almoner, and the King's Chaplains: the Dominican, Fr Hernando del Castillo and the Augustinian, Fr Lorenzo de Villavicencio.

Mariano was happy with the appointment of these assistant judges and came to see the Nuncio. However Sega, who really was motivated by anger though he denied it, shut him away in the priory of Atocha. He apprehended Jerome and he, being the ringleader, had him imprisoned in the Calced Carmelite priory in Madrid. I calculate that this would be mid-November 1578. All three, Jerome, Mariano and Anthony of Jesus, were now prisoners in Madrid. The Nuncio forbad them to celebrate Mass, telling them that they were excommunicated. They asked if they could hear Mass. The response was emphatic: *abstineant ab utroque*; that is to say, they were to refrain from celebrating or attending Mass. They were refused pen and paper to prevent any communication with the outside world. Of the three, it was Jerome who found himself in the worst situation. The Calced Carmelites from Andalucia continued to send fictitious stories and slanderous tales to the Nuncio. And Jerome lamented that the Nuncio believed them.

Conflicting voices could be heard in the Court; some happily spread rumours that the Order had committed serious offences: theft, insulting words and outrageous behavior. Others said that they had forged Bulls.

Jerome was horrified at the thought that not very long ago the Nuncio had two men hanged in Madrid for forging Bulls.

The most difficult period in the history of the Reform had begun. The Calced Carmelites entered into the Discalced Carmelite priories like a hurricane-force wind. The Chronicler wrote:

> The visitors entered the Discalced Carmelite priories like a victorius army, confident that the tide would now not turn against them, so that they could do what they had in mind to do. In the nuns' convents they altered what had been established by our holy mother St Teresa. If they discovered one minor mistake by a Discalced Carmelite friar, they would explode with fury and start a terrifying process and then report back to the Nuncio to exasperate him even more... Our holy Mother was kept informed by letter of all that was happening. No sooner had she read one report than another with more severe news arrived.

To crown it all, the Nuncio granted Tostado powers to make Visitations of the Order throughout Spain: it seemed to be the last straw.

Joanna Dantisco was upset when told that her son was leaving the Carmelite Order to join the Augustinians. She was not allowed to see him but strove to find a way to communicate with him. She managed to get a friend to pass a message to her son: 'They have told your mother that you are about to leave the Carmelite Order and join the Augustinians. If you have given this any consideration you are never to call yourself her son, nor see her, nor write to her, as she does not want to have a son who does not wish to suffer insults or trials for the Order of our Blessed Lady. If you think about what the Order merits and what you should do for it, you should consider yourself very lucky if they burn you alive.' Jerome replied via the friend: 'Tell my mother that such a thought has never passed my mind.'

The Count of Tendilla came to see him. He had had strong words with the Nuncio on Jerome's behalf. He told our man, with his hand on his dagger: 'They told me you want to leave Carmel and join the Augustinians. I swear that if you have given this any thought I will stab you,' and added: 'If you have any fear of what the Nuncio might do to you, I shall spend three thousand golden *escudos* and this very night I shall saddle six horses and arrange for you to escape from prison.'

Teresa, who was in Avila, wept.

Chapter Fourteen

After So Many Storms...

'Only two friends have stayed with me,' Jerome complained. In the darkness of his cell in the Carmelite priory, he felt his heart had been wounded; his world had become very black. Only his mother and the Count of Tendilla were on his side. His friends appeared to have kept their distance.

Some kept their distance because they did not want to get involved in matters concerning the friars and the Nuncio. Others because they reasoned that if so many bad things were being said of him some of it must be true; and it would be better for him to suffer in this life rather than in the next.

Some criticized him for having entered the Order, abandoning his parents and siblings whom he could have helped thanks to his good education and the support of the King. Others condemned him for getting involved in the Visitation of the Calced Carmelites; it would have been enough just to have visited the Discalced Carmelites. To try to reform the others was pure arrogance. Many different opinions about him circulated in the Court of Madrid. He awaited the ruling of the Nuncio who seemed to genuinely dislike him.

Louis Hurtado de Mendoza, Count of Tendilla, met Jerome in Granada in 1573 when he was Governor of the Alhambra and helped in the foundation of the Discalced Carmelite priory of *Los Martires*. Since that time they maintained a close friendship. The Count was by nature impulsive. He really wanted to support Jerome and, at the same time wanted the Discalced Carmelites to have a voice. He had had a stormy meeting with the Nuncio, who complained to the King that the Count supported the Discalced Carmelites who did not obey the Apostolic See nor the orders of his ministers. The King asked the Count to apologize to the Nuncio as he represented the most important of institutions.

The Count apologized in a letter dated 19 November. He added that he had to go to Mondejar straight away because his son was ill. He told the

Nuncio: 'If I have helped these Fathers, it was because I hold them to be good and holy.'

At this point the Count's Mendoza family comes into the spotlight. 'In the whole of Christendom there has never been a family that has served the Apostolic See more loyally than this family, nor has anyone achieved more or been more distinguished in the service of the Holy See.' How can the Nuncio say that a Mendoza supports the Discalced Carmelites in their disobedience to the Apostolic See? The Count continues in his letter, 'How undeservedly you have complained about me. If you understood that these friars are not very obedient to the Apostolic See nor to your Lordship, who represents them, I would be the first one to draw my sword against them.'

This Spanish nobleman continued to protest: 'Until the Apostolic See and your Lordship declare something contrary to what I have seen of the said friars, I shall continue to hold them in good esteem. And should your Lordship declare them not to be such I shall serve as your executioner, because my intention has always been to obey the Apostolic See, and I declare as a good and faithful Christian to live and die for the same See.'

Jerome was in his cell and only heard of the arrests (of the others) from the Count and from his anxious mother. Some searched for ways to alleviate his sufferings in prison and to calm the anger of the Nuncio. Teresa was in her convent in Avila, from where she wrote ceaselessly with petitions to the Court.

She was pleased with the efforts made by the Duchess of Alba who managed to get the Dominican, Fr Peter Fernandez, to be one of the Commissioners to accompany the Nuncio. He had been a Visitator of the Carmelites in Castile with the Nuncio, Ormaneto. Teresa saw this as a 'heavenly sign'. She pointed out that 'he knows both us and the Calced.' She pointed out to the Duchess: 'Please understand your Ladyship that what is at stake is nothing less than the protection of the Order of the Blessed Virgin Mary. The devil has waged a war against her and her Order.' Teresa asked the Jesuit, Paul Hernandez, to intercede with the President, Pazos, and with the Nuncio through his confessor. She asked for help from Roque de Huerta, the principal keeper of the King's forest… and she wrote to many others in the same way.

Jerome's case was discussed on 1 December, when the Nuncio met with the Judicial Commission, that consisted of the principal Chaplain, Luis Manrique, the Prior of Atocha, Fr Hernando from Castile, the Prior of St Augustine's and Fr Lorenzo from Villavicencio. They noted how the Calced

Provincials had gone to extremes during their Visitations of the Discalced Carmelite houses. They also observed that there was no substance to the judgments against Jerome nor did they appear to be true.

The Commission intended to deal first with the more urgent situation of the Discalced Carmelites and later consider the particular faults imputed to our man. However, the Nuncio stubbornly insisted: 'You must first substantiate Gratian's faults and afterwards deal with resolving the government of the Discalced Carmelites.'

'He was very strong and persistent about this,' claimed Jerome; 'there was no way that he could be persuaded otherwise.'

However, this became a matter of conscience for Jerome. If he denied the faults imputed to him, it would take a long time to follow the juridical procedure in establishing more facts about the case. In the meantime, the Discalced Carmelite houses would remain under the control of the Calced Carmelites leading to their total extinction. If, on the other hand, though innocent, he allowed himself to be condemned, if that is to say, he acknowledged the false testimonies imputed to him by the Nuncio, this would offend God. 'Some of the judges were in the same dilemma,' Jerome commented, 'they thought well of our Order and, being conscientious, they believed it would be a mortal sin to condemn it. They saw that to delay putting things right with the Order would play into the hands of the Nuncio and the Calced Carmelites who wanted the Discalced to remain always subject to them.'

At a certain point during the dialogue between the Commissioners, the Nuncio said to Luis Manrique: 'Your Lordship, you are not acting as a judge, but rather as a lawyer both for the defence and the prosecutor.' The King's Almoner replied: 'Your Lordship is not being impartial either, it is as if you were acting for the prosecution'. The Nuncio made clear to the Commissioners that Jerome was not punished for obstructing his jurisdiction when he obeyed the King, but rather for his insolence and excess behaviour, as testified by the friars in Andalucia.

The Commissioners knew that the Nuncio wanted to condemn Jerome and not the other Discalced Carmelites, and so, in order not to lengthen the process for the Discalced Carmelites, who longed to become an independent Province, the Commissioners suggested to Jerome that he accept being sentenced to appease the Nuncio and, at the same time, allow matters to advance.

Jerome later admitted that his conscience troubled him. 'Am I not obliged to defend my honour given my standing in the eyes of the people, and given the situation, would it not be a mortal sin to let them punish me though I am not guilty?' He consulted several theologians, especially Jesuits, who gave their opinions; some suggested one solution some another. It was Don Luis Manrique, one of the Commissioners, who helped him see clearly; 'Let yourself be punished as the Nuncio desires, otherwise the Discalced Carmelites will not be free from the government of the Calced. Thus you should be pleased to be like Jesus Christ who lost his honour for our sake and kept quiet before the false accusations.'

Jerome took his advice. The Nuncio submitted three folders containing charges against him, which revealed nothing new. They were more or less the same scandalous accusations that were found in the letter from Bro. Michael de la Columna and Balthazar Nieto, plus other ridiculous accusations from the Calced Carmelites in Andalucia. He refuted them one by one in seven folders. However, he declined to defend himself. In accepting the punishment he quenched the vindictive thirst of the Nuncio, Sega. He told the latter:'I am not guilty of any of the accusations that the Calced Carmelites bring against me, nonetheless I do not wish to defend myself but only to place myself in your hands. Do what you want, punish me as you think fit, whatever it is I will happily and fully comply.'

On 20 December, the sentence was read out in front of witnesses in the Carmelite priory, among whom was Balthazar Nieto, the Judas of the Discalced Carmelites. Jerome was to be permanently deprived of his office to govern and administer as Visitator and Reformer of the Carmelite Order, as well as any other office he held. The case was settled by the Court within the space of three days.

Immediately Jerome went to the priory and college of the Discalced Carmelites in Alcala de Henares. There he remained and submitted himself to the authority of the rector of that house. He fasted on Mondays, Wednesdays and Fridays every week. Over and above the ordinary penitential practice of the house he did even more. He was not allowed to write or receive letters from anyone, particularly from nuns. He had permission to celebrate Mass and preach and to write to his father and mother and to the Nuncio but to no one else.

He explained that what the Nuncio regretted most of all was that he had not been able to punish him for having impeded the latter's jurisdiction. However, the papal representative was 'greatly appeased and the trials came to an end.'

Not all of them; the Calced Carmelites made every possible effort to extend the Sentence to cover all parts (of Spain). In Andalucia various different rumours spread: that he had been burnt at the stake; that he had been put in prison for the rest of his life; that he had been put down a well and had starved to death ...

Teresa found out about Gratian's fate on Christmas Eve; the Christmas before she had broken her left arm. Now, a year later, she wept bitterly. According to her Secretary, Anne of St Bartholomew, 'that evening, throughout Matins, her eyes were like fountains, with tears cascading to the ground.'

The other two 'convicts' were more fortunate; Anthony of Jesus was let off by the Nuncio with having to recite certain prayers. Fr Mariano gave the excuse that the King was sending him to assemble some equipment in a mine in Jerez de la Frontera. Once out of sight the Nuncio soon forgot about him.

Sega wrote triumphantly to the Pope's Secretary: 'In a short space of time things have calmed down, to the extent that we shall not be hearing any more from the friars.'

However, all was not well in Seville. Fr Diego de Cardenas, Provincial of Andalucia, ignored the Decree of the Nuncio and got rid of the Prior of Los Remedios and replaced him with another. With the nuns he dismissed the Prioress, Mary of St Joseph, and replaced her with a crazy woman. Mary of St Joseph wrote in her book *Ramillete de mirra*, 'In the friar's priory, as they were men, the measures were not so extreme; but we, being poor women, had all the fury heaped on us.'

Mary of St Joseph, together with Anne of Jesus, who was Prioress in Beas, were the two female pillars of the Teresian Reform.

Teresa described Mary of St Joseph as someone who loved literature. In fact, Mary has left us two books written in the most exquisite Spanish: *Libro de las recreactiones* and *Ramillete de mirra*, as well as poetry and other writings. She was born in Toledo, the daughter of Sebastian de Salazar and Mary de Torres. She first met Teresa in 1562, when she was fourteen years old. The meeting took place in Toledo, in the Palace of Luisa de la Cerda, a friend of the Saint and Patroness of the foundation of the convent in Malagon. Mary entered this convent and became a Carmelite in 1570. Five

Mother Mary of St Joseph, Prioress of Seville.

years later she accompanied Teresa to the foundation in Beas and later to Seville where she became Prioress.

St Teresa had nothing but the highest praise for her; 'My fondness for her is beyond measure.' Mary of St Joseph was a strong character and sometimes confronted Teresa. 'I don't know how it is that in spite of all the trouble you give me I end up loving you even more when it's all settled; because then I forget everything and feel closer to you than ever.'

After Mary of St Joseph died, Anastasius praised her as 'a woman of the greatest purity, holiness, intelligence, prudence and discretion that, after Teresa of Jesus, the Order has known. Mary was insistent that the well-ordered legislation that Teresa had left should not be changed, and for this she suffered many trials and misunderstandings.' She too was afflicted with scandal, and like Teresa and Jerome was not spared malicious gossip.

When Teresa left Seville in 1576, the community consisted of five 'foreigners' (the name given to those who had come from Castile), and six locals. Two years later they were seventeen, the majority of them novices. 'Many are coming who want to be nuns, whose motivations vary, whose social backgrounds are different: none of them are right for us,' admitted Mary of St Joseph.

The first novice who entered the convent was called Beatrix de Chaves, a highly strung young lady whom Teresa had admitted, fooled by her affectionate ways and charm. A little later Mary del Corro entered the novitiate. She was in her forties, 'a real "holy soul" who had already been canonized by the entire city.' When, inside the convent walls, the applause for her holiness ceased, she left and denounced the Discalced Carmelite nuns to the Inquisition. Teresa, who was still in Seville at the time, had to endure the upheavals due to the subsequent Visitation by the Inquisitors.

Now, two years later, in December 1578, the convent of St Joseph in Seville suffered another crisis, only this time much worse, again involving denunciation and slander. In the picture were Beatrix de Chaves, together with a lay sister, Margaret of the Conception, and the priest, Garcialvarez, Confessor to the nuns; a man who lacked intelligence. Teresa had been grateful to him for introducing them to a house in Pajeria Street which became their convent. However, Mary of St Joseph described him as 'ignorant, confused and without learning or experience.'

Beatrix de Chaves told Teresa her life story which the Saint naïvely believed. Teresa recounted this in chapter 26 of the *Book of Her Foundations*. Beatrix had been disturbed by a troubled adolescence, particularly in the area of sexuality. When the time came for her to make profession she was filled with scruples. It was Teresa, writing from Avila, who told Mary of St Joseph to accept her for profession 'to end her temptations'. Mary of St Joseph obeyed knowing full well that this young girl was deceitful.

When Beatrix's parents wanted her to marry she rejected the suitor: 'They knew well that if she didn't want to get married it was not for a great love of virginity because she had neglected this gift when she was younger.' Her parents whipped her, she told Teresa. In the Saint's eyes she came across as a St Agnes, i.e. someone ready for martyrdom. Beatrix fooled Teresa but not Mary of St Joseph, who later wrote: 'She had painted us a picture of her parents, so that we all believed they were tyrants, telling us how they tortured her because she wanted to be good.'

This poor creature, unstable and disturbed, confessed for hours and hours in the confessional with Fr Garcialvarez who naïvely believed all her fantasies. She spoke with him about her revelations and the humiliations she suffered on account of the nuns when, for instance, they took her clothes off and laughed at her 'look at your body, so fat and white'.

The lay sister, Margaret of the Conception, who lasted about four months in Carmel, also went regularly to confession to Fr Garcialvarez. She caused havoc among the nuns and disturbed the life in the convent. The Prioress consulted Teresa who because she lived so far away could not see the danger and answered her: 'Don't be foolish, my daughter.'

The situation got out of hand. Fr Peter Fernandez, a Dominican, who had been a Visitator of the Carmelite nuns in Castile, arrived in Seville accompanied by his General. The Dominican said to Fr Garcialvarez: 'I am not leaving you to hear the nuns' confession anymore' and sent him packing. The reprimanded priest, his pride hurt, began to spread malicious rumours about Sr Mary of St Joseph in the city.

Fr Diego de Cardenas (the Calced Provincial of Andalucia) arrived in Seville. He had with him the Nuncio's Decree that allowed him to make Visitations of the Discalced Carmelite convents. He immediately restored Garcialvarez to his role as Confessor, and gave him a patent to hear the nuns' confessions even though this was against the will of the Prioress.

Fr Diego de Cardenas' entire Visitation was an exercise in nastiness. We have already seen this person preparing a letter with Balthazar Nieto and the simple-minded Michael de la Columna against Gratian, now he was undertaking the Visitation of the Discalced Carmelite nuns in Seville!

During confession Garcialvarez, 'called the nuns, one by one, and then by means of threats, exploiting their scruplosity, he incited them to say nasty things about Mary of St Joseph to the Provincial; the nuns never understood why he was telling them to do this.' Cardenas was in the chapel before the crucifix, kneeling before him was Mary of St Joseph. He mortified her for hours and hours, asking her questions at the top of his voice so that he could be heard in the streets. He called her a Judas among the Apostles, a wolf in sheep's clothing, a troublemaker, and other even worse things. He swore and cursed at the nuns urging them to declare that they were against the Prioress, against Gratian and Teresa. He referred to Gratian as 'that rogue' and Teresa as 'that old contemptible person'.

Cardenas removed Mary of St Joseph from her office as Prioress and guess who he put in her place? Exactly: Beatrix de Chaves! When Teresa realized what had happened, how she herself had made a serious mistake, she called Beatrix the 'black Prioress'. Beatrix, who did not know how to read, remained in bed most of the time and, when she felt like it, took a stroll in the streets outside, leaving the keys of the convent with a lay sister.

The account of the Visitation was sent to the Nuncio. Mary of St Joseph wrote later how the Nuncio uttered 'the most abominable and foul words imaginable, the kind that no nun should ever hear, nor will I dirty my pen to describe them.' I do not have any scruples in 'dirtying my pen' and will highlight the lies and slanders Cardenas sent to Madrid, which I quote word for word from the actual documents in our National Historical Archives.

I shall limit myself to the accusations against Jerome Gratian, who was accused of: dancing naked in front of the Sisters; being hugged and kissed by the Sisters during his Visitations; being seen alone with Mary of St Joseph; celebrating parties in the evening with the nuns behind closed doors; sleeping, one day, inside the cloister; being sent pillows made of fine material by the nuns when in Los Remedios and given turkeys to eat, etc. There were other, unedifying, accusations directed against Teresa, when she was in Seville, and also against Mary of St Joseph. When Teresa read this nonsense she said, 'Since they lie, it is much better they do so in such a way that no one will believe them, but rather laugh at them.'

The priest, Garcialvarez, and the new Prioress sent a letter to the Inquisition denouncing Mary of St Joseph. However, the Inquisition judged it wiser to ignore it. Garcialvarez muttered, 'that the Inquisitors ran like hounds after the heretics but dragged their feet when it came to something closer to home.'

Jerome was still confined to the priory in Alcala when the New Year, 1579, began. Mary of St Joseph was alone and neglected in a prison cell in her convent in Seville. She wrote, 'They kept a close watch on me, so that I could not speak nor engage with anyone, they would not even let me talk to the sisters.' From that time on the lives of these two figures were united in suffering and in slander.

When Jerome arrived in Alcala to complete his sentence, he met the Rector of the college, Fr Elias of St Martin, who was suffering from shingles. Jerome had thought that his stay in Alcala would help him find rest from his work so as to dedicate himself to prayer and study. However, the Rector, who was his friend and moved at his friend's torments, asked him to lead a Chapter with the friars.

Should the Nuncio, Sega, have been told of this? He was, in fact, told. Three wretched Discalced Carmelite friars wrote to the Nuncio to tell him that Jerome had disobeyed the orders depriving him of active and passive voice, and had continued to govern the Discalced Carmelites. The Nuncio wrote a letter to him in which he left Jerome in no doubt of his anger.

When Teresa learned of this she was upset and wrote to Jerome: 'I don't want to see you there. I'd rather you returned to "the Cats"!' 'The Cats', in Teresa's codified language, were the Calced Carmelites. Many years later, Anastasias, speaking about this with Cyril, remarked that her words were prophetic. 'The words of Mother Teresa were prophetic: returning to the Calced Carmelites, my life was more peaceful and they treated me with such love, respect and charity as if I had been with the Discalced Carmelites.'

Two of the friars who informed on him 'died that year from long painful illnesses' and the third received the habit but 'his life was ill-fated and unhappy,' commented Jerome in his *Historia de las Fundaciones*. However, immediately afterwards, he went on to exclaim 'enough about all the Order's problems' and continued: 'Let us start a new chapter, because the times we are entering are more peaceful after so many storms. The trials we endure must come to an end one day.'

The Dominican, Fr Peter Fernandez, called his legal advisors to a meeting. He reinforced the line taken by the Commissioners before the intransigent attitude of the Nuncio, when they had appeased Sega by imposing a Sentence on Jerome, his bête noir. The Advisors soon made the Dominican see that the best way to bring peace between the Mitigated and Primitive (Carmelites) would be for each to have their own government with two separate Provinces.

The Nuncio signed a document on 1 April 1579, contradicting his previous position. He decreed that a Vicar General should govern the Discalced friars and nuns, that it would be Fr Angel de Salazar, *ad tempus*, while they negotiated in Rome how the Discalced Carmelites could govern themselves. The (Calced) Provincials of Castile and Andalucia, who had governed their respective territories since 16 October of the previous year, following a Decree by the Nuncio, had that authority taken away from them. The Discalced were overjoyed when they heard this news.

Fr Angel de Salazar, a Calced Carmelite, had once been the Provincial in Castile. During his term of office he had disagreed with both Teresa and Jerome. However, he was a good man. His appointment to govern the Discalced would be like balm after the terrible times they had been through, especially in Andalucia where they had been under the cosh of the Provincial, Diego de Cardenas. Jerome praised Salazar: 'This Father was an honourable man, modest, calm and a good servant of God, and that is exactly what this poor Province needed at the time. During his days in charge Angel tried to support the priories and convents, endeavouring to bring peace and tranquility to the Order while awaiting its own government.'

The Decree did not mean that Jerome's detention in Alcala would come to an end, but the terms of his imprisonment were relaxed. He was able to give classes in the priory on the introduction to Sacred Scripture and on the book of Dionysius, *De mistica teologia*. He also preached in the main church and in the chapel of the University, where the most distinguished people in Alcala came to see him. Above all, he could write and receive letters, especially from St Teresa, so he could acknowledge that 'he had never been so privileged in his life.'

Jerome spent the year 1579 as a recluse in Alcala. He was never entirely absolved by the Nuncio until, apparently, the beginning of 1580. Meanwhile, Fr Angel de Salazar took the reins of the Discalced Carmelites and tried to repair the damage done in the previous months. He allowed Teresa to move around; she had been obliged to remain in Avila.

Free again, the Saint continued her round of visits to convents in Castile, accompanied by her Secretary, Anne of St Bartholomew. For now, there were no more foundations; Fr Peter Fernandez had warned her not to make a new foundation until she had a Province: 'He gave good reasons, as the Nuncio was so set against us, and as there was no one who could make him see reason, we could have got into trouble.'

However, there was an unjust situation in Seville Carmel. Fr Salazar studied the matter and, as he wrote to Mary of St Joseph, 'It was clear in my judgement that there was no evidence upon which to base their claims.' Fr Salazar reinstated Mary of St Joseph as Prioress with a Decree dated 22 June, and 'ordered her "in virtue of the Holy Spirit... to use and exercise her office as Prioress as she did before... and we order all our religious and sisters from the said convent, to obey the above-mentioned Mother Prioress and take her for their legitimate Superior as they did before."' The histrionic cries of the Provincial, Diego de Cardenas were forgotten, as was the slanderous nonsense levelled against her, Teresa and Jerome. The two nuns who made the accusations repented in the end. They were not thrown out of the Order but remained repentant and full of regrets.

The Nuncio's Advisors finalized a document that was approved on 15 July in which they asked the King 'in order to serve God and increase the regular observance, peace and tranquility of the Primitive and Mitigated Religious … we ask and request His Holiness to command that all the Discalced friars and nuns who profess the Primitive Rule of the said Order make a separate Province from the Mitigated, whose area is Castile and Andalucia. This Province is to be subject to the General of the Order as the others and is to be governed by a Discalced Carmelite Provincial elected by the said Province.'

Circumstances seemed to be brightening up on the horizon. The workings of the Imperial Curia was set in motion so that it was brought to Pope Gregory XIII's attention: 'How good it would be to support this Order and separate it from the Fathers of the Cloth.'

Teresa of Jesus was both anxious and diligent when she sent two of her Discalced Carmelite friars to Rome to pull strings with the Papal Curia. The two were John de Jesus Roca, Prior of Mancera, and Diego of the Trinity, Prior of Pastrana. They travelled secretly and incognito so as not to arouse suspicion. They even changed their names; John de Jesus Roca called himself Joseph Bullon and Diego of the Trinity, Diego de Heredia. Dressed as soldiers, they grew beards and carried swords, so that they looked like valiant army officers. Teresa, seeing John de Jesus Roca, taller and more elegant than Diego of the Trinity, said to him: 'Don't you look splendid!'

Teresa, being somewhat scrupulous, raised this matter of dress with the theologians of Alcala and Salamanca: 'Can one disguise oneself in secular dress? And if the reply is yes, how does one avoid scandal and defend one's honour from the malice of men?' The theologians replied unanimously: 'The general good of the Order is sufficient cause to disguise oneself in secular dress.'

The two friars were in Rome for almost a year. While there they used all possible means to obtain a papal Bull from the curial offices, which would separate them definitively from those of 'the Cloth'. They counted on the decisive support of the Spanish embassy. The Ambassador, the Duke of Sessa, was not in Rome but they received accommodation from the person entrusted with the matter, the Abbot Briceno.

In order to raise funds for the journey and the expenses that would be involved with the Roman Curia, Teresa had launched a general appeal to her nuns. The convents of Seville and Beas, with their respective Prioresses, Mary of St Joseph and Anne of Jesus, were very generous in supplying the necessary funds for the two men. In recalling this event, Mary of St Joseph expressed herself quite clearly: 'The Fathers owe their freedom to these convents of women. Each convent immediately offered them whatever money they could, as the friars know this to this day.'

The friars, on the other hand, were not so generous. Mary added: 'You will see later the way they repaid our holy Mother and her nuns.' It was a valid criticism of the Discalced Carmelite friars which the reader will soon see for themselves.

In January 1580 Jerome was set free from his confinement in Alcala, where he had been for over a year. The Nuncio, Sega, had visited the King who told him that, by now, it was enough punishment. And so the Nuncio lifted his Sentence. He was now free and without office. However, the friars in the priory of Los Remedios in Seville were quick to appoint him Prior. He was elected unanimously by secret ballot on 19 February. Angel de Salazar issued a Patent in Salamanca confirming his election, dated 10 March; this did not reach Seville until the month of November. On 10 April, another Patent from the Vicar General appointed him Commissioner and Visitator of the Discalced Carmelite houses in Andalucia.

The scenario had changed radically. All Jerome's privileges were restored, even though he still bore the suffering and slander in his heart. Salazar, whose health was delicate, could only visit the houses in Castile. Jerome revealed that 'the work of government was placed on my shoulders, so that I did everything that he [Salazar] could not do, who did nothing more than sign the patents I gave him; and not only did I deal with matters for the Discalced Carmelites but I even dealt with many matters for the Calced.'

In Jerome's annals of this year we read of two important visits; the first to the castle of Uceda (Guadalajara) to hear the confession of the Duke of Alba, Fernando Alvarez de Toledo. The brief account does not appear in the biographies of the famous Governor of the Low Countries; Jerome did not want it to go unrecorded.

The Duke of Alba, the most decorated General of the time, found himself confined in Uceda, about 30 miles (50 kilometers) from Madrid, on the orders of Philip II. Jerome visited him frequently on his way from Alcala to Uceda. 'He consoled me in my troubles and entertained me like a Duke, and I went to see him and the Duchess in their prison.'

On one occasion Jerome remained in Uceda for some time, as he caught a fever. This gave him the chance to relate to the Duke on more familiar terms. The Duke, 'even though a solemn man, was very happy to spend many days talking with him, sometimes on things of the spirit, other times on problems in the kingdom and, again, at other times on the wars in Belgium, with such familiarity as if the Duke were a simple soldier.'

Fernando Alvarez de Toledo, third Duke of Alba, had served the Spanish crown for forty years. Together with the Emperor Charles V he distinguished himself in Tunis, Muhlberg, San Quentin, and in the Peace treaty of Cateau-Cambresis with France. Philip II sent him to the Low Countries, where he ruled with an iron fist. It was for his unforgiving attitude at a notorious trial following rioting that he will go down in history with a tarnished reputation, as he became known as 'the butcher of Flanders'.

Then, because he allowed his son, Don Fadrique, to marry without the King's permission, to his first cousin, Maria de Toledo y Colon, he was banished to his castle in Uceda at the age of seventy-two. Twelve years before this, he had made a commitment that his son would marry Magdalen de Guzman, who was waiting in the convent in Toledo.

On 10 January 1579 a Royal Secretary had informed the Duke of Alba of the sentence. The Duke, who was in a wheelchair suffering from gout, was given four days to leave the Court. However, because of his pride, he left the morning of the following day. Jerome wrote:

> It is a great consolation to hear the confession of a man who was such a great soldier but whom the world considered to be very cruel, because when one of his soldiers walking through the country of a Christian land had been caught taking a handful of wheat against his orders, he had him hanged. He was considered haughty, often using familiar names to address high ranking officials, which did not make him popular at all with many people. Yet, on the other hand, when we examine his motives and look into his soul we find a man who had a clear conscience and was so humble that he would rather lose his life, honour and worldly goods than commit a mortal sin, and he would willingly suffer a thousand deaths and insults for Christ and for his Church. I was not the only one of this opinion, in

> fact all his confessors were, above all Fr Louis de Granada who, when he was going to hear his confession in Lisbon, said: I am going to hear the confession of that saintly soul, the Duke. This caused great amusement among the Portuguese, who were scared of him, and saw him as a latter day Nero.

The Duke's exile ended on 12 June 1580. King Philip II, urged by his councillors, appointed the Duke of Alba to be General of the army in its battle to conquer Portugal. The Duke wanted to bring Jerome to Portugal as his Confessor, but the latter responded: 'If the war were against the heretics or Moors, then I would gladly oblige, but being between Christians, I do not have the stomach to see Christians killing each other.'

Fernando Alvarez de Toledo, third Duke of Alba.

Jerome, who was occupied with his 'work with the friars, did not accompany the Duke.' Anastasius told Cyril, 'that at this time the Duke was a very saintly man, and if I told you some things about him, it would frighten you.' The Duke died in Lisbon on 12 December 1582.

Jerome's second visit, to the castle of Santorcaz, was of a very different nature. The Princess of Eboli, an enemy of the Duke of Alba, found herself in prison, but for a much graver motive. She and her lover, Anthony Perez, Philip II's Secretary, were involved in the assassination of John of Austria's Secretary, Escobedo. The Princess was arrested on the night of 28 July 1579, and taken to the Tower in Pinto, about three miles from Madrid. In February 1580, she was transferred to the Castle of Santorcaz, near Pastrana, where Jerome visited her. 'The King gave me permission,' recounted Anastasius, 'so that I alone could deal with the Princess of Eboli and the matters concerning her... which I did on many occasions. In doing this I had to be very astute, diplomatic and careful, given that this servant of God with her terrible reputation had very powerful enemies.'

In February 1580, the Princess of Eboli was transferred to the Santorcaz castle, near Pastrana, where Gratian visited her. *Engraving of the castle*

The poor Princess remained a prisoner in Santorcaz castle until March 1581. It was owned by the Archbishop of Toledo. The intense cold in the fortress weakened her so much that she had implored her nearest relatives, the Duke of Medina Sidona and the Archbishop of Toledo, to ask the King that she be transferred to her own palace in Pastrana. There she was to all intents and purposes confined to a wing of the palace. Her only contact with the outside world was a window that looked out over the river Hora. Just for one hour each evening she was allowed out on the balcony. The people of Pastrana were curious to observe the pale-faced, incarcerated Princess. She was confined there for eleven years until she died in February 1592.

Jerome met St Teresa in Toledo to discuss a foundation in Madrid, and at the same time to obtain permission for this from the Archbishop of Toledo, Cardinal Quiroga. Teresa had come from the foundation in Villanueva de la Jara, arriving at the imperial city on the afternoon of Palm Sunday, 26 March 1580. A little later, on Holy Thursday, she became very ill: 'I have rarely felt this bad in my life; I was paralyzed and had pains in my heart.' The Saint was confined to bed for a month. In the meantime, while waiting for Teresa to recover, Jerome made his way to Madrid.

He received a letter from her at the end of May asking him to return to Toledo. She had arranged for him to meet the Cardinal Quiroga, and Inquisitor General, on 2 June, the feast of Corpus Christi. The meeting took place on 6 June and was friendlier than expected. Teresa's book, *The Book of Her Life*, was in the archives of the Inquisition.

Jerome recalled the words Cardinal Quirogas had spoken about Teresa: 'I am very pleased to meet you, and you will have in me someone who will support you in all you intend to do. I would like you to know that some years ago your book was presented to the Inquisition and your doctrine was thoroughly examined. I have read it all. The doctrine is very sound, true and beneficial. You can send for it when you like. I am giving you the permission you want. Please always remember me in your prayers.'

How lucky can you get! Teresa had thought of writing a letter to ask for the return of *The Book of Her Life*, but thought better of it; that it would be better not to wake the sleeping lion that is the Inquisition. Now she had the approval of the General Inquisitor and together with the copy in the possession of the Duke of Alba they could make copies for the friars.

The following day, Jerome and Teresa left Toledo. He accompanied her as far as Segovia. In Madrid they were joined by the Vicar General, Angel de Salazar. They all travelled together over the steep mountain ranges of the Guadarrama. Teresa was happy to see how well they all got on; a Calced and a Discalced Carmelite in perfect harmony, confreres with the same goal: to find a way for the Discalced to obtain independence.

Jerome, together with Fr Diego de Yanguas, a theology lecturer from the priory of Santa Cruz, found themselves with the Carmelite nuns in Segovia. The two scholars studied the book the *Interior Castle*. 'We read the book in her [Teresa's] presence,' wrote Jerome, 'and I pointed out that many words were too colloquial. Fr Diego agreed with me. Teresa said we could make deletions. In this way, we deleted some things.'

Not long after this he gave the book to Mary of St Joseph, in the Carmelite convent in Seville. It survived certain upheavals but the original can still be found there today.

Jerome accompanied Teresa to Valladolid. While on his way to Medina he received a letter on 1 August from 'the Romans'. Frs John of Jesus Roca and Diego of the Trinity told him that Pope Gregory XIII had signed a Brief, *Pia consideratione*, on 22 June approving a separate Province for the Discalced Carmelites friars and nuns: it was the long-awaited Decree.

Teresa wrote to Mary of St Joseph and exclaimed: 'May God be praised, for giving us so many blessings; the least we can do is thank him.' The 'Romans', having fulfilled their mission, embarked by ship from Genoa, where they sailed to Spain in the galleys that brought the returning soldiers from Flanders to Portugal. Teresa's cause appeared to have triumphed. After so many storms… the weather had calmed down.

Chapter Fifteen

The Alcala Chapter

We can ask the question: had Teresa's cause triumphed? Everyone, including Teresa, was happy with the papal Brief, *Pia Consideratione*, which established an independent Province for the Discalced Carmelites directly under the General of the Order and definitively free from the harassment of the Calced. 'A joyous day for the nuns and friars,' exclaimed the Chronicler, 'who celebrated with all the exuberance that modesty allowed.'

However, not everyone was so happy; Mary of St Joseph, the Prioress of Seville, expressed a certain disillusionment, not for having obtained the desired independence, but for the wording of the brief. She complained: 'There is no mention of our Mother.' In fact, the pontifical text, with its copious detail, gave a succinct account of the Carmelite Order, a summary of the history of the Discalced Carmelites in Spain that numbered twenty-two houses, three hundred friars and two hundred nuns, but no mention of St Teresa. Mary of St Joseph complained that the document did not state that the nuns were founded first and then the friars, and that the foundress was called Mother Teresa of Jesus.

I really like this spirited woman who defended the cause of her Mother Foundress! Those were the days of male chauvinism, if you will forgive such a modern expression. Mary of St Joseph called them, 'troubled times'. She wrote that 'because it was a woman who had begun and was behind this achievement, many people poured scorn and spoke badly of what she had done, and this is why our holy Mother did not want people to remember that it was she and her nuns who had been behind the whole enterprise, but rather God.'

The fact that the papal Brief did not speak of Teresa, as Teresa had wanted, would have consequences later on. After her death her Reform would be extinguished with the last of her disciples. These I have reduced to three: Mary of St Joseph, Anne of Jesus and Jerome Gratian. The three of them were in disgrace and in exile, either externally or internally. All of this has been described very well by the scholar Donazar in his book *Principio y fin de una Reforma.*[1] The Saint's disciples were disapproved of, and 'Teresianism' would be diluted in the Discalced Carmelite Order.

Nonetheless, this was now the time to celebrate: the clouds had disappeared and the sky was blue again. On 15 August, the Brief arrived in Badajoz where the Imperial Court was being held. Teresa and Jerome were in Valladolid dealing with the foundation of a convent in the nearby town of Palencia. The Archbishop of Seville, Christopher de Rojas, a great friend of the Discalced Carmelites, had arrived at Cigales, just two miles from Valladolid. He was on his way to Lerma, his family home, but was struck down by the flu virus that was affecting the whole of Spain. The Archbishop asked Jerome to visit him. Jerome had witnessed with his own eyes how everyone had succumbed to this terrible flu: the Archbishop, the Marquis and Marchioness of Denia who were part of the retinue, the servants… and he himself caught it and had to return to Valladolid to recuperate.

Our Carmelite had just got out of bed and was still convalescing when he was summoned once again by the Archbishop. He went to meet him but saw that he was very ill. He gave the Archbishop the last rites and then he himself 'wrote a letter [for the Archbishop] that recorded all the good things that he [Gratian] had done.' Jerome had to hurry so that the Archbishop could sign it. On the night of 22 September he was with the Archbishop reciting psalms and doing what he could to help the man die well. 'At four in the morning the saintly prelate peacefully and with great fortitude offered up his soul to God.'

Jerome was grateful to the deceased Archbishop for his many acts of kindness to the friars of Los Remedios and to the nuns in Seville, as well as for the care he had personally given him. He recalled how, when he himself had been very ill, during his time as Visitator, the Archbishop took him into his palace 'where he visited him and looked after him.' Teresa had not forgotten her embarrassment when in Seville the Archbishop humbly knelt before her and asked for her blessing. He was buried in the college chapel in Lerma, which he had founded. The chapel was completed in 1617 by his nephew, the all powerful Duke of Lerma, and favourite of Philip III. The Duke was raised and educated by the Archbishop for whom he always had a great affection. A fine statue of the Archbishop, Christopher de Rojas, was placed on his tomb.

1 The beginning and end of a Reform. Written in 1968 in Colombia.

On 11 October, Luis Manrique, the King's Preacher, wrote to Gratian on the King's orders to inform him that the Dominican, Fr Peter Fernandez, Prior of St Stephen's in Salamanca, had been appointed to execute the Brief of Separation and asked Jerome to visit and tell him the news. Jerome was also to call a Chapter to create the new Discalced Carmelite Province. Manrique told him that 'his Majesty would be very upset if there should be some setback or difficulty that would prolong this affair.'

Jerome did not waste any time in getting to Salamanca, 'changing horses every two or three leagues.' However, when he arrived he met Fr Fernandez who was 'dying and unable to speak.' His joy now tempered by the sight of the dying man, he gave a very quick account of his administration, 'I did not delay. I did not even have time to reply to Mother Teresa who had written to me.'

Jerome arrived in Badajoz on 26 October, where he came across the Royal Court in mourning: Queen Anne of Austria, the fourth wife of Philip II, had died from the current universal epidemic.

The Dominican, Peter Fernandez, died a month later in November. The King had already asked Rome to write a new Brief that would confer the presidency of the Chapter of the Discalced Carmelites on two other Domincans: Frs John de las Cuevas, and Albert Aguavo. The choice of two meant that if one got ill or was impeded in some way then the other could go to the Chapter.

While waiting for the confirmation from Rome, Jerome made his way to Seville to take possession, as Prior, of the house of Los Remedios, 'that with all the turmoil had deviated greatly from perfection.' It was an arduous journey, made more difficult due to the heavy rain.

His arrival in Seville caused great excitement, especially among those who had spread malicious rumours damaging his reputation. Eight days before he arrived several ladies from a parish – I would love to know which one, but Jerome didn't divulge – had placed a bet on whether he had been burned at the stake by the Nuncio; some said yes he had, others no, he hadn't. Some were threatening to produce a paper bag with his ashes. When he arrived he preached at this parish church and the ladies who defended him said to the others: 'Come and see a miracle, you will see a man preaching who had been burnt at the stake.'

Maybe Teresa was referring to this anecdote when she wrote to Mary of St Joseph: 'We are delighted with what our Father's old lady friends are saying about him, and I praise God for the fruit that his sermons and holiness produce. I am not surprised at what he has done for these souls as he is so holy.' And she added: 'You are right to say he should cut down on his preaching, as he could make himself ill.'

On 9 January 1581 Luis Manrique, the King's Preacher, wrote to Gratian about the news from Rome. He was to go to the Court that was in Elvas, where he would receive letters for the new Executor of the Brief, Fr John de las Cuevas.

This meant another arduous journey in the middle of winter, 'enduring many trials... due to the heavy rain, the rivers and mud.' He took Fr Bartholomew of Jesus as a companion. In Elvas he was given four letters from the King: one for the Prior, John de las Cuevas, President of the Chapter, another for the Nuncio, another for the President of the Council of Castile and the last for the grand Abbot of Alcala de Henares. In the last letter the Abbot was told that the costs of the Chapter to be held in his city would be paid for by the King.

In the letter addressed to Fr John de las Cuevas, Philip II told him that he could trust Gratian, 'a religious of the said Order, who has known the Order since its foundation; he is very learned and very zealous for its well being, and you can have every confidence in him. Make full use of him; you will do well to listen to his advice about what has to be done, now and in the future.'

Jerome arrived in Talavera on 1 February, the day before the feast of the Purification. 'He was in such a hurry that he did not want to wait for the high water of the Guadiana River to subside. In spite of the clear and obvious danger he crossed the river in a small boat and could easily have drowned.' He wanted to arrive without anyone knowing, so as not to raise suspicions, and for that reason he lodged at an inn. A few days later, he wrote official letters notifying all the Discalced Carmelite Priories of the Chapter. Then, under the pretext that he had to go to the Dominican priory to celebrate Mass, he gave the letters to Fr John de las Cuevas to sign secretly, 'so that the Dominican friars would not know what was happening and tell others'. Two servants took the notification of the Provincial Chapter that would start in Alcala on 3 March; one went off to Castile, the other to Andalucia.

On his way to Madrid, Fr John de las Cuevas gave an account to the Nuncio of all that had been planned and, at the same time, gave him the

King's letter. Was the Nuncio happy? 'More resigned than happy, but then he could not interfere,' Jerome remarked. With a patent from Fr John de las Cuevas which appointed Jerome as his advisor, the latter set off immediately to silence the malicious voices in Alcala. There he began to prepare for the Chapter, unaware of the political manoeuvring among the Discalced friars.

Anthony of Jesus, the oldest Discalced Carmelite and together with St John of the Cross, the first of the Order, wanted to be Provincial. He had made this known even before the Brief had arrived from Rome. Teresa remarked, 'There must be something wrong with him.' Anthony had been elected Provincial in Almodovar in 1578, but this was annulled by the Nuncio and he was imprisoned. Now, in this new situation, Teresa was prepared to accept him as Provincial provided Jerome was Vicar General; it would give life to the old Macario – 'Macario' was the codename Teresa gave to Anthony of Jesus – to be Provincial before dying in peace, and by not having someone over him it would prevent him causing mischief.

However, when Teresa noticed that the Brief from Rome only allowed for one position, that of Provincial, she promoted Gratian's candidature. She reflected that if it could not be him then Nicholas Doria or even John of Jesus Roca, though she did not believe the latter had leadership qualities. She gave no support to Anthony of Jesus or John of the Cross, who did not even get a mention among her candidates. No, it was Jerome she backed; he was the man she wanted, her ideal candidate. He was also the King's choice, as well as the Commissioner's who would preside at the Chapter, the Dominican Fr John de las Cuevas.

However, there was a 'gang' – as Teresa dubbed them – that backed Anthony of Jesus. Ambrose Mariano, who from the Visitation of Andalucia had continuously tried to undermine Jerome, made it quite clear that he supported the candidature of Anthony of Jesus. Teresa wrote to Jerome about this on 7 November 1580: 'You should know that Fr Mariano has written to me and told me the important reason why Macario should be Provincial and that I should encourage his candidacy. Can you believe it! The two have become great friends.'

Jerome felt tired and wanted to be free of responsibilities, but Teresa did not agree with this. She fought to promote him and to have Fr Doria as his companion; Teresa had been blinded by the latter's intelligence and talents. The nuns were of the same opinion as St Teresa and prayed that their dear Fr Gratian would be the new Provincial. 'How anxious they are that you are elected Provincial! I believe they will be satisfied with nothing less. May

God protect you for our sakes; all the sisters send you their greetings.'

To have Nicholas Doria as his companion would be a poisoned chalice for Gratian. However, he accepted this in obedience to Teresa, who had been taken in by the Italian. She described Doria as 'very determined to follow him in everything.' She asked her man to accept him as a companion, 'even if only to please me.'

What did Teresa have in mind by 'companion'? If the post involved some kind of authority, it would be a first for any religious Order. If, on the other hand, the post did not involve this but simply meant a travelling companion, it would not be enough for the ambitious and deceitful man that Doria was, who, as yet, had not revealed his duplicity.

Ambrose Mariano continued to support the candidature of Anthony of Jesus. The evening before the Chapter, Teresa wrote to Jerome, 'I have spoken a lot with Mariano about his intention to elect 'Macario'. I do not understand the man…' And she warned her friend in a later letter, 'They told me that some of those who are going and have the right to vote want Fr 'Macario' to be elected. If this is what God wants after so many prayers then it will be for the best; His judgements are His own… May God guide them and may He protect your Reverence. However badly things might go, we have, at any rate, accomplished what is essential. May He be praised forever.' The Chapter began once the Priors and Delegates arrived in Alcala.

On Friday, 3 March 1581, in St Cyril's College, Alcala, founded in 1570, with St John of the Cross as its first Rector, the solemn opening took place of the first Provincial Chapter of the Discalced Carmelite friars. The event began with a formal academic ceremony led by the Apostolic Commissioner, Fr John de las Cuevas. In attendance at the ceremony, besides the twenty members of the Chapter, were the most distinguished people from the town of Alcala: the grand Abbot of Alcala, the Commander of the Order of Mercy, the Vice-Chancellor of the University, professors, students… Fr John de las Cuevas read the pontifical Brief and solemnly proclaimed that the Discalced Carmelites had separated from the Mitigated Fathers, and that the Discalced were to be subject to the Provincial elected at the Chapter.

Afterwards the same Commissioner addressed the assembly; Jerome wrote that he was 'very spiritual and learned'. In his address Fr John tried to dispel the apparent paradox created by the division. 'Is it less perfect to separate as perfection consists in unity?' 'This is not the case when division leads to greater peace,' argued the Dominican, Cueva. He referred to the biblical figures of Abraham and Lot, who separated so that there would be no arguing among the shepherds. Again, there was the case of Ss Paul and Barnabas... The Commissioner ended his address with the words, 'Therefore, it was right to go ahead; though you are separated there is more love and peace with the Mitigated Fathers'.

The Act that created the new Discalced Carmelite Province was signed by the Marquis de Mondejar and his brother, Enrique de Mendoza, a Doctor Torres, the Abbot of Alcala, Fr Jerome de Almonacid, Professor of Sacred Scripture, and Doctor de la Puente, Dean of the Cathedral Canons. Fr John de las Cuevas notified the Chapter members to meet with him the following day for the election of a new Provincial.

On Saturday morning, 4 March, after a Mass of the Holy Spirit, the voting began. First was the election of the four 'Definitors', as the General Councillors are called in the Carmelite Order. They were elected in the following order: Nicholas of Jesus Mary Doria, Prior of Pastrana; Anthony of Jesus Heredia, Prior of Mancera; John of the Cross, Rector of Baeza; and Gabriel of the Assumption, a friar from the La Roda community. Ambrose Mariano, who was not a Chapter member, was elected Secretary to the Chapter.

Around eleven o'clock in the morning the secret ballot for the election of the Provincial began. Jerome was elected by a small majority at the first ballot: of the twenty votes eleven were for him, seven for Anthony of Jesus, one for Nicholas Doria and another for Gabriel of the Assumption. Afterwards, to please St Teresa, the new Provincial chose Nicholas Doria as his companion.

It was not time yet to celebrate. In his governing team, apart from John of the Cross, who lived in his mystical world, the other three Definitors did not sing from the same hymn sheet. I don't know if Jerome was aware of this at the time but he would have to govern wisely. There had been no apparent contest at the Chapter, but the balance in the voting reflected a profound division in the way the Discalced Carmelite Order was to be conceived, a division that would be widened in the years to follow. On the one hand there were the 'Rigorists', who were very fond of Mother Cardona and her eccentric penances, and on the other, the 'Teresians'.

For the time being they were agreed on one thing: they had shaken off the heavy burden of the Calced Carmelites. However, Gratian very soon experienced the jealousy of those who saw him as the favourite of the Foundress; the young man who, ever since his profession had not ceased to be in authority without knowing what it meant to obey, or what it was to be poor… Already some were saying, he ate meat like the Calced Carmelites and that he was too lax.

When Teresa heard the news that her man had been elected she was very happy. She wrote him a letter ending with the following words: 'From your Reverence's servant, daughter and subject – and willingly so!'

On 5 March, the fourth Sunday of Lent, there was a procession from St Cyril's College to the Church of St Justs, passing the University and along the main street of Alcala. Accompanying the Discalced Carmelites from the University were the Religious from the other Orders, the Chief Magistrate together with the Town Council, and other dignitaries. At the front were the musicians playing their instruments. The Chapter of the main Church came out to greet them. Fr Anthony of Jesus celebrated the Mass and the new Provincial of the Discalced Carmelites preached; he was well known and liked in Alcala.

On Monday, 6 March, the Order of Carmel celebrated the feast of St Cyril; a legendary figure but who today has been omitted from the liturgical calendar. The friars of old had supposed he was General of the Carmelite Order who died in 1235. The Chapter agreed on this date to dedicate the College of Alcala to the Saint, which until that time had been called the Carmelite College but from now on would be called St Cyril's. The Chapter also agreed that all the houses of the Discalced Carmelites would celebrate a Mass every year for the needs of King Philip II and his family, in thanksgiving for his watchful care over the Discalced Carmelites. At the end of the Chapter it was agreed that Mariano would give an account to the King. The Monarch was also surprised and impressed with the little they had spent: a total of one hundred thousand coins (maravedies), which made Philip II exclaim: 'Those friars must have been on a strict diet!' On Thursday, 7 March, the Chapter members began to work on the Constitutions for the nuns and friars.

It is painful to reflect that the friars legislated for the life of the nuns but that is what happened in those days. Teresa was already anxious that the text of the Constitutions of the Discalced Carmelite nuns would be to her satisfaction rather than that of the friars. Jerome had already been instructed about this by Teresa in a series of delightful letters during the month of February. The Commissioner, Cuevas, had also been advised in a number of letters from the Saint. Even for the Constitutions of the friars she gave her counsel, because, although the friars weren't happy, it was her Reform, and being a friend of the learned and an enemy of the unbridled rigorists, she wanted her friars to be free and learned.

On Monday, 13 March, the two Constitutions, those of the nuns and friars, were approved. Those of the nuns were broadly based on the text Teresa produced for her first convent of St Joseph's, Avila, with a few masculine touches that the Saint had to tolerate. She had asked Jerome to have the Constitutions printed rather than copied by hand, 'in order to avoid differences, as there are Prioresses who, in writing them by hand, would omit and add whatever they wanted.' They were printed quickly, the same year 1581, and published in Salamanca.

Jerome noticed that the newly elected Definitors had a great influence on the friar's Constitutions. Teresa would have liked 'those [young friars] who had ability to go to university.' However, the Chapter legislated against this: 'that no friar of our Province could become a university professor, or be known as a Lecturer, Graduate or Presentator' and that no one 'can assume a Professor's Chair, of whatever Faculty, nor lecture any subject, nor vote in the election of a Professor.' Such a cult of ignorance would make Jerome feel isolated and question what he was doing in such a set up.

The Chronicler, glossing over this particular legislation, laid the blame at our man's feet: 'He aspired to Professorial Chairs for himself and his friars, though not for a salary, and he taught Sacred Scripture in Seville and Alcala… And so, consequently, was lax by permitting [too many] exits, in dispensing from fasts and abstinence from meat, in wearing fine clothes, in being absent from the Choir, in order to give time and space to those who were studying and dealing with lay people.'

The friar's Constitutions, with all these rigid tendencies, were also printed and published in Salamanca in 1582. The Constitutions were based on the Carmelite Primitive Rule that Albert, Patriarch of Jerusalem, approved and which were later confirmed by Pope Innocent IV in 1248. John de las Cuevas sent King Philip II a summary of the approved Constitutions that I will in turn summarize here:

> All are to wear coarse material, without linen clothes nor linen bedcovers, no one is to be different; everyone is to be without shoes, with only open rope-soled sandals; all are to sleep on boards without mattresses. They are to walk on foot, and in case of need or infirmity, on an ass or beast of

> burden. They are not to eat meat. They are to have nothing of their own, all to be provided by the community. All the lay brothers are to do some kind of manual work at prescribed times; those who attend choir, being without work, should exercise in order to maintain and preserve their health. They are not to go to the threshing floor to beg for alms in August, nor in the village streets; in the case of great need, a preacher may exit cloister with a priest, afterwards a lay brother is to collect the alms. No one is to leave the house to buy necessities, except the Superior and the Procurator and only when in urgent need; also the Preacher in order to preach, and a Confessor in the case of urgent need. Where there is a priory they are not to eat outside it, in the house of a layperson. There should be a spirit of recollection in the house. They are to remain in their cells praying and meditating on the Law of the Lord, leaving them only in the case of necessity, as well as at times of recreation; and they are to maintain silence from Compline till Prime. They are to fast every day from the feast of the Exaltation of the Cross in September until Easter Sunday; and every Friday of the year. As well as the Vigil of a religious feast. They are to examine their consciences before meals while together in the Choir in front of the Blessed Sacrament. There are to be some particular mortifications during the meal, such as kissing the feet of all those who are eating and other similar things. They are to discipline themselves every week on Mondays, Wednesdays and Fridays. The tasks in the dining room, such as washing and sweeping and the other humbler tasks are to be shared out equally among all, including the Provincial, Prior, or any other person. There are to be no teachers or graduates with degrees, no one is to be exempt from domestic duties; there are to be no special titles or other honorary titles other than your Reverence…

The Alcala Chapter 'ended on Thursday, 16 March. The Chapter members dispersed in order to be in their Priories by Holy Week.' Teresa was satisfied with the results: 'It seemed like a dream. However much we would have liked to think that this was our work we would not have done it as well as God did. May he be praised forever.' Humanly speaking it was the best they could do.

Teresa asked the new Provincial not to forget St John of the Cross. The latter walked to Baeza where he took up his appointment as Rector of St Basil's

College. 'You should know that in order to console Fr John of the Cross for the suffering he endures living in Andalusia (for he cannot bear those people), I told him that as soon as in God's providence we become a separate Province I would see to it that he came back up here. Now he asks me to keep my word – he is afraid they will elect him Prior in Baeza. He wrote begging me to ask you not to confirm it. If this is something you can do, it is reasonable to console him because he is tired of suffering.'

The request did not come about, and there are those who blame Gratian for this discourtesy to Teresa. In fact, John of the Cross will get even more involved in the land of Andalucia that apparently he could not stand, and with Anne of Jesus, the Prioress of Beas and foundress of Granada Carmel. Some time before, John of the Cross had gone to Avila to invite Teresa to the new foundation. However, the Saint had an 'old person's complaint', as she put it, and could not accept his invitation. On 29 November John of the Cross left Avila and made his way to Granada. It was his last farewell to her. He would never see the Foundress again in this life.

When the Chapter ended Teresa was keen to find out about the old Anthony of Jesus. She asked Jerome: 'How has "Macario" been?' 'Macario' was rather wounded when he left the Alcala Chapter; for what remained of his considerably long life he would not be very close to Gratian. However, this 'blessed old man', as Teresa called him on one particular occasion, was not dangerous. Jerome appointed him Vicar Provincial of Castile, and Fr Diego of the Trinity, Vicar Provincial of Andalucia, with vicarious powers that ceased when the Provincial visited one or other of the Provinces.

The danger for Jerome was alongside him, his Socius, Nicholas Doria. It was Teresa who had imposed Doria on him. Fr Nicholas of Jesus-Mary, Doria's religious name, was born in Genoa on 18 May 1539. His family was distantly related to the noble Doria family. He arrived in Seville in 1570 and like many other Genovese he was attracted by the city that looked out towards Latin America. He made a fortune by using his astute business acumen to trade with this far-off Continent. After leading a frivolous life, he changed his ways – they say after being saved from a shipwreck – and decided to embrace the life of an ecclesiastic. After two courses in Arts, Theology and Morality, he was ordained.

Thanks to his financial expertise he was able to resolve the complicated finances of the Archbishop, Cristopher de Rojas. His friendship with Mariano, whom he had known in the Priory of los Remedios, led him to embrace the Discalced Carmelite Order. Jerome gave him the habit on 24

March 1577, in Seville. One year after his profession, he was appointed Prior of Pastrana, and three years after that was elected the first Definitor at the Alcala Chapter and Socius to the Provincial. His was a career both rapid and brilliant.

Teresa was dazzled by this newcomer to the Discalced. She was impressed by his astute business acumen. They met each other in Avila, in June 1579. She wrote to Mary of St Joseph, 'He pleased me very much and I praise our Lord for giving this person with so much virtue to our Order.' Mary of St Joseph had known Doria in Seville but kept a discreet silence when Teresa sang his praises. Teresa was just as enthusiastic for Gratian:

> I am very consoled by the fact that your Paternity has now someone with whom you can deal with about matters concerning the Order and who can help you. I am happy about this; I have suffered greatly to see you so alone in this Order. He has certainly appeared to me to be a sensible and good advisor and a servant of God, though he does not have the great charm and gentleness that God gave to 'Paul' – there are few who are given so much at the same time. But he is certainly a man of substance; very humble and penitential and greatly values the truth, and he knows how to convince people. He will come to know very well 'Paul's' worth and is very determined to follow him in everything, which has made me so happy. There are many reasons (if 'Paul' gets on well with him, as I believe he will, even if for no other reason than to make me happy) why it will be very helpful for both of you to be always of one mind, which will bring me the greatest relief. Every time I think of the suffering your Paternity has gone through from those who should have helped you, I consider it, in part, to be the worst kind of suffering you have had. And so, my Father, do not keep him at a distance; for either I am being very deceived or he will be of great benefit to you in many ways…

You were being deceived, Teresa, and you will die without knowing the extent of this man's deceit. He was not honest. However, I do not wish to pass judgement, the facts will in due course speak for themselves.

Teresa was making a foundation in Palencia when Jerome visited her after the Alcala Chapter. She wanted him to remain constantly at her side, but he had a foundation of Discacled friars to make in Valladolid (4 May), in a garden and hermitage dedicated to San Alejo.

He moved on to Salamanca where, in an old hospital, called St Lazarus, he tried to establish a college for the university education of young Discalced friars, contravening the criterion of the rigorists that 'no friar can graduate.' Like all the hospitals for lepers it was on the outskirts of the city, on the far side of the river. Jerome liked the location, as it would not cost them anything: the houses in the city centre were very expensive. The hospital possessed a lovely chapel and had plenty of suitable space for the community. They would not have to leave there except to go to classes.

However, some friars didn't like it, because the place had a bad reputation, being 'a downtrodden area where many bad things were done that gave offence to the Lord.' It was separated from the city by a bridge. Due to its bad name, a brothel was located very close to the hospital and no college student from any of the principle colleges in Salamanca could ever cross the bridge wearing his college's gown. However, Jerome reasoned that 'if a castle full of soldiers were established there, soldiers who professed purity to the Virgin Mary against those abominable things that were practised there, it would be of great service to God. The priory being so close to the brothel would be off-putting for the clientele, and in time it might close. The many students who crossed the bridge looking for sin would be ashamed when they met the friars of the Blessed Virgin Mary at the entrance to the downtrodden area; and in fact this is what happened.' The local bishop was happy with the foundation and there were no problems. It took place on 1 June.

At the same time, Jerome was kept busy in Salamanca with the printing and publishing of the Constitutions. Teresa had wanted him to be present on the day the sisters moved into the house in Palencia; till that time they had been living in borrowed accommodation. The procession of the nuns to the new foundation, the hermitage of Our Lady de la Calle, took place on 26 May, the feast of Corpus Christi. However, Jerome had left Palencia days before in order to make a foundation in Salamanca, which had become urgent. He asked Fathers Doria and Roca to take his place. Teresa reproached him: 'You could at least have delayed your departure till we moved into our house, what would another eight days have mattered.'

Having done all she could in Palencia, Teresa set off for the new foundation in Soria. Much to her regret Jerome could not accompany her. It would be his Socius, Nicholas Doria, who would lead the party to Soria, where they arrived on 2 June. Doria endeared himself to the Saint and she praised him: 'In all this time I experienced his perfection and discretion; and thus he is one of those whom I love much in the Lord and who gives me great confidence for this Order.'

At the beginning of September Teresa arrived in Avila, where she met Gratian. The convent of St Joseph's was experiencing an alarming famine. Mary of Christ, a timid person, was 'a good nun but not a good Prioress,' wrote the Chronicler. Jerome saw the need for Teresa to take charge once more of the house and he encouraged Mary of Christ to resign. At the new elections the vote for Teresa, in spite of her insistent prayers, was almost unanimous. Jerome recalled:

> She, with the greatest grace in the world, reprimanded everyone, because we did not allow her to rest. When she wanted to explain why we should elect another prioress, I ordered her to kiss the floor, and when she was prostrated we began to intone the *Te Deum laudamus* with great relief and joy.

Teresa remarked with subtle irony: 'They made me Prioress because they were hungry.'

St Philip's Discalced Priory was founded in Lisbon, in October, with permission from the Provincial and prompted by Ambrose Mariano. It was so called in recognition of the King, who on 15 April had been sworn in as sovereign of Portugal. The Discalced Carmelite Order put down roots in the Kingdom of Portugal that had just formed part of the Spanish crown. The friars bought a Priory with a beautiful panoramic view looking over the sea. As Mariano was the first Prior, they were known in Lisbon as 'los Marianos'. The Discalced friars were well liked, as they were close to the Portuguese people and tried to intercede for them. However, not all the Spanish were well liked due to the political animosity between Portugal and Spain; the former seeing the presence of the Spanish as an invasion.

As the year came to an end Teresa asked Jerome to accompany her to the foundation in Burgos. He was in Salamanca at the time and agreed to accompany her. It was wintertime and the weather was severe. The journey from Salamanca to Avila was not pleasant, but it was necessary. Perhaps Teresa's urgent pleadings were a premonition of the little time she had left to live. She worried about Jerome's feet and asked him about his chilblains. She told him: 'Though I am tired I am reasonably well.'

Chapter Sixteen

The Inheritor of Teresa of Avila's Spirit

Jerome returned to Avila at the end of December to accompany Teresa to a foundation in Burgos, which had been delayed for a number of years. Seven years previously the Discalced Carmelite nuns had been asked to go there. Had the time finally come? Our man urged Teresa to obtain a Licence from the Archbishop before starting off. She replied that she had letters in which she was asked to make a foundation and a pledge from the Archbishop of Burgos to the Bishop of Palencia. When Jerome insisted on obtaining the Licence so as not to cause offence the Saint told him: 'Look, the things of God do not need so much prudence, would it be so seriously wrong to seek the things we need. That foundation will be of great service to God; and if it has to wait any longer it will not happen. Let us not say anything but take a chance. In the meantime the more we suffer the better it will be. The devil is using all his force to prevent us dealing with this foundation.' He agreed with Teresa's wishes and replied: 'Let's get going.'

They departed for Burgos on 2 January 1582. The weather was harsh, there was torrential rain then heavy snow. They passed through Medina and Valladolid, where Teresa became so unwell that 'they could hardly understand a word she was saying…' They spent several days in Palencia waiting for the weather to improve. It was there that Teresa received some inspiring words from the Lord: 'Don't be afraid, for I will be with you.'

On the way out of Palencia a charming scene took place. A knight, Suero de Vega, a benefactor of the Palencia foundation, was saying goodbye to the group. 'Though he was a knight with a cape and sword [Jerome wrote] he was very charitable and spiritually fervent, more so than many a religious.' This knight had been dying to see Teresa's face – she kept her face covered with a veil due to the great curiosity of the people. Jerome moved towards Teresa's coach and spoke to her through a small window: 'This is Sir Suero de Vega, so why are you covering your face? Lift up your veil.' Teresa lifted her veil and with a delicate smile said: 'May God reward you, Father; you have made me very happy.' She got out of the coach and greeted Suero de Vega, who, though a knight and a tough soldier could not stop his tears of joy.

Eventually after a twenty-day journey along muddy roads they arrived in Burgos. By this time Teresa 'looked a pitiful sight,' according to her Secretary and Nurse, Anne of St Bartholomew.

On entering the city, where 'it was raining so heavily that the streets had become rivers', the small party called in at the Augustinian priory to venerate the crucifix known as the Christ of Burgos, 'in order to commend our dealings to Christ and because it was getting dark.'

When Theophile Gautier (a French poet and dramatist, died 1872) gazed upon the crucifix in the Cathedral, where it had been placed after the expulsion (of the friars) in the 19th century, he described it as 'a long ghostly white crucifix.' It was an impressive figure of Christ, both majestic and at the same time repulsive, which drew people to adore it during those troubled times. When this crucifix was in the Augustinian priory, it was said to be made of flesh and bone and that it was seen to sweat. Also, it was said that the friars shaved it every fortnight and cut the toe- and fingernails. These were just old tales without much foundation. The figure on the cross is, in fact, made of wood covered with skin, with a false beard, hair and nails, and no older than the 13th century.

It was just as well that Teresa had entrusted their negotiations for the foundation to the crucified Christ as things would turn ugly. It was already dark, their clothes were soaking wet and in order to avoid being seen they went to the house of Catalina de Tolosa, a widow, who had prepared for them 'a nice warm fire.'

Accompanying Teresa were the seven nuns she had taken from Avila, Alba and Valladolid. Teresa was ready to confirm the foundation that very night. The house was suitable for a convent, possessing as it did a chapel: it had previously belonged to the Jesuits. Gratian and his companions, Fr Peter of the Purification and the lay brother, Alonso of Jesus, found lodging in the house of Peter Manso de Zuniga, a Canon at the Cathedral; he had been a fellow student with Jerome in Alcala.

Early next morning Gratian went to greet the Archbishop and ask his blessing. However, his Grace became 'upset and angry', and began to shout and complain about Teresa. If he had given his consent for her visit, it was in order to reach an agreement with her alone, not with a group of nuns. If they did not have a house with its own income, he would not give a Licence. As far as he was concerned, they could go back to where they had come from…

Go back?! When Jerome told this to Teresa she mumbled: 'In the state the roads are in and in this awful weather!' And so it was, that the things of God moved slowly and that Teresa would not give in. However, the Archbishop was even more resolved. He, Mgr Christopher Vela, son of the Viceroy of Peru, Blasco Vela Nunnez, refused to allow even Fr Gratian to say Mass in the oratory of the house of Catalina de Tolosa. The nuns had to go to a neighbouring parish on Sundays and feast days.

Jerome wrote that Teresa 'in her holy anger found it hard to take the formality and delay' of the Archbishop. Time passed and there was no way of finding a suitable house. The Archbishop justified his attitude that he had to treat everyone in the same way; he could not be partial to the nuns, given that the Discalced Carmelite friars and the Victorines had also made foundations in Burgos. Jerome was upset, feeling guilty for having brought them there without a Licence from the Archbishop. Teresa was angry and said that the devil who thwarted this foundation had to be 'the most stupid in hell,' because all this 'was so messy and no one knew what anyone else was doing.'

In the end, their tenacity won the day. Gratian recounted this in his *Foundations*:

> Just a few friends gave us their support. If Mother Teresa of Jesus' soul and spirit had not intervened, without doubt we would have gone back. Once again the Saint, with her determination and magnanimity of spirit, overcame all difficulties: she found a very good house at a very good price. Teresa of Jesus had all the correct paperwork, which pleased the Archbishop, and so founded her convent with authority and approval.

Jerome then made his way to Valladolid where he preached that Lent. He was 'very upset to have left Teresa of Jesus on her own in the midst of difficulties.' Perhaps he justified his departure when he thought of the slanders they had endured when together in Seville: 'The jealousy of many put a damper on the pleasure the two had in being together, and there was no shortage of people who gossiped about their close relationship.'

The Discalced Carmelites threw themselves into missionary activity. It had been agreed at the Alcala Chapter that the Fathers would go to the Congo to convert the local people. Jerome signed a letter in Valladolid, on 19 March – the first missionary document of the Discalced Carmelite Order – in which he authorized the first Discalced Carmelites missionaries to set sail to the Congo from the port of Lisbon. They were Frs Anthony of the Mother of God, who had been a Jeronomite, John of the Angels, Master of Novices, from the Los Remedios priory in Seville, Francis of the Cross, who was professed in Pastrana by Fr Gratian in May 1573, the deacon, Sebastian of the Angels, whom the Portuguese Chronicle described as an angel in human form, and the lay brother, Diego of St Bruno, who had been the infirmarian in La Penuela.

These five missionaries set sail from the port at Lisbon together with a flotilla of six Portuguese ships that were on their way to India. Jerome did not have much idea of geography, when he said his friars were going to 'the Congo and Angola, Kingdoms of Ethiopia', and later he said, 'to the Indias of Congo and Ethiopia.' However, he understood that they would land in the Congo, since the flotilla was to navigate around the coast of Africa until it reached India.

At six o'clock on the morning of 5 April 1582, the monarch Philip II gave the order to weigh anchor; the friars were on a vessel named after *St Anthony*. One night sometime after they had set sail a fatal accident happened: the ship's pilot was asleep. One of the other ships, called *Chaga*, collided with the smaller *St Anthony* causing it to sink straight away. The Discalced Carmelites were all drowned; the pilot and the captain were the only ones to survive.

This sad event was a big blow to the Discalced Carmelite friars. Some of them saw the disaster a sign from heaven to suspend all such activities, but the majority did not agree. Jerome saw the tragedy as proof that the missionary activity of the Discalced was pleasing to God and that this misfortune was all part of the redemptive work of Christ; besides, it was the will of the King that the Reform would contribute to the propagation of the Catholic faith.

The following year, in 1583, Jerome sent five more missionaries: Fathers Peter of the Apostles and Sebastian of St Andrew and the Brothers Bartholomew of St Gabriel and Luis of St Paul, together with a lay brother. There was another disaster, only this time it wasn't a shipwreck, instead the friars fell into the hands of English pirates. At first they were about to hang them, but later decided to abandon them, naked and hungry, on the island of Cape Verde. Sometime later they were rescued and made their way back to Spain.

After this second incident the number of voices who disagreed with such missions increased. However, according to Jerome, there were also those who remained in favour. In the year 1584 a third expedition of friars was sent out and eventually arrived safely in the Congo. There they began their missionary activity that showed great promise. However, it all came to an end when our man was no longer in charge of the Discalced Carmelites and was replaced by Nicholas Doria.

What had happened to Jerome's Socius? Nicholas Doria was in Pastrana, where he had exercised the role of Prior, a role that did not satisfy his ambition. He felt exiled and in March 1582 he wrote a letter to Teresa, from which it was clear that he was suffering from scruples while being in charge of a small community. The basis of his letter was a complaint against Jerome; he also implied that he felt neglected. Teresa explained to him why the Provincial made him Prior in Pastrana: 'there must have been a very good reason why our Father had to separate himself from you.' She reproached him: 'Don't be sanctimonious, and do not stop writing to our Father to tell him whatever is on your mind.'

In May of that same year Jerome sent Doria to Italy to present to the General of the Order the respects of the new Discalced Carmelite Province and to confirm his appointment as Provincial. This task, which should have been an honour, was interpreted by the Discalced Carmelite Chronicle as an attempt by Jerome to distance himself from his Socius. Rumours spread among the Discalced Carmelites that Jerome could not abide having this valiant man near him; a man capable of standing up to him, and who was so observant of the Rule that it showed up his (Jerome's) laidback attitude.

These rumours reached Teresa's ears. She told her man about them, so that he would be aware of what was going on: 'They have told me that it has been noticed that your Reverence does not like having with him someone of substance.' Jerome attached little value to the rumours and did not suspect anyone of being malicious, whether his name was Mariano or Roca. He responded by saying that he had sent to Rome someone who had the necessary qualities: was he not Italian, with a famous surname, and was he not an able diplomat?

Doria would not have missed this opportunity to go to Rome for anything, though he let it be known he was reluctant to go by ship. He arrived in Genoa where he made contact with his family; he learned that his mother had died. He waited there for the General of the Carmelite Order to arrive, which he did a few days later. His name was John Baptist Caffardo, the successor of Rossi, who had died in September 1578. Doria stayed with the Calced Carmelites in their priory, where he was offered all kinds of things, including the position of Prior, if he would transfer over to them.

The General, Caffardo, was very happy with Doria and all he had to say. He gave him a document making him Procurator for all the Provinces of the Discalced Carmelites; it would turn out to have disastrous consequences. When Doria wrote to Teresa about this document she was not aware of all the implications. She later wrote, 'He [the General] made him his Procurator for all the Provinces of the Discalced Carmelites, both friars and nuns, so that everything going to the General must pass through his hands and be submitted to his counsel.' The letter was written to Tomasina Bautista, the Prioress of Burgos, on 3 August.

Teresa could not have understood that the ship of her Reform had just been hit by a torpedo below the waterline. A Procurator of the General of the Order within the new Discalced Province had not been envisaged in the Constitutions, nor did it respond to the spirit of Alcala. From now on Doria saw himself in a different light, no longer the Socius at the side of the Provincial, but rather a Superior in his own right who was placed between the General of the Order and the Governor of the Province.

From Genoa Nicholas Doria went on to Rome to obtain confirmation of the Discalced Carmelite Constitutions from the Pope. He later returned to Spain days before Teresa's death. The definitive absence of the Foundress would further Doria's ambition for power.

Jerome Gratian left Valladolid when Lent was over and returned to Burgos. In this city Teresa had been able to establish a foundation in a way that satisfied the Archbishop. On 18 April, Wednesday of Easter Week, Mgr Cristopher de Vela agreed to give her a Licence: 'to you, Mother Teresa of Jesus and the Religious of the Discalced Order of Our Lady of Mount Carmel, so that in the place and houses that have been bought… the Order can make, plan and construct a convent…' The new convent, which was the

Saint's last foundation, was dedicated to St Joseph and St Anne.

On 29 April there was a Chapter and election of offices, Sr Tomasina Bautista was elected Prioress. Jerome reached Burgos in May. Days later he said goodbye to the nuns and to Teresa. Neither Teresa nor he knew that this would be their last goodbye. However, they perhaps guessed, because Teresa's health was very poor and, now that the foundation was sealed in Burgos, she wanted to return to her convent in Avila.

Jerome left Burgos on the morning of 7 May. He was in such a hurry that he could not say goodbye to his friend, Peter Manso. It would be Teresa who made excuses for him:

> Our Father Provincial has asked me to tell your Honour how he had received a letter from his father, who is going to Rome, and said he (his father) would stop to speak with him in Soria, on his way. So he could not wait any longer, and for this reason he had to go this morning. He would very much have liked to have seen you, but yesterday he was so busy that he was not able to. I beg your Honour to commend him to God.

Was Gratian's father, Diego de Alderete, who was about ninety years of age, really going to Rome? Whatever for? And why did he want to see his son in Soria? Why not in Madrid where he lived? This is what Teresa says in one of her letters that is to be found among the collection of her letters. Truly, the father's story remains difficult to believe. Nevertheless I mention this because it is such an unusual and surprising event, but also because I have not come across any reference whatsoever to this by any Teresian scholar.

In Soria (I don't know if he saw his father as Jerome made no reference to him) he continued his Provincial Visitation of the houses. It is not easy to trace his itinerary, nor does Teresa know where he was at any given time. She told Anne of Jesus, Prioress of Granada: 'From here he went to Soria, and from there to many other places on his Visitation; no one knows for certain where he will be, nor when we shall have news of him.' However, it seems she worked out that in a few months he would have done the rounds of all the houses.

From Soria he travelled to Alcala, Pastrana and Toledo. In June he appeared in La Roda. In July he visited Daimiel, where he planned to make a foundation, then Malagon and Almodovar. He continued on to Andalucia. Teresa begged him not to go to Seville, where a plague had been ravaging for over a year. Fr Diego of the Trinity, whom Jerome had made Vicar in

Andalucia, had died from this terrible plague in the month of May. On 8 July, Fr Fernando de Pantoja, Prior of la Cartuja, died; he had been a great friend of St Teresa. In August Jerome visited Granada where John of the Cross was Prior of the Discalced friars and Anne of Jesus was Prioress of the Discalced nuns. He asked Anne of Jesus to write a history of the Granada foundation.

Teresa had left Burgos and was in Valladolid. There she wrote to Gratian who had by now arrived in Seville. It was Saturday, 1 September, the moon was full, and Teresa of Jesus had spent a night 'that was truly wretched and so too is the condition of my head.' 'Tomorrow, as the moon wanes, this indisposition will pass.' It was a long emotional letter… 'I don't know why your Reverence has to spend so much time in Seville, for they told me you will not be returning until the Chapter… Don't think of becoming an Andalucian; you don't have the temperament to live among them.' She concluded: 'May Our Lord answer my prayer and protect you, and keep you free from all dangers, Amen. From your Reverend Servant and Subject, Teresa of Jesus.' It was the last letter that Teresa wrote to him.

Teresa died in Alba de Tormes on 4 October and Jerome Gratian, her dear Father, was far away, in Andalucia. He arrived in Beas the following day. 'Because I had to go to Beas to put out the fire there,' he complained, 'I was not with the holy Mother when she died.' He had gone to Beas to put out 'a fire' that could have attracted the attention of the Inquisition; 'a very terrible entanglement of the devil, which made the nuns very anxious and uneasy. He had gone there as quickly as possible to undo this knotty problem…'

Jerome had ordered Teresa to go straight to Avila. However, when she was in Medina, Fr Anthony of Jesus, Prior of Mancera, was with her. In Jerome's absence he had the latter's faculties; in other words, he could act as the Vicar Provincial. Anthony made Teresa go to Alba de Tormes, where the young Duchess was about to give birth. St Teresa was 'sick to the point of death' when she arrived in Alba.

At the same time in Beas, a pious Discalced Carmelite friar had gone to the convent and encouraged the nuns to participate in a devotional game during recreation. It consisted of reciting and counting with one's fingers: 'I believe in God, I hope in God, I love God, I fear God, glory be to God…'

A scrupulous nun complained to the Vicar Provincial, Diego of the

The signature of Teresa of Jesus.

Malinas Carmel, 17th Century

Trinity (who died in Seville of the plague during the month of May), of feeling compelled to this form of entertainment. The Vicar ordered the game to be suspended during recreation; it was hardly recreational. Some nuns confessed to priests from the town of Beas and accused themselves of acts of love of God that had been forbidden by the Vicar. One of them, who was very scrupulous, confessed: 'Father, I have sinned mortally against obedience because I said, "I believe in God, I love God..."' The astonished confessor asked her: 'Why have you sinned?' 'Because the Vicar Provincial had ordered me not to say this.'

The story got out and scandalized the public. The clerics were astonished that the Discalced Carmelites had ordered the nuns not to believe in God or love Him. They cried out: 'We are looking at a case for the Inquisition.' Jerome came to resolve this problem and calm the atmosphere. On 22 October, while in Beas, he was informed of Teresa of Avila's death. 'On this day, at four in the afternoon, "Eliseo" found out that "Angela" had gone up to heaven to the joy of God.'

It took eight days for Jerome to learn the news of Teresa's death. I am not mistaken, because her death coincided with the reform of the calendar by Pope Gregory XIII. That year, 1582, lost ten days, as the calendar jumped from 4 to 15 October. King Philip II accepted this reform straight away and issued a Royal Decree to this effect in Lisbon on 4 September for all his Kingdoms. Jerome, in his turn, sent a circular (25 September) to the houses of the Discalced Carmelite Province in which he inserted the text of the Royal Decree and ordered that it be established as the new calendar.

When they gave Jerome the letter with the sad news, he was inside the enclosure (Beas Carmel), as the Prioress, Catalina of Jesus, was very ill. They were all very shocked when they heard the news but, being beside the bed of the ill Prioress they tried to control their feelings. However, seeing the sadness on the faces of her nuns, the Prioress asked them: 'Why are you so sad?' They did their best to conceal the pain on their faces, but the sick nun insisted: 'Please tell me the truth. If you are sad because our holy Mother, Teresa of Jesus, has gone to heaven, it is not news for me; it does not upset me, even if this is what you have to tell me.'

Gratian asked her: 'What do you mean, Mother?' The Prioress replied: 'The day you came and said Mass in our convent, the day after the feast of the glorious St Francis, our holy Mother, Teresa of Jesus, appeared to me during Communion, beside the altar. She was just like she always was when she received Communion, and said to me: "Daughter, you see me already in Heaven; therefore, do not be sad at my parting, as I shall help the Order from there more than from here, and do not concern yourself over the cause of my death, for in the end it was prayer that carried my soul away."'

That same evening Jerome wrote down his most intimate thoughts on paper, which he entitled *Dialogo de Angela y Eliseo;*[1] these were names they used as codes that they had agreed among themselves. Teresa was 'Angela' and Jerome was 'Eliseo', like the Prophet; he was also known as 'Paul'. He did not mention the specific details of Teresa's death for the obvious reason that he could not have known them. These would appear later, with more precise information, in some of his other writings: *Tránsito y última jornada de Ángela,*[2] written in the first months of 1583; *Diálogos del tránsito de la*

1 Conversations between Angela and Elias.

2 Angela's passing and last day.

madre Teresa,[3] written towards the end of 1584; and the chapters 13 and 14 of his *Historia de las Fundaciones,*[4] in the year 1589.

He admitted that the news left him stunned; it was the biggest shock of his life, quite frightening. He visited the Blessed Sacrament where he tried to calm his soul, 'even though his body was cold and shivering, in his interior there descended a dense fog and a sense of loneliness; it seemed that a very heavy weight had fallen on him, and now with the absence of Angela new trials and cares had been placed on his shoulders.'

Jerome believed he was the inheritor of Teresa of Avila's spirit. That same evening he attempted to change his name in religion: Jerome of Jesus instead of Jerome of the Mother of God.

'Angela' told him as in a vision: 'I haven't gone away. We shall always be together, and now I shall truly help you.' And Eliseo answered: 'Since you have gone away and are happy, Angela, let me inherit the gifts you had here, since I have been left to look after your daughters.'

> So it seemed that Eliseo wanted to change his name and call himself Jerome of Jesus. Suddenly, the Virgin Mother Mary appeared, laughing and exchanging knowing smiles with Angela and with Christ. All were smiling and seemed to be enjoying themselves. The experience made poor Eliseo so ashamed when he saw his sins; knowing that Angela already knew them. He was so overwhelmed that he wanted the ground to open up and swallow him. He shuddered to think that Angela now knew his wickedness. He spent a great deal of time, with great impetuosity, making acts of contrition for his sins to please Angela and to be worthy to speak with her.

He could not sleep that night. He rose before dawn and prayed before the Blessed Sacrament to 'Christ and the Blessed Virgin and to Angela that they would give him the gifts that Angela had here in this life, since there she did not need them, she was already happy and safe. And thus, he began to list Angela's gifts so that they might be given to him.'

Jerome remembered that it was in Beas, in the year of 1575, that Teresa of Jesus made the decision to obey him in all things and how, later, in Ecija, she turned this into a vow. 'And from here below he boldly called upon her and ordered her (even though she was in heaven) that she help us a lot.'

3 Conversations about the passing of Mother Teresa.

4 History of the Foundations.

He knew well what it meant to be a needy orphan and to lack the support that from now on he would not have in the leadership of the Discalced Carmelite Province. However, he felt he had inherited Teresa of Jesus' spirit, and in this she would not fail him.

Chapter Seventeen

The Almodovar Chapter

'Oh my God, dear people, the feet of this saint smell of fragrant fruit, of lemons, citrons, oranges and jasmine!' A servant of the Alba house kissed Teresa's feet, exposed in a coffin in the chapel of the Discalced Carmelite nuns in Alba de Tormes. Fr Michael de Carranza was equally expressive in recalling this time: 'The smell was so pleasant and pervasive and consoling, that it seemed to me more pleasant than an aromatic shrub and the sweet smell of resin, perfume, musk and amber, remained for a very long time.'

The funeral took place the morning after her death, 15 October, with a large number of people in attendance. The old Duchess of Alba and her daughter, who had just given birth, 'prepared the funeral with lots of candles, adorning the chapel with brocaded drapes.' The burial took place quickly at midday; the body was placed between the two grilles of the lower choir. She had died thirteen hours before. Why such a hurry? The day before she died, on the night of 3 October, Anthony of Jesus asked Teresa: 'If Our Lord should bring you to himself, what do you want us to do: do you wish to go to Avila or is it your wish to remain here?' Teresa replied: 'Oh Jesus, what a question to ask, Father. Have I got to have my own house?'

To Joanna of the Holy Spirit, who was holding her, she said: 'Would they not give me a small piece of ground here?' A small piece, no, but a lot of earth and lime.

The stonemason, Peter Barajas and the carpenter, Nicholas Hernandez, were told to dig a deep hole, as deep as the height of a man and fill it in, in such a way 'that even if anyone wanted to take her out they couldn't.' Thus, 'they packed in so many stones, lime and bricks, that they broke the coffin and all of this material entered in', with the blessing of the Vicar Provincial, Anthony of Jesus, who knew that Jereome wanted and decreed that Teresa be buried in Avila.

The people rose up in anger. The cleric, Peter Gonzalez, moved with pity and with tears in his eyes, said, 'I was very upset to see the way they treated the body of such a one as our holy mother Teresa of Jesus.' The sister of the Saint, Joanna de Ahumada, complained that 'it wasn't done with respect.' Her husband, John de Ovalle, protested to Anthony of Jesus that a provisional resting place had been transformed into a grave. Fr Anthony replied: 'It should not be a provisional resting place, but a grave; here she will remain forever.'

Yet another reason to bring torment to the Discalced Order: not only her spirit, but also her body was to be involved in a tug of war.

'She was my refuge, solace and comforter. When she was present she consoled me with her beautiful and saintly words and now she is not present her letters do the same.' Jerome held on to Teresa's letters which he formed into a thick book. He wrote so much about her that his life became a projection of the saintly foundress, 'If I were to tell you what I heard her say, how much she loved me, her gifts of soul and body, what we suffered together as we journeyed together to make foundations and, finally, what I know of her myself, which perhaps no one else has heard, I could write a book bigger than any written before.'

He missed 'her natural and supernatural graces, her gentleness, discretion and prudence.' However, in his solitude he felt her presence. Not with any interior voice or imaginary vision; God did not lead him along this path. He did not doubt the wonderful signs that occurred at her death, because 'just as God blessed her with wonderful phenomena in this life, He also showed such phenomena at her death, which will serve to encourage her daughters, fill them with spiritual fervor and give authority to her words of counsel, her example and the warnings she left in her writings.'

Even though our man was so close to the Saint, he had not received such gifts. He was a highly qualified intellectual but, he acknowledged, he never experienced the visions or apparitions of Teresa. 'I never saw her with my bodily eyes, nor in any extraordinary imaginary vision, but rather I sensed her help. It is like what happens to two people who speak to each other in the dead of night, or when nuns speak to you from behind the veils they wear.'

Jerome put the following words in the mouth of Anastasius: 'I have to believe in the miracles of the canonized Saints, because the Church requires them for the canonization of a Saint; and regarding other special revelations or visions, I would not dare call them lies or inventions if the Church does not judge them as such, [but] I would look at them closely before I believed them.'

Anne of St Bartholomew, Teresa's nurse, told us that she 'did not leave any directives, nor did she say anything about where she was to be buried.' Neither did she speak of her successor, though she gave an indication of this in a letter to Mary of St Joseph, Prioress of Seville, on 17 March, months before her death, in which she considered Mary as her successor. 'You say everything so well that if they respected my opinion you would be elected Foundress after my death. Even if I were still alive I would be eagerly in favour, for you know much more than I do – and are better; that is the truth. I have an advantage over you in having a little experience. But not much attention should be paid to me anymore, for you would be startled to see how old I am and how little I am capable of.'

Jerome declared 'that it was not necessary to have another Foundress, nor to appoint anyone to take over her role.' Teresa of Jesus was the Foundress of the Discalced Carmelite Order, of nuns and friars; though the latter, in their struggle to oust her man, would have also (tried to) erase the memory of Teresa of Jesus. Has there ever been a Congregation of men born of a woman? It should also be considered a grace that Teresa of Jesus died on the day of St Francis of Assisi, 'who founded a Religious Order.' Jerome noted that she 'was a Foundress and devoted to this Saint.'

Gratian ended the year with Visitations to houses in Andalucia. When he had finished his stay in Beas he made his way to Caravaca, where he arrived on 21 November. The nuns begged him to make a foundation for the friars, but the town was small and the Jesuits and Discalced Franciscans were already there. He moved to Granada to meet John of the Cross, Prior of Los Martires, and Anne of Jesus, who was elected Prioress of the Discalced Carmelite nuns on 1 December; he had presided at the elections. In the new year of 1583 he appeared in Seville, where 'there was no shortage of calumnies and malicious gossip about him.'

Cristopher Gomez, a little known artist from Seville, painted the figure of Jerome Gratian onto a large canvas that is kept in the convent of the Carmelite nuns in Seville. It seems we can date this to the month of February in the year 1583.

He appears standing, with a book in his left hand; the index finger of his right hand is pointing to the Blessed Virgin Mary of Mount Carmel who is

Jerome . *An oil painting by Cristobal Gomez, 1583. Discalced Carmelite nuns, Seville.*

in the upper right hand side seated in glory. The ribbon or streamer issuing from the lips of Fr Gratian contains this caption: *Accessi ad Prophetisam*; i.e. I have drawn closer to the Prophetess (Our Lady).

The Carmelite nuns in Seville have the honour of possessing the two original paintings of St Teresa and Jerome Gratian. That of the Saint, by

Brother John of the Miseria, has immortalized the painter. We cannot say where Brother John was at the time (of the persecution), because when the persecution by the Nuncio, Sega, and the Calced Carmelites worsened against the Discalced Carmelites in 1578, he disappeared as if by magic, leaving Teresa worried about him, believing him to be abducted like John of the Cross. However, the very simple Brother John of the Miseria had searched for a safe-conduct to Rome, where he threw himself at the feet of the General of the Order and became a Calced Carmelite. Later he would join the Franciscans and then once again the Discalced Carmelites, living in the priory of St Hermenegildo in Madrid, where worn out by the years, he died in 1616.

Cristopher Gomez, who painted Gratian's portrait, was an artist who lived at the end of the 16th century; very little is known about him. Two of his works are known: the portrait of our man and an Immaculate Conception that he signed in 1589, which is to be found in the Archbishop's palace in Seville.

Two years had passed since the Alcala Chapter. The friars had to hold an interim Chapter, midway through Gratian's term as Provincial, to elect new Definitors. It was seen to be important in gauging the temperature of the friars now that Teresa was no longer in this world. Jerome convoked the Chapter in Almodovar, the geographic centre of the priories in Castile and Andalucia, for 1 May, the fourth Sunday of Easter.

Jerome went to the Chapter in Almodovar with the feeling that if he had problems with the Calced Fathers, he was also going to have them with the Discalced.

In an inn in Toledo, on the road to Almodovar, he ran into Nicholas Doria, whom he had not seen since the latter's return from Rome. Jerome arrived riding on a mule with his travelling companion, Brother Gregory of The Holy Angel. Doria had ridden on a little donkey without any other adornment other than an old saddle. In greeting them Doria could not suppress his character. He really shook the Provincial with the following words he had to say: 'Yesterday your reverence gave us a law that we were not to ride with a saddle. How is it that you and your companion have broken that law so quickly?'

Jerome rode on a mule because it was a long journey, one he had completed many times with Teresa, and the Foundress viewed it to be correct (to use saddled mules) 'for long journeys or when there was great need.' This reprimand from his Socius touched Jerome deeply. He smiled and humbly ordered someone to take away the saddles.

Nicholas Doria was showing yet another sign of disloyalty. When they reached Malagon the nuns prepared for them a meal of chicken, partridge and other little goodies. Seated around the table, once again his (Doria's) zeal blazed forth. He took a turkey leg and lifting it up high, like a flaming sword, he shouted: 'My Fathers, are we going to the Chapter to reform the Order with these meals. Let anyone who wants to eat meat eat it, as for I, I would be happy with some eggs; that is, if you have them.' He got up and left the table.

This was Doria… Teresa of Jesus was dead and his histrionics now came sharply into focus.

The Chapter members from Andalucia and Castile had arrived in Almodovar. On Sunday, 1 May, the interim Chapter of the Discalced Carmelites began. As he was Provincial Jerome presided; in total there were twenty-six chapter members. The new Definitors were elected: Fathers John of Jesus Roca, Ambrose Mariano, Augustine of the Three Kings and Ambrose of St Peter. The four were opposed to Jerome, especially Roca and Mariano. Our man was either not aware, or did not want to be aware, that they had him trapped.

One fundamental defect in Jerome Gratian, or perhaps his great virtue, was his inability to gather a team of collaborators who could shoulder the work of government. He held no malice and perceived no malice in others. In his simplicity he lacked the political instinct and ambition of a Doria, these being so obvious in so many of the latter's mean attitudes. However, I like Jerome, seeing him as I do as a noble soul, a Don Quijote de la Mancha, even before Cervantes had conceived of the character and lost his hand in the battle of Lepanto.

During the Act of correcting Priors, Jerome accused Fr John of the Cross, Prior of Granada, of not visiting the laity enough; as these visits were very helpful in obtaining alms for the priory. Jerome had been told this by Fr Diego of the Trinity, when he was Vicar Provincial in Andalucia: the latter died of the plague a year before the Chapter. Jerome reprimanded the saintly mystic, who kneeling down, humbly received the reprimand.

When he was allowed to speak, Fr John of the Cross said: 'Father, if the time I should spend in visiting these people and in persuading them to give alms I occupy in our cell asking Our Lord to move these souls so that they do for Him what they should do by my persuasion and with this His Majesty supplies my priory with what it needs, why do I need to visit, if there isn't a need nor work of charity?' The Provincial and the Chapter members agreed before the Prior of Granada's logic.

Jerome invited Doria to give an account of his trip to Italy and his meeting with the General of the Order, John Baptist Caffardo. Doria told the assembly how the General was 'very understanding' of the separation between the Calced and Discalced, and how the General commissioned him to be his envoy in Spain, to look after things here for the good of the Order.

An envoy of the General? Another Tostado? Doria was taken aback by the murmurings of disapproval. He excused himself cynically: 'Believe me, my Fathers, in accepting this commission I am serving your Reverences' interests; but if you do not believe this, then that's fine by me, I would be much happier in a cell than being engaged with many business affairs; there is more peace in a quiet place than in the midst of activity.' Will Gratian perceive the duplicity of this man? No, he does not see it…

The Assembly continued with its debates. Jerome raised with the Chapter members the issue of expanding the Discalced Carmelites into other countries that were either developed or missionary. An initial expedition into missionary lands ended tragically; none should expect the works of God to go always according to plan. A second expedition fared no better; it was leaving Lisbon in April 1583 when it was intercepted by pirates. However, news of this event had not yet reached the Chapter. Jerome pointed out that the apostolate of souls was something Teresa really cared about, and also the King, the Protector of the Discalced Carmelites. The Chronicler expanded on this point when he wrote: 'It was evident that this was the will of the King who showed it in so many ways that it was understood as an order. He said many times to his closest minister that the new plant of Carmel, detached, recollected and fervent, was the most suitable for the propagation of the faith; and to oblige it more, he denied other Orders this undertaking in order to give it to ours.'

John of the Cross raised certain objections to this desire to expand. He advocated for solitude and recollection. He feared that the Discalced Carmelite life, essentially contemplative, would disfigure its spirit by going to other countries. The Chronicler suggested that John of the Cross feared that it was too heavy a load for the fragile Discalced Carmelite Order to carry, and that it would divide the members; so many would be needed to go to the many foundations. The proposal to expand prevailed: Doria would go to Italy to establish a priory for the Discalced and the Council planned new expeditions to the Congo.

At the last session there was the correction of faults of the Councillors, as had been established in the Alcala Constitutions. It meant reviewing the conduct of the Provincial. Once again it was Doria who spoke out and attacked Gratian. He recalled the incident of the mules, the meal in Malagon… He shouted: 'You are destroying the Order with your naïvety and lack of rectitude in government.'

This outburst aroused other zealots to join him against the Provincial. It was so bad that the Definitory wanted to remove him. Nicholas Doria, having lit the fuse, fearing the consequences of the Provincial's removal, took the floor again to calm the situation. The Chronicler put the following words into his mouth: 'What the Provincial has done, between us, is reprehensible; but he has his excuses, so that his preaching is seen to benefit people, he leads many ladies to perfection, he mends lawsuits and makes friends, he lectures in universities, he is always speaking of God, he gives good advice to everyone … and unless we can prove the opposite to everyone there is a real possibility that we shall be hated by all. Your Reverences, control your zeal and be satisfied with a warning… He has less than one year left, any one of your Reverences, when he takes over, will be able to pull up the darnel, since it will not have had time to take deep root.'

The Definitory, buoyed by Doria's cynical words, decided not to dismiss the Provincial but gave him an order: do not preach, except on rare occasions. It was then that Jerome reacted; a ban on preaching sounded like the Inquisition. 'You can never forbid me from preaching except if I should preach false doctrine; in this way you slander both the doctrine and the person. It would be better if I quit the office than to be slandered while governing.' He was willing to step down as Provincial.

The Council members amended the Decree with a fraternal warning to try to limit his preaching, 'to certain feasts, very few, and on very precise occasions.' Thus the Chapter came to an end, where the Definitors led Jerome to understand that 'even though he was Provincial, there were those who, in the name of the entire Order, could give him orders.'

The Chapter came to an end and Jerome continued his role as Visitator to the houses. He had, in fact, two years left as Provincial; he felt keenly these signs of dissension. Such dissension he did not find in the convents of the Discalced Carmelite nuns, where he experienced the same warmth and appreciation Teresa had shown him. In July, he visited Alba de Tormes; nine months had passed since the death of the foundress. The nuns there 'had scruples about what to do with the holy body', and they urged him to open the sepulchre.

It took them four days to open the hole and take out the stones and lime that covered the coffin. When they opened the said coffin, 'they found the lid broken, half the wood had rotted away and was full of mould; there was a strong smell due to the amount of damp.' It was Fr Ribera, the Saint's first biographer, who described the following details. 'The clothing had also rotted and smelt of damp. The holy body was covered with earth that had entered into the coffin, the latter being full of mould, but her body was sound and intact as if they had just buried her then… They took off almost all her clothes (because she had been interred with all her habits) and, they washed the body and removed all the earth. There was a wonderful strong scent that filled the entire house, which lasted for several days.'

Jerome admitted that 'the clothes, removed from the body, smelt awful and ordered them to be burnt; when they were on the body they smelt good.' He added the following regarding her incorruption: 'She was so intact, that my companion, Fr Cristopher of St Albert and I went outside while they took off her clothes. When they had done this they called me in, keeping her covered with a sheet. I was astonished to see how full and firm her breasts were.'

Everyone who saw her body spoke of the pleasant odour that came from it. However Anastasius, many years later, wanted to make his opinion known about the scent and incorruption of Teresa's body:

> Many things are natural, and it is because we do not know the natural causes that these seems miraculous; that it is quite possible for a body to be preserved without corruption, as they said of the body of Tulia, the daughter of Cicero, which was found intact after many years when they discovered her tomb in Rome. Many times it just happens that an illness disappears in a particular part of the body, and at that stage, looking back, it is assumed that something that had been done was the cause of the cure. Also it is very normal for someone to imagine hearing knocking or noises when on their own; due to our weakness these occur in the mind. Or some

> people, who like mysteries too much, imagine they hear or see miraculous things, and afterwards recount what happened but in such an exaggerated way, that they claim something was miraculous which was nothing of the sort. Finally, in the time we now live in, there is no way that I would want to hear of anyone talk about miracles, because our faith being deep-rooted does not need them, as I said at the beginning; although the scent from the finger cannot be denied (maybe it is natural), I would not want to be drawn on the other 'miracles'; maybe the lime caused the body to remain intact.

The finger Anastasius refers to Jerome kept with him as a relic all his life. It was the little finger on the left hand that he cut off for himself at that time.

When he was taken prisoner by the Turks, they took the finger from him. He had to recover it 'for some twenty *reales* and some gold rings and encrusted rubies that were on her finger.' Towards the end of his life, March 1610, he left it as an inheritance to the Carmelite nuns in Seville. He wrote to his sister, Sr Juliana of the Mother of God, from his exile in Brussels: 'I have written that I have it [the finger] on loan, that it belongs to the convent of the

St Teresa's left hand conserved in a reliquary.

Discalced Carmelite Priory of Ronda, Spain

Discalced Carmelite nuns in Seville, and thus without fail it will go there.' However, at his death the reliquary of the finger remained in Brussels. He also cut off the left hand that he left at St Joseph's, Avila.

> This hand – he wrote – I carried in a piece of cloth with paper, and out of the finger oozed oil that stained the papers. I left it in Avila in a sealed casket, and within this casket was the key of the chest where the body was to be found.[1] I told the nuns to guard that casket for me, as it contained some relics. Anne of St Peter asked me whose relics they were that I had brought in that casket. I asked her why she was asking me this question. She said that when she entered the choir she had seen mother Teresa with her own eyes, who told her: 'Take care of that casket, as her hand is there.' When other nuns went to kiss the relic they saw a hand blessing them.

This hand had quite a history. In 1585 Gratian left it with a foundation of Discalced Carmelite nuns in Lisbon. However, after many vicissitudes it returned to Spain and today it can be venerated in the priory of the Discalced Carmelite friars in Ronda.

Jerome was in Soria for the month of September, perhaps October, preparing for a foundation in Pamplona, when Nicholas Doria arrived looking for Patents and instructions to go to Italy. The annoying Italian then disappeared and would return to Spain only to put himself in charge of the Discalced Carmelite Order.

In December 1583 our man was in Pamplona. He had come early in order to be there for the arrival of the nuns from Soria. They arrived in two carriages. It had been a difficult journey for them through rain and snow. At the head of this group was Catalina of Christ, who would become Prioress, whom Fr Gratian considered a 'great saint'. When Teresa made her Prioress for the foundation in Soria, he said to Teresa: 'Mother, why do you want to make her Prioress as she does not know how to read or write very well?'

The Chronicler wrote that Catalina's parents did not teach her to read and write in order to avoid the danger of a Protestant sect. This is what it

1 Teresa's body had been moved from Alba de Tormes to Avila.

was like in those days with some parents! Teresa replied to the Provincial: 'She lives a saintly life, and that is enough.' Now it was Jerome who placed her at the head of a group of nuns chosen for the foundation in Pamplona.

The day of the Immaculate Conception he preached in the Cathedral and announced that that evening the nuns would enter the city. The Bishop invited him to dinner and told him of his desire that the nuns would come directly to the Cathedral and from there, in procession, they would be accompanied to their new house, the convent of St Joseph of the Most Holy Trinity. The following day, 9 December, the Bishop placed the Blessed Sacrament in their chapel. The Act of foundation, written by Jerome, gives an account of the details of the foundation.

The Provincial also discussed with a nobleman, Martin Cruzat, Lord of Oriz, about a foundation for the Discalced Carmelite friars in Pamplona: this would not begin until August 1587. Jerome gave the nobleman, Cruzat, who was one of the principle rulers of that city, the habit and the name, Martin of Jesus & Mary, and sent him to Pastrana for his novitiate.

Gratian's fame as a preacher kept him in Pamplona for more time than expected. On New Year's Day, 1584, he preached in the Dominican church, only after this did he leave that city. On the Feast of the Epiphany, having left Castile, he preached in the small town of Estella, in the Basque region. In that place a monastery of Benedictine nuns asked to be admitted into the Discalced Carmelite Order. Jerome agreed on condition that they got permission for this transfer from the King and the Pope.

In the town of Santo Domingo de la Calzada Jerome had a strange experience. It was Sunday evening and he was visiting the cathedral, which was full of the memories of St Dominic. It was in this place that the great saint experienced his vocation. Here too Dominic's holiness grew when he welcomed pilgrims on their way to Compostella. Perhaps he had stood under the small henhouse – something quite unique in a Cathedral – in which were a white cock and hen, reminding the visitor of one of the most beautiful legends, captured in the phrase: 'Where the hen crowed after it was roasted.'

A woman came up to Jerome and asked him if he was a lawyer. He replied: 'Why do you ask?' The woman answered: 'You gave me the impression you are. I know of a case that I tell you no one on this earth can resolve.' She spoke of a theologian, a Professor in Alcala, who had been accused of an abominable sin. Among those who had slandered the man was her husband. The woman believed in conscience that an injustice had been done to the man who, it was said, had fled to the land of the Lutherans to avoid arrest by the Mayor of Calahorra.

Gratian was prepared to help this lady and spoke to a Chaplain at the Cathedral, who told him that the accused had not fled, but was being held prisoner in that same Cathedral. The Chaplain allowed Gratian to talk with the man who was behind bars and in chains. He saw that the man was distraught and upset. 'It was like a miracle,' Gratian recounted; that by revealing what he needed to do to resolve his problems and escape from that accusation he should expose his rivals. They (Gratian and the Professor) agreed that he, Gratian, should speak to the Archbishop in Burgos and with the King in the El Escorial and other people. The Professor was freed from this disgrace thanks to our man, 'who had uncovered the malicious lies, and so the Lord was served and everything was left in order.'

Jerome returned to Castile where he prepared a new missionary expedition to the Congo; it would be the third attempt. This time the saying, third time lucky, rang true. The missionaries left from Lisbon on 10 April 1584. Anastasius tells us what happened:

> Friars had been sent to the Congo to convert the native people. These friars did great work, even though there were only two of them they had baptized more than five thousand of the indigenous people. One of these two was Father Francis of Jesus, the Unworthy, of whose holiness, spirit and zeal one could say a great deal. On two other occasions he [Gratian] had sent [missionaries] on the same expedition to Ethiopia on the orders of the King of Spain, and at the request of Alvaro, King of the Congo; the first missionaries drowned, the second returned naked, robbed by Lutherans, until the third group, Father Francis, Father Diego of the Blessed Sacrament and another, arrived and bore fruit as I said.

The same Anastasius defended himself against criticism stemming from the zealots among the Discalced Carmelite Order:

> They accuse me of making a big mistake in sending those friars. There are some souls for whom perfection as Carmelites consists in not going out of their cell nor making a mistake in choir, even though the whole world is burning. For them the good of the Order consists in multiplying our priories in small villages in Spain and forgetting about everyone else. Any other attitude they call restless and lax. God did not call me to this but

> rather to save souls; even those souls who have to serve in small places, establishing with them priories in the most important cities in different kingdoms for the true expansion and benefit of the Order. And since I spoke at great length and in a spirit of close friendship with mother Teresa of Jesus, whose spirit was zealous for the conversion of all the world, so her way appealed more to me.

The expedition was made up of three friars: Diego of the Blessed Sacrament, born in Toledo, a contemplative who was highly intelligent, he was to be the Vicar; Diego of the Incarnation, born in Cangas and very charitable; and Francis of Jesus, a lay brother who adopted the pseudonym of *Unworthy*, he was highly praised in the Chronicles for his holiness. They left Lisbon together with Martin de Ulloa, who had been appointed Bishop of St Tome.

In June Gratian was in Malaga to finalize the foundation of the priory of St Andrew de los Percheles, located on the banks of the estuary of the river Guadalmedina, in an area notable for its fishing. The previous year the well bred Fr Gabriel de la Penuela, old and suffering from gout, had come to Malaga. The town, Los Percheles, so called by the fishermen, offered him the hermitage of St Andrew. The plague had devastated Malaga and more than ten thousand of its inhabitants perished as a result of this terrible scourge. The place they chose to bury the people, outside the city walls, was next to the hermitage so that surrounding it was nothing but a graveyard. Fr Gabriel dedicated himself to taking care of the infected in a hospital that had been built near the hermitage. When the plague ceased, he wanted to commence the foundation, but the Dominicans alleged that it was too close to them, and the Bishop, who gave them support, did not dare give his permission.

Fr Gabriel wrote to his Provincial, who was in Granada, and asked him to obtain a lawsuit from the Chancery against the Bishop and the Dominicans. Gratian turned up in Malaga. Along the way he had thought that nothing is achieved by legal wrangling, but rather with humility and faith.

He visited the Bishop, who was called Juan Pacheco, and spoke to him frankly: 'They have asked me to take out a lawsuit against Your Lordship, but what I would prefer to do is to appeal to you that, if it is to serve God and you are happy, a Discalced Carmelite Priory be founded in the area of St Andrew de los Percheles, since in that area there are buried the bodies of more than four thousand souls who died from the plague, and it happens that dogs and other animals dig up pieces of flesh from those tombs. For this reason it would be good to have a priory that encompasses this area, and where one can intercede for the souls of the dead. Also since many people from los Percheles and those that call here with their fishing boats are without Christian doctrine, they would have someone they can confess to and say Mass for them.'

The Bishop, Jerome noted, looked at him from head to toe and after a long silence said: 'Come and eat with me and then the next day you can preach in the cathedral.' At the meal the Bishop told him frankly: 'I and my priests are supporters of the Dominicans, and so I have to favour them and oppose you in this lawsuit. However, be at peace and do what you believe is for the greater service of God, and He will help you.'

Jerome understood the Bishop's words to mean he had been given verbal permission. He took over an empty house where he placed his friars. The people helped them with alms; they placed a bell in the hermitage. The same Dominicans led a procession with the Blessed Sacrament where they left it in the Church of St Andrew. It was 27 June 1584. The priory was, for Jerome, one of the most pleasantly located in the Order, 'being next to the sea and on the beach, and though not in the city, not far away. Sometimes, for recreation, the friars would throw out a net from the door of the priory, and then haul it in full of fish, which they cooked for dinner and ate as many as they wanted.'

Jerome came to an agreement with the Bishop of Malaga for a foundation of a convent of Discalced Carmelite nuns; something he had not expected. It was founded on 17 February 1585, six months after that of the friars. Six nuns were recruited from convents in Granada and Beas.

At the end of the year the Provincial found himself in Seville, ready to accompany some nuns to Lisbon, the next foundation.

Chapter Eighteen

Lisbon

When the Portuguese dynasty died out King Philip II claimed to be the rightful heir to the Portuguese throne as the Grandson of Manuel the Unfortunate. The other claimants were Anthony, Prior of Ocrato and the Duchess of Braganza. Though Philip II had a legal right to the throne, he had to overcome a certain resistance before being acknowledged as the new Portuguese Monarch. The Duchess of Braganza came to an agreement with him as long as he respected her feudal rights and lands. However, the Prior of Ocrato put up a resistance, later fleeing to France where he sought refuge. The might of the Spanish army, commanded by the Duke of Alba, and the fleet, led by the Marquis de Santa Cruz, opened the gates of Lisbon to the Spanish Monarch.

In the court of Tomar (15 April 1581) Philip was solemnly sworn in and acknowledged as King of Portugal. He swore to maintain the laws, privileges, customs, and liberties of the Portuguese people. In this way Portugal was united to Spain in the figure of the King. The former country remained completely autonomous as, in fact, there was no territorial, administrative or juridical unification by Spain. Philip II made his solemn entrance into Lisbon on 27 July 1581.

It was months later, in February 1582, that the Discalced Carmelite priory was founded in Lisbon; Ambrose Mariano was the first Prior. The Priory was called after St Philip, in honour of the Spanish Monarch. Once Philip II had consolidated the Portuguese throne, he left Lisbon on 11 February, 1583, to go to the El Escorial. He entrusted the government to his nephew, the Cardinal and Archduke, Albert of Austria, son of his sister, the Empress Maria, widow of Maximilian II. Cardinal Albert, as Viceroy of Portugal, was also Apostolic Nuncio, principal Inquisitor of Portugal and Legate a *latere* of Pope Gregory XIII. For the Portuguese the fact that Cardinal Albert was the great grandson of King Manuel I and the Papal Legate softened the blow that Portugal was now subject to a foreign King.

A nationalist feeling rose among the ordinary people against the Spanish King, in contrast to the nobility. As a result or this, before leaving Portugal, Philip II had to establish Spanish garrisons in certain cities. We shall see later how the Carmelites would take on the role of peacemakers, and in particular, Jerome, in this political turmoil.

Among these noblemen was Don Duarte de Castel Branco, the Count of Sabugal, Don Luis de Alencastre, Commander in Chief of Avis, Don Joao Lobo, Baron of Alvita and, especially, Cardinal Alberto, who would be the great benefactor of the Discalced Carmelites.

Fr Mariano, encouraged by the Cardinal, went to Seville on 15 October to speak with the Provincial in order to recruit nuns for this foundation. Mariano had been ministering to Dona Isabel de Castro, the Countess of Sebugal, who was very close to death. Torn between obedience to the Cardinal and the spiritual needs of the Countess, he said goodbye to her with these reassuring, prophetic words: 'Do not say anything, my Lady, you will not die until I return.'

The Portuguese Chronicler, Melchior of St Anne, wrote that 'this was the first marvel, because all the Doctors stated that, barring a miracle, she could not live more than a few days… The Countess held on until Christmas Eve, the day Fr Ambrosio Mariano returned from Lisbon. He was with her during that night, and was with her when she died at three o'clock in the morning.'

Jerome Gratian, who was in Seville, approved of the project and was pleased that in this way St Teresa's longed-for dream to make a foundation in Portugal would be fulfilled and arranged that four nuns be transferred: Mary of St Joseph, Prioress of Seville, and Teresa's favourite disciple, as head, then Mariana of the Saints, Blanca of Jesus and Ines of St Elijah, who were also Teresa's disciples. Jerome himself was to accompany them together with Anthony of Jesus at the time Prior of los Remedios in Seville and Ambrose Mariano. Peter Cerezo Pardo, a benefactor of the Carmelite nuns in Seville, covered the cost of the transfer. He also joined in the journey, accompanied by a servant and by Henry Freile, a Portuguese man, and father of SrBlanca of Jesus. Also in the party was Bernadine de Mena, a brother of the subprioress of Seville.

The small group left on the morning of 10 December. In order not to draw attention to themselves the nuns put on black mantles and were accompanied by 'four female VIP's.' They left St Joseph's convent exiting the city by the nearby Triana gate, where they followed the river bank. They made their way to the bridge that was made out of boats, which they then crossed. Once over the bridge they took the road that led to the priory of Los Remedios, where they were met by Anthony of Jesus and Mariano. There they celebrated Mass and, after communion, went to a garden next door, where they waited for Fr Gratian to arrive. He had celebrated Mass in the convent of the nuns who had left and consoled them for the loss of their companions.

I am being meticulously detailed about the journey because the day will come when Gratian would be accused of breaking the friar's enclosure by allowing nuns to enter it. This is really stupid, but if anyone is to blame, then the blame should go to Anthony of Jesus or Mariano, who let the nuns into Los Remedios, and not our man, who was still in the city.

The next morning, the party left early without taking breakfast, and took to the road to Extremadura. Near Olivenza, already in Portugal, a tragic incident occurred. A rabid dog crossed their path; 'at that time of the year dogs did not ordinarily have rabies; this happened during the summer when all was dry and the animal thirsty,' Jerome recounted. The dog was walking in front of Fr Anthony of Jesus when it attacked the mule he was riding. Next it bit the mule that the lay-brother, Fr John Baptist, was riding; he was a companion of Fr Anthony. When the dog attacked Jerome he managed to avoid it. Next the dog bit the nose of Cerezo Pardo's mule at which point the rider thrust his sword into the dog's mouth and through its heart.

Fr Anthony fainted when he learned that the dog was rabid, and refused to go any further until he had seen a doctor. They found one in Olivenza, or rather, a quack who dedicated himself to healing and preventing rabies by breathing on the wound, using his saliva and invoking certain invocations and formulas. However, he told them 'that all that was necessary to cure was a hair of the dog, that no one would be in danger, only the mules that had been bitten would die. He gave some of them a loaf of bread to eat that he had half eaten, and with that he bade them all farewell.'

As they approached Lisbon Fr John Baptist's mule started to bite the other mules and shortly afterwards died; as did the mule carrying Peter Cerezo.

The last stage of the journey was by sea and they disembarked in Lisbon, next to the Discalced Carmelite priory that was located on a low hill overlooking the estuary of the river Tagus. Fr Mariano, who had gone on ahead to prepare for their arrival, was there to greet them. It was midday on Christmas Eve, the bells tolled in preparation for the feast. In the Discalced

Carmelite church the nuns joined in Midnight Mass and spent the night in the church. Mary of St Joseph recalled, 'the nuns were exhausted and I myself was in a bad way and none of us had as much as a pillow on which to lay our heads. This was the hardest thing any of us had done in our lives, as we had to be seen by all those who came to matins.'

At 8 o'clock on Christmas morning, as the Carmelite nuns did not have their own house, and at the suggestion of the Dominican, Fr Luis de Granada and the insistence of the Cardinal, they were offered hospitality in the Dominican convent of the Annunciation. It was in this place that Sr Mary of the Visitation, the nun famous for her stigmata lived; she was at the height of her miraculous powers.

At a later date Gratian would again be blamed for allowing nuns to eat with friars in their priory, even though it was Mariano who had brought them into the refectory. When Fr Gratian at the end of his Mass, came into the refectory, the nuns were already sitting down having a meal. He looked a bit anxious so Mariano told him: 'Don't worry, mother Teresa also ate in the friars' refectory in Pastrana.'

Mariano had brought to Seville some bits of cloth with five drops of blood from the five wounds of Sr Maria of the Visitation, the Prioress of the Annunciation convent whom he seemed to greatly venerate. The effect on Mary of St Joseph, recounted Jerome, was one of 'revulsion and horror,' and if she were in charge, she would have advised the King to watch over the Kingdom of Portugal with greater vigilance.

As Mary was staying in the same convent where the stigmatized Prioress lived she was able to get to know her. Since 7 March, 1584, the feast of St Thomas Aquinas, Sr Maria of the Visitation was seen by her nuns to bear the wounds of Christ's passion. Days later, the Dominican Provincial, Fr Anthony de la Cerda, wrote a summary of the miracles that God had worked in Sr Maria of the Visitation. Fr Luis de Granada visited her and was taken in by the virtues of the nun. Cardinal Albert and the Archbishop of Lisbon also went to visit her. The Cardinal wrote a report of this miraculous phenomenon and sent it to King Philip II and Pope Gregory XIII, so that the fame of her stigmata spread throughout the whole of Europe.

The Carmelite nuns did not spend long in the Dominican convent, in fact, less than a month. Mariano managed to obtain for them a house next to the priory of the friars. The convent of the Discalced Carmelite nuns was inaugurated on 19 January 1585, under the patronage of St Albert.

Whereas the priory was called St Philip in deference to the new King of

The fortified Tower of Belen that guards the Tagus estuary represents one of the most typical images of Lisbon

Portugal, the convent would be in honour of Cardinal Albert. It was to break an unwritten rule of St Teresa's: that all the Carmels would be dedicated to the Patriarch, St Joseph. The Discalced Carmelite nuns in Avila complained that the first Patron of the Reform (Joseph) had been downgraded to a secondary level, but Mary of St Joseph who, like Teresa, was an excellent poet, answered her critics with a few lines of verse:

> Joseph, Great Patron of Carmel,
> we should not wonder
> that you are considered unparalled,
> in Portugal, you are second
> in Castile, you are first...[1]

Before she left the convent of the Visitation, Mary of St Joseph was able to expose the nun with the wounds for the fraud she was. 'One day, Mary wanted to see the wounds of the crown of thorns that the nun said was on

1 José, Patrón general del Carmen,
no es maravilla
que juzgue por desigual
ser segundo en Portugal
siendo primero en Castilla...

her head,' Gratian wrote, 'so she pulled off the prioress' veil who had tried in vain to stop her, and saw that on her head there were no wounds nor any sign of a crown of thorns.' Mary also insisted that the Prioress show her the wound in her side as she had shown the Bishops when they examined her. For several days the nun refused, but in the end she gave in and showed Mary the wound… 'This has been painted on!' exclaimed Mary of St Joseph.

Mary told this to Fr Luis de Granada, the holy friar who, in his old age, fell for the lies this deceitful nun. She also told Fr Mariano and wrote a report of what she saw to Cardinal Albert: 'There was no wound in her side or crown on her head.' However, as a consequence of what Mary had done she was branded suspect, and fell foul of those devoted to the nun. Jerome, who would also suffer as a consequence, advised Mary of St Joseph: 'It would be better not to appear to be against this woman whom everyone esteems so highly, as you are in a strange country and you are just beginning a foundation.'

One of Jerome's penitents in Lisbon was the highly decorated aristocrat, the Marquis de Santa Cruz, Don Alvaro de Bazan, first Marquis of Santa Cruz, Lord of Viso and Valdepennas, supreme Captain of the high seas, a member of the Order of St James and, as such, Commander in Chief of Leon and Villamayor and permanent Mayor of Gibraltar. The man had spent his life in the navy and had been involved in a thousand naval battles. This same Marquis approached Jerome to be his confessor.

The two became friends and our man was invited to dine with him. Jerome recounted later, 'The Marquis came to trust me so much that he showed me the despatches that came from England and the letters the King wrote him. He also consulted with me about his business affairs, about matters concerning his soul and conscience, as well as matters concerning his government over war and peace.' As a result of this friendship the man came to see the Castillian troops in a new light and, from what Jerome told him, saw what their needs were.

Jerome was also friendly with Cardinal Albert, who entrusted him to preach during Lent and to hear the confessions of prisoners, of whom many were political.

Gratian's four year term as Provincial came to end. He convoked a Chapter in Lisbon for the month of May; the third of the Discalced Carmelites.

There were thirty members who came together in Lisbon for the Chapter that began on 10 May. 'Two were excluded who did not have the proper credentials,' according to the Portuguese Chronicler. On the first day, the twenty-eight members with active voice elected the Definitors of the Order: Jerome Gratian, the outgoing Provincial, John of the Cross, Prior of Granada, Anthony of Jesus, Prior of Seville, and Gregory Nazianceno, Prior of Valladolid. Anthony of Jesus declined on the grounds of poor health, so John Baptist, the Prior of Malaga, was elected instead.

The time arrived for the election of the Provincial. Jerome, with a noble magnanimity and with an economy of words, proposed to the assembly the candidacy of Nicholas Doria. The latter, who was in fact the Prior of St Anne's, Genoa (Italy), was not at the Chapter. He was elected with an overwhelming majority: of the 28 votes cast he won 26. The other two votes went to Mariano and Alonso of the Angels. John of the Cross, commenting on the results of the election with other confreres, said in a voice that Jerome could hear: 'He has elected a Provincial who will expel him from the Order.' History would confirm the truth of the saintly Carmelite's prophetic words.

The Chapter authorized the foundation of a priory in Mexico and designated two friars, Peter of the Purification and Christopher of St Albert, who were in Genoa trying to find the new Provincial. Afterwards Jerome, in his farewell address, read a long report in which he gave an account of his four year tenure as Provincial and in which he shared in all conscience the hurts and slanders he had experienced. His *Apologia* began like this:

> The desire for the greater glory and honour of God and the salvation of souls, the expansion of our holy Order, and the need to tell the truth, and to enlighten others as to how they should proceed in the government of this Province, and the advice of some spiritual persons who have greatly touched my conscience, and my own sense of duty, moves me to give an account of the things that have happened in this four year period of my being Provincial, the houses that have been founded and the contradictions and calumnies I have endured. I wish to declare my reasons for some of the things I have done, which in the eyes of those who do not understand will appear dubious and deceitful, so they will see that, for fear of falling into error, I could not have done otherwise. If it appears that what I am doing in defending myself is an imperfection or due to a desire to sing my own praises and that I am not exhibiting as much mortification or humility as anyone who wears this habit should, I want you to understand that when

> things are made public and the person is well known, he is obliged, under pain of mortal sin, to defend his honour and tell the truth, since the honour is not his own but that of the entire community, and nor is the dishonour his problem alone but rather everyone's. It was not right that I should explain myself before but, now that I am leaving office, I need to do this.

In his account, the ex-Provincial recorded how he had worked hard for the Discalced Carmelites and the houses that had been founded. He said that the Reform could, at that time, count some forty houses of friars and nuns, and that the number of friars had to be more than five hundred. He gave thanks to the fact that in the last four years the Order had established itself in other Kingdoms: Portugal, Italy and, what he called, the Kingdom of Ethiopia, 'so that Our Lady be served and known throughout the world, and of her children, it is said, that *in omnem terram exivit sonus eorum*'; i.e. *their cry goes out through all the earth.*

He complained about the slander he suffered. They (his detractors) branded him as being 'negligent and remiss in punishing and giving penance', that for this reason the Order was lost; and of 'favouring and giving refuge to those who did wrong and were lax.' They accused him of having spent too much time preaching and, as a result, neglected the government of the Province. They criticized him for having placed his (own) sisters in the Order without dowries; he argued that such an accusation imputed also Mother Teresa of Jesus.

'There was no need to respond to such ungrateful and small-minded hearts'; but the Provincial did respond. His sister, Mary of St Joseph, who was professed in Valladolid in 1579, 'brought five hundred *ducados* that had been given her by the King.' His other sister, Isabel of Jesus, who was professed in Toledo in 1584, and his sister, Juliana of the Mother of God, still not yet professed, 'will bring their dowry once their parents have passed away.'

The slander that disturbed him most was the gossiping from a small group of friars who said, 'nuns, nuns, he deals a lot with nuns, and has many friends who are nuns.' 'In the end these suggestive and malicious rumours became public and spread through the city, filling the minds of the simple people. The world we live in wants to believe such malicious and deceitful gossip; instead it should give no credence to these rumours.'

Jerome realized that 'major superiors [of the Order] are like cities on the mountain tops and consequently would be exposed to the fury of the wind.' In his *Apologia*, he naïvely named a few of the more senior members of the

Discacled Carmelite Order at the Chapter with whom he had had problems. The effect was to arouse their hackles. For example, Anthony of Jesus was one of these: he [Jerome] had to summon him from Seville to Toledo the previous summer, of 1584, for having an improper relationship with Dona Beatriz of Avila, the sister of Fr Peter. Jerome also accused him of being responsible for 'slanders that issued from Seville.' These were fresh slanders that had gone to Rome, and all because he, Fr Anthony, was upset that 'he had not been made Provincial.' Another senior member was Mariano who 'was an accomplice and a zealous witness', a troublemaker who 'readily and willingly received letters from friars giving credence to the slanders therein.'

Neither Anthony of Jesus nor Mariano would forgive him for being so forthright. However, a certain person was coming from Italy, someone 'zealous and reformed', who would put the Reform in order following the previous 'relaxed' government.

The Lisbon Chapter was suspended at this point, to await the arrival of the new Provincial. Did the Chapter suspect that Nicholas Doria might not accept the task, in all humility? In order to persuade him, the emissaries brought letters of supplication, one of them from Fr Luis de Granada. The Province felt consoled when it found out that Nicholas Doria had accepted.

As first Definitor, the ex Provincial would remain at the helm of the Discalced Carmelite Province until the new Provincial, Nicholas Doria, arrived. Jerome tried as quickly as he could to implement a directive approved by the Chapter: to make a foundation in Mexico. A month before, on 9 April, he had signed an admirable *Letter of Brotherhood* with the Franciscans in Lisbon, so that the two Orders would help each other in their ministry to non-believers. He also wrote a pamphlet, entitled, *The Stimulus of Faith*, to encourage the friars to engage in missionary activity. It upset him to see only 'a few who felt motivated to convert others, and the many religious and secular priests who had no heart for this.' When the said pamphlet came to light a year later, Doria would use it against him.

Before the new Provincial had stepped foot in Spain, a fleet of ships set sail in June from the port of Sanlucar de Barrameda (near Cadiz) to Mexico. On board one of the ships was the Marquis of Villamanrique, the Viceroy of New Spain (Mexico). Also on board and bound for the 'Indies' were the first Discalced Carmelites. There were twelve in all, like the twelve Apostles.

The Chronicler described this foundation in Mexico as 'the crown of his [Gratian's] Provincialate' and 'his last achievement.' It was fortunate for the Discalced Carmelites that Nicholas Doria had not yet taken over the helm, as he would put a halt to the missions: another cause of conflict.

Jerome had carefully prepared the missionary expedition. He had received a letter from Fr John of the Mother of God, the Rector of St Cyril's College, Alcala, in which he asked Jerome for permission to go to Mexico to do some business on behalf of relatives. Jerome made it clear he would not give permission to look after the man's family, but he was willing to let the man travel with four religious to convert New Mexico.

Gratian negotiated for a licence with the Council for the Indies, which proved to be very generous. Anastasius recounted that 'informed of the spirit of the Order and how it intended to live, they gave provision for twelve friars to travel, in honour of the twelve Apostles. They gave them foodstuffs, animals and stores from the ship that they seldom gave to other religious. They wrote to Father Jerome, who was still Provincial, encouraging him to send these missionaries with their strong faith and hope, who with God's help would bear much fruit.'

In June, Fr John of the Mother of God and his companions embarked for South America. At the end of September Nicholas Doria disembarked in Barcelona – it was already too late to abort the mission – and convoked a Chapter in Pastrana for 17 October. Thus the members continued the Chapter that had been interrupted in Lisbon.

As the Definitors had already been elected, the Chapter had only to focus on various problems affecting the Reform, and listen to the proposals of the new Provincial. Doria had decided to divide up the Discalced Carmelite Province into four Districts or Semi-Provinces, with a Definitor acting as a Vicar Provincial, at the head of each one. The four Definitors were: Gregory Nazianceno in Old Castile, John Baptist in New Castile, John of the Cross in Andalucia, and Jerome Gratian in Portugal, who was also appointed Prior of St Philip's in Lisbon.

Jerome wrote: 'I wanted to rest a little from work and government, but I could not do this because I was quickly sent to Portugal to be Vicar Provincial.'

The Pastrana Chapter finished with the new Provincial setting out his programme for the government of the Province. The trumpets that brought down the walls of Jericho blew. The Chapter members shook at the sound of his (Doria's) voice: 'Strict observance, my Fathers! We will quickly go astray with the little observance your Reverences have seen. What has caused this? Is it not the faintheartedness that the habit of forgiveness has instilled? Yesterday strong, today weak; yesterday persevering, today fallen; yesterday brave, today timid. Oh what a miserable state our family is in! If we want to improve then let us be observant. If we want to edify our neighbour then let us be observant. If we want to gain souls for Christ then let us be observant. What fruit can be gained from relaxing our laws? Who has captivated us so that we have turned away from the true path we had begun?'

The Chronicle does not tell us where Nicholas Doria's withering gaze was directed, but his words were obviously a bitter reproach against the previous Provincial. Much later, Gratian was to write in his Lisbon *Apologia*: 'the truth is that I am more inclined to gentleness than to rigour, to love than to hate, to peace than to revenge, and to do good rather than bad; but, believe me, nothing in conscience and justice, would stop me from punishing another when it was my duty to do so.'

Doria continued with all the ardour of a novice: 'Fathers, I cannot live with my conscience if I did not continue to repeat this. I want you all to understand that I must speak like this, it is my concern and my undertaking. I trust in God that, even after my death, my bones will cry out: "Regular observance, regular observance!"'

Our man remained silent, not rebutting the implicit criticism. However, he wrote an article which circulated among the Discalced Carmelites entitled *Apologia in defence of charity, against those who, under the heading of observance of laws, cause it to become lukewarm and upset life in Religious Orders.*

On 17 October, Fr John Carrillo, a Canon and Treasurer in Avila Cathedral, appeared in Pastrana; he had been sent for by the Bishop of Palencia to attend the (Carmelite) Chapter, in order to deal with the translation of Teresa's body to St Joseph's convent, Avila. Alvaro de Mendoza, Bishop of Palencia and formerly Bishop of Avila had been a friend of St Teresa's. He had acquired the patronage of the main chapel in St Joseph's and adorned it with two lavish sepulchres: one with a gospel for Teresa and one with an epistle for himself.

Canon John Carillo, the Bishop's envoy, arrived after dark at the Chapter and was welcomed by Doria and Jerome. The two Carmelites, knowing why he had come, considered it more discreet to deal with the matter in secret, rather than at the Chapter. They met up the following evening, the feast of St Luke, approved the request by the Bishop of Palencia and swore to keep the actual translation (of Teresa's body) as secret as possible, and to leave in Alba de Tormes a significant relic of the Foundress. Fr Gregory Nazianzen, Vicar of Old Castile, was chosen to execute the plan.

On 13 November, Gregory Nazianzen, who was in Valladolid, wrote to Canon John Carrillo with details as to how he was going to remove Teresa of Jesus' body. They did not want to disturb the nuns in Alba, 'who were very anxious; they had been praying for the success of the Chapter': not even the Duke of Alba could prevent this. 'Assuming that it must be done in secret, there ought to be no noise or exposure.'

He (Fr Gregory) went to Alba on 24 November, the evening before the feast of St Catherine, where he lodged in a house opposite the nun's convent. Jerome also showed up with the reliquary of Teresa's left hand that he had recovered from Avila where it had been deposited.

Gregory Nazianzen and Jerome entered the convent that same evening and, with the approval of the nuns, opened the coffin to look at Teresa's body. The habits were worn but the body remained flexible and intact. The nuns, with the Prioress, Ines of Jesus, processed into the choir to recite compline. It was then that Gregory Nazianzen read out to them the Patent from the Chapter, signed in Pastrana on 27 October:

> Nicholas Doria, Provincial of the Discalced Carmelites, and the four Definitors from this our Provincial Chapter in Pastrana. With this Patent we give permission to Father Gregory Nazianzen, Vicar of our District of Old Castile, to take the body of our good Mother, Teresa of Jesus, that presently lies in our convent of nuns in Alba, and to place it in the sepulchre that his Illustrious and Most Reverend Lord Bishop of Palencia has prepared, being more respectful to the virtue of the said Mother, and being the first convent that she founded and being Prioress of the same at the time she died and to which she went when ill, and for the great deal that is owed to his Illustrious Lord Bishop and for the great devotion and desire that he has for this, and for many other reasons that move us...

The nuns were shocked. Gregory Nazianzen cut off the left arm from the shoulder joint as a relic for the convent in Alba: the arm that Teresa could not use after the fall on Christmas Eve 1577. One hand was missing which

Gratian had cut off in 1583, which he carried around with him. They took the body to the place where Fr Gregory was staying, opposite the convent. Gregory Nazianzen with a small and silent cortege left Alba before dawn, with the body of the Saint on a mule, taking the road to St Joseph's convent, Avila.

Jerome left Alba de Tormes to go to Lisbon to take charge of his new mission as Vicar of Portugal and Prior of St Philip's Priory. He may well have thought that by going away at that particular time, and so far from Castile, that his life would be peaceful and calm, but he would have been wrong. Doria's reach was very long.

Chapter Nineteen

Woe to St Teresa's Hens...!

At the end of the 16th century Lisbon had a population of over one hundred thousand inhabitants, with a considerable presence of slaves from various countries. The city was adorned with beautiful buildings constructed during the reign of Manuel I, in a style called 'Manuel', the best example of which was the monument known as the Batalha Monastery. The Tajo river estuary was a multicoloured vista of Portuguese and foreign vessels. Perched above the estuary and outside the city walls were the two Carmelite houses: St Philip's for the Discalced friars and St Albert's for the Discalced nuns.

On his return to Lisbon Gratian continued the same religious and political activities: on Sundays and Feastdays he preached in those parishes with 'the blessing of the Order and enthusiasm of the Portuguese for things Castilian.' He was confessor to the Naval Commander, the Marquis de Santa Cruz. He maintained the friendship and support of Cardinal Albert. He visited the barracks of the Spanish soldiers and heard the confession of prisoners, including two famous ones: the Bishop of la Guardia, captured in Setubal, and the Dean of Evora Cathedral, Alfonso Enriquez.

In 1586 he opened a house for reformed women, together with Captain Cespedes, and this a year before the first institution for the redemption of prostitutes was established in Madrid. He also housed in St Albert's convent twenty-one Franciscan nuns who had fled from Belgium due to the religious struggles. Later, with the help of Cardinal Albert, he assigned these nuns their own convent. Finally, he brought spiritual comfort to Spanish soldiers in their hospital, where many 'died in despair.'

Gabriel de Zayas, Secretary to King Philip II, wrote to Gratian from Madrid on 25 February 1586, with two pieces of information; first, that a foundation of Discalced Carmelite Friars had been made in the Priory of San Hermenegildo, Madrid, and, second, his brother, Thomas, informed him that 'our holy old father', Diego Gratian, ninety years old, had remained

View of Lisbon *by G. Braun and F. Hogenberg en their study Civitates Orbis terrarum. 16th century, Madrid.*

in bed because of the cold weather, had only eaten and drunk very little, but was happy and looked well.

Diego Gratian died on 2 March. He had been looked after, spiritually, by two Discalced Carmelites. The news of his father's death arrived from the same correspondent, Gabriel de Zayas: 'This morning God brought him to Himself in a way that was so Christian, just as he had lived.' He died surrounded by his children and grandchildren while reciting pious verses in both Latin and Greek. The Carmelites who were with him said to him a little before he died: 'Remember your good friend, the holy Mother Teresa of Jesus.' To which Diego replied: 'Dear Fathers, she has been with me now for some time.'

Diego had been a good man who had been happy with his salary that supported his many children while other Royal Secretaries somehow managed to accrue fortunes and large estates. Gabriel of Marmol, who wrote these details in his biography of Jerome, said that 'he [Diego] was a generous almsgiver; a poor person never left his house without alms and being consoled. He kept accounts with cooks, bakers and all those others who dealt with food, shoe makers, tailors, and clothes, and he would pay for food and clothes, especially for those who were poor yet upright. Afterwards these traders would come to him with the accounts for their money. His wife said to him: 'Lord, how can you pay these expenses with such a limited salary that can't support so many children?' He replied to her with great earnestness: "My dear, these needy people are also children; God will give enough to everyone." And in this way his last wishes were settled, since he left everyone in an honourable state and owned nothing to any man.'

The fact that Teresa of Jesus' body was lying in her convent in Avila had now become well known. Miracles attributed to her circulated around the Court in Madrid. Laguna, President of the Council of the Indies, who would later die as Bishop of Cordoba, asked permission from the Provincial, Nicholas Doria, 'to see the saintly body with the aim of making a report to his Majesty about what is to be seen, because already it has become public that her body is miraculously intact and there comes forth a pleasant odour.'

On 1 January 1586, Professor Laguna, accompanied by Professor Contreras, Judge of the Royal Council, and Fr Diego de Yepes, Prior of St Jerome in Madrid, who went for devotional reasons, together with the Bishop of Avila, Peter Fernandez de Teminno, were able to examine Teresa's body. The Bishop of Avila had called these people, together with a team of medical doctors and lawyers, who would testify to the correctness of the procedure. Fr Diego de Yepes stated, 'It [her body] was intact, without any form of corruption and with a very pleasant odour.'

When the people of Avila found out that Teresa's body had been returned there they were filled with joy, but the Duke of Alba, Anthony Alvarez of Toledo was angry, as was his uncle Fernando, the Prior of St John's. The two of them vowed to return the body of the Saint to Alba. Their protest reached Rome with such force and persuasion that Pope Sixtus V ordered the Discalced Carmelite friars to return the body of Mother Teresa to Alba, without delay, under pain of excommunication.

On 18 August, the Nuncio, Speciano, sent the order from Rome to Nicholas Doria and to Mary of St Jerome, Prioress of Avila, obliging them to carry out the order within the space of three days, and 'if anyone claims the right (to reverse this decision), they will have to appeal to the Pope.'

Doria arrived in Avila, under great pressure from the order from Rome. He entrusted the transference to Fr John Baptist, Prior of Pastrana, and Fr Nicholas of St Cyril, Prior of Mancera. They had to transfer the body by night and without fuss or noise. On the morning of 23 August, Teresa's venerable body was buried, once again, in the convent in Alba de Tormes, after nine months in Avila.

The nuns in Avila appealed to Rome and began a hard-fought lawsuit. In the end the house of Alba, being very powerful won the case. On 1 December

1588, the Nuncio, Speciano, declared in favour of the house of Alba. This was confirmed by Pope Sixtus V on 10 July 1589.

Mary of St Joseph, the Prioress of St Albert's in Lisbon, so wise and intelligent, predicted that a storm was looming. Ambrose Mariano, before leaving Lisbon for the Chapter in Pastrana, had left with her a chest of papers to be sorted and sent on to his new abode that was none other than the Priory in Madrid.

She recounted in her book, *Ramillete de mirra*, how among those papers was 'a document belonging to a certain Religious Superior who was among those who were now in government. In it the said Religious pointed to more than thirty things that should be changed in the nun's Constitutions, all of them to destroy the said Constitutions, which our holy Mother had wanted to be kept permanently unchanged.'

In reading this document, Mary of St Joseph heard alarm bells. She realized that the Constitutions given by Teresa to her daughters were in danger; that is to say, the Carmelite Reform in its most authentic sense. She wrote: 'The friars have this characteristic; they cannot live without inventing new things.'

When, a little later, she noticed the first indications of persecution against Fr Gratian, whom they had sent to Portugal to keep him at a distance, and the look of Doria's new Government, she expressed, prophetically in verse what would become of the Teresian Reform:

Oh, oh, Dear Carmel,
Watch out, the fox is around,
attentive and covetous,
and wanting to take away your peace!
...
Woe to the poultry yard of Teresa,
If help does not come soon
From the great Shepherd of the sheep,
it will be seized and the hens scattered!
...
We are women!
I ask: How shall we be heard?

> We will be heard less if we are put down
> In the foreboding ill
> I forsee may happen!
> ...
> In the year eighty-six,
> As you know, I am telling you this now;
> Some one will be the witness
> Who will endure the storm.

On 19 July, Jerome obtained permission 'from the holy Inquisition' and from Cardinal Albert to publish a pamphlet *Incentive for the Propagation of the Faith* that was printed in Lisbon. When Doria would later come to read it he would feel insulted and would send Jerome a letter strongly condemning the pamphlet. However, Doria had not as yet read the text when he convoked a meeting of the Vicar Provincials, for 13 August, in Madrid.

Jerome, being Vicar Provincial in Portugal, had asked to be excused as he was so far away and did not appear. John of the Cross, Vicar Provincial of Andalucia, left Granada with Anne of Jesus, who was going to her new convent in Madrid as Prioress. John fell ill in Toledo and delayed his arrival. A rumour spread that this meeting would be anti-Gratian and that John did not want to take part. The Chronicler deduced that John of the Cross 'felt that they were out for the life of someone who had given life to many.' However, John of the Cross, though late, arrived in Madrid and signed the Act on 16 August. The meeting stretched over twenty days, until 4 September. From 19 to 28 August they suspended the sessions when Doria travelled to Avila to fulfil the Pope's mandate of translating Teresa's body [back] to Alba.

The meeting of Definitors resulted in three important agreements: a change of liturgical rite, to have a General Procurator of the Province in Rome, and the printing of Teresa's books.

The Discalced Carmelites adopted the Roman breviary and abandoned the old Jerusalem rite, in order to widen even more the gap between them and the Calced Carmelites. John of the Cross and another Definitor did not agree with this, but Doria's motion was carried. Months before Doria had initiated diplomatic manoeuvers aimed at King Philip II to obtain from Rome a new Brief to confirm the one given by Pope Gregory XIII in 1580 in which the Discalced Carmelite Province was erected.

Doria feared that the General of the (Calced) Order, unhappy with him for the foundation in Genoa, would have the Brief revoked and the

Discalced Province suppressed. Thanks to the influential recommendation of Philip II, Pope Sixtus V issued a Brief, *Quae a praedecessoribus nostris*, on 20 September, which confirmed the erection of the Discalced Carmelite Province as agreed by his predecessor, Gregory XIII. Doria also obtained the presence of a Procurator in Rome, John of Jesus Roca, Prior of Barcelona, which meant a further step towards the independence of the Discalced.

The agreement to print Teresa's books was important. Anne of Jesus, who had just become Prioress in Madrid, was entrusted with compiling Teresa's works. She, in turn, handed them over to Fr Luis de Leon, who published the 'first edition' with the publisher, Guillermo Foquel, 'the first printer in Salamanca', in 1588.

If in the meeting of Definitors there was a certain hostility towards Gratian, this was not reflected in the Acts. The storm intensified towards the end of this year, 1586. The pamphlet *Incentive for the Propagation of the Faith* deeply irritated Doria. His letter to our man has not been preserved, but from the response we can deduce the Provincial's anger. He reprimanded Jerome for having published the pamphlet without permission and told him testily that 'if there is so much to be gained by conversions, he should have been the first to ask permission to go on them [the missions] and not be satisfied with encouraging others while he remained in Spain.' He ordered Jerome to prevent the book from being circulated.

However, the book had been distributed; it wasn't possible to retract it. Gratian pointed out to Doria that if it was a question of permission, he had got it from the Cardinal who, in Portugal, was (Papal) Legate *a latere*, 'to whom all friars and nuns looked to as their General or Pope; I did not believe that more permission was necessary.' If it is a question of the book's doctrine, 'it is universal and is suitable for everyone.' If Doria considered it 'scandalous or bad doctrine… your Reverence should write giving reasons why you are against the book, and do not be a judge but accept another's opinion.' It was the first slap from Doria (as Provincial) against Gratian.

On 19 February 1587, Jerome wrote a warning letter to the Discalced Carmelite nuns. He was prompted to do this by 'a particular responsibility that Mother Teresa entrusted to me.' He recommended them to ask at the next Provincial Chapter that Teresa's Constitutions be left untouched, as she 'arranged them with much reason and spirit, advice and holiness.' 'I warn you [he wrote to the Prioresses] as someone who knows well, that there are many Religious who feel called to reform the nuns; and as they do not have your experience, they believe that many things in your Constitutions would be better expressed in another way; and if two or three of them get together at a Definitory meeting, they can alter things that will be the beginning of much discontentment.'

Mary of St Joseph was certainly disturbed from the time she had read the document that was among Fr Mariano's papers. She also wrote to some Prioresses she knew, alerting them to the 'danger we are in', persuading them 'to stick together, and ask the new Provincial, whom we trust, to help us and look after our interests. Let us ask at the first Chapter they celebrate that our Constitutions be confirmed, and for further legislation that would support the same.'

Mary of St Joseph still had faith in Doria. He had been her confessor in Seville and assured her that he would support the nuns against certain fickle friars who liked to invent new things. However, she would become aware very quickly that the fury of an angry Doria could also fall on her. Doria had convoked the interim Provincial Chapter in Valladolid for 17 April. Some Prioresses, prompted by Mary of St Joseph, would ask the Chapter not to change the Alcala Constitutions that Teresa had left them. The Chapter responded: 'Your request came as a surprise to us, given that we are ready to preserve your laws, out of the love and respect we have for the good Mother Teresa.'

There was a deliberate postscript: 'It may be that some friar has made you anxious.' The friar they were alluding to was none other than Jerome Gratian, who had left Lisbon and turned up at the Chapter in Valladolid.

Forty six delegates had gone to Valladolid. They began working on Saturday, 18 April; the Chapter lasted a week. John of the Cross ceased to be Definitor and Vicar Provincial of Andalucia and was elected the Prior of Granada for the third time. Jerome ceased to be Definitor and Vicar Provincial in Portugal and was assigned Vicar of the new province of Mexico.

Is this a reward for all Jerome's work? No, it is a subtle way of getting rid of an adversary by sending him far from the peninsula; a banishment to far away Mexico. In recording later the persecutions he experienced Jerome would write in 1590 that the intention to send him to Mexico was not out of missionary zeal but to 'banish him from Spain.' At a certain moment Jerome let the word 'grudge' slip out; the grudge that Doria had against him. Doria began to stake his territory, and this was, to remain in power and get rid of any dissenters. The first and most important of these, though not the only one, was Gratian. At the end of the Chapter he was appointed Vicar of the new canonically erected District of Mexico; Doria and the Definitors had signed a Patent to that effect on 25 April. Some days later, on 3 May, Jerome, and other Discalced friars, were given another Patent ordering them to embark on the first available ship leaving for Mexico.

A good many of the Chapter members were aware that Doria's order to send Jerome to Mexico was simply to expel him from Spain. Gratian went to Seville, ready to do as he was told. However, it happened that no ship would leave that year for Mexico. In April, the pirate Drake, had attacked the port of Cadiz and harassed the Andalucian coast with a fleet of thirty ships. Queen Elizabeth I of England knighted this pirate on the bridge of his ship, raising him to a Knight and when, the following year, 1588, King Philip II sent his 'invincible' Armada against England, the result of which has gone down in history, Drake would fight as a Vice Admiral in the battle of the English Channel.

Doria refused to let Jerome leave the port until Drake's flotilla of ships went away. A rumour went round Seville, where he (Jerome) was well known, that he had sought to escape to spite his Superiors.

Augustine of the Three Kings, Vicar Provincial in Andalucia, was not happy that Jerome was present in Seville, because he felt threatened by him. Together with certain friars who had sharp tongues, he revived some of the old gossip that the Calced Carmelites had disseminated throughout Seville.

Knowing in Portugal that Gratian had not left for Mexico, the Marquis of Santa Cruz and Mgr Teutonio de Braganza, Archbishop of Evora, asked Doria to let Jerome go to Lisbon. The Archbishop pleaded that he was needed to fulfil certain ministries. However, the Provincial responded to him by saying that Fr Gratian had been ordered to remain in Seville by the Chapter and, therefore, he could not give him permission to leave.

Doria was not telling the truth. The Chapter had not decided such a thing. It was Doria, with the complicity of the Definitors, who wanted to banish Jerome to Mexico.

Immediately afterwards, at the insistence of Augustine of the Three Kings, Jerome was thrown out of Seville and sent to Ubeda and Jaen to establish new foundations that had been requested by these cities. He would denounce the way he had been treated when he came to write his defence against the things that Doria accused him of, 'they threw me out of Seville, accusing me of causing scandal and for other failings.'

If Fr Gratian was responsible for such grave scandals in Seville, which obliged the Vicar Provincial, Augustine of the Three Kings, to send him away, why was he sent to Jaen to make new foundations? Jerome submitted and travelled to Jaen saying: 'Close your eyes to the slanders, be concerned for obedience and the good of the Order.'

While the Chapter members debated in Valladolid, Anne of St Bartholomew, Teresa's nurse and Secretary, had a vision of 'how all the Discalced Carmelite friars were full of grace and the love of God, and that above the Priory where they were gathered, there was a cloud that shone like the sun, in the midst of which was our Father Saint Elijah, holding his cape spread over them.'

I must confess that I do not find Anne of St Bartholomew a particularly nice person. However, she confirmed in her book, *In Defence of Teresa's Inheritance*, the vision she had had of the Prophet Elijah with his cape stretched over the Chapter members in Valladolid, all of them 'full of grace and the love of God.' The reality was not really like this. Although the majority were good friars some of them, beginning with Doria, were full of resentment.

After the Chapter ended, Doria turned up in the convent in Avila. When the Prioress told him of Anne of St Bartholomew's vision, he replied: 'To all of us this (Chapter) seemed to have been inspired from above. From the beginning everyone agreed with whatever I said.' In this he was absolutely right. He was determined to impose his own autocratic style of leadership on the Discalced Carmelites, whom he would govern with an iron fist.

The nuns asked Doria about the previous Provincial, he replied cynically: 'Father asked permission to go to Mexico to preach. In all charity we refused him, and showed him how sadly he would be missed. However, Gratian was not persuaded by us and so we left him to do what he wanted.'

Doria was Machiavellian. He was a very able administrator with exceptional gifts for things financial but whose theological formation was somewhat lacking. 'He had no other thought in his head other than an obsession with putting the world to right,' said Ephrem Montalva.[1] The latter wondered, as Donazar had before him, whether there was not some sort of sexual anomaly behind this. Montalva suggested that Doria was a kind of narcissist who saw himself as a Reformer, and as such, wanted to remain in power, using any means, in order to erase every trace of what Teresa of Jesus and her disciples had achieved.

Without revealing anything to the Chapter, Doria had been negotiating with the Court of King Philip II to ask the Monarch to obtain from Rome a new Brief that would raise the Discalced Carmelite Province into a Congregation. Pope Sixtus V issued a new Brief without much delay. On 10 July 1587 the Congregation of Discalced Carmelites was erected, under a collective government, called a *Consulta*, with a Vicar General at its head and six Councillors to assist him on a permanent basis; all bound to secrecy.

This new Brief, created by Doria, was made to measure for him. The new Congregation would divide into as many Provinces as necessary, each one led by a Provincial. At the Chapter in Valladolid Gratian had made sure that this kind of government, the *Consulta*, was turned down. However, now, with the authority of a Papal Brief, Doria made sure that he was in charge.

At the end of November, Doria met with the Definitors in Madrid to give them an account of the Papal Brief. He presumed that after the Brief had been read by the Secretary of the Apostolic Notary of Madrid, it would come into effect immediately; that he would become Vicar General of the new Congregation of Discalced Carmelites. However, the Definitors told him 'that according to the Brief a General Chapter of the entire Discalced Congregation should take place, and that in the Chapter the Brief should be read and accepted by everyone, or, at least by the majority of the members. For such an important matter that was of interest to everyone, it was only right that everyone should know about it. No one should complain that they had not been told or suspect something surreptitious', as the Chronicler commented.

The issue of Gratian arose, a difficult rival (to Doria). The attempt to send him to Mexico had failed. However, Doria would endeavour to deprive him of both active and passive voice so that he could not be elected: a Machiavellian move that would catch Jerome Gratian by surprise.

Jerome found himself in the land of Jaen (southern Spain) where he was

1 Ephrem Montalvo was the author of two books on St Teresa, published in Madrid in 1973 and 1975.

welcomed kindly by the Bishop, Francis Sarmiento. The latter 'knew Jerome to be a man of great learning and discretion, and invited him to discern the authenticity of many spiritual people in his Diocese, whose conduct the Bishop was not entirely happy with.'

During this time Jerome founded the Priory of the Archangel Michael in Ubeda, where four years later St John of the Cross would die. The Vicar Provincial of New Castile, and first Definitor, Fr Elijah of St Martin, called to see him on 10 November; Elijah had been sent by Doria and had with him all the evidence that was needed for criminal proceedings against him.

How did this come about? Doria had not reproached Gratian openly at the Valladolid Chapter that had taken place six months earlier, at which he had been appointed Vicar Provincial for Mexico. Why criminal proceedings, as the accusations against him were based on some old gossip by the Calced Carmelites? It was simply because Doria wanted to have him excluded from the Chapter that was to elect the Vicar General of the new Congregation. As Vicar Provincial Gratian had every right to be present.

Fr Elijah of St Martin, in conformity with the legal document received from Doria, asked Jerome on oath 'by virtue of the Holy Spirit and holy obedience' to respond truthfully to everything he was asked. There was nothing new in the accusation against him; it was the same old story:

> That in Lisbon he frequented the nuns...
>
> Again, that in Seville he continued the same frequenting and dealings...
>
> Again, while in both Lisbon and Seville, in the convents of nuns they washed his clothes and sent him sheets made of fine wool which he slept between. He [wore] linen shirts.
>
> Likewise, that in the convent in Lisbon the nuns of Saint Albert often sent him special food that he accepted and ate.
>
> Again, he has always been a source of irritation to the Province when dealing with our nuns. The Province has taken note of all the gossip that has arisen from his dealings with the said nuns. He is fully aware of this as the Province has often warned him but, in spite of this, he ignores us and carries on.
>
> Again, he was in Lisbon, in the convent of Saint Albert and often stayed there until one or two in the morning.
>
> Again, while in Lisbon and in Seville, even though not in bad health, he normally ate meat, wore linen, often slept on a mattress with linen or

> serge sheets. Even though he was ordered not to sleep with sheets made of serge, he, nevertheless, continued to sleep this way. While eating with lay people and travelling, he normally ate meat, even on days when the Church forbade it.
>
> Again, all the time he was in Seville he went and ate outside the Priory every day and often ate meat with lay people in the garden of our priory at night time. This was the way he behaved there.
>
> Again, he printed a book on the Brotherhood with the Discalced Franciscans, in which he gave very indecent names to those Fathers of the Province who did not agree with him, and disobeyed the Provincial and did not want to retract as he was ordered to…

Doria extended this list with the contributions offered by Anthony of Jesus, Vicar of Portugal and Augustine of the Three Kings, Vicar of Seville. These additions were, once again, the same old gossip.

Gratian complained that he was given only three days to respond. He told Fr Elijah: 'I swear on my word as a priest that I will tell the whole truth about what I know and have heard about these false testimonies.'

His response was lengthy. It showed what a shrewd mind he had, and his extraordinary talent for debate. He didn't hold back. He exposed those who slandered him and mentioned them by name. He admitted that he responded 'with more anger than he should have, that he called Doria and Anthony of Jesus and others, slanderers and prejudiced.'

However, I shall not delay with the points made in Gratian's response. Doria became aware that he himself had gone too far. When he met with the Definitors on 25 November, to receive the Brief, he made known to them only the last accusation that referred to the book published in Lisbon; he kept silent about all the other charges referring to the nuns.

Doria told the Definitors how a book written by Jerome the year before, without permission, had come into his possession. How it contained provocative statements against the Superiors whom he called 'visible demons,' who 'do not wish to leave Spain but themselves eat up the alms given by the poor.' Doria asked that Gratian be deprived of active and passive voice at the next two General Chapters.

He was not successful this time, but the field had been prepared to achieve his objective. With the approval of the Definitors, he sent Jerome a letter on 28 November 1587, signed in the priory of St Hermenegildo, Madrid, by Fr Nicholas of Jesus & Mary, Provincial, Fr Elias of St Martin,

Vicar, Fr Anthony of Jesus, Vicar, Fr John Baptist, Vicar and Fr Augustine of the Three Kings, Vicar. The letter, edited by Doria, was a warning for the future, in which they asked Gratian to apologize for the past and observe the regular life, especially in the matter of what he ate, his dress, his bed linen, and to use restraint in visiting the nuns. Jerome considered the text of this letter as 'a very grave and heavy reprimand.'

The whispering became a scream among the Discalced Carmelite nuns. Word went round that the ex Provincial had been accused of unseemly behavior with the Discalced Carmelite nuns. However, voices were raised in his defence.

The first of these was that of Mary of St Joseph, Prioress of Lisbon. She wrote to Anthony of Jesus that she was surprised at what was said 'of the dealings and conversations Father had during his stay with us as Vicar Provincial'; because, not only does this question the honour of the Father, it also questions that of the nuns. She invited him, as Vicar Provincial, to make a thorough examination of the way they live.

She wrote a similar letter to Nicholas Doria, in which she also invited him to carry out a rigorous examination of the way they lived. 'The greater rigour with which your Reverence makes this examination, the greater the favour and benefit it will be to us. And your Reverence will be fulfilling the obligation you have for the things of our holy Mother Teresa of Jesus; to look after the honour of her daughters. And though we no longer have the protection and defence she gave us in the world, we have not lost the zeal and recollection that she taught us. And so we are willing to have a thorough examination of our way of life.'

What did Mary of St Joseph and the other nuns who signed the letter achieve by this? She reveals this in her book *A Bunch of Myrrh*: they were called 'perjurers and liars'.

Other friars from Lisbon wrote to Elias of St Martin praising highly Fr Gratian's holy life and the fruit of his pastoral ministry. Michael of the Resurrection wrote: 'My conscience obliges me to say that, in faith, in all the time I have known him, which must be more than ten years, I have never seen anything in him that might be an imperfection, because he has always behaved in a way that was holy.'

Fr John of the Conception wrote, 'Your Reverence will be really appalled that I have written you this letter. The reason that motivated me is that I have heard that there have been some false testimonies made against our Father Gratian. As I accompanied him all the time he was in Lisbon, I saw in him much perfection and heard from him much holy doctrine. He gave good example in this place and brought blessings to many souls, both religious and lay people. It seems to me, I dare to say, as someone who knows him well, that nothing they say is true. I witnessed with my own eyes how some souls who with good fortune, have ceased to offend God, thanks to his holy teaching and good example. Others are now further along the way of perfection and are more enlightened. I would not have told of the beneficial things this saint has done, had I not seen it for myself. It pains me that those who accuse him do an injustice to themselves, and not to Father Gratian, because, just as God rescued the saintly Susanna, He will rescue him… Let them say what they like, they put themselves in hell, but him they raise up to heaven.'

Others supported Gratian with similar praises, including Fr Thomas of the Holy Spirit, Fr Anthony of Jesus Mary (not to be confused with Fr Anthony of Jesus, the Vicar Provincial), Fr Francis of the Cross, Fr Michael of the Virgin and Fr Albert of St Peter.

However, these testimonies mattered little to Doria. His objective was to destroy Gratian's reputation. If he could not banish him to Mexico, he would deprive him of authority by taking away his passive and active voice, and what was worse, his honour.

Jerome left Ubeda for Jaen at the beginning of 1588. He had been invited by the local Bishop since a Canon from the Cathedral wanted to give to the Carmelites a house and garden for the foundation of a priory (Ubeda).

Jerome remained in Jaen until the end of Lent. The Bishop, Francis Sarmiento was delighted to have him as a guest in his palace, whom he invited to dine, happy to listen to what our man said. Every day he discussed matters with his Carmelite guest for more than two hours.

While Jerome was getting the foundation ready he dedicated himself fully to the task of preaching as well as examining certain visionaries who were disturbing the life of the diocese, a task the Bishop had asked him to do. 'There were some "holy women" [wrote Jerome] who believed they had reached perfection, because seeing themselves as female demons, they believed they had to suffer carnal relations with the devil, who would force himself on them without their consent. They would lose all reason, becoming crazy, possessed women, until eventually their mouths were opened so they could receive the Blessed Sacrament. The principal instigator of this *alumbrados* novelty was a priest from a parish in Jaen, called Gaspar Lucas.'

Jerome wrote a book about this priest which he entitled, *Crazy Fantasist.*[2] He also informed the Inquisition in Cordoba of the stupidity of these women and of the Curate who encouraged them.

Time went by and Doria saw that he had to convoke a Chapter to fulfil the innovations contained in the Brief from Rome. As yet he had not succeeded in preventing Jerome from attending the Chapter; and, because Spain had concentrated all its fleet in Lisbon in preparation for its attack on England, no ship would be leaving for Mexico that year.

Doria had somehow to find a way of getting rid of Gratian. Mariano, a fellow Italian, suggested an ingenious way to deceive him: that Jerome's family asks him to go to Madrid for an urgent matter. Then, when he appears at Court, without written permission from the Provincial, he will have incurred a grave penalty of disobedience, and this according to the Discalced Carmelite Constitutions.

2 The title of the book in the original Spanish: *Higuera loca*.

Chapter Twenty

An Ill-Fated Year

Anastasius said to Cyril: 'You were right to call the year '88 a dreadful year. It has been the most fateful of our times, when many revolutions have occured... During this year the Chinese have fought fierce battles with pirates and Tartars; the Japanese have been tyrannized by Uchondon; Persia has fought battles with the Great Turk; a new sect has arisen in Turkey and spread as far as Egypt; there has been a great insurrection among the Sultan's private army which set fire to more than forty thousand houses in Istanbul; in Tripoli, the Marabout came with their armies and destroyed Azambaxa; in Hungary, Zenan has brought much suffering to the Hungarian people; in Italy, there is no shortage of rumours and fears; in France, their King has died; in Spain, the Armada that set sail for England was defeated, and yet they plan to send their ships to Portugal in the year '89.'

Many Religious Orders were deeply worried. In the Discalced Carmelite Order, for example, a new form of government, known as a *Consulta*, had been introduced; this was to bring much suffering to our friend.'

'Our friend' is Jerome Gratian, against whom they (the members of the Consulta) have formed an alliance. He wrote, 'I believe that all the stars and their nefarious influences have turned against me: because I have suffered greatly, and the sum total of my trials and persecutions went from bad to worse that year.'

Jerome began the year peacefully enough in Jaen. There he preached and was involved in some kind of pastoral activities, encouraged by the Bishop and spurred on by the faith of the people. On 8 February, he wrote to his two younger brothers, Peter, who was twenty-three, and Laurence, eighteen: both had joined the Discalced Carmelites in Pastrana. Peter, for reasons of ill health, would leave after eleven months without taking vows; he was ordained later as a diocesan priest and became rector of a hospital in Madrid, where, in 1599, he died caring for plague victims. Laurence remained in the Discalced Carmelites and took the name 'Laurence of the

Mother of God'. He had to witness the entire iniquitous process against his older brother, and in the end saw him expelled from the Order.

'Never neglect your prayers, he [Jerome] told them, so that our mother and our other brothers and sisters, who are not in our Religious Order but who live in the world, may be pleasing to this sovereign Lord.'

Their mother, Joanna Dantisco, now a widow, lived alone in her house in Madrid. Her husband, Diego, had died two years earlier. Two of Jerome's older siblings had also died: Anthony in 1576 and Luke in 1587. The latter had worked as a lawyer in Madrid, marrying Joanna Carrillo, in 1576, a noble lady from Toledo. When Anthony died, Luke was entrusted by King Philip II to catalogue the books of the El Escorial monastery. He wrote a book entitled, *Galateo español*. It was a treatise on good etiquette, replete with stories and amusing anecdotes, a kind of code of conduct for the Court. It was first published in Madrid in 1582 and went through no less than twenty-six editions, the last was at the end of the 18th century.

Jerome was now the eldest in the family. Thomas, the next eldest, was Secretary to King Philip II. He, like many in the family, inherited a facility for languages. Thomas wrote a treatise on the art of writing letters which Cervantes referred to in his books *La Galatea* and *Viaje del Parnaso*. Thomas' wife, Laurencia de Zurita, was very well versed in Latin. She was a good calligrapher and an accomplished musician. Lope de Vega[1] in his book *Laurel de Apolo* wrote about her.

The other brothers and sisters, in order of age were: Justine, who was educated at the College for Noble Ladies in Toledo: she took over from their mother in running the home and looking after her younger siblings. She later married Peter Zapata del Marmol, a Secretary at the Royal Council and Clerk to the King's Royal Chamber. After Justine there came Joanna, who married a governor from Segovia: she died within a year of getting married. Then came Louis, a student at Alcala University, who married Ines de Barrionuevo. He became a Secretary to the wife of the Viceroy of Sicily. He died aged just thirty-two in Madrid, in 1596. The other four daughters entered the cloistered life: Adriana joined the Jeronimites in Madrid; Maria, Isabel and Juliana, the Discalced Carmelites.

In the same letter that Jerome wrote to his two brothers, Peter and Lorenzo, both now novices, he congratulated them on being accepted into the Discalced Carmelite Order, dedicated to Our Lady, and encouraged

1 A Spanish poet and writer, second only to Cervantes in reputation.

them to persevere in the Order until they died. After some spiritual advice about the novitiate, he wrote that one day he would like to sail 'full of good intentions to a place where he hoped to give his life for God, or, failing that, he would drown on the way or, if he arrived, that he would die at the hands of pagans.'

However, Jerome would never have to endure the martyrdom he longed for on the other side of the world. Instead, he would suffer martyrdom on his own soil and by the hands of his (Carmelite) brothers. Jerome told Peter and Lorenzo not to worry about the rumours circulating about himself. 'Do not be upset if you hear some people spreading rumours, since you cannot thread a needle without using your teeth to bite thoroughly the end of the thread. However, on the day of judgement these things will all come into the open. I am happy to be going [to Mexico] and I go at the express wish of the entire Chapter and with permission from the King. I pray to God that this year the ships will not be impeded from sailing as Drake impeded them long ago.'

Jerome wanted to say goodbye to his mother before leaving for Mexico, as he knew that once he set sail he would not see her again. However, the Provincial did not reply to his request (for permission to visit her). Doria saw Jerome's request to go to Madrid as an opportunity to catch him committing an act of grave disobedience. In the Discalced Carmelite Constitutions it was laid down that whoever went on a journey without 'written' permission was to be deprived of active and passive voice. Doria persuaded Gratian's mother and some friends, including Anne of Jesus, Prioress in Madrid, to write inviting him to come quickly and visit them in Madrid.

Doria wrote provokingly to Joanna Dantisco: 'I know that he does not want to come, that now he knows he is going to Mexico he doesn't want [his relatives] to dissuade him.' In the same letter he added, 'For the sake of his honour he should come, because he has preached things about revelations that were ambiguous and now the Inquisition has got involved.'

However, Jerome did not pay heed to these appeals, not even to his mother's. He knew well that he would need written permission from the Provincial.

Mariano wrote to him, 'When your Reverence receives this letter you should leave everything and go to Madrid... It is important that you set out without waiting to finish those Lenten sermons... I am telling you this out of my great love for you; should anything go wrong let it fall on my shoulders... *Servus inutilis*, Fra. Marianus, *peccator*' (*Your useless servant*, Bro. Mariano, *a sinner*).

Gratian suspected that they were preparing a 'trap' by means of this letter to him in Jaen. A lay brother had brought the (Mariano's) letter to him. On learning from the bearer that the Father Provincial had given him the letter his suspicion was confirmed. If he had asked Doria for written permission, as demanded by the Constitutions, why did Doria hide behind a cunning letter from his friend Mariano? In the end Doria gave him written permission to travel, 'full of orders and restrictions that were difficult to fulfil'. It was dated 1 April:

> When you receive this patent, within twenty days of this present month of April, you are to leave Jaen or wherever you are and come directly to Madrid. Within eight days of your departure you are to present yourself in this priory of Saint Hermenegildo, where you are to remain for no more than six days. When these days are over you will leave Madrid and have ten days to get to Seville by the most direct route, going to our priory of Los Remedios. There you will wait for and embark on the first ship that sets sail for Mexico... 'If the 2nd of this month [May] has passed without Fr Jerome having received this patent or if he has not complied with it and left, it follows that it loses all authority either for him to leave [for Mexico] or to come to the priory in Madrid. The patent is ineffective for all the other details as well. In order that it might have carried more authority it and all its contents were issued with a warning about his being rebellious and disobedient to his Superior's orders!'

It was the beginning of May when Jerome arrived in Madrid, Easter had come and gone. Juan Lopez de Velasco, a friend of the Discalced Carmelites, came to meet him and invited him to stay in his house. It was thanks to Jerome's father that Juan Lopez had a good job in the Treasury. Although Jerome did not know that this Velasco was another Judas Iscariot in the service of Doria, he did not fall into the trap, but instead went directly to the San Hermenegildo Priory, as decreed in the Constitutions.

The (following) conversation he had with Velasco revealed the kind of traps that were being set for him. Andrew of Marmol, Gratian's first biographer, noted that this Velasco, 'whose position he owed to Fr Gratian's parents, should not have treated him like this.' He describes how Velasco cynically said to Gratian, 'What a good thing it is to live peacefully and harmoniously with one's superiors and not be the cause of anxiety for the Order'. To which Jerome replied, 'It is what I want more than anything'. Velasco continued, 'Father Provincial complains that you are proud, ambitious and that you want to be a Superior.' To which our friend replied, 'I am very far from wanting to command or to aspire to positions of authority, as nothing would please me more than to be in a priory where I could study. Let him tell me what humble words he wants me to use, or whatever it is I should say.' He asked Jerome if he could write down what he had just said. Jerome replied, 'Write whatever you like and I shall sign it,' upon which, Velasco, that Judas Iscariot, vanished from his sight. Velasco went to his home, Jerome to the Priory.

The following day, 2 May, Gratian visited the nuns. While he was in the parlour with Anne of Jesus, the Prioress, Velasco appeared with a note written by Doria and asked him to sign it. Jerome saw that the text was asking him to renounce the office of Vicar Provincial of Mexico, and to be deprived of 'active and passive voice'. He told Velasco that he would be willing to do this only under obedience, which would be a very different matter, and asked for paper to write to Doria to this effect. Velasco told him, 'I don't have any other paper, just amend what is written in the letter I have.'

Anne of Jesus, the Prioress, intervened, 'Sign it Father, for your own sake. Let us stop going round in circles. Why not make this act of humility. It will shut them up and everyone else when they see your humility.' Fr Gratian presumed that Velasco would show the document to the Provincial, who would not keep it. He made some amendments between the lines, adding 'if I am ordered by obedience, I shall renounce my position' and signed the document. Velasco then ran to St Hermenegildo priory with the piece of paper in his hands, where Doria and Mariano were waiting for him.

Jerome had fallen into their trap. Doria held up the piece of paper as though it were a trophy. The Nuncio was the first one he showed it to, 'Look, my Lord, it is true, what they are saying about the offences he has committed, since he confesses to them.' The Nuncio was keen to see this man who humbled himself in this way.

When Gratian arrived in St Hermenegildo, Doria had prepared a written text on the reverse side of the paper that he (Gratian) had just signed, on which he was ordered to renounce his right to vote and his office. He wrote in his autobiography: 'This really opened my eyes…'

Jerome thought it would be sinful to sign the new letter, because, besides there being no grounds, he would have been bringing dishonour on himself (and therefore his Order). He asked for the letter so that he could tear it up, but Doria did not give it to him. Velasco, that Judas Iscariot, turned up again and offered to intervene. Jerome told him angrily not to interfere in matters to do with the friars. And this is the way the matter remained. Jerome recorded, 'Doria wrote and signed the document that said in the future I would renounce (voice and office), and the other side of the document he wrote the order of renunciation, which I did not sign.'

Jerome remained in Madrid during those long and hot summer days. Obviously he must have wanted to visit his mother and say goodbye to her, but he makes no reference to this in his autobiography. Following a request from the Nuncio, Speziano, to come and visit, he went accompanied by Fr Mariano. When the Nuncio asked him 'if he wanted to go to Mexico,' and Jerome replied that he did, the Nuncio responded, 'As I need you to do something for me, it is not a good idea for you to go to Mexico just now.' To which he responded, 'I will do whatever I am asked.'

Such willingness to do what he was asked did not go down well with Mariano or with Doria. On the following day, Mariano went to see the Nuncio and asked him, 'Why did my Lord wish to interfere in our Father Gratian going to Mexico?' Mariano told him that it would be better for him to go because of the scandals, and that he spent a lot of time with the sisters, as well as spending all his time preaching. He went on to say that Jerome had let the Order become lax and that he enjoyed his food and drink as could be seen by his size…

The Nuncio responded to Mariano, 'If this man is as you say he is then surely it does not make sense to send him to Mexico. He suggested instead that Doria send him to Evora (Portugal), where the Archbishop, Teutonia de Braganza had asked for him. However, Doria ordered Gratian to go first to Seville, where he was to arrange his passage to Mexico. Then, before his ship left, he could fulfil the Nuncio's wishes by visiting the Archbishop in Evora.

It was around 6 May when Jerome left Madrid. While he was on his way to Seville, Doria called together the Vicar Provincials for a meeting, at the conclusion of which they pronounced the following sentence against Gratian:

> On the eleventh day of May, fifteen hundred and eighty-eight, being together at a Definitory meeting, the Reverend Fathers, Provincial and Definitors, wishing to decide on the matter of Father Jerome Gratian of the Mother of God, in view of his disobedience, abuse of jurisdiction and the

> many defects in his regular life as listed in the [juridical] process, as well as the abusive words he used in his statement, in which he called calumnious the charges made against him and said the witnesses were melancholic, malicious and false, going on to say that the Provincial is blind, lacks understanding and is prejudiced, but without offering any proof or giving a satisfactory explanation, before confessing to many of these charges which he calls calumnious...
>
> The Provincial and Councillors, having seen all the above, propose the following sentence: that Father Jerome Gratian agree to the request and charges made against him, that he be ordered to retire to a priory designated by Father Provincial, where he can take care of the good of his soul, as he himself has asked. He is to be deprived of active and passive voice in the Province and Congregation of our Order; that is to say, he cannot vote nor be elected to any position of the same, save in the priory where he is; only there has he his position and active voice with regard to the business of the priory. The privation of active and passive voice is to last until the Chapter of the Congregation of our Order, when it is to be returned if he is seen to be peaceful and quiet. They [Provincial and Defninitors] will remove him from the position of Vicar of the district of Mexico to which he was elected at our Chapter held in Valladolid... but he may keep his position to lead a group of Fathers who are to go to Mexico with the next fleet, because it would not be right to change the offices that His Majesty [King Philip] has taken an interest in...

The sentence was signed by Nicholas of Jesus & Mary, Provincial, and the Vicars: Elias of St Martin, Anthony of Jesus, Augustine of the Three Kings, John Baptist and also that of the Secretary, Gregory of the Holy Angels. However, Jerome was not to be told of this sentence. Why not? The idea was to tell him about it only when he was in Mexico, from where he could not appeal. Over there he would find himself deprived of his position as Vicar of Mexico and reduced to a simple friar. They also kept the decision quiet in order to produce it at the next Chapter when Jerome's supporters would ask for an explanation. They had the document that Jerome had signed declaring his desire to go willingly to Mexico.

Gratian arrived in Seville on 16 May. He went straight to the booking office to process his passage to Mexico. However, he found that the money given to the friars had already been allocated elsewhere. This did not trouble him unduly as he had a promissory note from the Treasury. And while awaiting financial assistance from Madrid and the ships were being prepared, he went to Evora.

Soon after he left Seville the General Chapter was convoked in Madrid for 18 June. (At the Chapter) he was ordered not to leave Seville unless it was to embark on a ship: an order written and signed by the Provincial together with his Definitors. 'The Chapter was quick,' recounted John Vazquez del Marmol, Secretary to the Nuncio, 'so that no one could complain that they had waited until he [Gratian] left Spain to call the Chapter, and also because they said the Pope might change his mind and later revoke the Brief.'

Mgr Teutonio de Braganza, Archbishop of Evora, welcomed Jerome with open arms. He knew of the order that he was not to leave Seville, but did not tell him. 'I had to keep this very secret from the Father, so that he did not go back and leave me', explained the Archbishop. Gratian, unaware of Doria's latest order, told Mgr Teutonio that the permission given him to be in Evora would expire at the end of May and that he would then have to return to Seville. The Archbishop remarked, 'The Nuncio wrote to me to say that you had to be here. Does your Provincial think that I and the Nuncio are naïve, that we must be taken in by these Genoan and Italian tricks, as you have been?'

The Archbishop and Gratian had first met a long time ago, maybe when they were in Salamanca, where Mgr Teutonio also knew Teresa. He was the son of the fourth Duke of Braganza. As a young man he entered the Jesuits and was then sent to Rome where St Ignatius of Loyola wanted to meet him. Ignatius questioned him and told him that he was destined 'to adorn the Church,' but did not let him continue in the Jesuits. In 1578 he was appointed Auxiliary Bishop to the Cardinal Prince, Henry, the Archbishop of Evora. That same year, Mgr Teutonia took on the role of Archbishop when the Cardinal handed over to him the reigns of the government of Portugal.

Archbishop Teutonio wanted Gratian in his diocese to resolve some problems he had with Illuminism: 'both men and women who were engaged in prayer with some indications that supernatural phenomena were involved.' The Bishop of Jaen had already entrusted our Carmelite with a similar mission. Mgr Teutonio wanted to make use of his gifts of discernment.

When the Discalced Carmelite friars from Portugal passed through Evora on their way to the Chapter in Madrid, they invited Gratian to accompany them. Still unaware of the order of May 11 (not to leave Seville) he excused himself, even though he had every right to go as Vicar Provincial of Mexico. When the friars had left he admitted to the Archbishop, 'My Lord, I always try to do everything in this life for the greater praise of God. I taught almost all the friars of our Province and gave them the habit; they are very fond of me. If I go to the Chapter, they will look to elect me. It could well be that there are those at the Chapter who believe it would be a service to God to elect Father Nicholas. If I was at the Chapter and there were divisions and factions among those blessed friars they would lose the simplicity and openness they now have. I think that it would serve God better to let them be, since they have not summoned me while inviting the others. Besides, I am happy to be released from such a great responsibility and not to lose this favour which God is granting me.'

Mgr Teutonio alerted the Nuncio that Doria did not intend to invite Gratian to the Chapter. The Nuncio, for his part, wanted him to be present. The Provincial (Doria) made the Nuncio aware of the document that Gratian had signed, in which he indicated that he saw his vocation and spirit to be missionary. The Nuncio was suspicious of what was behind the document and warned Doria. The latter crossed his arms under his scapular, responded to the Nuncio that if he wanted Gratian to come to the Chapter, he should compel him, at the very least, to observe the laws of the Discalced Carmelites. The Nuncio responded, 'I see that you are persecuting a saint, a man I consider to be very humble and, as such, he will obey your order and any other graver order that you give him.'

The Nuncio asked that he, himself, be allowed to dictate the order (to bring Gratian to the Chapter). Doria had dictated it to the Nuncio's Secretary, Barnabas del Marmol, who, coincidentally, was the brother-in-law of one of Gratian's sisters. The Nuncio noticed some harsh words in the said document and amended them; later telling his Secretary, 'I gave this order to keep the peace and in exchange for their calling him to the Chapter, although it will soon be revoked.' The Nuncio signed the formal document on 17 June (it was revoked thirteen days later) and told Doria that he did not need to see it. The Nuncio, like Gratian, was naïve.

The General Chapter of the new Congregation of the Discalced Carmelite friars began the following day, Saturday 18 June, in the priory of St Hermenegildo in Madrid. Gratian, being in Evora, was not there, and nor was Peter of the Purification, Prior of Genoa; he had been summoned late to ensure he would not arrive. Also absent was Christopher of St Albert, Prior of Caravaca, a close friend of Gratian and destined to go to Mexico; he was replaced at the Chapter by a staunch supporter of Doria.

Doria used every trick in the book, including irregular methods of election, to bring to the Chapter certain members of the Order who should not normally have been there. 'The Socii ... were not appointed in the ordinary way, but were somewhat insecure people, and for this reason, could more easily be manipulated. There were some who were very young and with little experience and with less time in the Order than the Constitutions decreed.' These were just some of the accusations levelled against Doria in the file 4515 in the Spanish National Historical Archives. In the same file it states that a young Discalced Carmelite, Thomas Aquinas, went around 'bribing the friars to vote for the Vicar.'

As predicted, Nicholas Doria was elected Vicar General of the new Congregation. However, in spite of his manipulation, there was a certain amount of opposition. Of the 58 votes, ('a much higher number than had been anticipated or that assembled afterwards') he obtained 32 votes. Before the election Doria exhorted the friars to elect the most worthy candidate, but expressly excluded Jerome Gratian, as he had been deprived of active and passive voice, arguing 'it would not be right to have a Provincial who is so lax.'

There were protests and heated debates concerning Jerome's absence. Those who protested wanted to know why he had been punished. The Prior of St Gabriel's and the Prior of Daimiel were expelled from the room. In order to restore calm Doria read the first draft of the document he had written; the one the Nuncio later amended:

> To you Father Gratian of the Mother of God, for as much as has come to our attention of some of the things that concern your person, of which it seemed to us right to remedy to avoid problems and their consequences.., we order that from here on you live a regular life with the observance that the other friars of your Province live; a life in common, [keeping to your] cell and cloister. Nor are you to deal with people outside the Order, nor write to anyone without permission from your Superiors... All of which it is right that you fulfil and each article in this document we order you to keep and fulfil in virtue of holy obedience and under penalty of excommunication...

'You see, the Nuncio thinks along the same lines as the Chapter,' remarked Doria. He then took out a large pile of documents and began to read from the time Jerome received the habit until the present day, adding, 'We find something new every day.' And yet, in spite of the imposed silence and the impact that resulted from the Nuncio's order, and the vitriolic denouncements against him, the results of the voting for the Vicar General of the new Congregation gave Doria only 55 per cent of the votes; i.e. he won with only a slender majority.

The Nuncio, Speziano, turned up at the end of the Chapter and asked why Fr Gratian had not been called. Doria replied that the Father wanted to go to Mexico, and showed the Nuncio the document Jerome had signed. However, Doria's intention (and the Nuncio was taken in again by Doria) was to make him his Socius in the same way that, years before, he had been Fr Gratian's Socius.

Speziano did not know that Jerome had been deprived of his right to vote: silence had been imposed in the Chapter regarding the situation of the accused. The Nuncio, believing everything had been put right, wrote a letter to our Carmelite dated 20 June: 'Those Fathers who came together at the Chapter have elected Father Nicholas as Vicar General. And he, for the good of the Order and to calm things that occurred in the past, has resolved to elect your Paternity as his Socius... For this reason the sooner you come the better.' On the same day, Doria sent Gratian a patent so he could travel.

Anne of Jesus, the Prioress of Madrid, when told that Gratian had been called to Madrid, was full of joy and wrote to the Prioress of Avila:

> Your Reverence will already be aware how God has blessed us, that we are all united under the government of our Father Vicar General, who has chosen for his companion Father Jerome Gratian, who will be the second person of our government, and as they must work together, everything will pass through his [Gratian's] hands; and so he will no longer be going to Mexico. Our Father Vicar General has arranged that he be contacted in Evora and asked to come immediately, as he does not want to do or say anything without him.

Four Definitors were appointed at the Chapter: John of the Cross, Augustine of the Three Kings, Anthony of Jesus and Elias of St Martin, and six Councillors: Anthony of Jesus, Ambrose Mariano, John of the Cross, John

Baptist el Rondenno, Louis of St Jerome and Bartholomew of Jesus who, at the end of the Chapter, just disappeared.

Bartholomew had been a friend of Jerome's, and was one of those who, when passing through Evora, had invited him to accompany them to the Chapter. He was elected sixth Councillor to the displeasure of Doria, who had Bartholomew ejected from the room when meeting privately with the six Councillors to discuss Batholomew's conduct during the visititation of Andalucia. Angered by Doria's attitude, Bartholomew left and the Vicar General, against all the rules, replaced him with Fr Gregory of the Holy Angels, a man as short of intelligence as he was faithful to the dictates of his boss.

This was the way that Doria's government, now called the *Consulta*, functioned: a government of seven friars. John of the Cross was among its members. When would John come down from the heights of Mount Carmel and become aware of the character of this sly Italian?

Jerome arrived in Madrid in mid-July. In spite of the summer's heat the atmosphere inside the priory of St Hermenegild was cold; no one said a word to him, no one took any notice of him, he was just ignored. Resigned to this, he told the Nuncio, 'In order to be the Socius, deprived of voice, I might as well be a lay brother.' On the first night he saw linen sheets on his bed. He asked the others what this meant. They told him that the Provincial had ordered them under obedience to do this.

However, Cardinal Albert wanted Gratian in Lisbon. When Philip II learned of the latter's arrival in Madrid, he urged him to return to Portugal. On 22 July, the King's Secretary, Cristopher de Moura, wrote to Doria informing him that the King wanted Gratian to return to the service of the Cardinal Archduke; this meant that Doria's plans to banish Gratian to Mexico were now, definitively, at an end.

Doria was not aware of any danger; he had been elected Vicar General of the new Order, he had six years ahead of him… he had enough time to finish Gratian off. In order not to upset the King, Doria signed a new patent on 26 July, that allowed Gratian to proceed to the city of Evora to await further instructions from His Majesty the King. 'This patent replaces the one that had been sent allowing you to come to Madrid to be my socius.'

When Gratian received the patent he got ready to leave once again for

Portugal. However, Doria did not give him a travelling companion or a mule. 'Since he is going into the service of his Majesty, the Order has no obligation to look after him. It is up to his Majesty or, the Nuncio, to give him a companion. He behaves like a layman, then he can look after himself like a layman.'

John of the Cross approached Brother John of St Albert who was in Madrid seeking justice against a sentence of expulsion from the Order; another macabre story of Doria's 'justice'. John told the Brother, 'Go with Gratian to Lisbon, and see how you get along together.'

John of St Albert wrote later, 'At the time I did not understand why he said this to me, because I didn't know that he was angry with the said Father, but as time went by I understood the malice with which he had said this.' He replied to John of the Cross, 'Why do I have to go Father? I suspect that when I arrive in Lisbon they will take the habit off me and, if that is the case, I would rather not go, they can take it from me here.' 'You will be all right, you have my word', replied John of the Cross, 'when you are far away the case against you will be forgotten.'

The Brother returned to Jerome ready to accompany him on his journey. However, when he told Jerome that he had received the order (only) from the third Councillor, he refused to to take the Brother. 'We shall both be lost; I for taking you and you for leaving without a patent from the Vicar General.'

The Nuncio was not happy with the decision to let Fr Gratian go without a companion. 'He was very annoyed,' Jerome said, and asked his Secretary, Barnabus del Marmol, to accompany him. The Secretary would use the visit to Portugal to find out about the situation in that Kingdom and, at the same time, about the things of which Gratian had been accused. The Nuncio's term of office would come to an end in August, when he would return to Rome, taking his secretary with him. In this way Gratian would be able to count on this man to defend him in the Roman Curia against the inferred offences.

Jerome Gratian and Barnabus del Marmol left Madrid on 26 July, the feast of St Anne, at two o'clock in the morning. That same morning, John of the Cross came across the lay brother, John of St Albert, and asked him, 'Why didn't you go with Father Gratian?' Brother John explained, 'neither he nor I dared [go together], since they did not give me a patent from the Vicar General.' Fr John of the Cross replied, 'That's not the reason, he is someone who is very much above himself, but he will not get anywhere with this attitude.'

Jerome and Barnabus had hardly left when Doria and Mariano arrived at the Escorial, where they told the King and his ministers that Gratian had gone to Lisbon because a nun wanted him to be with her: they were referring to Mary of St Joseph, Prioress of the convent of St Albert, Lisbon. This slanderous remark did not come from the ordinary friars of the Discalced Carmelite Order but rather from the very top. The slander was overheard by others…

Jerome had undertaken a lot of travelling in the space of a few months: from Jaen to Madrid, from Madrid to Seville, from Seville to Evora, back to Madrid and again from Madrid to Portugal. In the meantime the imperial politics of King Philip II were moving under the same ominous shadows as this ill fated year.

The 'Great Armada', that has ironically gone down in history as the 'Invincible Armada', weighed anchor in Lisbon on 30 May, determined to invade England. The execution of Mary, Queen of Scots, the 'martyr Queen', in February 1587, was the determining factor that drove Philip II to invade the island. The inexperienced Duke of Medina-Sidonia took charge of the fleet because of the death of Alvaro de Bazan, Marquis of Santa Cruz, a friend of Gratian. The storms and the attacks from Howard and Drake

Portrait of the Cardinal Archduke Albert, *by Rubens. The Prado Museum, Madrid.*

turned that venture into a disaster with the loss of half the fleet. The phrase, attributed to King Philip II when he learned of the disaster while praying in the choir of the Escorial, is proverbial, 'I sent my ships to fight against men, not against the elements.'

Gratian had returned to Portugal at the end of September with a patent to do whatever Cardinal Albert requested. He found himself in Evora when he received three letters from the Cardinal asking him to come to Lisbon, where a delicate task awaited him.

Having no idea of what lay ahead when he arrived there at the end of September he discovered that he had been given the responsibility of Apostolic Visitator of the Discalced Carmelite nuns in Portugal.

For some time he tried to free himself from this awkward task that he had been given by the Cardinal and King Philip II. There was a rumour among the Spanish soldiers that the friars had an arsenal of weapons in a Carmelite house. The Prior of this house, Fr Anthony Calderon, had been abducted as a supporter of Don Anthony, the Prior of Ocrato, and Pretender to the Portuguese throne, and been taken to the castle of San Gian.

Jerome began his Visitation in the middle of January 1589. However, before the previous year ended, which we have called 'eventful', he had received new blows from Doria. The latter, it seemed, had lost none of his obsession to undermine Gratian.

On 15 August, before he reached Lisbon, Doria had sent a letter to Mary of St Joseph, Prioress of St Albert's, in which he ordered her to have nothing to do with Gratian. 'In the judgement of our *Consulta* it seemed right to give you the following order: that neither you, nor anyone else, are to write, talk or have anything to do with Father Jerome Gratian, nor receive letters from him, nor are you to become involved in any business concerning him.' This is all to be, 'under pain of excommunication, *latae sentenciae*; for which you will be held accountable.'

When Mary of St Joseph received this order from Fr Gregory Nazianzen, the Provincial of Portugal, she later acknowledged, 'I was astonished!'

This Fr Gregory was another Judas Iscariot who had been bribed by Doria. He was received into the Order and professed by Jerome in Beas. He had accompanied Teresa and Mary of St Joseph to Seville in 1575. Now he played Doria's game and, very subtly stirred up trouble in Lisbon against Jerome and Mary of St Joseph. Fr Peter of the Purification, who was in Genoa, would later write (13 March 1589) in a letter defending Jerome: 'Above all I feel that his sons, whom he raised, nurtured and taught, fail to tell the truth for reasons of personal gain, and avoid what is right. Oh, Father Gregory, if I could write down what is in my heart, what wouldn't I tell you!'

This Fr Gregory harassed Mary of St Joseph with impertinent letters to extract some secret from her that would compromise Gratian. 'Manifesting that he was my friend, pretending to be upset, he wrote me very long letters, telling me that people were saying this and that about me.'

What exactly were they saying? 'That I have disturbed this country with letters trying to entice Fr Gratian to come here.' 'That there is a deep disordered friendship between myself and the Father'... They also sent her a document with the foulest of questions, such that 'are not to be put down on paper, nor should chaste ears hear.'

> They have tried in every possible way to get me to lose my good name, though I know well they are not doing this to get at me. It's impossible to say how many tricks and inventions they have thought up in order to get me to admit that this Father has done something wrong, or that he said or did something that was damaging to the Order. I can really and truly say that they have tormented me for more than three years, sometimes with a stick, sometimes with a carrot. However, I place my hope in the Lord that neither one nor the other will make me deviate from the truth.

As they could not catch her out or make her sign a letter, 'as they had caught out the other saintly and sincere Father' (Mary of St Joseph was alluding to Gratian) they imposed on her the order to stay away from him. When Gregory Nazianzen presented her with this order, she wrote on the same piece of paper: 'I have been notified of this order, which I will in all humility and with my all heart obey, as I understand that it is the will of my Superiors, not because I have requested it. I have asked nothing for myself, since there is nothing on my conscience that should cause me to be given such an order.' She then signed it.

However, the slanders did not end there. Doria and his Councillors came to the General Chapter in Madrid, and began a visitation of the houses. In each house they read out the process they had begun against Jerome, and the faults for which he had been deprived of active and passive voice. Carmel was disturbed by all this. Many naïve souls were taken in by the scandal not knowing what to think. The Chronicler could not disguise the anxieties felt by the Order: 'A terrible storm blew up with this new government that all of a sudden disturbed the calm waters of the Order. Friars and nuns discussed among themselves this state of affairs. The voices of upset friars and nuns could be heard complaining; in the classrooms, during recreation, in face-to-face conversations, in the most humble offices.' Those in Lisbon, who knew Mary of St Joseph and Fr Gratian, disclosed that their unbecoming relationship had taken place in Seville. In Seville they stated that it had taken place in Portugal.

Doria's obsession was nothing less than to finish him off. However, Gratian would escape from him once again. Cardinal Albert, Viceroy of Portugal, had appointed him Vicar Apostolic of the Carmelites in Portugal which meant that he would reside in Lisbon for a period of more than two years.

Chapter Twenty-One

Apostolic Visitator of the Carmelites in Portugal

No sooner had Jerome arrived in Lisbon than he was embroiled in a case involving the Inquisition and the Prioress of the Annunciation convent, Mary of the Annunciation; a nun who claimed to have the stigmata. Her trial began on 9 August. She was very thin, pleasant and pious. She had been elected Prioress of the Dominican convent of the Annunciation in Lisbon in 1583, at the age of 32. A year later, on the feast of St Thomas Aquinas, the wounds of the Lord appeared on her body. Every Friday red stains that looked like blood were seen on her hands, feet and side. On Thursdays, while saying the Hail Mary, she felt the pains of the crown of thorns on her head. It was even said that she levitated and a mysterious light shone from her body.

For four years people were taken in by this inveterate liar, even the Dominicans were taken in by her. Fr Luis de Granada, such a venerable mystic, wrote about the marvels of the nun with the stigmata to St Charles Borromeo, Archbishop of Milan and to St John de Ribera, Archbishop of Valencia. Fr Luis, after looking at the wounds of Sister Mary, could be forgiven because of his advanced age. However, when Mary of St Joseph first came to Lisbon and lived with her, she was not deceived. Nor when St John of the Cross came to the Provincial Chapter in Lisbon in 1585 was he deceived. Fr Augustine of the Three Kings, another Chapter member and Provincial of Seville, invited him to come with him on a visit to the nun with the wounds, whom, they said, produced many miracles. John of the Cross told him, 'Why should I go to see something deceitful? Stay quiet and you will see how the Lord will reveal all.' Nor was Jerome Gratian fooled.

Jerome saw that his life was in danger from the followers of Don Anthony, the Prior of Ocrato (the Pretender to the Portuguese throne: who saw Sr Mary as a patriot), when they got hold of a letter he had written to Sr Mary of the Annunciation, in which he advised her 'to be careful about some things that people were saying about you, that you should know what is going on.'

In order to satisfy Cyril's curiosity (about the threat to his life), Anastasius told him:

> It's a long story. Suffice to say that because I revealed to Cardinal Albert certain secret things upon which depended the peacefulness of that Kingdom and which would prevent the Lutherans from entering it, and taking responsibility of matters concerning the Prioress with the stigmata, I was forced to flee at night and take a roundabout path to Castile so as to avoid being killed by the followers of Don Anthony. Having escaped I gave a report to the King at the Escorial Palace, where he asked me through Don Christopher de Mora (after having given him a full account of what was happening in that Kingdom) if it seemed a good idea for the Inquisition to take charge of establishing whether these wounds were authentic or not. I replied that the matter was not canonically contrary to faith but rather to the Bishop, but I considered it right for the Inquisition to intervene, given that it was so serious and unusual, and there was the fear that Lutherans could enter the country and damage the faith. The King ordered my Superiors to let me go to Lisbon as soon as possible. I returned and, shortly after my arrival the wounds were discovered to be false…

At the trial by the Inquisition, initiated by Cardinal Albert, fifty-nine witnesses gave evidence, the vast majority were against the nun. In the middle of October, Sr Mary of the Visitation was the last to be questioned, and refused to confess. However, a bowl full of hot water, a bar of soap and a piece of cloth made the 'wounds' disappear. Faced with this evidence the nun confessed; thus ended the fabrication that had half of Christianity under her spell. She did it, she admitted, for vain reasons, because she had been taken for a saint. Once her hands had been washed the tribunal had no need to continue with the washing of her feet and side.

On 8 December, in Lisbon Cathedral packed with members of the public, the sentence was read out: the nun was to be banished to another convent. Cardinal Albert apologized to Rome. The Roman Curia showed its displeasure by replacing the Nuncio and deposing the Dominican General. Fr Luis de Granada died days later on 31 December, perhaps from such an upset: he had just written a book entitled *A Sermon on Fallen Public Figures*.

The devotees of the Prioress and the followers of Don Anthony, who had held her up as a herald of messianic patriotism, said 'that a demon in a Carmelite habit had brought some powder that King Philip had given him, with which he had made the wounds disappear, wounds that our Lord God had sent as a gift from heaven to his holy Prioress.'

'Then I was persecuted for a second time, Jerome recounted, but as the Inquisition was involved and Cardinal Albert supported me, I was not too anxious.'

Gratian arrived in Lisbon on the feast of St Michael, 29 September. He had come from Evora, where Mgr Teutonio had welcomed him into his palace. The Archbishop had written to the Court and spoke highly of the virtues of this friar and friend: 'He has been a great servant of the Lord during the time he spent with me. He preached every holy day, and often twice in the main church as elsewhere. The local dignitaries flock to see and hear him, and his preaching has borne much fruit in them. As a result we have seen many people receiving the sacraments, giving good example and amending their lives. Those whom we thought of as suspicious in the Archdiocese, have resolved their own problems and accepted that, as the Father said, all their revelations were pure figments of their imagination. He taught them well and now they are great servants of Our Lord.'

Mgr Teutonio would always remain a great defender of the goodness of this Carmelite friar, as would the Cardinal, Albert of Austria, who recalled him to Lisbon.

The day after Jerome arrived he had a meeting with the Viceroy. The latter gave him his orders that he reluctantly accepted, which were to carry out an Apostolic Visitation of the Calced Carmelites. The General, Pedro Enriquez de Azevedo, the Count of Fuentes, and Judge by royal appointment, also hoped that Jerome would continue the apostolic ministry he had begun in Lisbon before he had had to leave for Madrid.

Gratian asked Nicholas Doria in a letter dated 1 October: 'I have been asked to deal with soldiers and prisoners, not to mention other matters of the King, concerning his castles and hospitals.' He informed Doria that he had come to this Portuguese Kingdom 'with a patent from your Reverence to do what Cardinal Albert ordered me to do.' As his new ministry would be incompatible with some laws and mandates of the *Consulta*, he wrote, 'I would like to do the right thing in every way, and to obey as sincerely and perfectly as I can.'

In spite of his willingness and desire to keep his Vicar General informed, and also to seek his approval for what Cardinal Albert had asked him to do, Doria remained silent. He did not respond to any of Jerome's insistent letters. However, he did manage to say, eventually, that he should do whatever the Cardinal ordered him. Thus, after three months of persistent efforts and with the consent of his Vicar General, Jerome accepted the task given him by the Cardinal: to be Apostolic Visitator of the Portuguese Calced Carmelites. He would say, 'I have been given the task of a Superior of the Portuguese Calced Carmelites, having experienced the ascerbic nature of the Andalucians.'

The role that he had been given gave him independence from Doria, since he was now under a higher authority. However, it did not make his relationship easy with the Discalced Carmelite nuns in Lisbon nor with Doria and the *Consulta*. We have already seen how Doria had hurriedly sent an order to Mary of St Joseph, before he arrived in Lisbon, to forbid her from having any communication with Jerome.

In that letter Doria accused the Prioress of having encouraged the Cardinal to ask Gratian to come to Lisbon. He wrote that the reasons for this were shameful and which he would be disclosing later; for example, that Jerome had had at least three children with Mary of St Joseph!

In the Discalced Carmelite priory of St Philip, Doria had spies who would regularly inform him of every move Jerome made. 'The Fathers here told many lies about me, for example, that I had been condemned by the Nuncio, Speziano, that I was in Portugal without permission from the Order, that I behaved scandalously with nuns, and other things of this nature.' It was his fate never to be free from calumnies, nor from Doria's evil intentions, as the latter continued to seek his downfall.

Doria had been to Seville where he visited the priory of Los Remedios. He took every opportunity to speak badly about Jerome to each member of the community, including novices. On one particular occasion a friar stood up and said to Doria, 'Father, look at the way you are treating Father Gratian. We all know him here and know he is a good man; do not dishonour him.'

Doria bit his tongue and from then on did not mention Gratian's name again. Fr John of St Joseph, who had stood up to him, ended his account with this exclamation, 'Let's see where this disgraceful and wicked behavior will end up; this is not the end of it. The Lord will remedy everything as only He can.'

While he went around visiting the houses of Andalucia, Doria had left John of the Cross in charge of the *Consulta*, which was based in Segovia. In his naiveté John supported the Vicar General. When, later, the holy mystic became aware of Doria's deceitfulness, it was all too late. However, thank God he did not tarnish his reputation in support of a wretched Vicar General, who endeavoured to use the Saint's guilelessness as an instrument to cover up the deeds of a shameful dictatorial regime.

There is one testimony we should not overlook, which comes from an account by John of St Albert, the lay brother whom Jerome did not want to take with him on his journey to Lisbon some months earlier. The Brother was in Segovia, in the same location as the *Consulta*. It was the day before or after the feast of St Francis of Assisi, 4 October, in 1588; he did not remember the exact day. That night the lay brother discovered 'how angry they were with Fr Jerome.' While the friars were in the choir reciting compline he entered Fr Anthony of Jesus' cell to tidy it up. Just then he heard raised voices coming from the meeting of the *Consulta*. Brother John of St Albert went closer to listen. They were talking about Gratian, who had asked for permission to accept a role given him by Cardinal Albert. Brother John heard, 'The devil has dressed himself in this man's clothing in order to destroy our Order. If we do not give him the permission he asks for he will assuredly complain to the Prince Cardinal who will think badly of us, and so will his Majesty.'

Brother John could distinguish the voice of Fr Gregory of the Holy Angels, who apparently said, or rather shouted, 'Fathers, let's get rid of this man once and for all, which is something we should have done a long time ago. Do not give him permission, instead let us complain about him to the Cardinal, then this will come to the attention of his Majesty. When the Cardinal asks us why we refused to obey his Majesty we can reveal all, showing his Majesty all the legal processes against this Father. Let us tell him [the Cardinal] that in order to serve his Majesty we have concealed a lot about the said Father, and so as not to allow him to carry on in this way we do not want to give him the permission he is asking for. With this [argument] and we can quote the Constitutions that state that no member should seek favours from people in authority, we have enough power in our hands and evidence to throw him out of the Congregation or to lock him up from where he will never again emerge.'

John of the Cross stated, while substituting for Doria at a Discalced Carmelite Council meeting:

> It would be better that we advise him [Doria] to personally request this dispensation [to allow Gratian to be Visitator of the Calced in Portugal] from the Cardinal, in his position as Vicar General of the Order. With the excuse that Fr Vicar is absent, our Council will not grant the permission and in that way we will remain in His Excellency's good graces. If he [Gratian] should make use of his office [as Visitator appointed by the Nuncio and Cardinal], the Council may then proceed against him, if this seems appropriate. If his Excellency confirms the appointment, we can appear to agree, thus safeguarding ourselves in the whole affair and protecting ourselves on all fronts. However, we must maintain our opposition to this shabby way of asking our permission.
>
> This is not the way a subject should make a request, rather it appears he is commanding us as our superior – making the request public and asking for confirmation that we have been notified, as though undertaking a legal action, something he cannot take against anybody without our permission, least of all against ourselves. Moreover, he is endeavouring to compel and force us, his superiors, by constraint or through fear of him, to legislate for something that would undermine our laws.
>
> All this should be carefully recorded, and in order to come to the most favourable conclusion he should be ordered to present himself here and inform us of what exactly the King or Nuncio wants of him – which might all turn out to be his own fabrication! We will then try to grant him his freedom, even to the extreme of expelling him [from the Order] which seems to be what he really wants and is looking for. It would be better to lose him than he ruin ourselves and the whole Order, which he loves very little and could end with him if we don't curtail his steps.

Strong words from Fr John of the Cross. The little Brother John of St Albert continued with his precise account:

> I don't know how I could have remembered this report, and many other things that I have forgotten, of what Fr John of the Cross said if I had not noted them down.

Brother John of St Albert remembered some more things. Two months later, in the middle of December, around the feast of St Lucy, two Calced Carmelites, who had come from Avila to be ordained by the Bishop of

Segovia, were put up in the Discalced Carmelite Priory. During recreation that evening, John of the Cross asked them what they thought of Fr Gratian's Visitation to the Calced Carmelites in Portugal. The two replied, discreetly, that it was not their concern what happened in another Kingdom.

However, John of the Cross insisted, 'It was done very badly and cannot be lauded. He obtained it by his own hand and manipulation. He managed to achieve it despite the caution of the Council and without our understanding. He neither had the Council's good-will or permission for it and this cannot be tolerated. Our Fr Vicar General is in Madrid insisting that the Council resist and block this Visitation in every way possible. I have a letter of his [the Vicar General] in which he states how he had informed him [Fr Gratian] about how he had punished him, he and the Council, by depriving him of office for his faults. Because of this punishment, our Council can, among other things, block the execution of this Visitation, given that he accepted that role without the permission of the Council.'

John of the Cross stated at the Council meeting later that evening: 'Don't think that those were just throwaway remarks of mine at recreation. They were quite deliberate so that those Fathers [of the Community] would understand that we could not defend Fr Gratian but had to contradict him in advance. They themselves will not be afraid to resist him now and will see that it is good to embarrass him seeing that he has kindled a fire that endangers so many others. The more distanced he is from us who might have helped him, so much greater will be his exposure and the greater the war we must wage against him. We must not grant his request; that we give him permission to accept or continue this Visitation. It is down to him either to continue or to abandon this task. He cannot look to us to decide what he should do. Let us wait and see how the whole affair turns out.'

These words were spoken by John of the Cross in Segovia, in the heat of the sessions of the Council. They were harsh and betrayed an erroneous attitude towards Gratian, which is not found in the standard biographies, except in the work by Father Donazar, who wrote that 'John of the Cross's discourse on Father Gratian is very harsh, almost cruel… One could say that it smacks of the malice of Father Doria.'

It would not be long before John of the Cross finally became aware of the game he had, unwittingly, been part of. Nor would it be long, once he had distanced himself from the government of the Council, that he would also be hated and scorned by Doria and his supporters. John became a reactionary. Doria and the others denounced his friendship in Segovia with Anna de

Penalosa and her niece Ines del Mercado. They poked fun at him and began a slanderous legal process… Ambrose Mariano mocked his venerable bald head: 'Father John, he said, you have a pumpkin for a head; when is it going to ripen?' John of the Cross replied, 'It will ripen in God's good time and not before, even though it remains unripe until I die.'

Jerome began his task as Visitator at the Carmelite Priory in Lisbon. This priory, in the city centre, prided itself on its ancient history and its founder, Nuno Alvares Pereira (1360-1431), who was the overall commander of the Portuguese army that defeated the Spanish at the battle of Aljubarrota (14 August 1385). At the time of his [Jerome's] visit to Lisbon, there was a rumour that a revolt (against the Spanish army) had been planned in the Carmel on Christmas Eve, and that six thousand muskets had been hidden inside the walls, which were to be handed to the people when the English arrived.

The people expected the English to arrive because Don Antonio, the Prior of Ocrato, had sought help from Queen Elizabeth in the form of a pact that promised submission to England, in return for annual payment of 300,000 *ducados*, and the opening up of trade routes between the British and the Portuguese Indies (Brazil). The Queen of England had thought it would be easy to take Portugal; the English fleet was assembled in the English port of Plymouth. The Prior of Ocrato counted on the local people rising up against the Spanish army that was laying siege to Lisbon. The Spanish were suspicious of the Carmelites, in fact, the guns from the castle were trained on the Priory and every night companies of Spanish soldiers patrolled it, watching out for any suspect activity.

Jerome had a difficult mission. He was a simple friar who entered into the Priory with no other intention than reforming it. However, Philip II, who was far away in the Escorial Palace, and Cardinal Albert of Austria, urged him to perform a special, political mission: to find out what was happening inside the Priory? Was there an arsenal of muskets? Was the source of the rebellion by the people based on the hope that the English would come?

There were Spaniards who, fearing for Gratian's life, advised him not to enter the Priory without a detachment of soldiers. However, he dared to cross the threshold. With his companion, Fr Baptist of the Trinity, who was his Secretary, he entered on 10 January 1589. He presented his credentials and, at a Chapter meeting, accepted the obedience of the friars. 'Everyone did what they were asked to do, without any dissent,' he wrote to Cardinal Albert, 'and so that your Highness will be sure of this, I ordered them to sign their names; I, and my companion, also signed the document which has been sent to your Highness.'

'I ate, slept and stayed with them for a long time,' said Jerome. The priory contained about one hundred friars, about forty of them novices. He took a cell next to the novitiate. The fact that he was a Spanish Visitator could have created a certain prejudice, but he need not have worried. He discovered that the rumour about the muskets was false. Those friars who were more restless and supporters of Don Anthony he moved to other priories where he gave them respectable positions, and so, in this way he carried on with the Reform in peace.

However the English came. On 13 April an English fleet of one hundred and twenty ships set sail from Plymouth, under the command of Francis Drake, who transported 20,000 men led by John Norris. On 4 May they sighted La Coruna and attacked it. A breach was opened in the old city, the English standard bearer climbed up to the highest point of the walls, his flag in hand. However, Mary Pita, a heroine in the defence of the city, shot the man. The English soldiers were demoralized and retreated to their ships. Mary Pita, who had been married four times, when widowed for the last time received from King Philip II for her heroic actions the pension of a standard-bearer plus five *escudos* every month and permission to export mules from Spain to Portugal.

After the attack on La Coruna, the English fleet sighted the coast near Lisbon on 26 May, where the Prior of Ocrato was to be found. The English disembarked in the southern bank of the bay of Peniche. When, in a field near Lisbon, it seemed that the battle was about to begin, the Spanish army retreated and took refuge behind the walls of the city. Jerome made his way to the battlefield, 'to hear the confessions of the soldiers. The Cardinal did not believe that any Portuguese would go to confession.' Jerome saw panic sweep through the (Spanish) army: 'it made my nerves shrink and my throat tighten.'

What Jerome did during this battle was interesting. The Discalced Carmelites of St Philip's Priory, located outside the walls and near the sea, were put up in the Priory belonging to the Calced (for their safety). The Discalced Carmelite nuns of St Albert's convent, who had made a vow not to leave the cloister, and were ready to die for the faith at the hands of the heretical enemy, were persuaded by Jerome to leave for their own safety. He led them to the castle of St George; 'It was an edifying sight to see the Sisters processing behind a big crucifix, carrying crosses in their hands, their veils over their faces and accompanied by the Discalced and Calced friars and a troop of bodyguards; it raised the morale of the soldiers as they passed by.'

Francis Drake.
Anonymous portrait. The National Portrait Gallery, London.

Jerome also went looking for the Bernardines de Odivelas, who were a mile and a half outside Lisbon and just half a mile from where the English army was camped. Some nuns stayed behind 'waiting for Don Antonio with some food and drink as though he were their King, being his supporters.' Jerome brought inside the city the 'Philipine' nuns, (supporters of King Philip II) not without grave risk; his friends told him off him for doing this. However, as he admitted, 'My zeal to prevent these brides of Christ from being violated by the Lutherans spurred me on.'

On 1 June, the feast of Corpus Christi, there was no procession. The English, seeing that there would be no battle in Alcantara, seized the outskirts of Lisbon and lay siege to the city. The Priories of St Philip and St Albert and other churches outside the city walls were requisitioned by the English to accommodate their soldiers. Jerome wrote later:

> The enemy remained three days outside the walls of Lisbon. My life at this

time was to go at night time to my Carmelite priory where one hundred Calced Carmelite friars were shut up in an upstairs dormitory, because all the rest of the house and chapel, the cells and offices were full of lay men and women, more than two thousand, who had taken refuge there with their household goods. I was tormented to see these poor people suffering from hunger and misfortune, because in their fear they did not think to bring any food, so we had to help them lest they perished. During the day, I and my Discalced confreres heard the confessions of the soldiers.

On the third day, when it seemed the enemy would enter and all would be lost, my Portuguese Calced Carmelites were afraid and left the dormitory without taking any notice of what I told them. When I saw this, I asked a group of up to fifty Portuguese musketeers to go to the upper dormitory and ask the women, who were relatives of the friars, to leave. I told the soldiers, in Portuguese, to take the shot from their muskets, so that they were more or less unarmed. My Portuguese words really caught their attention and they gaped at me for a long while, repeating them in front of me.

There was so much to do. There was the constant danger of death and so little time to sleep. I confronted those arrogant Portuguese soldiers without any fear; they had invaded the convent to fight (God only knows what they intended to do) but this was the greatest danger we encountered. Although there were more than 8,000 armed Portuguese, they all simply disappeared, leaving only the Spanish on the field. The Portuguese captains themselves admitted that when their soldiers saw that the English were prevailing they started to actually assist them and slaughtered their own people. It turned out that we clearly had 30,000 English enemies. Of the 80,000 Portuguese who were enlisted for the war, we had no idea where 8,000 of these armed men were.

At this time it would have been so easy for one of them to stab me; as I had sworn at them to get out of the Priory. The same Spanish soldiers reprimanded me for daring to climb over the roofs at night with a burning torch to get to my Priory to protect it. I could easily have been shot. However, to tell the truth, at such a time when a man decides to die, he sees no danger.

Francis Drake was with his ships in Cascaes. After a three-day siege with much fighting and many wounded he ordered a ceasefire. He had put his faith in the promise of the Prior of Ocrato: that in reaching the walls of

Lisbon the gates would be opened and his soldiers would be rewarded with eight times their wages, but this never materialized. Drake was not really interested in Lisbon; he was, however, more interested in not losing his fleet.

> He was missing many soldiers, some, though few, killed at the hands of the Spanish, but many more of them by the hand of God when they were struck down by a sudden illness. This was caused when many of them, hungry and tired, left their ships and sought to fill their stomachs with Portuguese marmalade. On the outskirts of the city they came across a place that made soap, the kind they used in that place, it was soft and gooey and looked just like marmalade. It made them very thirsty but the combination of soap and water gave them diarrhea and a fever. Many of them died within a day and others were so ill they could not fight.

On Monday morning, 5 June, the enemy retreated. Cardinal Alberto asked Jerome to go out with a company of soldiers and identify the dead.

> As I went out I saw the dead, it was a terrible sight. There were more than three hundred Spaniards, whose bodies we turned over, with their faces up, and we crossed their arms to show that they were Catholics. There were more than eight hundred Lutherans, whose bodies we turned face down, facing hell, where their souls were burning. Their bodies would be burnt.

The siege had ended and peace returned to Lisbon. 'Though not for me, lamented Gratian, for whom new wars were only just beginning.'

There was a war going on against Jerome Gratian in Madrid, where Doria and Mariano continued to undermine him. In the Royal Court they (Doria and Mariano) had won over Garcia de Loaysa, Almoner and Chaplain to King Philip II and Tutor to Prince Philip, and with him they had also won over the King, who liked to hear of observance, obedience and strictness among the Religious Orders. Doria knew exactly how to sell his style of leadership. He and Mariano had called Fr Carranza, a Carmelite of the Ancient Observance, to come from Valencia in order to turn him against Jerome: Fr Carranza had been appointed by the General of the Order as Apostolic Visitator of the Spanish and Portuguese Provinces. Doria and

Mariano told him about all the malicious rumours levelled against our man, who was at that time in Portugal as Apostolic Visitator. Consequently, he was outside the Order's jurisdiction. Jerome had been judged critically by the Nuncio, Sega, when he visited Andalucia and was deprived of his voice by the Discalced Superiors, who claimed that his attitude was upsetting the observance of the Discalced Carmelites... In a paper that Gratian wrote we read:

> On Sunday evening [12 March 1589] his Highness [Cardinal Albert] requested to see me. He began by asking me how the Visitation was going and we spoke at great length. He then told me that I should continue with this and because he would support me come what may, I should have no fear of anything or anyone. The day before I had received a letter informing me that Frs Mariano and Carranza had spoken to the King in order to stop it [the Visitation]; and without doubt they must have sent something there [Portugal]. I do not know how much further this charade can continue, everyone understands that it is coming from the very opposite attitude to the one they ought to have. Thus, the Calced Carmelites say they are writing to express their concerns, and that this is because Fr Mariano is jealous.

There was an exchange of letters between Carranza and Jerome. The former told him that he should step down as Visitator of the Carmelites in Portugal; that it was, by right, his concern (Carranza was Vicar General of Portugal). Jerome replied that he was willing to step down if ordered to by the rightful authorities, and that his conscience was untroubled. It had not occurred to him to offer such resistance but 'if anything needed to be negotiated then it was up to the Cardinal to do so, whom as Legate, *a latere*, I hold in the place of God.'

Gratian felt uneasy and asked Cardinal Albert to release him from the Visitation, but the latter ordered him 'to carry on and not worry about anything.' Gratian wrote to Carranza: 'Blessed be God who one day will show us that place where all hearts will understand and come to know the whole truth, since this is now hidden from us. There you will know that I am a true son of your Paternity and so, like many in the Order, desire your wellbeing.'

When Carranza arrived in Lisbon Jerome met him in the Carmelite priory and gave him 'the respect that the General of the Order usually receives.' Shortly after he arrived Carranza fell ill and almost died. Jerome kept vigil at his bedside and when he recovered gave him an account of his Visitation and handed over all his paperwork. Gratian had wanted to return to his Discalced Priory to let Carranza finish the Visitation he [Jerome] had started. However, Cardinal Albert did not agree to this. The two friars ended up by carrying out the Visitation of the Calced Carmelites in Portugal, in complete harmony, 'and when the Visitation was ended, Carranza rushed to Aragon when Antony Perez had begun his revolt, and I returned to my Discalced Carmelites in peace and quiet; though this was like the quiet of a screaming child who takes in breath before screaming again.'

By December 1588, Barnabus of Marmol, who was told by the Nuncio, Speziano, to accompany Jerome Gratian to Evora and Lisbon, had returned to Madrid. There he found out how Doria had so secretly and cunningly used the Decree of the Nuncio against Gratian. It was a Decree that Speziano would regret signing; in fact, fifteen days after he had signed it he annulled it and forbade Doria to apply it. The latter informed the priories and convents that Gratian had been punished by the Nuncio; that the only reason he had not been sentenced was because he enjoyed the protection of his Highness, the Cardinal, and, that he had gone to Portugal without any permission from the Order.

There were many letters written by different people involved in this messy affair but it would be too much to quote all of them. While Jerome continued his Visitation to the Calced Carmelites in Lisbon the level of persecution against him gradually increased, without any end in sight. He kept patient and suffered in silence but, in the end, he lost the battle.

A lay brother, who lived with him in Lisbon, heard him cry out when the mail arrived from the Royal Court, 'Praise God, there is no shortage of slanders from Madrid!' Fr Luis de Leon, now well on in years, encouraged Jerome to defend himself. The famous Augustinian had himself been the victim of jealousy and slander and, as a result, had been locked up in an Inquisition's cell for five years. He told Jerome that as 'head of the Order he had made it grow.' So why did he now want to go to Mexico? Gratian had once again resurrected a plan to flee to Mexico and desist from defending himself.

Fr Luis de Leon, in Salamanca, wrote to John Vazquez del Marmol, the brother of Barnabus, who was also a priest, and who defended our

Carmelite's interests in Madrid. When the Augustinian friar (Luis de Leon) heard Jerome argue that in his absence others would stand up to defend the Order, he exclaimed, 'he must be joking!' 'If they don't dare stand up now when they are well armed and have a Captain [Gratian] in their midst, do you think they will stand up when they are not armed and their leader is no longer with them, when those others [Doria and his followers] remain as absolute rulers?'

Fr Luis de Leon had just published the works of St Teresa. Thanks to Anne of Jesus, to whom he would dedicate his *Commentary on the Book of Job*, Luis was well aware of the difficulties of the Discalced Carmelites. He had no doubt that 'the Tower of Babel had to collapse', referring to the *Consulta*, 'because it is of human origin and founded on very mean principles. I would already like to see the end of it and help him in any way I can.' Clearly Fr Luis believed that Gratian should defend himself for the good of the Order; that if this government of the friars should triumph it would destroy fraternal charity, simplicity and openness which are the most important virtues, and the Order would decline. Fr Luis de Leon exclaimed, 'Another Teresa would have to rise up to reform it.'

Barnabus de Marmol accompanied the Nuncio, Speziano, to Rome after Speziano had completed his mission in Spain. In March 1589 they arrived in Genoa where they told Fr Peter of the Purification, Prior of the Discalced Carmelites (in Genoa) about Jerome's misfortunes. Fr Peter was outraged and wrote a stinging rebuke to Gregory Nazianzen, the Provincial of the Discalced Carmelites in Portugal. He accused him of being on the side of those who persecute the just, and he found it very hard to accept (this situation) given how well Fr Gregory knew Fr Jerome. Remember that he had received him into the Order in Beas, but now Gregory was a cunning enemy who hid his real intentions. However, Peter of the Purification unmasked him and blamed him in part for the 'tricks, lies and wickedness' against 'my Father Gratian, who has been an honour to the Order, and an example of virtue and goodness… And they are suggesting that he is a gourmand, a drunkard, is voracious and dissolute; that this is what he is like with lay people; besides this, they said he complains to the laity, and that all this comes from a diabolical ambition!'

> The worst of all is that with their odious words they question the honesty, purity and honour of his person, and drag that angel [Mary of St Joseph] into it, to bring her down. Oh infernal mouths and incarnate demons, from

> whom I constantly sense such great wickedness! Are you not aware who he is? What kind of person he was as a layman and how he has lived as a Religious? I have been his travelling companion on journeys to houses of our friars and nuns, I have had dealings with him in secret and in the open, inside the confessional and outside the confessional, and I did not find anything to criticize but on the contrary, I found much goodness (if goodness is to be criticized). I weep for him and shall continue to weep for him as one who has benefitted from his company and his teaching, and if I can I shall end my life in his holy company.

Fr Peter concluded his letter:

> And finally, they told me to my face that all this intrigue was carried out by your Reverences with the goal of getting rid of Fr Gratian in order for your Reverences to better your own positions.

This letter from Fr Peter written in March 1589 crossed with one Doria had written to him. Doria knew that the Nuncio, Speziano and Barnabus del Marmol, would pass through Genoa, or had already passed through, and wanted to contradict whatever news they had shared about Gratian. Fr Peter said that Doria wanted him to return quickly to Madrid, because Gratian had sent the King some letters contradicting the laws of the *Consulta*. 'This upsets me (having to go to this meeting) and to see that even before I arrive they have already made up their minds, and written to tell him (Gratian) that he should not be in charge of a group of lax friars, that he will not get away with it, because his Majesty has ordered us to favour the best.' Fr Peter lamented: 'It pains me to see Father Gratian so exhausted by this trial. He [Jerome] has been helped (so they tell me here) by Doctor Marmol who is now on his way to Italy with the former Nuncio to try to make a case that should not need defending.' He had one last recommendation: 'Commend Fr Gratian to the Lord, he will need this.'

Barnabus de Marmol was to be a good agent in Rome for what concerned our man, and especially for the nuns. Jerome limited his communications to the Brothers Marmol, Barnabus and John; one in Rome, the other in Madrid.

Doria and his Council counted on the support of many people in the Royal Court and, to crown it all, the King had come out in favour of Doria. Nicholas Doria had won the trust of King Philip II who had become convinced that he was the ideal Superior for the Discalced Carmelite Reform.

'Let Fr Gratian live the regular life [Doria wrote to the King] since he has made his profession and besides the Rule is not so hard since friars who are much older and less healthy than he can do so, as well as the Superiors of the Order. And above all let him not have anything more to do with the nuns and especially the one with whom his relationship is most notorious, who is in Lisbon [Mary of St Joseph].'

Jerome reasoned that it would be better for him to go to Rome, given that the road to the King was now closed to him. We read in one of his letters: 'I am resolutely determined to go to Rome, since this route is more secure. Where there is doubt concerning ecclesiastical matters one should always go to the head, which is what the Saints did of old, like Saint Anthony of Padua when there were problems with Fr Elias. I will get permission from the Cardinal in order to go to Rome so that I can argue my case.'

The more intelligent nuns were also unhappy with Doria. They feared the Constitutions given by their holy Mother, Teresa, would undergo modifications. Anne of Jesus, who watched the vicissitudes of the *Consulta* from Madrid, had herself experienced Doria's deceitfulness. Shortly after the Madrid Chapter ended he had visited her on 1 July 1588, and shared with her at length how he would look after the government of the nuns. Anne was very happy at this and rejoiced. The following day she wrote to the Prioress of Avila about 'the gift that God has given us, that we are all behind the leadership of our Father Vicar General, who chose for his companion Father Jerome Gratian, who will be the second person of our government and, as they must work together, everything will pass through his hands.'

It was a joy that was short lived; in fact, it lasted only a couple of days. Doria had lied to her about Jerome and confirmed this on 5 July when he published the *Acta for our Sisters the Discalced Carmelite nuns*. In the *Acta* the *Consulta* reserved to itself the right to govern the nuns and to appoint their confessors and procurators. It forbad friars to enter the nuns' convents or speak with them without their written permission. It also prohibited the re-election of the prioresses without first obtaining permission from the *Consulta*.

With one stroke of the pen Teresa's Constitutions were destroyed. The *Consulta* centralized all the problems of the nuns, even the most insignificant, something the Saint detested, as she wanted convents to be places where the superior was to be a mother for her nuns.

Anne of Jesus, brave woman that she was, hastily published the 1581 Constitutions, approved in Alcala and accepted by Teresa, and sent copies to all the convents. Published in Madrid by Peter Madrigal in 1588, they contained two letters that Jerome had dedicated: 'To our most holy Mother, Teresa of Jesus, Foundress of the convents of the Discalced Carmelite nuns' and 'To the holy Discalced Carmelite Mothers and Sisters'. The publication was endorsed by the Nuncio, Speziano, who confirmed that the Constitutions, given by the competent Superiors, 'were written by the late Teresa of Jesus, the first Institutor and Foundress of your Order under the guidance of the Holy Spirit.'

As Doria carried doggedly on regardless (of the nuns' complaints), Anne of Jesus resolved to turn to Rome. Mary of St Joseph, Prioress of Lisbon, supported her as did other convents. John Vazquez del Marmol, in Madrid, wrote to some Prioresses, though not to all,

> send me your backing as soon as possible, in the name of Doctor Barnabus del Marmol [secretary to the Papal Nuncio] and whoever he replaces, so that he can do all the negotiations on behalf of the Order, and especially obtain Apostolic confirmation from His Holiness and from the Holy Apostolic See, of the holy Mother's Constitutions that the said person [Barnabus] will carry with him. This should be done as secretly as possible because we are dealing with people who are very clever; and so, seeing that not all the nuns are of the same mind as you, Reverend Mother, it is better to avoid any repercussions and avoid provoking them. It should be enough for you, Reverend Mother, to support this, and perhaps two or three others, though it would be even better if as many as possible did. If, perhaps, your Reverence does not want to help in this matter, let it be of no consequence since the reason why we are keeping this secret is not that there is anything to hide but that what has to be done is done with minimal fuss.

Silently and without fuss, Doctor Marmol was commissioned (by the nuns) to place this matter before the Roman Curia. A year later it bore fruit. On 5 June 1590, Pope Sixtus V signed the Brief *Salvatoris* in which he confirmed the Alcala Constitutions, which forbad the Superiors (of the friars) from introducing any modifications; it also stated that the nuns were to have their own Commissary to govern them. A eulogy appeared in the Brief, which would have made Mary of St Joseph very happy: 'a mother called Teresa of Jesus... to whom sixty priories and convents, more men than women, honour her as Mother and Foundress.'

'Mother and Foundress'... also of men; furthermore, the Brief retroactively revoked the laws that had enabled the nuns' Constitutions to be changed and prohibited the Vicar General from modifying them in future. The Brief made clear that there was to be a General Commissary, 'mature in age, prudent and knowledgeable,' who would be responsible for the government of the nuns and would occupy a position second only to the Vicar General.

When Doria found out about the Brief he was furious. However, cold and calculating as he was, he used the resources he had at his disposal, and knowing what they had hatched in Rome before the Brief materialized, he convoked an Extraordinary Chapter in Madrid for the month of June 1590. The Chapter was not due to meet until the following year, but, it seemed, he was above the law.

Chapter Twenty-Two

Locked up in an Inhospitable Cell

On 9 June 1590, the General Chapter convoked by Doria began in the Priory of St Hermenegildo, Madrid. It was at this meeting that they completed the establishment of the laws and the new government, the *Consulta*. The members also spoke at length about Jerome Gratian; the latter was at the time far away in Evora (Portugal), making Visitations of the Carmelite nuns.

The following day, after our Carmelite celebrated the Mass on Pentecost Sunday, a pious and very elderly lady came up to him. Her name was Anne Martinez, a woman of prayer and penance from her childhood; she asked in her native Portuguese tongue: 'What is the matter, my son, what is troubling you'? He replied: 'There is nothing troubling me. Why do you ask?' 'Because the moment you raised the Blessed Sacrament I saw with my own eyes our Lord Jesus Christ putting a very heavy cross on your shoulders.' When Jerome recalled this incident he thought to himself: 'I could not understand what cross she meant, until later that is when I experienced it.'

There were no elections at this Extraordinary Chapter in Madrid. It finished on 2 July with the promulgation of the new Constitutions that endorsed the Government of the *Consulta*. 'Take note,' said Jerome, 'that there being approximately a thousand people in this congregation, only seventeen were found at the Chapter, and that twelve of them were made up of seven Councillors and five Provincials; the same ones who made the rules at the last Chapter in 1588; of these, eleven will retire at the intermediate Chapter which will be held in the year 91. The Religious of this Congregation are offended that the Chapter should be brought forward by a year. They believe that it was done to ratify these laws while there were people of the same opinion, and so close the door to anyone who thought differently, who could have been elected and voted had the Chapter been held at the right time.'

These Constitutions that ruined those of Alcala were immediately published. On 11 July a shorter version (of the same) was published. The new regime, imposed by Doria, codified in 26 chapters was called the *Consulta*. In the prologue we see the signatures of the six Councillors, among them, Fr John of the Cross. However, the two basic issues that motivated Doria to convoke the Chapter were: first, in what way could they entirely remove Gratian's influence and, secondly, how could they get those nuns back into line who had reacted to the *Consulta* by going directly to Rome, i.e. those who had defended Teresa's legacy and who were friends of Jerome Gratian: namely Anne of Jesus and Mary of St Joseph.

The Chronicler wrote that one of the concerns of the Chapter was 'to bring Fr Jerome Gratian of the Mother of God back from Portugal, in order to take a firm stand, because from there he had encouraged the nuns in their plans and anyone else who conspired against the Council.' Of the seventeen Chapter members, only one raised his voice to object: John of the Cross. What they said about Gratian and the nuns appeared scandalous to John, and for this reason he protested, even though his protests fell on deaf ears.

Doria read out all the previous legal proceedings, the letters and documents with the charges leveled against Fr Gratian. He did this to get the Chapter to issue a new Sentence condemning him, which would ratify the Sentence the Vicar Provincials issued three years ago. There was a huge stack of paperwork. Among these was a very recent testimony forced out of the young Brother Francis of the Cross, made between February and April 1590. If I dwell on this, it is only to illustrate the perverse methods Doria and his supporters used.

Brother Francis of the Cross had been Fr Gratian's Secretary for a year and a half. The Chapter members had made the young man come to Madrid to question him, without even allowing him to say goodbye to Gratian. Doria tackled him: 'Brother Francis, for the sake of peace and quiet and for the sake of the truth about Fr Gratian, the things he vehemently denies, tell us what you know about his dealings and communication with the nuns in the convent of St Albert in Lisbon and, in particular, with Mary of St Joseph. We shall give you a minute to think about it. You can take it for granted that we have more than enough information on this matter. We would like to hear from you about who else knew these things and who spent a lot of time in his company. We know only too well that he ate meat, wore clothes made of linen, visited the nuns of Udivelas and many other convents, particularly our own; we have a small pile of papers on this. We are not saying that he has mortally sinned or even venially, but rather that we know he is refusing to admit the truth.'

Francis of the Cross made a half-hearted attempt to rebel. He reminded the Vicar General that there was an order from Cardinal Albert, issued under pain of excommunication, in Lisbon on 29 November 1589, 'in which one was ordered not to say or write anything, nor process anything against Fr Gratian during his Visitation, unless it were in a message entrusted to a legate.' In other words, 'that no judge or anyone else worry or disturb Fr Jerome Gratian of the Mother of God during the commission he was given from his Highness to make a Visitation of the Carmelite Order in Portugal.' The lawyer, Francis de Arratia, pointed out the same to the Council a month later, on 29 December.

Doria replied to Francis of the Cross, 'This [order] has no authority outside the Kingdom of Portugal.' His point was enough to convince Brother Francis. He was sworn in, and then Doria took him to the Secretary, Fr Gregory of the Holy Angels, so that the latter could record the answers to a questionnaire they had given Brother Francis. When the Secretary gave the lay brother the written record of his responses, the Brother Francis noticed 'that there were many things that did not sound right', and told the Secretary to cross out the parts he pointed out; something that Fr Gregorio was not happy to do. 'What I wrote makes sense, and is in conformity with my conscience,' recounted Brother Francis. This did not seem right to Fr Gregory who crossed out some sentences and made annotations.

The formulated questions could only come from the mind of a sexual obsessive, which is what Doria was: 'If you know of any talk or rumour among religious or secular persons about the relationship and intimate communications between Father and Mary of St Joseph or if there has been any scandal, tell us what you know.' 'If you know that after he was given a ruling not to have any more dealings or communicate by writing or speak with the said Mary of St Joseph or go to the convent, that he was there, and did speak with her, tell us how many times and when. Tell us what you know...' Fr Mariano took Brother Francis of the Cross to a cell where he was locked up. He escaped and later appeared in Lisbon and, in the end, left the Order.

Jerome Gratian was formally condemned by the Chapter. It meant that it could never be said that this was the work of an individual Superior, but that the Order as a whole, united in Chapter, condemned him, after having seen and examined the evidence against him. In order to silence the voices of those friars who were concerned about Jerome, Doria imposed 'a penalty of excommunication, that no one is to have anything to do with Fr Gratian, nor write to the Father, and that if anyone knows of someone who is writing or has dealings with him, he is to be denounced under the same penalty, and if they see Fr Gratian or one of his friends writing any letter, that they be obliged to send it to the *Consulta* under the same penalty.' Mariano was entrusted to visit the King to notify him of the Chapter's resolution on Gratian and to obtain from the King an order to expel him from Lisbon.

The nuns were also taken to task. Doria, homosexual and misogynist, could not tolerate a rebellion by some nuns who bypassed him by going directly to Rome. Of course, in Doria's mind, Jerome was responsible for this lack of respect by the nuns. From now on he had both Anne of Jesus and Mary of St Joseph in his sights; the two who represented the vision and inheritance of St Teresa.

The proposal that was made by Doria and approved by the Chapter was truly hard: 'that as in the small and the great concerns, in the juridical and the paternal, in the elections and observances, the nuns are to be dependent on the *Consulta*.'

However, the Brief, *Salvatoris* (which protected Teresa's Constitutions), which reached Madrid in August, a short time after the Chapter ended, annulled all that had been decreed at the Chapter. This Brief was accompanied by another, *Nuper iustis*, in which Mgr Teutonio, Archbishop of Evora, and the Augustinian, Fr Luis de Leon, were appointed executors of the first Brief. Both were given faculties to convoke a Chapter for the execution of the Brief, *Salvatoris*, 'if the Discalced Carmelite Superiors postpone the convocation of the said Chapter more than a month.' These pontifical documents were made known to Doria, as Vicar General, via a notary, on 26 August 1590. The next day, Pope Sixtus V died in Rome.

Doria moved rapidly to counteract the *Salvatoris* Brief. Firstly, he told the King what the impact of the new Brief would be, 'that it will totally destroy regular life.' 'They asked for it,' Doria said, 'the ex-Prioress of Madrid, the Prioress of Lisbon and Seville because they were not re-elected nor able to enjoy anymore the liberty they had grown accustomed to in their way of life. ... It is true that the two Prioresses were able to contact Pope Sixtus V and ask him if they could themselves go to Rome and be able to take with them the friars and nuns whom they choose without any Superior being able to stop them.' Doria's letter ended: 'You see, Your Majesty, if you have never heard anything like this since the time nuns came into the world, then consider Your Majesty, that if they get away with this, all the other nuns from other Religious Orders will negotiate in the same way with Rome.'

King Philip II did not wait long to react. On 17 August, he ordered his Ambassador in Rome, the Count de Olivares, to get the *Salvatoris* Brief suspended. Some days later, on 21 August, Doria sent a long and threatening letter to the Discalced Carmelite nuns, in which he told them how upset he was by their applying for a pontifical Brief, and the problems that this would cause: a Commissary to replace the *Consulta* in the government of the nuns and the freedom that it would give to Prioresses to choose confessors and preachers. 'Oh Sisters! I am upset to see how quickly Discalced Carmelite nuns call liberty holy! How much better if you insisted more in calling obedience holy, something that is part of the Order!' Doria threatened them, that if they were not willing to obey him, he would have nothing to do with the government of the Discalced Carmelite nuns, and leave them to their fate.

The nuns were thrown into confusion. Doria had managed both to intimidate and divide them. Some wrote to the King begging him to support the Brief, others, bowed down humbly before Doria. Some wrote collective letters, others wrote individually. The friars also got involved. In Madrid and Barcelona, for example, the friars refused to celebrate Mass for the nuns. However, there were also those who were happy with the Brief and demanded Fr Luis de Leon to execute its resolutions quickly. Mary of St Joseph wrote from Lisbon to the Prioresses of Avila and Valladolid to encourage them not to give up.

> You all know that I am ready not only to suffer similar trials, prison, hunger, thirst, beatings and slander, but more, even death if it were necessary, for the smallest detail of the Constitutions that my holy Mother left. If God does not take away the light He has given me then all hell together will not make me change; His light will not fail, and thanks to his mercy I shall not lose faith, for the surest and safest path is to follow the saints and obey the Vicar of Christ. Hoping to please him, I am happy to endure much for writing this, as I am sure this will be the case, because no matter how it (my suffering) is used it would afford me joy to know that I might encourage my Sisters to rise up and follow our holy Mother, Teresa of Jesus, who is our head and captain; no other voice should be heard in her houses.

Mary of St Joseph was a woman of extraordinary courage. 'I would prefer to die than believe that what they said was true: that there are some of our houses that do not want the Constitutions of our holy Mother to be confirmed.' She was ready to raise her voice so that everyone would hear her, even though she would be punished. The Carmelite nuns in Vitoria were opposed to the Brief, and requested King Philip II to ask the Pope to revoke it, because 'of the thirty-two convents of this Order in the Province of Spain, only six have received the Brief, *Salvatoris* by Pope Sixtus V…'

This claim was not certain, the Carmelite nuns were divided, those in favour of the Brief were the convents of Barcelona, Beas, Caravaca, Cordoba, Malaga, Medina del Campo, Sabiote, Sanlucar la Mayor, Seville, Soria, Zaragoza, Lisbon, Huete, Madrid, Palencia and Salamanca. Those against were: Burgos, Malagon, Pamplona, Segovia, Villaneuva de la Jara, Avila, Cuerva, Granada, Toledo and Vitoria. It is not easy to be clear about where the convents stood, not all of them spoke with one voice, some were in favour others against, and some, like Valladolid, were initially in favour but then against.

Doria did not delay with the lesseer-known nuns, he went straight to the leaders to strike them down, who were none other than Gratian, Anne of Jesus and Mary of St Joseph. However, like the clever calculating person he was, he would wait for the right moment.

Mgr Teutonio, Archbishop of Evora, left the execution of the Brief in the hands of Fr Luis de Leon, who on 25 November, notified Doria and his Definitory that they should convoke the Provincials and Socii to elect a Commissioner for the nuns, 'mature in years, wise and knowledgeable.' He dared to propose these names: Jerome Gratian and John of the Cross.

To hear Jerome's name was to Doria like being bitten by a snake. John of the Cross, already in disgrace, was shut away in his priory in Segovia and would never again attend the meetings of the *Consulta* that had transferred to Madrid. However, the fact that he was proposed for Commissoner of the nuns placed him on the list of those who were considered suspect, those who had conspired to obtain the Brief, even though the mystical poet had nothing to do with this.

Fr Luis de Leon was very disappointed. On 25 November no more than three Provincials appeared in Madrid, so he was obliged to postpone the Extraordinary General Chapter until 2 February 1591, the feast of the Presentation. Now Doria was in the driving seat. He asked the King to reject the Augustinian friar from the Brief's resolutions, since 'he has had a close and very familiar relationship, of four years standing, with Anne of Jesus. Such is this relationship that few days pass when he is not in the said

Fr Luis de Leon.
Engraving by Pacheco.

convent four or five hours with her alone, locked in the chapel or parlour, and keeping his mule at the door.' Once again the obsessive Doria resorted to similar kinds of slander.

On 26 January 1591, King Philip II received a report from the Council Chamber on the matter of the Brief *Salvatoris*. Very much under Doria's influence, the report advised the King not to allow the Superiors of the Discalced Carmelite friars to abandon the government of the Discalced Carmelite nuns; it warned Anne of Jesus and Mary of St Joseph to obey their Superiors; Doctor Marmol and his brother, were no longer to get involved in this matter and, as one of the brothers wanted to return to Rome, he could not leave the Kingdom without permission from his Majesty. Peter Cerezo Pardo, the Sevillian Knight, who helped Teresa a great deal with her foundation in Seville and had given money for the expenses in Rome, 'has been ordered by the assistant and the Regent of Seville, that he is to have no further dealings in this matter, nor is he to be an occasion of anxiety for the nuns'. To Fr Luis de Leon, 'that he leaves here to look after his office as Provincial'; and, as Fr Luis de Leon had convoked a Chapter for 2 February (concerning the said Brief), 'orders the Vicar General (Doria) to advise those who should come to the said Chapter to delay their visit,' now that the Count of Olivares is negotiating the withdrawal of the Brief in Rome.

Jerome was also damaged by the report. 'The reason why Fr Gratian and the two or three nuns who have raised this (*matter*), was because he had been punished and the nuns because they were not given the chance to be reelected. They were very upset about this, and this came out later in various things they did and by their disobedience.' Further on we read: 'It was understood at this meeting that Fr Jerome wants to go to Rome concerning the Brief of the nuns, as he is encouraging them and, with the other two nuns, mentioned above, has been the principal occasion of this discord.'

Doria's malice had induced the Chamber to believe that if Anne of Jesus and Mary of St Joseph had acted in this way it was because they had not been re-elected as Prioresses. Certainly, Anne of Jesus had not been Prioress since 18 November 1589, when Mary of the Nativity was elected for the convent of St Anne in Madrid. Mary of St Joseph stopped being Prioress on 17 January 1590 in the convent of St Albert in Lisbon. However, what motivated the two of them, unknown to the Chamber, was their desire to defend what they inherited from St Teresa.

On 25 April 1591, the new Pope, Gregory XIV issued the Brief, *Quoniam non ignoramus*, that substantially annulled the former Brief. Doria saw it as a triumph, though not everyone praised him and his *Consulta*. The office of Commissioner for the nuns was annulled, but his jurisdiction did not fall back into the *Consulta* but rather went to the Provincials. As for the Confessors, there were enough Provincials to provide for a free election by the nuns.

Days later, at the beginning of May, with the closure of the Portuguese Provincial Chapter of the Discalced Carmelites, Jerome's Visitation of Portugal came to an end. Now what would become of him? Would he return to Madrid to place himself at the disposition of Doria? On 25 May he was in Santaren (just north of Lisbon), where he preached in the Church of the Holy Miracle. This recalled a local 13th century legend about a consecrated host that was stolen by a woman at the instigation of another, who was of the Jewish race, and was seen to have miraculously changed into blood.

Our Carmelite returned by boat to Lisbon, with an ulcer on his leg and a bruise on his nose. On 29 May he wrote to the Discalced Carmelite nuns in Madrid:

> I am waiting to hear where the Fathers of the *Consulta* will send me, as I have finished here now. Glory be to God that I am ready for anything,

> because everywhere there are sacraments to celebrate, God to be loved, a pulpit to preach in, pious ladies to direct, melancholic ladies to scold, couples to marry, friendships to make, gossip to endure and letters to write. Thus come what may, even though we lose our lives, we must always strive for the greater glory of God and the increase of our Order, which one moment the Superiors of the Order help, the next they do not help.

Doria called him to Madrid. The time had come for his revenge. Anastasius tells Cyril:

> I was wary of going on this journey. From Lisbon I could have sailed to Rome. I was so naïve and obedient. My desire was for peace and humility. I thought to myself that if I went to the *Consulta* and gave them the reasons I had difficulties with this new government that they would believe me. But when they did not believe me and refused to budge from their attitude, I told them I would give up and not speak anymore about it, rather I would obey them in everything and I would help (I had done everything my conscience told me to, in writing to the Pope, to our Protector and our General, telling them what I thought) and, that I would go peacefully to whatever priory, serving the Order in my role as confessor and preacher and keep to my studies.

Gratian was as intelligent as he was naïve. A letter from Fr John Baptist assured him that the Superiors 'would receive him and treat him very well and all the worries of the Order would come to an end.'

He could have gone to Rome; he had permission from the General of the Order, Fr Caffardo, to give an account of his Visitation to the Portuguese Carmelites. However, he preferred to place himself at the disposition of his Superiors in Madrid.

Mgr Teutonio de Braganza, who was in Madrid, wrote to the Cardinal reminding him of his promise to send Fr Gratian to his diocese in Evora and, in this way, he would avoid the reprisals of his Superiors. As far as Mgr Teutonio was concerned, Doria and Mariano were 'people whose judgement is not at all sound.' However, Jerome had decided to go to Madrid. In his bag he carried various letters of praise for his work in Portugal. The General, Count de Fuentes, extolled his apostolic endeavours among the soldiers and political prisoners, above all during the siege of Lisbon by the English. Cardinal Albert honoured him with a Patent that thanked him for his work during his two years in Portugal. Likewise the Provincial and Carmelite Fathers in Lisbon formally stated 'how Father Gratian had lived a regular life all the time he was with them. Consequently, the Discalced Carmelites cannot suggest that he has lived in a lax way because he was not in their houses where they could have seen the kind of life he led.'

On 3 June Doria sent a Patent to Jerome, in his usual abrupt style and with typical urgency. 'I order you to present yourself in this Priory (of St Hermenegildo) within 25 days, counting from the date of this letter.'

The Discalced Carmelites had come together in Madrid for an intermediate Chapter that began on 1 June. Elections were held at this meeting and those elected divided up the offices. Jerome later pointed out that in the Chapter the elections were made in such a way 'that whoever was a friend of Father Gratian, or had supported him in any way, was overlooked, thereby manifesting to the horror of all, the strength of their feelings.'

John of the Cross was left without an office. He wanted to return to Segovia. The Chapter members proposed he go to far-off Mexico. In the end, he was sent to the Andalucian Province. On 19 August, the Saint wrote to Anna del Mercado that he had taken the road from 'the desert of La Penuela, six miles this side of Baeza, from where it took me nine days to arrive.' 'My only thought is that all this has been ordained by God,' he told her. Diego Evangelista, resentful and bad-tempered, had risen to Definitor at the Chapter. This man would make the last days of John of the Cross' life a misery with a defamatory process that would spread to Fr Gratian. John's death, his peaceful death, saved him from a ruling that might otherwise have found him expelled from the Order, as would happen to Fr Gratian. Providentially, Fr John of the Cross died on 15 December 1591, in Ubeda.

Jerome left Lisbon on 11 June, the Tuesday after the feast of the Blessed Trinity. He took the road to Madrid and on the way called into the Priories of Maqueda and Toledo. In both of these he perceived that the friars were scandalized by the government of the *Consulta*. The Prior of Toledo, Elias of St Martin, warned him that Doria's true intention was to expel him from the Order. When he reached Getafe, he met his two friends, John and Barnabus Marmol, who told him that Doria and Mariano 'were on such good terms with the King' that the letters he [Gratian] had from Cardinal Albert and others would be of little use.'

With these bad tidings he reached Madrid on 28 June, in time for vespers of Ss Peter and Paul. He went straight to the Priory of St Hermenegildo. He looked for the Vicar General who was in the garden walking up and down with John Lopez de Velasco, the layman who was also a Judas Iscariot – remember it was he who had made Jerome sign that shameful document. Mariano, who was there, told him that he 'had a face like a Velasco portrait.' Jerome greeted the Vicar General. He kissed his scapular and the Vicar General then blessed him. He then went to eat something and, as he was feeling so tired went to his room, where 'he found rest in sleep and in everything.'

Two days after the feast of Ss Peter and Paul, Jerome went to the Vicar General's room very early in the morning, where he got on his knees and kissed his scapular. Doria, seemingly disdainful, heard him say: 'I give you my word, Father, that you will have no subject who will obey you more truly, and no friend who loves you more; I beg you to order me to do anything you like. You don't need to consult others, who always are going to disagree with you.'

Doria replied to him: 'Father, I do not want to speak about anything concerning your Reverence, because I see you as a soul rejected by God and the most false there is.' Doria said this to Jerome who answered humbly: 'Despite all this, it would be my consolation to do whatever you may order, for a soul, no matter how lost to God, can turn again to Him.' Doria, with a stern face, dismissed him with these words: 'Live a regular life, and if you don't, we can already see what will happen. Go to Fr Blas of St Albert, who is one of the Definitors and is now Provincial of this Province.

Fr Blas gave Jerome lots of advice: 'Try not to miss going to choir and, though it seemed good, do not remain before the Blessed Sacrament at night time, but go to bed…' A shocked Jerome replied: 'I will do whatever will be for the greater glory of God. In time all shall be revealed; all I want is peace for my soul.'

Jerome's brother-in-law, Peter Zapata del Marmol, arrived at the Priory; he was married to Justina Dantisco and brother of the other Marmols, John and Barnabus. He had come to collect Gratian and to take him to see his mother. Fr Blas told him it was very early to be leaving the house. Jerome told him that people were going to think that he was being held prisoner. In the end, after a long wait, the *benedicte* arrived; i.e. permission from the Vicar Provincial. Fr Blas went with him. On the road Jerome said to Fr Blas, 'You know by now Fr Blas how much I like and esteem you; but your lack of trust damages both our hearts.'

Fr Blas was moved by the sincerity of Jerome's words and began to cry. Even though he was very much part of the *Consulta* he acknowledged that Fr Gratian was a good servant of God. He revealed to Gratian the orders of the *Consulta*: he was not to leave the house except on rare occasions, then always accompanied by one of the Councillors; was not to preach except in St Hermenegildo and never in a nun's convent; he was not to speak to anyone about his business… Jerome concluded: 'By the things he told me and seeing the scheme [at work] I would have to climb over walls to lead an evil and shameful life.'

It was three years since Jerome had seen his mother, and when he did he embraced her. She was old by now. Over and above the weight of her sixty-four years, she also carried her son's cross. In Joanna's house the family came together, a small intimate circle, to discuss matters. They agreed to approach the King; why shouldn't the King hear from the son of his Secretary? And if the King did not listen to him, he would go to Rome.

That same night, Sunday 30 June, Doria and Mariano went to the Escorial to speak to the King; they gave him the news that Gratian had arrived. 'I was determined to keep my counsel [recounted Gratian] until they [Doria and Mariano] came, and then ask them for permission to go there [to the Royal Palace]. And if they do not give it to me, let us see what will be the right thing to do. If they give permission, I shall tell the King that these Fathers have oppressed me, and request that his Majesty asks Religious Superiors from other Orders to hear me. Or if it seems fit that I should turn to my Superiors, and have permission from them to deal with matters that are extremely important.'

Jerome was aware that 'in those three or four days that I have been here they had begun to use some cruel tactics'; for example, they prevented him from visiting Mgr Teutonio de Braganza, the Archbishop of Evora, who was in Madrid and gravely ill.

Peter of the Purification, who was a member of the Spanish Province of Biscay, had arrived at St Hermenegildo's the night before. He had been in the novitiate with Jerome in Pastrana, and had defended him from distant Genoa, where he was Prior. Before coming to Madrid he had visited Rome in order to support Jerome's cause.

Peter was not able to speak with him in St Hermenegildo's where he remained for just six hours. That same night of 4 July he was sent to Segovia where he was put into the Priory's prison cell; he was accused by the *Consulta* of going to Rome without permission. He showed the Licence he had received in his Priory in Genoa from the Roman Cardinals, but they took no notice of it; as he said very expressively: 'They took as much notice of this as if I were the man in the moon.' If you mess with Doria, this is what happens to you.

Did Gratian meet John of the Cross? Donazar offers the following supposition: 'As he arrived in Madrid on 28 June and Fr John of the Cross did not leave Madrid until after 6 July, we think they would have met in St Hermenegildo's, where Fr John of the Cross said goodbye to Fr Gratian. However, it cannot have been an emotional farewell as history, or we, would have liked. Fr John of the Cross was perhaps not prepared to understand Fr Gratian. Also, could he (Gratian) trust Fr Doria's former Councillor, of whose deeds in recent months he was unaware? Above all, we should not forget that certain individuals in the Order, like despots who carried censures with them, strongly forbade anyone from speaking with Fr Jerome. It was a formal meeting, perhaps only their eyes met; besides, the saints bear their souls in opaque bodies.

How did Jerome find life in St Hermenegildo's Priory? With naïve optimism he admitted to being calm and happy, though he was also quite angry. On 5 July, John Vazquez del Marmol sent a note warning him, 'Don't send letters except with your brothers or people you trust entirely. All the letters and papers we will send you read them and then return them, because you are not meant to have any.' The note ended: 'Suffer in silence, be hopeful, let us see that whatever comes later from the Escorial is meant to be.'

On 23 August 1591, Fr Luis de Leon died in Madrigal. His death prevented him from executing the Brief *Salvatoris*. Months before he died he had already given up, having had first-hand experience that it was not easy to fight against Doria. He also realized that Jerome Gratian was not as simple as he had supposed. His death meant one less enemy for Doria.

A canonical Visitation of the Discalced Carmelite nuns in Madrid had begun. Fr Blass of St Albert, sent by Doria as the Visitator to St Anne's convent, behaved like a true tyrant. The Visitation, according to the Constitutions should not exceed five days, but this went on for a month. What the Visitator was most eager to establish was, 'Who was sent to Rome to confirm their Constitutions, who helped and gave advice, who was responsible and who paid for it?'

At the end of the Visitation Fr Blas called a community Chapter. The Prioress, Mary of the Nativity, was bereft and worn out. Mary of St Jerome, who was brought from Avila (to replace her as Prioress), tormented all the sisters on the orders of the friars. According to a report, 'She does not behave like a Prioress but rather like a tyrant.' Anne of St Bartholomew, who was St Teresa's secretary, was her companion, and managed to lessen, in part, the severity of the Prioress. 'They make us say one hundred thousand penances,' one of the nuns admitted, 'that we would never be able to finish saying. Those seemed like days of the Last Judgement and during a time when everything was known at Court.' Anne of Jesus came off worse; she was confined to her cell, forbidden to have visitors, deprived of daily Communion and of active and passive voice for three years.

Mary of St Joseph, far removed in Lisbon, was for the time being at least, free from Doria's vengeance. He was focused on Madrid and on how, finally, he could finish off Gratian. Mary would eventually be imprisoned in a convent cell and also deprived of active and passive voice. On Good Friday, 1593, she would write from her cell, *A letter from a poor Discalced Carmelite prisoner*. It was a calm and, at the same time, heartbreaking account of her afflictions. She wrote it for her 'dearest Sisters and Daughters,' who were as disconsolate as she was for the way she was being treated. 'Not content with this' – that is to say, with the expulsion of Fr Gratian – 'a year later they ordered me to be thrown into a locked cell, no sister was allowed to speak with me or have anything to do with me, under the gravest penalties. I am not able to hear Mass, only on holy days of obligation, nor go to confession, nor receive communion except once a month.'

Jerome wrote a letter to John Vazquez del Marmol from his prison cell on 20 July 1591:

> I am doing what I am ordered, which is to keep quiet and keep away. Yesterday, they wrote down what I told them about the charges of Mary of St Joseph, without giving them to me first; now they say they will give them to me. I do not believe that the reply will please the Vicar [General] at all, because it was the supreme truth and they are supreme liars, and therefore, I don't know how they can go on; not with much conviction, I believe. Peter Gratian told me that he went to see my mother. I believe that now they would like Velasco to enter into the affair to try and make peace. It is best just to keep quiet and continue to listen to them, and give evidence openly at their tribunal until they know what the situation will be like in

> a week's time, as I believe they fear a revolt; and so, yesterday, when I was with groups of friars, they were all very solicitous and told me this and that, etc. I am keeping my counsel and my thoughts to myself.

Doria made six accusations against Jerome which clearly reflected his greatest obsession: the relationship between him and Mary of St Joseph. The first five, referred to distant events: the transfer of the nuns from Seville to the foundation in Lisbon in December 1584; that taking the nuns from the Seville convent, 'among whom was Mary of St Joseph', he placed them in the cloister of Los Remedios Priory; that upon arrival in Lisbon, he introduced the nuns into the Priory enclosure, where they ate in the refectory with the friars, sung in the choir and were given accommodation for two days and one night; and when in her convent, 'he went to see Mary of St Joseph every day in a place that had a window without a grille or door, that he entered the cloister, and that there he often entered inside the enclosure and at other times he entered with some merchants in order to buy certain serge…' The sixth charge referred to his recent meeting with Mary of St Joseph after she had been given an order not to have any dealings with him.

Our man responded in writing to these charges three days later, on 22 July. He had only to give an account of the first five because they occurred when he was Provincial and, since then, there had been 'six Provincial and General Chapters, and more than eight meetings of Vicar Provincials who came together to check the sins committed up to that time.' In actual fact, the one who made these accusations should, according to the Constitutions, have been the one punished. However, he responded to them, 'not to free myself from any trial but rather to clarify, for those who do not know what happened, so that they do not make rash judgements.' He made clear that it was not he who placed the nuns in the friar's cloister in the Seville and Lisbon Priories, and reminded Doria and his accusers that this was done by Mariano and Anthony of Jesus. If he entered into the cloister with merchants it was 'to fix a price and deal with the sale' of some bundles of serge that the nuns sold for alms. The door or grille belonged to a house they called 'the library' that they had bought. 'And in order that the nuns do not have to go outside to see the books, they made a door where, if sometimes the said Mary of St Joseph came with another nun, it was to read the books and nothing more.'

The next day, 23 July, Doria and the Definitors ordered Jerome not to write nor receive letters without permission from the Vicar General, under pain of excommunication, 'now it is evident that this Father's writings are a cause of anxiety in the Order and of scandal for the laity.' Jerome found himself cut off from the world.

On 26 July he was presented with eleven new charges that referred to his behaviour during the Visitation of Portugal, where he was accused of disobedience and of having defied his Superiors, also that he sowed discord by his letters and the words he spoke against the General Chapter and the *Consulta*; that he had dishonoured the Vicar General and Definitors by writing offensive words, saying that 'they were liars, jealous, ambitious and other similar insults', that he had disobeyed the Constitutions issued by the General Chapters, that he had sowed the idea among the Discalced Carmelite friars that it was good for them to lead 'an easy life, to have a government in which there was no [juridical] process, and to be on familiar terms with nuns…'

Days later Jerome submitted an extensive reply to each of the charges they imputed against him.

His brother Thomas came to visit him, and brought some letters. However, he recalled Doria's order and so did not accept the letters nor write any. Out of obedience he did not want to read them though he did get his brother to give him an account of them. He encouraged Thomas to obtain for him an audience with the King, something he had been trying to do. It is hard to understand why the King could deny an audience to the son of his employee and old servant, when he had given them repeatedly to Jerome's adversaries; if the King, 'who represented justice on earth' did not listen to him, then it would be time to go to Rome.

Joanna Dantisco, 'saddened by the problems of her son', wrote a begging letter to King Philip II at the beginning of August. 'I fear that they are about to dishonour him more than when they will take away his habit as they have told me they will,' she told the King. 'He would very much like to come and kiss the hands of Your Majesty and give you his account, but they will not give him permission even though he has asked. Have pity on me, Your Majesty, and remember that my good husband served Your Majesty and His Serene Emperor, and my good son Anthony Gratian.'

There will be no reply from King Philip II. Broken-hearted, Joanna was still not allowed to see her son. They put him in the most uncomfortable cell; it was a real prison. And in the Royal Court the most outlandish rumours circulated.

Chapter Twenty-Three

To Rome 'Dressed Like a Criminal'

'We can't have a situation where a friar says the Order is telling lies,' argued Doria, 'and now we have said he is lax we must prove it.' Doria was not going to let this issue go. Later he said the same thing only more explicitly: 'No individual friar should accuse an Order of lying. It is better that the friar should suffer'.

The accusations levelled against Jerome on 22 and 26 July did not appear to be enough (to expel him from the Order). Doria and the Council needed new witnesses. To this end they looked to Lisbon and Seville. However, the questioning (of witnesses) in Lisbon did not take place because the Prior, Fr John of Jesus, refused to collaborate and pointed out that the Cardinal had already testified on Gratian's behalf.

The Council then sent someone called Fr Diego Evangelista to Andalucia on 15 August with all authority to resurrect the old accusations levelled against Fr Gratian by the Calced Carmelites. Diego was a friar without shame. He first went to Granada where he intimidated both friars and nuns alike, and also attempted to incriminate John of the Cross.

Diego's file on this mystical Carmelite (John of the Cross) was stitched inside the habit of a lay brother so that it would reach Madrid. The Vicar General, Doria, made out that he was horrified when he read its shameful contents, but he did nothing to control Diego's perverse conduct. John of the Cross, as we have already said, was fortunate to have died in December. However, Diego Evangelista did not hesitate to say, 'If he had not died, his habit would have been taken from him and he would have died outside the Order.'

Diego Evangelista was from Seville and it was from Seville that he embellished the report on Gratian which was then taken to Madrid in installments. It contained not only the old fabricated stories from the Calced Carmelites six years earlier, but also included those from the Discalced Carmelite friars.

Diego listed thirty-nine new charges that were read out to Gratian on 9 November: the same night that news arrived in Madrid of the death of Pope Gregory XVI. 'They are thirty but they could easily have been three hundred,' he remarked sarcastically. The charges included the previously mentioned abominations that he and other lay people, including Peter Cerezo, were purported to have committed against nuns; needless to say, the names of Anne of Jesus and Mary of St Joseph were also among those accused.

The charges were read out without interruption from start to finish. Jerome wrote, 'They accused me and some lay people of the greatest stupidity and indecency with Discalced Carmelite nuns, saying things they wouldn't say about prostitutes.' He covered his ears and begged them to stop slandering the brides of Christ. His accusers told him that the charges were endorsed by more than seventy witnesses. One of the accusations was outlandish: that Jerome's younger sister, Juliana, who had been professed in Seville Carmel aged eighteen was, in reality, his daughter by Mary of St Joseph.

On being informed about her daughter's alleged paternity, Joanna Dantisco retorted, 'They did not go through the labour pains I did in giving birth to her.' She was forbidden to visit her son in his cell in the priory of St Hermenegildo. Then malicious rumours reached her that in order to avoid further difficulties with his own Superiors, he wanted to leave the Discalced Carmelite Order. As a result she sent him the following resolute message, 'I have been told that you want to leave the Order of Our Lady. If this idea has passed through your head, never speak or write to me again, nor consider me your mother. I do not want a son who lacks courage; who, because he has been persecuted wants to leave such a Mother as the Blessed Virgin Mary and turn his back on the Order to which he so willingly gave himself and to which, later, I offered you up.'

His mother's words upset him deeply, but later he found heart when he realized that the Lord and the Blessed Virgin would support him through his trials. Peter Zapata, his brother-in-law, was the only person allowed to visit, a privilege not given even to his brothers and sisters. It cost Jerome a great deal not to be able to preach at the first Mass of his brother, Peter. John Vazquez del Marmol complained about what was happening, 'These people are vindictive and cruel. What hope is there, given that they have the upper hand?'

People were speaking about Gratian's situation in the streets. The Royal

Court was alive with rumours. The members of the *Consulta* told a certain Prelate about the accusations levelled against him, and made it clear that they didn't believe there was any sin involved. The Prelate, blessing himself, told them, 'I don't understand you, Fathers. You say there is no sin, and yet you cause so many rumours and scandals? Put an end to this!' The same Prelate made some inquiries and then reached the conclusion that the two Italians (Doria & Mariano) were not of sound judgement. 'It can happen,' he said, 'that a man can be wise in most things but totally off his head in one particular instance.' He was referring to Doria.

They kept Jerome securely locked up in a small room that was used by the servants. There was no light, and the lock was on the outside, his only companion was his breviary. Afterwards they took him to a cell in the novitiate, even though, according to him, 'I was not able to see anything or speak to anyone, except when they brought my food. In order to get away with what they were doing to me no one must know what they were doing nor could I speak out in my defence.'

King Philip II was confused. He had received petitions from Jerome's supporters that the judges be impartial. Jerome himself had asked the King to be given such judges, or, to be allowed to go to Rome, now that he had permission from the General of the Order as well as the Cardinal Protector 'to speak about these grave matters.' He asked him 'as a son and brother of his [the King's] employees.' However Doria, with Machiavellian diplomacy, had managed to win the King's trust by rendering him an important service, as Anastasius recounted, 'which was to remedy the damage incurred to Spain by the contracts with the Genovese who had drained all of Spain's money through their financial dealings'. Thanks to Doria's intervention a decree was issued against the Genovese, and the King, in his gratitude, would have made him an Archbishop and given him 'anything he wanted'.

However, all Doria wanted to do was to carry on governing with his *Consulta*: Jerome was his stumbling block who had to be removed. In order to achieve this he and Mariano visited the King. He told the monarch, cynically, 'My Lord, we like and love Father Gratian as much as we love life itself, and whatever we can do for him we shall do. Should he do what we ask of him which is only right and fitting, and what we are supposed to do, he will remain in our hearts. However, if he does not, we have a duty to our Order.'

That a subject be obedient, submissive, observant, quiet and humble sounded all very good to the King. It was for this reason that when Jerome's friends went to see him he told them, 'Had he done what his Superiors wanted, which was the right thing to do, then I would be on his side, but he did not. Do you want me to support him even though it would be against his Order and against all reason?'

What did Jerome's Superiors want? i.e. what did Doria want? He wanted our man to confess that he was guilty as charged. He would be ready to pardon all the charges against him, knowing they were false. However, he (Jerome) was not to go to the Pope in Rome, which was contrary to the wishes of the *Consulta*.

Jerome gave in; he had become ill in that cell with a severe headache. He confessed to the *Consulta*: 'I beg you very earnestly, for the love of Our Lord, do not damage the honour of the Order and of these servants of God [the Carmelite nuns].' He asked them not to continue with a trial that would bring into the public domain those abominable charges. He was ready to sacrifice himself and to leave the Order quietly.

Doria, however, rejected this offer. The trial had to go ahead, and be held before the King and his Court. There could be no going back. Doria was very confident of the King's support and that the accused would be destroyed.

His accusers oppressed Jerome with incessant questioning, they tore up the notes he had written, made him sign a letter to the King in which he admitted to being content to accept the sentence from those he had called overly zealous… Doria was worried that impartial judges might annul the case.

They (the members of the Consulta) persistently asked him if he had in fact written to Rome. Jerome replied, 'Can't a Religious be advised by and consoled by the Vicar of Christ?' Doria shouted in front of all the Fathers of the *Consulta*: 'No, no, no, this man must be possessed by a thousand devils!' Jerome realized that such words merited to be heard by the Inquisition, and to this end he asked to see a Consultor from the Holy Office. The Inquisitor, John de Mendoza, came to see him. The man listened to the concerns of the accused and noted the shameful conditions in which he was forced to live, he ordered the *Consulta* to moderate the harsh treatment and allow him to assist at Mass at least on Sundays and feast days.

At the turn of the New Year, 1592, Jerome was convinced that his luck had run out. Then there came a ray of hope. His face lit up when he found out that the King had appointed two external judges to the Discalced Carmelites: Fr Francis of Segovia, ex-General of the Jeronimites and at the time Prior of Madrid, and Fr Bartholomew Munoz, a Dominican, ex-Provincial and, at the time, Rector of the College of St Thomas. Gratian felt quite overcome when he wrote to them: 'After hearing the judges and having discerned what they have said against me, please judge me objectively with the documents and evidence I have at hand.'

However, he was deeply disillusioned when those two wise friars told him they were not empowered to judge but were simply there to assist and to witness the judgement. When he saw that there was no alternative for them but to condemn him, he threw in the towel.

Disconsolate, he asked the two Judges appointed by the King to show him the grave accusations against him. He was submissive, advising them only of the weaknesses in the process: the accusations were anonymous and there were no names given for the witnesses. However, they told him that they lacked the authority to revise the judgement. They informed the King that the accused was ready to be sentenced, and that the Order could proceed. When the condemnation by the Vicar General and the Definitors was given, it was grave and disproportionate (there were 'seven blank votes').

The document (condemning Jerome Gratian) was signed in St Hermenegildo Priory, Madrid, on 17 February 1592 by all the members of the *Consulta* as well as the two Priors of St Thomas and St Jeronimo. The Secretary, Fr Gregory of the Holy Angels, read out the sentence to Jerome in his cell. He then wanted to take his habit from him but our man wouldn't let him, he wanted to do it himself. He took off his capuche, scapular, and finally, habit. He then put on a soutane and mantle that he had kept since he entered the Novitiate. 'Only one who has suffered such an event can describe what it feels like. I entered the Order of the Discalced Carmelites believing I had a vocation. I suffered a lot before I could establish a Province and now those to whom I have given the Order's habit are taking it from me.'

After eight months of house arrest in St Hermenegildo's he went out the main door and made his way to his mother's house. There he took off his soutane. She made him a new dark-coloured habit with material that wasn't as coarse, as well as a short cape worn by hermits and pilgrims.

Ephraim Montalvo, in his book The *Teresian Inheritance*, wrote that the entire condemnation was based on sex. He argued that Doria was obsessed with it.

Jerome was condemned for the following reasons: as Provincial he allowed lay people to enter the nuns' cloister and also allowed nuns into the cloister of Discalced Carmelite friars; he was over familiar with one of the nuns; he sowed discord in the Order and against his Superiors; in spite of the cautions received from his Superiors he remained incorrigible, an attitude that took root when he was a novice. Even as a novice 'they wanted him to leave the Order.' 'And thus they declared him to be incorrigible and, therefore, ordered him to remove his habit, and to leave the Order to which he could not return.'

News of the sentence spread like wildfire in the Court of Madrid. However, by contrast, within the Discalced Carmelite Order there was a dreadful silence. Anastasius lamented:

> I felt abandoned by people within and outside [the Order]: all those who could have helped me abandoned me when they saw my rivals persecuting me. Those who did not know me believed what they [his enemies] said. My friends turned their backs on me, and when I turned to them for support and advice, they shrugged their shoulders. One of my most saintly and oldest acquaintances said to me: you do not have any other choice but to go to a mountain or a desert where you will never see people again.

He did not go to a mountain, but rather to Rome, 'because the Sentence contained threats of excommunication so that he had to see the Pope.' The Nuncio, Peter Millino, released him from the censures contained in the Sentence, for six months. This meant that he had time to go *ad pedes pontificis* (to the Pope's feet).

There was a new Pope in Rome. On January 30, Cardinal Aldobrandini was elected Pope, taking the name Clement VIII. He would govern the Church for the next thirteen years. Austere and vegetarian, he went to confession on a daily basis, almost always falling into a trance. During the consecration of the Mass he would shed tears. Jerome, wearing the habit of a pilgrim and carrying many letters of recommendation from members of the nobility, set out to meet him.

On 27 February, ten days after his expulsion, Jerome made his way to Alicante where he got on board a ship. In a long letter to his sister, Adriana, a Jeronimite nun, he described all that had taken place on the journey. A mile and a half from Madrid, he and his mule fell crossing a river, 'where I got soaked in the water and covered in mud. Then a strong bitter wind arose and I thought I would die if I had to go another couple of miles; but I felt much better when I reached the lodging and washed myself by the fire.'

Two laymen accompanied him; one of them was called John Palacios. However, they left him when they reached Alicante. Anastasius recounted:

> When the Lord saw me sad and alone at the port, He provided me with a companion in the form of a servant, the son of the landlady with whom I had stayed in Alicante, his name was Joachim Lafonte. He was so kind, so capable, with such good handwriting, and used to travelling [he had already been to Rome accompanying a bishop], so faithful, so virtuous, so very suitable, physically big, so loving and diligent. I could never have imagined I would get someone like him. God inspired his mother with the idea of taking him with me so I could help him to prepare for ordination, which is what I did.

There were no ships leaving Alicante so he made his way to Valencia. 'It was Lent, and I was very sorry that I could not preach or hear confessions: I was not allowed to wear my habit, preach nor be seen with a crowd of people. According to the Sentence I was not allowed to preach or hear confessions until I had joined another Order outside the Discalced Carmelites, nor was I allowed to join the Calced.' He spent Holy Week in Valencia 'with the desire to hear the singing and look at the monuments that are better than any other city in Spain.'

Though he could not preach in Valencia, he found some consolation; 'Our Lord arranged that he should be in a hospital for fallen women with whom he could talk and he converted many. There is nothing so regrettable in this situation than that a man should go around, unjustly deprived of his ministry, when he could be using his gifts for the honour of God.'

On Easter Sunday, 29 March, Jerome Gratian left Valencia for Tortosa where a ship was loading linen on its way to Italy. On the journey he encountered a funeral cortege that was carrying the body of the Master of Montesa, the Viceroy of Catalonia. 'I envied him because we were on different journeys; I so longed to have done with the trials of life.'

Just as he was about to set sail from Tortosa, he received a letter from Alex Cerezo, the cousin of Peter Cerezo, asking him to return to Vinaroz so that they could both sail together to Genoa. This is what he did. Alex Cerezo was carrying a million *escudos* from the King for the wars in France.

When he got on the ship he was surprised to find that two of Doria's envoys were on the same vessel. 'I embarked in Vinaroz,' he recounted, 'on the same galley as two Discalced Carmelite friars going to Rome who were going there to solicit support for all the sentences and legal processes against me, and to justify their case were I to appeal. I engaged with them in a friendly way as if nothing had happened, without saying a word about what I was doing, no one on the ship knew.'

He felt an inner happiness once again, all resentment had gone. He treated the two in a familiar way, knowing full well that they were going to Rome to ask for his dismissal. We know their names, Luis of St Jerome and, the wicked, Diego Evangelista, Doria's enforcer: the man who had recently tormented both Jerome and John of the Cross.

It was pouring with rain when they arrived in Genoa on 16 May, the vigil of Pentecost. Gratian tried in vain to find lodgings. It was already dark so he tried his luck at the Calced Carmelite priory. 'I went there fearful that they would not accept me,' he recounted. However, they did accept him 'with the greatest kindness and gave me the most comfortable room and bed that I could have wished for. They brought me up to date as to all that was happening to the Order in Italy.'

Embarking on a papal galley from Genoa he arrived at the port of Civitavecchia (the port of Rome founded by Emperor Trajan), on the feast of Corpus Christi. As he was disembarking from the galley, there were two infirm and penniless young men from Navarre who asked him for thirty gold coins with which they thought they could survive in Rome. Jerome said to himself: 'It's never wrong to do good.'

He handed them twenty-four gold coins. In exchange the young men gave him a bill of exchange with a value of two hundred gold coins that they thought could be cashed in Rome in compliance with a covenant.

Jerome Gratian entered Rome in early June wearing, as he himself described it, 'the habit of a common criminal.' He could not cash the bill from the two Navarre men as the banks would not accept it, explaining that if the young men died it would not be paid. He found himself shut away in an inn, 'tired of walking, alone and without any money. I felt afflicted and anxious, not knowing when the negotiations would begin [at the Vatican] nor to whom I should turn.'

He knocked on the door of Cardinal Peter de Deza with an introductory letter addressed to the Cardinal from Lady Luisa de Cardenas. The letter stated: 'I beg your Illustrious Lord, as earnestly as I can, to please grant me the favour of listening to him and supporting him, in a way that his just cause be heard, seen and upheld, as one is accustomed to do in this Court.' Jerome would have been satisfied had the Cardinal simply offered him a crust of bread, but the latter insisted that he join him for dinner, and made him a guest in his house for as long as he remained in Rome.

Born in Seville in 1520, Peter de Deza had been a Canon at Seville Cathedral, an Archdeacon of Toledo and Judge at the Chancellery of Valladolid. He had also been an advisor to the Inquisition, and President of the Chancellery of Granada, where he showed his zeal for the conversion of the Moors and, in the end became President of the Chancellery of Valladolid. In 1578 he was created Cardinal by Gregory XIII and joined the Roman Curia in 1580. He assisted at the Conclave of seven Popes. If he did not attain to this position himself, it was, according to a contemporary expression, 'because of the sin of being Spanish.'

Jerome was very happy to stay in the palace of Cardinal Deza and to join him at meals. It was unusual in Rome for Cardinals to allow friars to eat with them. 'The friars in Italy are not as esteemed as they are in Spain,'

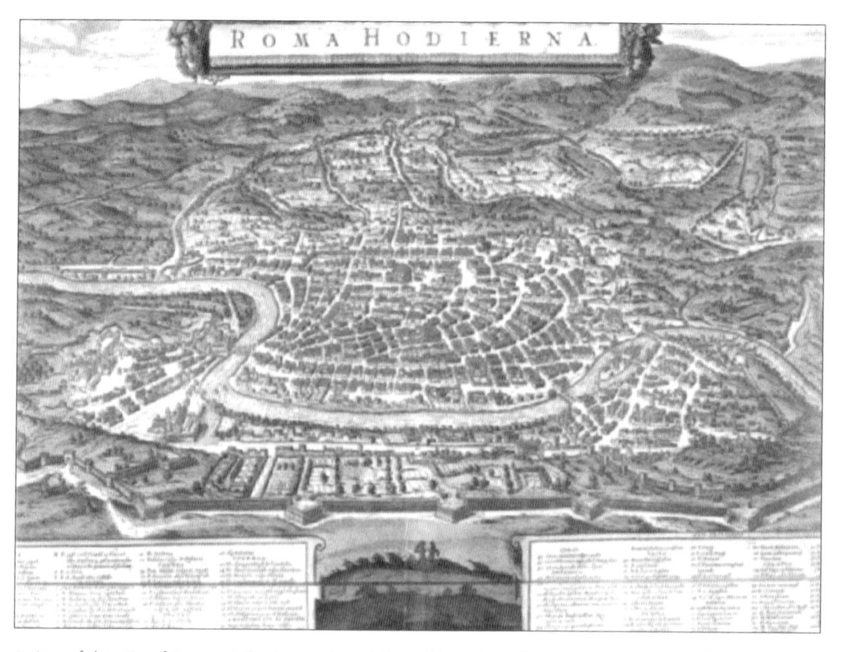

A view of the city of Rome at the beginning of the 16th century. *Engraving from the work Theatrum Orbis Terrarum, 1570. The Estense Library, Modena.*

Jerome noticed. In the meantime he was not short of money. The young men from Navarre were able to return the money they borrowed. Peter Cerezo sent him five hundred gold coins from Seville, which he left in the bank. 'I was cross to see myself with so much money, but afterwards, four hundred coins would serve as my ransom, buying me my freedom; which, had they not been available, I would not have been freed. The other hundred I spent on my travels until I was taken prisoner.'

Doria's henchmen had reached Rome ahead of Gratian and told everyone about his trial and sentence. What was worse, they produced some shameful letters prepared by the Secretary of the *Consulta*, Fr Gregory of the Holy Angels, which described at length his relationships with the nuns as despicable. Gregory presented the events of Jerome's journey from Seville to Lisbon in this way: 'He took some nuns out of their convents and put them with some friars in their Priory, and there he committed the worst kinds of acts of indecency with them.'

However, the Romans were tired of hearing insults and of the persecution of friars, and usually said: *Cose fratesche!* (Things concerning friars!)

As Gratian recalled, 'In a certain sense there had been [in Rome] another honest and persecuted friar. Everyone knew that Pope Sixtus V had come to Rome to get away from being persecuted by friars and rose to be Pope.' For this reason, Romans were reluctant to listen to friars who came singing about the shamelessness of fellow members and eventually in early July, the (Spanish) Ambassador, the Duke of Sessa, ordered the two Discalced Carmelite friars, Diego Evangelista and Luis of St Jerome, to leave. Consequently, they left Rome for Genoa.

However, Jerome had not won the battle in Rome. Back in Madrid Doria was anxious and had prompted the King, Philip II, to send an urgent letter to his Ambassador, saying, 'If Father Gratian turns up there, ask the Pope to ignore him and to have nothing more to do with this matter.'

Philip II was not loved in Rome but he did hold a great deal of power. At the time the Cardinals were careful not to upset the Spanish monarch in order to defend a simple friar.

Jerome attempted to introduce his case quietly and without litigation. He asked himself, in order to obtain the revocation of his Sentence, would it not be better to avoid litigation, with its tribunals and judges, and just trust in the grace of God. Shouldn't he forget the past and hope that the Pope would lift his excommunication and give him faculties for confession and preaching.

Jerome had dealings with some important people in Rome who encouraged him to visit the Pope and ask for two Religious who knew the situation in Spain and who would deal with his case 'so that he could achieve peacefully, without injury to anyone the greatest service to God.'

The Cardinals, Peter de Deza, Jerome's friend, and Dominic Pinelli, the Protector of the Carmelite Order, spoke about him to the Pope. Pinelli, Genovese like Doria, had heard all the gossip about this man and, as a result, judged him badly. He told the Pope that, if they were to avoid difficulties, it would be better if Jerome did not return to the Discalced Carmelites but was accepted by the Calced. The Pope replied that it was only reasonable to expect difficulties when his intention is to live with the greatest perfection. He told the two Cardinals: 'See what he wants and help him, and tell him to come and see me so we can talk.'

Cardinal Deza explained to the Pope that he had held him [Jerome] back 'until he really understood what he had to say.' He added, 'Can he, a person in the public eye, renounce his honour just to keep the peace? The answer is no, following the example of Christ, and the teaching of St Thomas [Aquinas].' Cardinal Deza spoke very highly of this Carmelite while Cardinal Pinelli on the other hand maintained a disturbing silence.

King Philip II, for his part, had given orders to his Ambassador to prevent Jerome from turning to the Calced or the Discalced to avoid his being a cause of concern or anxiety. However, in other respects, he should be supported. Jerome described his situation very graphically as being 'between a rock and a hard place: the King and the Pope.'

On 16 August, Gratian was finally able to speak with the Pope, Clement VIII, as he was walking in the gardens of Montecavallo. He gave the Pope a formal document that explained his case and asked to be absolved from the censures contained in his Sentence of expulsion from the Order. The Pope handed the document to his Confessor, Fr Alexandre, who referred it to Fr Toledo, later to become Cardinal. Fr Alexandre was hard on Jerome and put a lot of pressure on him to join another Order; he appeared to be a prejudiced Judge, who 'took the other side.'

Gratian was told that he had to enter another Order. He asked to join the Carthusian monastery of Our Lady of the Angels but they turned him down. He knocked at the door of the Capuchins and the Discalced Franciscans, but they too turned him down. Anastasius explained: 'None of them wanted me. I was seen as a person rejected by all the Orders, and as the vilest Religious in the world.'

The Pope, encouraged by Gratian's adversaries, ordered the Dominicans to accept him in the Priory of the Minerva (Rome). However, the Vicar General of Spain, who at the time was Fr John Vincente, threw himself at the feet of the Pope and pleaded: 'If he has sinned and is a bad man and was deservedly expelled from his Discalced Carmelite Order, what sin has the Order of St Dominic committed that it should be forced to take in someone who had been expelled from the Carmelites.' Gratian lamented:

> The Pope did not say anything. Then something prevented me from taking that habit. From heaven, the Blessed Virgin Mary and holy Mother Teresa must have seen that it was not the way for my salvation to be forced to become a Religious with another Order, no matter how holy. It was not right to join for purely human reasons, nor when there was no divine calling. In all my life I had never been in such distress. I really feared that I would be sent to the galleys. Who knows maybe they [his opponents] had hatched a plot against me, for they wrote to Spain saying that I had been thrown into the galleys by the Pope for being rebellious to the Apostolic See. The Pope's galleys were full of unruly friars, as I was then [considered], who for the least reason had been punished in this way.

Jerome resigned himself: 'When I saw such a terrible and hostile wind, I reduced the sails, hunched up my shoulders, kept my mouth closed and turned to God.'

He met St Philip Neri in the house of the Marquise of Rangosa, a noble lady from Rome. The Saint had grown old; in fact he was coming to the end of his life. One of Neri's disciples described him as 'a handsome, elderly man, fresh faced, his white hair seemed like ermine. The skin on his face was soft and without lines, and when he raises his hand you can see the sun through it like alabaster.' Philip Neri was an undoubted apostle of Rome. This old saint, the founder of the Congregation of the Oratory of Our Lady of the Vallicella, who discerned hearts with his penetrating gaze, told Jerome: '*Fratello, non dubitate*' (Brother, do not doubt).

'How did he understand,' Jerome recalled, 'the anguish I felt at the time. His gestures and words brought me such deep consolation and my heart was filled with such peace, the like of which I have never known in my life. May the Lord be blessed who gives so much grace to His servants and in this way consoles the afflicted.'

Fr Alexandre, the Pope's Confessor, told him that it would be good for him to join the Augustinian Order, and after a certain period of time, he could return to the Order of Carmel. Gratian interpreted the words of the Pope's Confessor to be the will of the Holy Father. However, he was not sure that the Confessor was well informed. 'He who knows about interior turmoil will know that you cannot explain the great quandary this turmoil creates in the heart.'

Gratian was bewildered. He knew the radical position that the Court in Madrid had adopted. Philip II had given orders to the Duke of Sessa, his Ambassador in Rome that on the part of the Discalced Carmelites and in what concerns Fr Jerome's case, 'you must be ready, after a sentence passed in full agreement and by such people and causes, that nothing comes along to contradict it. And so I charge you to carry it out…'

Jerome had also become disillusioned (with the Vatican). He decided, reluctantly, 'to please his friends who wanted him to find honour in the Augustinian Order, to be free from his rivals, to obey the Pope and to use his talents.' When a Jesuit, Joseph de Acosta arrived in Rome, Jerome shared with him all that was in his heart, for they had studied together in Alcala and Joseph was a learned and pious man. He advised his old friend to let things be and not request to join the Augustinians, because he would live afterwards with the greatest of scruples as a consequence. Joseph advised him to 'leave Rome so that the rumours be forgotten; let it be known where you can be found so that the licences might be sent to you there.'

At the end of 1592, while waiting for a reply from the Augustinians, whose General had left Rome, Jerome went to Naples.

Joanna Dantisco, Jerome's mother, suffered as she watched her son suffer. On 21 September while in Madrid she wrote in her will: 'Widow and mother, wife of Diego Gratian, who was a servant of His Majesty, now deceased. I am ill from the illness that our Lord is best served to give me, but in my judgement and natural understanding…'

In one of the clauses of her will she stated: 'Also, I bequeath that Mr Francis de Morales be reimbursed for all he has paid for carriage of letters and dispatches that have come from my son in Rome.'

In his biography on Jerome Gratian, Andrew de Marmol recounted how Joanna suffered a grave internal injury that put her in danger of death. When the doctors gave her only a few hours to live she was given the last rites. However, she asked for silence and those present saw a light around the bed of the dying woman and heard the voice of Teresa of Avila who asked the Blessed Virgin Mary: 'Our Lady, give life to her, my friend.'

Joanna recovered and lived for another ten years. She would be comforted in her final hours by her son, Jerome.

The Viceroy of Naples did not receive Jerome graciously because the visitor was out of favour with King Philip. 'Stung by the off-hand way I had been treated,' Jerome complained, 'and troubled by the thoughts within myself, since I did not know anyone in that city (Naples), I left and getting on my horse gave it free rein to go where it pleased, like the adventurous knights of old, when desperate or afflicted.'

He embarked on a galley bound for Sicily, arriving there sometime in February 1593. There he found the Viceroy, the Count of Olivares. The Countess felt sorry for him and put him up in the Spanish Hospital in Palermo, where he lived for eight months. He dedicated his time to writing books, 'because I did not have anything else to do apart from prayer and study, and sometimes, during recreation, going to speak with the wounded soldiers.' One of these books, for which he had already written a draft in Portugal, was entitled *Mystical Harmony* that touched upon matters of perfection and the spirit. He also wrote a *History of the Carmelite Order.*

> Treated like an Armenian bishop, I was given a room in the hospital containing a small bedchamber with embroidered hangings. I felt that a hospital steward called Simon, who had been a servant of my father, was far too generous to me, so I reprimanded him for what he spent. But he told me that the hospital gave me much less than ordered by the Viceroyals, and so he dipped into his own purse. Simon ate and dined with me, and the captains and soldiers were also very fond of me, because I preached and heard their confessions and understood their problems. In sum, I had a very quiet and good life there; I wrote a book on the Order called, *Flores Carmeli.*

At the beginning of July the Countess of Olivares received the Brief, *Uberes fructus*, from Pope Clement VIII, that had been issued in Rome on 27 January. It was addressed to 'my beloved Sons, the Vicar and Definitors of the Discalced Carmelite Congregation'. The Papal Brief was definitive and a terrible setback to Jerome, confirming, as it did, the Sentence of expulsion. He was obliged to join the Augustinians or another Observant Order. Under no circumstances was he to be received back into the Discalced Carmelites.

> The case of the aspirations and complaints of the same Jerome has been examined by our dear son and theologian, Master Alexander de Francisco, to whom we entrusted the examination of the said case and to report to Us [his conclusion]... once the case had been disputed and on several occasions presented to Us with due diligence, the above mentioned Sentence [that he be expelled from the Discalced Carmelites] was approved and confirmed by Our authority, command and knowledge; the same Jerome promises to enter the Order of the hermit friars of Saint Augustine, whom he himself has chosen.

It got worse, when he was branded a fugitive for not being in Rome.

> As the said Jerome, having then neglected his salvation and his state [as a Religious], turning his back on the fear of God, disregarding the fulfillment of his promise, and going around in a secular habit and without any concern to enter into another Order, We, approving and confirming the said Sentence, and the processes that formulated it... by the present we entrust and order that the said Jerome, under pain of excommunication, *latae sententiae*, and other graver penalties, including corporal, which you yourselves, (or by means of other Prelates, local Ordinaries, or Nuncios of Our Apostolic See, if required by the said Vicar General, or other Prelates or Superiors of the said Discalced friars) can apply to him, strongly oblige and order him in the name of Our authority, to enter the Order of the hermit friars of St Augustine, which, as has been said, he himself has chosen, or enter another of the approved Observant Orders, within the timescale given him, any excuse, appeal or complaint not being permitted; but in such a way that, not having as yet entered into an Order, he cannot come personally to the city of Rome, nor remain in it for any motive or pretext whatsoever, under the same penalties.

As well as the Brief, the Countess de Olivares also received some letters from the General of the Augustinian Order addressed to the Augustinian

Provincial in Sicily, accepting Jerome into the Order. The compassionate Countess, not wishing to inflict on him any more distress, kept the news of the Papal Brief to herself. She hid from the unhappy friar the resolution from Rome. At the same time she begged him to accept the habit of the Augustinians and gave him the letters for the Priors of Messina and Catania (Sicily).

On 13 August, Jerome arrived in Catania where he presented himself to the Prior of the Augustinians. In his pocket was a letter from their Provincial telling them to give him a habit and accept him into their community. However, on checking that he had been expelled from another Order, the Prior advised Jerome to visit the General of the Order in Rome. After this he travelled from Catania to Taormina (Messina region), where he met with the same result.

He sailed back to Naples on the flagship of the Pope's fleet. On board, he met up with a Discalced Augustinian who had letters for him from his (Augustinian) General. These contained the news that they were awaiting him in Rome, where they wanted him to make a foundation of a reformed priory in St Peter's and St Marcelino.

For fear of highway robbers he was reluctant to continue his journey (from Naples) to Rome by land. So after visiting some relatives in the port of Gaeta, he made up his mind to go by sea.

On 11 October 1593, while celebrating Mass very early in the morning, 'he decided, with a happy heart', that he would belong to the Augustinian Order. He put on the black habit and grey capuche that he had been carrying. With this habit on, that looked Augustinian but wasn't, he embarked in Gaeta on a frigate of the Inquisition that was going directly to Rome. It was captained by the owner, Anthony de Leiva. Jerome was 'torn apart,' he admitted, 'by the appeals both of the Blessed Virgin Mary and holy Mother, Teresa of Jesus' appeal not to leave their Order, but now I was taking the habit of the Discalced Augustinians.'

> When the wind calmed down the sailors set sail. About ten o'clock in the morning, when we were ten miles out of Gaeta, near the Circeo mountain, the crew saw a Turkish galley in the distance with smoke coming from its mast: the signal that these were pirates. Fear seized the crew and they began to cry out. The galley came close and fired muskets and cannon balls to get our crew to surrender.
>
> Our frigate stopped moving and the Turks came on board and in no

> time they robbed everyone on the boat. They made us all climb on board their frigate. Besides myself there were nine sailors, five passengers and a servant who had become attached to me. When I saw people dressed in blue and red and with white headdresses it did not look good, especially when two or three of them surrounded me saying 'asperos, asperos', which meant money. They asked me to give them what I was carrying. The only thing I understood was the desperate situation I was in.

Jerome quickly found himself stripped of all his clothes,

> stripped of the habit of Saint Augustine that I had put on that day… I gave thanks to God and to the Blessed Virgin who so quickly punished me for the decision I had made four hours earlier, after my Mass, to take off the habit she had chosen for me. However, I was happy with the habit that Adam had given me, no one could take this from me, except by skinning me.

'Because this was the end of my time as a Discalced and the beginning of my time as a captive,' Anastasius lamented bitterly, and 'to avoid making mistakes and in order to catch my breath, let us leave the account of my captivity for another day.'

Chapter Twenty-Four

A Captive in Tunis

Jerome Gratian was stripped of the Augustinian habit he had put on that very day, and 'happy to put on the habit that Adam gave me.' He covered his private parts with a linen cloth. Once he had got over the initial shock he reasoned that 'he would surely not survive in the galley, it would be nothing other than a slow death. It was possible to survive in a Christian galley, especially the Pope's, but those of the Turkish galley meant death.' When he was in Rome he had been afraid he might end up in a papal galley.

He felt the loss of his possessions but above all his writings, including his *Mystical Harmony*: a spiritual dissertation that he had written in Palermo and which he had brought with him to publish in Rome, but now the Turks used it to clean their weapons.

The prisoners were put in the hold of the galley, where they met other captive Christians, all with their hands in chains, everyone crammed in together. The galley continued on its journey, the heat and smell were unbearable. The prisoners were fed a vile black biscuit and just a little foul smelling water to drink. After a few days at sea, during which the Turks had captured more Christians, they arrived at the island of Ventotene. From there they intended to return to North Africa in order to avoid the perilous winter weather and to restock their food supply.

Ventotene, in the Province of Naples, was a small island, just two miles wide. It had an ancient history, including, among other stories that of Ulysses who heard in the breakwaters the singing of the mermaids.

The captives were allowed to step on land and eat a milky pudding made with maize and drink as much as they liked from the pools of dirty rain water; water that wasn't foul smelling as the water they had been drinking.

One of the Turks, seeing Gratian almost naked, took pity on him and gave him a covering of coarse wool so that he could survive. A fellow

Christian from the galley gave him some old sandals; a Moor, who had been a slave in Madrid to the Secretary, Matthew Vazquez, gave him a blue cap that covered his bald patch. One of the Turks gave him a piece of sweet bread that was not as black as the biscuits he had eaten, which he shared among his companions. 'The taste of that sweet bread and the dirty rainwater was such at the time that all the tasty morsels and gifts that one could imagine could not compare. ... I enjoyed the sweet bread more than almonds, the water refreshed me much more than sweet wine.'

He remained calm in the midst of his misfortune, convinced that this situation would lead to his death. However, 'he experienced an inner calmness and a light that dispelled all the darkness and disturbances that had been tormenting him. He hoped by undergoing martyrdom for Christ that he would soon see him. As long as he had to live he would accept whatever suffering he had to endure as a slave.'

The anxieties and the turmoil that had troubled his heart now ceased and all the problems of the past were forgotten: where was Doria and the *Consulta* and the Pope…? He foresaw that he would not return to the land of the Christians, that death awaited him at the hands of the enemies of Christ, but it was, he admitted, 'a real cross, when servants of God, without scruple or fear, do wrong.'

The bad weather got worse and the Turks feared being cut off and left without food. They offered up prayers and invocations to Mohammed. They called on the '*papaz*': the Turks used the term *papaz*, (Pope) to address Christian clerics. They got Jerome to sit down in their midst, forcing him to sit on a stone. Our Carmelite was alarmed by this and had no idea what they were up to. They asked him to lift up one of his feet. There was a fire burning nearby. One of the Turks took a red hot iron from the fire and immediately branded a cross on the sole of his foot, and then the same with the other foot.

Some time later Jerome asked some Christians who had spent a long time as prisoners of the Turks why they did this. They explained: 'Father, it's a Turkish superstition that when the weather is bad and they see they are in danger, and with their hatred for the cross of Jesus Christ, they brand a cross onto the soul of any priest they find. We must warn you Father, that if their circumstances don't improve you will surely be burned alive, since this is what they do.' Jerome prayed that the weather would improve. He had grown up wanting to sacrifice himself for Christ, but he now trusted that his prayers would be answered and they would reach North Africa.

Indeed, his prayers were answered. That same night, three galleys from the Pasha of Tunis together with some small sailing boats from Bizerta sought shelter from the bad weather near the island of Ventotene. They brought with them fresh supplies of food and an abundance of biscuits. The pirates chose as captain of this small fleet the man in charge of Gratian's galley, as he was the most experienced. When the weather calmed down, they set sail to do more pillaging before they returned to North Africa.

At midnight they caught sight of Gaeta. They had intended to plunder it, but a woman spotted them and began to shout and scream so the alarm was sounded from the castle. Later, during the day, they anchored between Gaeta and Naples, and plundered two hermitages that were in the open country and stole livestock. The following day, in the Bay of Naples, they robbed small boats that were on their regular route from the ports of Torre del Griego and Castelamar. The pirates reached the island of St Peter (off Sardinia), where the prisoners were untied so that they could be deloused and refreshed.

However, the pirates then spotted four galleys from the Grand Duke of Florence which were coming in their direction. Everyone had to quickly scramble on board. The wooden ladder to the galley was taken up so quickly that Jerome almost fell into the sea, and then they immediately cast anchor. The Turks had a great piece of luck when the main mast of the flagship of the Grand Duke broke, which meant it had to give up its pursuit. They arrived eventually in Bizerta, 'which is the port of Tunis and the largest in Barbary. The captives were happy to get some rest after their terrible trials at sea.'

Barbary was the historic name given to the Muslim countries of North Africa; Morocco, Algeria, Tunisia, Libya and Egypt, and today is known as the Maghreb. The Berber kingdoms had become weak, their power undermined by the feuding between the nomadic tribes and town dwellers, and between the interior and the coastal cities; the latter were occupied by nests of pirates who infested the Mediterranean waters and attacked the business interests of the European nations.

The Mediterranean, whose waters lapped the Barbary coastline, was the link that united the three then known continents: Europe, Asia and Africa. The Mediterranean was a place of communication and trade routes, being half *mare nostrum* (our lake) and half 'Turkish lake'. It was considered vital to control the African coastline, as it was a refuge for pirates of the Ottoman Empire who devastated the Mediterranean coastal towns. By the 15th century the blocking of the commercial route to India and China, known as 'the spice route', caused the Portuguese to explore new ways through the seas to India. By hugging the African coastline they discovered a new spice route that avoided the Turk controlled Mediterranean.

Portugal conquered Ceuta (today a Spanish enclave bordering Morocco) in 1415, and began its maritime expansion along the African coast. Spain, then ruled by the Catholic Monarchs (Isabel and Ferdinand), conquered Melilla (a Spanish enclave bordering Morocco) in 1497, to counteract the activities of the Berber pirates. The Catholic Monarchs believed that the re-conquering (of Spain), which culminated in the sacking of Granada in 1492, would not, in fact, be completed until they had incorporated the territories of the old Tingitana Mauritania (northern Morocco). Spain then conquered certain enclaves in North Africa: Melilla in 1497, Mazalquivir in 1505, the rock of La Gomera (Canary Islands) in 1508, Bugia (Algeria) in 1510... All these cities were situated along the western coast, stretching from the city of Oran (Algeria) to the Atlantic.

Apart from the said coastal cities there were the eastern cities of Argel (Algeria) and Tunis. In the first half of the 16th century Argel was the seat of the powerful Barbarrosas. With the protection of the Ottoman Empire they transformed this city into a haven for piracy. An expedition against the city by the Emperor, Charles V, ended in disaster in 1541.

Tunis, a vassal of Spain, was attacked and taken by surprise by the pirate Barbarrosa in 1534. The Sultan, Mulay Hassan, took refuge in the Court of Charles V where he asked the Emperor for help. The Imperial forces invaded Tunis in 1535, reinstated the Sultan and restablished it as a vassal state of Spain until 1574 when it was occupied by the Ottoman fleet. However, from 1591 onwards, two years before Jerome's arrival the Ottoman domination of Tunis was purely nominal and its governors capitulated to the pirates in the Mediterranean.

The galley that took Gratian was controlled by two strong men: Elisbey, a Captain from Bizerta, who owned the vessel, and Durali, who had his house in Argel. Both of them had been pirates for more than twenty-five years. The two divided up the spoils, more than sixty captives, between themselves. They drew lots for the Christians, pairing them up with those of similar age, height and build. Jerome was paired up with a clean shaven young man from Genoa, called John Baptist Almiroto, who 'after being captured offered fifteen hundred gold coins as a ransom. He did not have that amount with him at the time but he was very well off. He had a kind face and the Turks believed they would get a good price for him.' As luck would have it the young man was taken by Durali and Jerome by Elisbey, the captain of of the Bizerta. Jerome was indeed lucky, 'because though this Captain treated his slaves very badly, at that time he needed money desperately, and was prepared to haggle. The mention of ransom was all that the new slaves wanted to hear.'

Elisbey was poorer than Durali and for this reason Jerome imagined that there was a much better chance of being ransomed quickly. The pirate had some thirty captives whom he took to his 'bath': the place where the captives were locked up was called a 'bath'. The word came from Constantinople, where the Christian prisoners were crowded together in the old (Roman) baths that were wide and with high walls. Elisbey's 'bath' was 'a small broken down pen, with some rickety wooden rails. In the middle of the "bath" there was a flour mill; a small donkey led by a blind apostate turned the stone.'

The Turks left their captives without food or drink for a long time. Only eventually did they bring 'a bowl of hot stew made from boiling a cow's head for all thirty captives; I was given a piece of the nose. It happened that Christians whom they [the Turks] convinced to renege on their faith, or who had already begun to be abused in an abominable way, were set apart and given good food, but they forgot about the rest of us.'

Anthony de Leiva, the owner of the frigate that Jerome had been on at the time of his capture, wept bitterly over his loss. He died of melancholy and sadness.

Rumours spread (among the pirates) that Fr Jerome Gratian wasn't just any priest but rather an Archbishop with an income of twenty thousand gold coins, who was going to Rome to become a Cardinal, and that among the Christians he was considered a great *marabuto* (which is what the Turks called their preachers and religious men) and a relative of King Philip of Spain.

'Praise be the Lord who restores my honour,' Jerome exclaimed. 'In the land of the Christians I was greatly dishonoured and humiliated, to the extent that I was not deemed worthy even to be a cook in any Order of the world, but in the land of the Moors I was exalted to the level of a great Archbishop who was going to Rome to be a Cardinal. In no time I would be "the Great Priest": the term they used for the Pope. I have actually been made an Archbishop and Cardinal and potentially the Pope; they call me "*papazquivir*", which is what they call a great Prelate'.

When the Pasha in Tunis heard these rumours, he wanted Gratian for himself; Tunis was just ten miles from Bizerta. There was a law among them that when an important person was captured the Pasha, or the Great Turk (the Ottoman Emperor), could take such a person. Elisbey, who lived in Bizerta, seeing that he could not keep his man because he was a subject of the Pasha, handed him over to Durali, whom the Pasha could not touch because he was a citizen of Argel (Algeria), over which the Pasha had no jurisdiction.

The Pasha sent the Envoy or Ambassador of the Great Turk to Durali. His name was Zambali. He asked Durali for the priest. The Ambassador was escorted by soldiers on horseback with lances and muskets. However, Durali, who was very arrogant, told the Great Turk's official that he would throw him down the stairs if he asked for the priest. Zambali told him quite calmly: 'Look, Durali, I forgive you this time, because I know that you are drunk. Do what I say or on the head of the Great Lord, I shall drag you by the tail of my horse! No more drinking wine today. We shall speak again tomorrow morning.'

The following morning, 12 November, Zambali ordered Gratian to get ready to go to Tunis.

> The only thing I had was an old breviary given to me here in the Durali 'dungeon', and a striped coat, which is like a poor person's mantle of different colours, which I wore against my already frayed skin: this happened due to the coarseness of the sackcloth in the galley; also I had a small blue cap that covered half my head: that was then the dress of the black archbishop.

Jerome lost all hope of a quick ransom.

> Some Christians told me that they took important captives to Constantinople, to the towers of the Black Sea, keeping them there like exhibits for a long time until they died. Just as other Kings usually have cages for lions or exotic birds, the Great Turk has a wooden cage full of important men, surrounded by a very strong wall. In the end, I lost hope of being ransomed and in my mind I saw myself as another bird in that cage. I've been told by the Christians that it is so cold [there] they cut the feet off many who are suffering from frostbite, so that they do not die.

When the party reached Tunis, they took Jerome to the Pasha's castle where he was made to kneel down in front of the ruler. The Pasha asked him about life in Spain and news of the King. Jerome had no desire to speak (about these things), as all he wanted was to speak about a ransom and gaining his freedom.

He was then led to the store cupboard, which served as the palace's prison. 'The first thing he heard were loud groans and the crying of a Christian called John Casaz, to whom they had just given eight hundred lashes, breaking every bone in his body.' Jerome spent the night in that place. The following day the 'eunuchs' came to visit him. This is what they called 'the young shaven men whom they kept as "ladies" for their abominable amusement. These men dressed very elegantly, were clean shaven and wore perfume, as those engaged in such a bad profession were obliged to do. They were kept indoors, under lock and key, others did the same with their female friends.'

One of these men, called Gonzalo Machuca, from Cordoba, was a slave to Abraham Aga. Gonzalo heard the voice of his master: 'Machuca, come here to your priest; kiss his hand.' 'This I shall willingly do,' he replied, and fell on his knees in front of Fr Gratian who gave him an 'archbishop's' blessing, as if he really were an archbishop, while the others laughed.

Machuca leaned forward and whispered in Gratian's ear: 'Father, don't even think about a ransom nor speak about it, even if they do, but rather tell them that you must die here, that there is no one who remembers you in the land of the Christians, because you don't have any other way of achieving freedom (than to become a muslim).' 'I was not expecting to hear these words,' Jerome said to himself, 'I did want to talk about my ransom as soon as the Pasha called me, and I had nothing else in mind other than to be free as soon as possible from this land.'

When the *rengil* Abraham Aga (the Turks called 'rengil' or 'woman's blouse' those Turks who liked to dress their men slaves as women) saw that Machuca spoke to Jerome secretly, he said to him in a loud and angry voice: 'What are you saying to him, you dog? Are you persuading him not to be a Moor?'

The Pasha did not summon Jerome and there was no talk of a ransom. He was taken to the 'bath' with the other captured Christians where a blacksmith put iron chains on his feet, which is what they did with a Christian they intended to ransom.

Cyril asked Anastasius: 'What was a "bath" and what was your life like in that place?' Anastasius replied: 'They call a prison a "bath", a place in which they kept captured Christians, it could just as well be called a dungeon or an underground cell, for that is what it was: a subterranean prison, a kind of well, in which they kept the captives. It just had a vent for light. The door was very thick and had many locks. It led out into a small yard where the soldiers stood guard with their weapons. There was another heavily locked door that led to the citadel or fortress of Tunis, from where they kept a strict watch over the Christians so that they could not escape. When the sun sets the Christians go to bed and the door is closed. At sunrise they open the door to let the Christians out to work.

'It was a very narrow place to live in, so that we were all squashed in like sardines. In order to accommodate the six hundred Christians who were there, they made places, like wattles, used to breed silkworms, one over another, which they called "communes". In the "bath" we created a space that served as a chapel with two altars. We also slept there; that is to say, my friend, Fr Luis, Canon of Lipari in Sicily, and I. The Pasha had bought Fr Luis from another Moor and kept him locked up so that he could say Mass for the Christians.'

'Oh my God! Did they allow you to say Mass?' Cyril was surprised. 'Yes, and with such readiness that, when they discussed my ransom, the Pasha, my owner, said: "I do not want to give away my Priest for any amount of money, as he makes my Christians happy." He said this because I preached to them every night after they had come together and eaten. I sat in a makeshift pulpit, a barrel from the galley, at the door of our chapel, where everyone in the "bath" could hear. At the same time we also recited our evening prayer, accompanied by a lot of guitar music and similar instruments; all the Christians sang together without much respite (from their suffering).

'Whenever I preached I would criticize Mohammed and his sect in order to encourage some weak Christians who were about to renege on their faith. However, on one occasion a Turkish guard (some guards were located in the "bath") went to the Pasha to complain that the priest had said bad things against their holy prophet, Mohammed. The Pasha responded by severely scolding the guard: "Dog, who told you to listen to what the priest was preaching? Do you, by chance, want to become a Christian? Leave them alone. Aren't they in their own place? Do you expect them to say good things about Mohammed?"'

The 'bath' was a tight squeeze for the six hundred Christians who lived there, the majority of them in chains. 'There was a lot of noise, a foul smell and all kinds of fleas that loved to feed quietly on our bodies. I don't know what more to say other than to tell you that any Christian prison would be like paradise, in comparison with what that place was like.'

Most of the captives went to work outside every day. Anastasius explained to Cyril: 'I never had to do this. I remained always in the "cloister", together with some twenty or thirty old and worn out people, or those chained with heavy irons (as I was). We Christians made these mats which we shared with a companion, out of palm leaves. They served as a blanket, mattress and sheet. I was in agony with the kind of chains they put on my feet, which later they took off, I couldn't sit up straight and when I said Mass I could only kneel with a great deal of effort. I usually found it easier to pray and study lying down than in any other position.'

Jerome had spent more than a month in the Pasha's 'bath', when on Christmas Eve of that year, 1593, a Portuguese man whom the Turks called the '*Papareta*', because he was small in stature, (a man often criticized for being a terrible liar), fell on his knees before him. Taking hold of Jerome's hands and, with tears in his eyes, he began to kiss them, telling him: 'Father, may your faith remain strong, look at Jesus Christ and the Blessed Virgin Mary, keep your eyes fixed on your eternal reward…' Jerome was taken aback and asked him: 'What's happened that you are preaching to me *Papareta*? Why are you telling me this, my brother?' He replied, 'Don't you know, Father? I don't want to be the first to tell you the news.'

The man wanted to walk away without telling him anything but Jerome insisted that, for the love of God, he tell him what was happening.: 'This morning,' the man told him, 'the Janissary [the elite Turkish guard] had a meeting of their council. They sent their representative to tell the Pasha that they know you are an Inquisitor in the land of the Christians and have burnt more than fifty apostates. This is why you were on the frigate belonging to the Inquisition; you were transporting those prisoners in chains and fetters to bring them to justice. They are asking that you be burned alive. You should know by now that the Pasha will not object to what this council orders. These dogs do not burn people like we do in the land of the Christians, but rather they place the fire at a distance so that the body is roasted slowly.'

The Janissary consisted of more than four thousand soldiers who guarded the land for the Sultan of Constantinople. The soldiers had met at the custom's office to discuss Gratian, whom they accused of being an Inquisitor. Our man knew how insolent the Janissary could be towards the Pasha. He also was aware that they had burned Fr John Vanegas, a Calced Carmelite from Toledo, in Argel, because he told them he had a cousin who was an Inquisitor.

> Immediately my nerves shrank and my throat tightened, the blood in my veins turned cold; blood that would later be burned in the fire. The rest of the Christians returned from their work, closing the door of the 'bath', they all came to sympathize with me. They were in tears when they confirmed the news about the fire. I began to pray as if I were a martyr, since I was going to die for the faith at the hands of those who hated the Inquisition, which the Christian world upholds. I tried to remember the many good intentions I made in prayer to be a martyr for Christ; especially two days earlier, when they had stoned a Jew to death, all because he said, 'I hope you have a bad journey Mohammed'! I was very envious that he had died, but sorry because he died a Jew. I desired to be in a similar situation to attain glory and leave behind so much misery, and bring to an end my trials and persecutions.

Jerome feared he would give in at the thought of such a cruel death: 'They put the fire all around the Christian until he slowly roasts.' He made his confession to Fr Luis, the Sicilian Canon from Lipari, his companion during his captivity. He celebrated the three masses that a priest normally celebrated at Christmas.

Dawn came. Any noise turned his stomach with the thought that they were coming for him. A captive, named Montilla, wanting to comfort him, told him that he had given an apostate friend ten gold coins to stab him in the heart to save him from the torments of the fire. The plan was, when he was tied to the stake, the man would approach him and, before anyone could stop him, would kill him.

Midday arrived and still no one had come for him. He forced himself to eat. 'It is one thing,' he said, 'to think about martyrdom but quite another to be so close to the real thing.' The waiting continued for several days. He grew tired of making so many acts of martyrdom. Afterwards he learned why the Janissary wanted to kill him: they had abducted him from a frigate belonging to the Inquisition so they had presumed he was an Inquisitor, being the most important person on the ship, the others were sailors or poor people. He also learned why the Pasha had defended him.

The Pasha spoke in the following way to the Janissary: 'I, myself, would willingly give you my priest for you to burn and all my Christians if you want, and also my own self. However, I ask you to consider two things: first, that my Priest is not of such low status that he would be an Inquisitor, but is an important Archbishop who was going to Rome to become a Cardinal and shortly afterwards was going to become Pope. And second, as you already know, the Great Lord [the Sultan] has ordered me to obtain the release of Amatarraez, a Provincial Governor, from captivity, who is a prisoner in a castle in Naples, and also Caudali, an Arab soldier, who has been forced to row in the Spanish galleys. They [the Christian authorities] would exchange these two for the priest, or, failing that, they will give me thirty thousand gold coins for his ransom, and this money would pay for their release. However, that said, if you have information that he really is an Inquisitor then burn him as soon as you like.'

The fury of the Janissary abated, 'because the Turks [the Janissary] were placated, the rest was easy to remedy. And so the *Papaz* escaped the fire.'

Lent of 1594 arrived and Jerome doubled the number of prayers he said and went more frequently to confession. On Easter Sunday a Spanish prisoner, an apostate called Mami, arrived in the 'bath'. He was from Fuente del Sauco, six miles from Salamanca. He was dark skinned, with a wart on his right cheek, his right arm wounded by a musket shot. He was captured in Rio de Oro and taken to Tetuan and from there to Argel by a Moor called Majaluf, who was from Granada. His owner forced him to be circumcised and gave him the name Mami. For fourteen years, till the present day, he had dressed like a Turk.

Jerome tried to learn the Turkish language from Mami who knew it well. In between classes they had long talks about the perdition of his soul. Eventually he returned to the faith when Jerome converted him. 'However, he could not do this without having to undergo a real test, after which many had died for Christ.' In other words he had to confess publically his faith in Jesus Christ which he had denied.

After making his confession, Mami called on the most important people in the 'bath', Jacob and Baptist Espelares, Anthony de Maruella, Alonso de Ojeda, Fr John Ruiz, a Calced Carmelite, and some others to accompany him. They went out onto the patio, and standing before Zali Mamet, the Pasha's private guard, and other Turks who were there, he openly proclaimed: 'I, gentlemen, am a baptized Christian, who was given the baptismal name of Alonso of the Cross. Afterwards, being ignorant and a bad man, I reneged on my faith in Jesus Christ and adopted the perverse sect of Mohammed. Now I state publically that I deny the sect of Mohammed that I hold to be wrong and deceitful, and I confess that the faith in Jesus Christ is true and holy and I am returning to it.'

After he spoke these words the Christians took him quickly to the 'bath', watching his back lest he be killed. Zali Mamet, angry and upset, shouted at him: 'How can this be, since you were circumcised according to the law of our saint?' And shouting even louder he said: 'Does your Priest think all of us must become Christians?' And added, 'You will soon see what will happen to you,' before going off to tell what had happened to the Pasha.

According to their law an apostate who returned to Christianity, should be killed straight away. Alonso of the Cross, now no longer Mami, awaited martyrdom. The priest, Jerome Gratian, was to be beaten with a stick fifty times. He had been saved from being burned at Christmas, thanks to the Pasha's greed.

The Pasha told Zali Mamet: 'And what business is it of yours if he becomes a Christian? We have a spare oar in our galleys [for you]. Just ensure that the Mufti, who is like a bishop, doesn't find out. Don't let his secretary find out either, as he is like the chief magistrate of the city. They shall not burn our priest. As for the other one, let him be.'

Zali Mamet returned and shouted: 'You, the Priest and Mami, come here!' The two of them stood up, swallowing hard, both afraid of the pain that was surely to come. They were then taken to the blacksmith next to the guards' room. The blacksmith did not say a word, but Zali Mamet ordered him to take the chains off the priest and put them on Mami. 'It was such a relief,' wrote Gratian, 'to see my feet without that metal bar; I had longed to see myself one day without those irons and be able to cross one leg over the other.' However, they then put an iron chain on him, a very rusty one, which they called Magyar-chains: the Magyar's usually put them on Turks they captured. 'The new chains were very thick and heavy. My ankles were clasped with big shackles that weighed twice as much as the original irons.'

Jerome and his companion returned to the 'bath', but always anxious: 'Mami of being burned and the Father, of being beaten.' Some time passed before Mami was condemned to row in the galleys and Jerome was left with 'a ton of iron'.

'The temptation to apostatize was obvious,' Gratian wrote in his book, *The Chronicles of a Captive*, so that 'more than half, and even three-quarters, reneged on their faith.' It would be a miracle if any of the boys and clean-shaven young men escaped. Even though they were only cabin boys or very small and poor, nonetheless the Turks bought them at excessively high prices for their own corrupt ways. Once the young captive had been bought his owner dressed him in fine clothes, fed him delicious food and offered other delights, thus persuading him to become a Muslim.

The anxiety that came from being held captive and the fear generated from seeing other Christians suffer meant it was all too easy to be persuaded… And when they (young Chritian captives) found themselves dressed in silk clothes, with as much delicious food as they could eat and adored by their owners, who had bought them for their own evil purposes, it did not seem so bad to renege on their Christian faith, whose doctrine they had never really understood. If, however, some managed to persevere without reneging on their faith, at the harvest banquet, when the Turks were drunk, the latter grabbed hold of their (Christian) waiters and forcefully circumcised them; it didn't matter how much they shouted or cried out.

Sodomy or 'the unspeakable sin' as it was called at the time, was customary among those people. Many of the bad men preferred to 'renege in order to avoid going to the galleys, which were insufferable. Others reneged in order to enjoy a comfortable but depraved lifestyle. If they escaped these two options, the cunning ingenuity and false testimonies of the Moors led many others to fall.' Without doubt, it was difficult for these men to go through the pain involved in circumcision, but it was even harder to lose all hope of being ransomed and of being set free; which happened when there was no reply to their letters.

What did Jerome do all day in prison? He heard the confessions of fellow Christian captives and sought to comfort them when they had been beaten. He mediated when there were arguments and visited the sick. He offered their captives money to pardon those whose ears or nose they were going to cut off. As a result of his efforts on their behalf he was shown the greatest respect by all the Christians. They gave him their money so it wouldn't be squandered away on gambling. And when money was given by Turks who were ill to be cured by their sick Christian playthings, it was not given to the latter but to Jerome. 'Here *Papaz*, take these ten gold coins. If Doctor Peter heals me after a number of days give them to him. If not, give them back to me. You see we are not so foolish as the people of your country, since we give money to the doctor not just to treat us, but to heal us.'

Acting like he was an archbishop Gratian wrote letters of pardon for those Christians who approached him because they had reneged on their faith. With the letter he gave them a certificate, written in Latin, adding names they used of Mohammed, so that if they got to the land of the Christians, it certified to the Inquisition and archbishops that they had his blessing. He helped many Christians in this way. With the money that was given him and his status as 'archbishop' he had authority to arrange the ransom of Christians.

His companion, Fr Luis, celebrated Mass at daybreak for the six hundred Christians in the 'bath' before they went out to work. He, on the other hand, said daily Mass for the Christians in the prison belonging to the Janissary and other special slaves, of which there were more than one thousand six hundred in Tunis. He said Mass secretly for the Christian women in the prison and for the many men and women who reneged on their faith.

> One of them gave me twelve coins in case I wanted to buy something for myself; another gave me a cotton shirt. The female captives from the prison gave me, via a captive who served them, a linen shirt, like the kind they wear in Holland; afterwards I learned that they did this on the orders of the Sultan's wife, herself an apostate. Afterwards, in order to keep me dry, the Christians made a white coat especially for me. They shared with me what little food they had; placing a roasted patridge on a stone they could divide it up into nine pieces. All the bakers are Chritian. The Pasha's baker gave me a loaf every day; it was the whitest and tastiest bread I have ever tasted. The Janissary's baker gave me six white loafs for the women's prison. The Christian women as well as the women who had reneged on their faith sent me bread from the Sultan's table and many other presents. I was also bought presents secretly by some individuals who had reneged. They came to me to play music and entertain me and to share with me things they had written to the Viceroys and to the Christian world. I allowed them to do this because I did not want to miss an opportunity to re-convert some.

'In the end, I had a comfortable life, like a bishop,' Jerome acknowledged, 'as I did not lack presents or money. I was able to exercise my talents on behalf of the people who were so needy, and which bore obvious fruit.'

During his time in captivity he did not cease to write. Some letters he wrote to friends and benefactors asking for money to ransom him have been preserved. There are also three letters he wrote to his mother, Joanna, who in her old age lived with her son Thomas in Madrid, opposite the Church of St Martin: Thomas was a Secretary to King Philip II.

It would take too long to write about the thousands of incidents Jerome recorded in great detail for us to reflect on, about his experiences during his captivity in Tunis. I would just like to ask him, like Cyril: 'Tell me how Jerome were you ransomed? I really want to know?' Anastasius replied: 'There was a rich Jew from Tunis, called Simon Escanasi…'

However, before we get to that, he recounted how, many years before, when he was living in Lisbon, he had saved the life of a Jew from soldiers who had been sent to kill him. His name was Abraham Gebre. He was so grateful that he wanted to give his saviour three hundred gold coins as a reward, but Jerome told him: 'Whatever good I do for someone I don't do it for money. God will repay me by the hand of another Jew.' He rememberd this event now because it would be a Jew that would free him from captivity.

It happened like this. Simon Escanasi, a rich Jew from Tunis, was on his way to Naples to sell his merchandise. At the port of Gaeta, he was taken prisoner and his property seized. Jerome's relatives, who lived in Gaeta, one of whom was Jewish, knew that Simon Escanasi was a powerful figure in Tunis. They managed to get his merchandise released and, giving Simon six hundred gold coins, begged him to do what he could to ranson their relative. The Jewish merchant was grateful to these relatives. He took the ransom money to a Genovese family called Lomelines, who earned their living through commerce and fishing: they lived in Tabarka, near Tunis.

The Pasha, who had returned from a hunting trip, owed a month's salary to the Janissary soldiers. The latter were so bold that they told the Pasha: 'Give us our money or give us your head.' Faced with this predicament the Pasha asked the Jewish merchant, Escanasi, to lend him some money, adding, 'Do you want the Janissarys to kill me?' The Jewish man replied: 'I don't have any money. However, there could be no better solution than to release the priest and pay the Janissary with his ransom money. If you delay any longer, given the way you treat him, the only thing you'll get out of this is a bag of bones. I have come from where he lived and have been given six hundred coins for his ransom. I spoke with his relatives and they told me who he is. Although he is a great servant of God and preacher and Religious, his Order won't give anything for him; he does not occupy a position of any authority nor possess any income other than that of a poor friar; he has managed to fool you.'

The Pasha was convinced by what the Jewish merchant told him. He asked the merchant to speak to the *Papaz* and agree a ransom price. Escanasi told Jerome: 'If this opportunity passes and the Pasha finds money elsewhere, you will have no hope of being freed.' Jerome replied: 'I have no other money than the six hundred gold coins you tell me you've deposited in Tabarka.' The Jewish man said: 'Let's get the iron chains off for now, then we'll see… God is great!' Jerome agreed to this and said: 'If this Jewish man says God is great how could I say otherwise?'

Jerome Gratian and Simon Escanasi sought to borrow a thousand gold coins from the Arabs and Jews; the amount they needed to meet the ransom demand. On 11 April 1595, after eighteen months of captivity, the Pasha of Tunis signed a letter of freedom for Jerome,

> Fr Jerome, a Spanish priest, and my Christian slave, has given me a thousand gold coins, in exchange for which I give him this letter of freedom. With this letter it is to be understood that from today onwards he is free and can go wherever he wants without any hindrance or without contradiction. He can leave to go to the land of the Christians from any port, door or land in north Africa that he chooses from this day that I have given him his freedom. This was written in the moon of Xaaban, in the year one thousand and three. Mohammed, Pasha of Tunis.

The Turks took the chains off Jerome's feet. The blows from the hammer were very painful but eventually he was free. The Jewish merchant hid him in Tunis because he foresaw what would happen. Indeed, the Pasha, no longer pressurized by the Janissary, having paid them off with the money, regretted freeing his priest. He felt that he had been fooled and said that Jerome should give him at least six thousand more gold coins and searched throughout Tunis to get him locked up again.

Simon Escanasi went to see the Controller and the Mufti, where he produced the said letter of freedom. Jerome, safe in his hiding place, trembled at the thought of going back to prison. In the end the Jewish merchant succeeded in his dispute with the Pasha. He brought Jerome to the French Consul's house where he remained for a month, until he could leave Tunis for Tabarka. It was in Tabarka that the agent of the Lomelines' family, Stephen Salinier, who was then in charge of the fortress, handed over the six hundred gold coins to Simon Escanasi which the latter had carried from Gaeta for Jerome's ransom. Salinier himself gave another seven hundred which completed the ransom, not only for Jerome but also for a priest and lawyer called Utiel, who had been ransomed with him. Jerome insisted on staying in Tabarka with this money and more besides, until two thousand *ducats* was raised to rescue those who had been held captive with him. He revealed that twelve Christian captives had been ransomed in this way, with the four hundred gold coins that a certain Diego Rodriguez had lent him for his own ransom, and with some more gold coins that some of the apostatized had given him and other Christians had lent him.

He reached Tabarka at the beginning of May, where he remained until he was able to embark on a ship bound for Genoa. He reached the Italian port on 18 August.

Chapter Twenty-Five

Cardinal Deza's Theologian

In Genoa, Gratian stayed in a place near the Dominicans. Although making him welcome, Fr Ferdinand of Our Lady, the Discalced Carmelite Prior of St Anne's, could not invite him into the Priory. Jerome recorded this very graphically in a letter to his sister, Mary of St Joseph, a Discalced Carmelite nun in Madrid:

> I am here in this garden belonging to Jacome and Beatrice Marengo, because the Fathers have orders not to allow anyone who has been expelled to enter the Priory. I am like a deer that comes out from among the bushes, exhausted by the chasing pack of dogs; its ears pricked, it leaps back at the least sound of a crossbow. They are like men aiming muskets, waiting to see if it is a wild beast or a man that is making a noise among the bushes before firing or lowering their guns.

In Genoa, he was able to get details of the many events that had taken place during his captivity. Doria was dead, as were some others who had signed the Sentence that expelled him. Anastasius reflected on this:

> The truth is that in the first year I was held captive God raised to heaven almost all those who had been my judges, who had expelled me and those who had wanted to see me expelled from the Order. Now they will have to give an account to God for this. Those who remain will have cause to be fearful. Rumours circulated among the people that this was the righteous judgement of God. We shall all have to go before the judgement seat of God when the secrets of our hearts will be revealed.

Mary of St Joseph, not Jerome's sister, but the Prioress of Lisbon, was more explicit; she had also suffered from Doria's axe-wielding when she was locked away in a cell in her convent:

> Practically the entire Order was placed in the greatest predicament that anyone has ever seen. There was almost no hope of getting away from his [Doria's] tyrannical leadership… Our Lord was pleased to set his little flock free and guide it along the [right] path. And later after him others died… in fact of those who collaborated in these matters, six have died within a short space of time. With their deaths, all the threats vanished like smoke, leaving the whole Order, and even the whole of Spain, astonished to see that all in that group had met their end.

We need to retrace our steps to see what occurred in the Discalced Carmelite Order after Gratian had been expelled.

On 3 April 1592, the General of the (Calced) Carmelite Order, John Baptist Caffardo, had died on a journey from Italy to Spain. On 6 June 1593, Pentecost Sunday, the General Chapter of the said Order took place in Cremona, when Gratian was in Palermo. At this Chapter a new General was elected. Doria had been present as Vicar General of the Discalced Carmelites, accompanied by a group of five Provincials, each one with two Socii. The former Vicar General (of the Calced), Fr John Esteban Chizzola, was elected as the new General. He was taken aback when the Discalced Carmelites brought him a petition at the end of the Chapter seeking independence from the Carmelite Order. This created a huge commotion at the Chapter. In order to avoid a long drawn out legal battle he therefore proposed to 'sacrifice something now so as not to lose everything.' He knew that Doria was power hungry and that he enjoyed the protection of the Spanish Monarch, so that sooner or later he would have his way.

In a secret ballot the General, Chizzola, and his Definitors approved the separation that Doria longed for. This was achieved more easily than was expected. On 20 December 1593 (Jerome was by now a captive) Pope Clement VIII confirmed the agreement in Cremona with the Brief *Pastorales officii* by which the Discalced Carmelite Order became independent of the Carmelites of the Ancient Observance, and Doria was appointed its first Superior General until the first Chapter of the new Order. This would take place in May 1594. When death came knocking on Doria's door he was at the height of his power and conceit: he had been General of a new Order in the Church.

At the beginning of April 1594, shortly after they had celebrated the General Chapter of 'The Discalced Brothers of the Order of the Blessed Virgin Mary of Mt Carmel', which was the title of the new Order, Doria retired to pray at the newly founded Priory in Bolarque, near Pastrana. It was a remote place near the river Tajo. During the meal, they read in the refectory a book on the excellence of penance but which also contained warnings and objections against blind and imprudent penances. When Doria heard this he was furious and wanted to burn the book. The community told him that the book did contain some valuable points. However, he responded: 'What good can it be, if it has this chapter? Throw it away, your Reverences, and don't read it here again. Penance, Fathers, penance; all this prudence and discretion lead to us losing souls!'

The pathological aspect of his character became more evident at the hour of his death. His obsessive behavior made him tense and anxious. He usually went through the cloisters at St Hermenegildo with his fingers crossed and would reprimand those who passed him: 'Brother, *in fine hominum denudatio operum*.'[1] As he walked through the garden, he made odd movements with his hands that seemed to suggest he had lost his head; his anxiety for power had made him quite neurotic.

While on his way to Segovia, where the General Chapter was to be held, he fell ill in Alcala de Henares. A small bone in his foot caused him to take to his bed from which he would never arise. When some Fathers visited him on his sickbed he launched into his obsessions: 'My Fathers, the time has come to speak about important principles. If we wish to live and die with solace then we must practise penance, be observant and all must live as equals. And so as not to delude myself, I testify before the Lord who must judge me, that though I am not worthy to govern this Order, I am not aware of having been jealous or bitter towards anyone, and that everything I have tried to introduce into the Order was not for any other motive than to please God and improve the Order's observance and primitive perfection.' One sentence alone summed up all that Doria was trying to say: 'Fathers, from the grave my bones will preach this message. This is the way I have lived, and this is how I shall die.'

Doria died in the Priory of Alcala, on 8 May, at five o'clock in the morning. He was just nine days short of his fifty-fifth birthday; he had been in the Order for nineteen years.

Shortly before he died Doria confessed he had not been jealous or bitter towards anyone. When those who had condemned Gratian were dying, they cried out that he was innocent. Anastasius said: 'While they were dying

1 At the end of the day examine what you have done.

they said for all to hear that I was innocent. They did this both to restore my reputation, in so far as they could, and to free themselves from the fear they had for having slandered and humiliated me. There is no more compelling testimony to my innocence than when my adversaries acknowledge it.'

Jerome was referring especially to Fr Thomas Aquinas, from Seville, who was professed in Los Remedios. While travelling from Madrid to the Escorial he fell and 'ruptured a vein. Within a few months he became consumptive. One morning his confreres found him dead; he had died alone.'

The (General) Chapter was celebrated in Madrid, not in Segovia, at which the Nuncio, Caetani, was present. Fr Elias of St Martin, then Prior of Toledo, was elected General for a period of six years, with nine votes in favour from a total of fifteen.

Mary of St Joseph showed her joy at the election of Fr Elias:

> Our Father Elias of St Martin was elected without fuss and very amicably by the entire Order. We hope with him not only that peace will be fully restored but also for the return of those the Order has lost. That saintly man, Father Jerome Gratian, has been a great loss to the entire Order. May the Lord rescue him from captivity which came about due to the persecution of his enemies, who, as men of power, pursued him over land and sea until he fell into the hands of the Turks. There he does what he has always done, which is to free the souls of those who apostasized from the power of the devil, restoring them to the faith. It is for this reason that the Turks are prolonging his time in prison and the trials he has to go through.

The Nuncio wrote in his report to Cardinal Aldobrandini, the Secretary of State of the Holy See, that Fr Elias, the new General, is 'one of the oldest members in the Order; he is prudent, discreet, learned and leads an excellent life.' He added this curious note: 'The death of Fr Doria has not caused any alteration, but rather has had a good effect, because, though he was infinitely worthy, his election to govern in perpetuity as General would not have been right. His leadership had begun to be much disliked and once again created divisions in this Order.'

At the Madrid Chapter the members read out the 1593 Brief, *Uberes fructus* that confirmed the expulsion of Gratian and prohibited him from being readmitted to the Discalced or Calced Carmelites. The entire Assembly approved the resolution unanimously. The new General, Elias of St Martin, was a good person, and seemed to renew the hopes of the Order, but…

Gratain first wrote to Fr Elias of St Martin from Tabarka, then later from Genoa and later again from Rome, where he had arrived by the middle of October. He begged him to reply to his requests in writing to be allowed to return to the Order. However, his letters were met with deathly silence. 'After I had been rescued I wrote to your Paternity from Tabarka that now I have returned to the land of the Christians, I would like to die in my Order even as its most insignificant novice. The past is past and all forgotten; I ask to be admitted in order to serve my brothers. I wrote the same from Genoa.'

He was now in Rome for the second time. He began to plead to be readmitted after his time spent in captivity. With the scars of his torture visible on his body, the figure of Jerome touched people in the Eternal

Pope Clement VIII

City. He wrote an article, A *Treatise on the Redemption of Captives*, which he dedicated to Pope Clement VIII, in which he recounted vividly the pitiful situation of Christians in North Africa.

This time what he said was received much more sympathetically (by the Pope). On 9 January the Pope acceded to his request and wrote a Bull allowing him a period of three years to pay back both his own ransom-money and that of the other twelve ransomed from captivity. He was given permission to beg alms 'in any church, monastery or pious place and from door to door'. He had agreed to pay back the money lent by Turks, Jews and captive Christians. He owed 'more than one thousand three hundred gold coins, most of it incurring interest. I had agreed that when I came to the land of the Catholics I would seek their [the twelve captives] freedom and return the money.' The Bull described him as fifty years old and with a greying beard.

On 6 March, Pope Clement VIII retracted the 1593 Brief in which he had confirmed Jerome's sentence of expulsion, and with a new Brief, *Apostolicae Sedis benignitas*, restored him to the Order of Discalced Carmelites. 'We grant you,' declared the Pope solemnly in Latin, 'and give you permission to return to the Order of Discalced Carmelites and once again be received into it, and that you can exercise and enjoy all the graces, privileges, indults, favours, prerogatives, active and passive voice, as if you had never been expelled or deprived.'

After suffering so many trials our Carmelite felt encouraged by this. The Church had spoken through the mouth of the Pope, that his life, 'is clear of all stains or trace of incompetence or ignominy of which you had been accused. We restore you to the pristine state in which you lived before.' The Pope had spoken. So be it.

However, all was not straightforward. On the contrary, there were problems that once more dogged his life. The Duke of Sessa, Philip II's Ambassador (in Rome), received an explicit order from the King: 'Ensure that the Sentence given by Sixtus V [*sic*] against Father Gratian, forbidding him from ever returning is not altered; were it to be altered it would create difficulties for the Order.'

The King got the Pope's name wrong. It was not Sixtus V but Clement VIII who ratified the Madrid Sentence and who had now exonerated Gratian. However, in Madrid fear of Jerome's return spread. The King wrote of the 'difficulties' that his return would create.

The new General, Elias of St Martin, wrote to Jerome eventually, on 21

March. In his letter he confirmed that there were difficulties. He apologized for the tardiness of his reply, as his letter 'would not be comforting for your Reverence.' Jerome already knew, since he had been in a position of authority, 'that the Superior had to put the good of the community before all else.' If he returned to the Order there would be no peace among the religious. 'I [Fr Elias] found clear signs that your return would cause great discord and division which, as head, although unworthy, I am obliged to avoid insofar as I can.' Therefore, he asked Jerome, 'since you have been and are a great son of the Order and the same has a great love for you, allow yourself, for the sake of the good of the Order, to be separated from it.'

In short, they did not want him back. They did not respect the Papal Brief. 'Those who were then in charge, the architects of the sentence of expulsion, did not wish to obey the Brief,' Jerome said. Fr Angel of Jesus, the Prior of Lerida, wrote to him in a letter dated 5 July 1596: 'I have always been a true son of your Reverence, this so well known in the Order that I am not known by any other name other than "Fr Gratian's companion", which I am proud of, and do not regret for the little time I have left.'

Fr Angel offered a brief resume of the Discalced Carmelite Order's attitude to the Papal Brief. 'I passed through Toledo a fortnight after the announcement of the Brief and found out almost everything that was going on: how it was not received well by some Definitors, yet who nevertheless did not want to be considered Jebusites. I had lengthy conversations with some Definitors who spoke well [of you] but did not act accordingly, saying that they wanted to accept [the Brief] and that they are pleased your Reverence has done so well, but that they are doing what is best for the Order by ignoring the Brief.'

To speak highly of Gratian and, later, for the honour of the Order, disobey the Pope's authority by not admitting him, is called hypocrisy. The Carmelites postponed the decision whether or not to deal with his admission to the General Chapter that was to be celebrated in 1596. In this way they prolonged the problem… When the Chapter was held Jerome would not be readmitted. However, the Prior of Lerida tried to console him: 'You have many sons in the Order who are very fond of you.' One of them, Peter of the Trinity, in the same Lerida priory, wrote to him: 'Your Reverence should not forget that, in Christ, you have been the cornerstone of the Order.' These letters left him with a grain of comfort in the midst of so much ingratitude from those who governed the Discalced Carmelite Order.

When the Pope and Cardinal Pinelli, the Protector of the Carmelite

Order, 'saw the problems in Madrid, they delicately invited Jerome to join the Calced Carmelites. He went to the [Calced Carmelite] Priory of St Martin in Montibus [Rome] where he was given a warm welcome and put up in the General's room. On 6 April, he received a patent from the Vicar General of the said Order which allowed him to live with them and put on their habit, while at the same time, to observe all the rules of the Discalced Carmelites.'

> When I was ransomed, I put on a habit of white linen. I had a greyish brown capuche, the kind galley-slaves wore, I also put on a cap and I wore a cross around my neck. In this way it could be seen that I was a ransomed captive. As I went on my journey I wore a cloak with black and white stripes which I took with me from North Africa. After my efforts in Rome to negotiate (my re-entry) I made a cloak and dyed it black and a cassock of the same material; like a Priest freed from the land of the Turks. I had thought to put on my Discalced Carmelite habit, (as stated in the Brief), but instead put on the Calced Carmelite habit. Very saintly and learned men in this Order have worn this habit and are still wearing it. I saw no reason to go on denying myself.
>
> My friends congratulated me when they saw me in this habit, and consoled me with words that I had been greatly blessed by God by not returning to the Discalced Carmelites, because those who now governed thought no differently from those who had expelled me. Among them were some who might treat me badly again. It is very wrong when a humble Religious does not have respect for his Superiors. This was true for me too, even though I began to see that I was in trouble. I knew they were zealous for the Order, and that they had to respect the honour of their predecessors, and to keep those whom they considered troublemakers quiet. So they searched for new reasons why I deserved to be expelled, or at least, to force me to go to some small isolated priory, where the only ministry I would have would be to hear the confessions of pious women and say my prayers. [However] God does not want us to keep our light under a bushel but rather on a lamp stand, to enlighten many to achieve greater freedom and obedience, as I have since experienced.

He did not stay long in St Martin in Montibus. Cardinal Deza, the Secretary to the Holy Office, appointed him to be his personal theologian. The Cardinal gave him a place to stay in his palace, where he was to reside for five years, till he left Rome. 'I served him for five years as his theologian, writing and publishing books. I preached in Rome and because the Cardinal, my Patron, was one of the oldest in the Congregation of the Holy Office and Protector of Spain, I took part in some very important and sensitive matters concerning the Inquisition and other grave issues.' He dined with Cardinal Deza but, he told his sister, Mary of St Joseph, how much he missed the 'fish in St Martin in Montibus, which Brother Michael cooked with onions and garlic.'

The process for Teresa of Avila's canonization began in Salamanca in 1591, nine years after her death. It was then that the Bishop, Jerome Manrique, a great friend of the Saint, interviewed twelve people who had known Teresa and in this way began to gather information. In 1595 King Philip II asked the Nuncio, Caetani, to gather information from a broader perspective, i.e. from other parts of Spain. This (canonization process) was for several reasons: her incorrupt body, her reputation for holiness and the miracles that they said had been worked through her intercession. Centres for this purpose were set up in Avila, Toledo, Madrid, Valladolid, Zaragoza, Palencia, Salamanca, Seville, Valencia, Segovia, Medina del Campo, Huete, Villanueva de la Jara, Malagon, Cuerva and Sanlucar la Mayor. The reports were submitted to the Apostolic Protonotary, Doctor Barnaby del Marmol, and reached Rome by 1597.

By this time Jerome had already begun to advance things (for the beatification) in the Eternal City. He wanted nothing more than to get Teresa canonized, as it would be a loud and clear vindication of her person. In Rome, Cardinals and other influential figures had read her books and the biography by Fr Ribera. Jerome observed that there was a great desire to canonize this 'gadabout' saint from Avila. When Cardinal Deza read her biography he said to Jerome: 'Let's really try to ensure she is canonized. I, as the Protector of Spain, must ask his Holiness. I commend you to study books dealing with this [process of canonization], and to write to Spain that they ask his Holiness to canonize this holy woman.'

At the beginning of 1596 Gratian wrote a circular letter to the Discalced Carmelite nuns in Spain in which he gave instructions as to how they should proceed. He instituted a process based on that used for the canonization of St Diego of Alcala, who was acknowledged a saint in 1588. The first step was the *vox clamorosa*; in other words, to get people to write many letters to the Pope urging him to promote her canonization. 'The letters that had the greatest influence were from his Majesty and the Empress as well as The Infanta. There were letters from the Duke and Duchess of Alba, where Teresa's body lay; from the Bishop of Avila and the Bishop of Salamanca; a letter from the city of Avila and its Church Council; a letter from the town council of Alba de Tormes and from the people around Avila and Alba; and finally letters from some noble ladies who had known Teresa well during her lifetime and knew of the miracles that occurred at her death…'

In short, the *vox clamarosa* or reputation for holiness, 'is the first thing that is required if her cause is to get into the [Vatican] Consistory. Once there, and if it is appropriate, it is put forward as a cause for canonization… These letters are the first documents that are required.'

Jerome's position as theologian in the house of Cardinal Deza, Secretary at the Holy Office, allowed him to observe certain factions within the Roman Inquisition that tried to brand Teresa's doctrine as heretical. He got his hands on the points they wanted censured and wrote a thirty-page treatise that he entitled, *A Defence of the Doctrine of the Mother Teresa of Jesus*. 'It is the greatest service I can offer to the Order at this time. If I were in a Discalced Carmelite habit or in another habit as I am, it was all for a purpose,' he told his sister, Isabel of Jesus, a Discalced Carmelite nun in Cuerva.

Gratian's Discalced Carmelite vocation was such that nothing could make him give it up. He saw that it would be good for the Order to expand into Italy and France; something that Doria did not want nor, apparently, his successors who also opposed any expansion of the Reform.

In Rome Gratian helped a Spanish priest from the Oratory, Francis Soto, a member of the Papal Choir, to establish a Discalced Carmelite convent. They bought a house near Montecavallo, arranging it 'in the way that Teresa used to furnish her convents.' Neither the Discalced Carmelite nuns in Genoa nor those from the Carmels of Spain would give them nuns, yet they began to take in vocations; the first five aged between eighteen and twenty. An Augustinian nun from St Martha's convent offered herself, but Jerome thought that 'she would do damage by teaching the others the customs of her own Order, which was lax.' He searched for 'two of the most experienced souls on this earth.' One was Spanish, Leonor de Molina, 'who for twenty years had carried Teresa's Rule in her bag' and had come to Italy with her brother, a Captain from Naples. When she heard about the foundation she offered to join, as she had a great desire to see the Order grow.

The other was an Italian, Lady Ursina, the Marchioness of Rangona, a woman of 'the greatest spirit, prudence and humility'. He taught the two women how to put Teresa's Constitutions into practice, and thus the convent of 'St Joseph, Head of the Family'[2] began to function, under the jurisdiction of the Holy See, with a Bull of foundation dated 9 February 1597.

Fr Peter of the Mother of God turned up in Rome together with a companion from the Discalced Carmelite Priory in Genoa. Jerome invited them to make a foundation in Rome, 'where the Head of the Church is to be found'. 'If not, I shall found it myself,' he told them.

The Discalced Carmelite Superiors learned that he was instrumental in founding a convent in Rome and that he was employed as a theologian by Cardinal Deza and was well known to other Cardinals. In order to counteract the foundation made by someone as bold as he, whom they had expelled, they decided quickly to found the Priory of Our Lady de la Scala, in Trastevere; a poor suburb of Rome. Anastasius recounted, 'This was the beginning of the Congregation of the Discalced Carmelites in Italy, which, as I have already said, followed the same Rule and Constitutions as those in Spain. However, whereas the Spanish were more recollected and more concerned for their own self-perfection, the Italians were more concerned with winning souls for God by their zealous ministry'. The Discalced Carmelites in Italy separated definitively from those in Spain in the year 1600.

While the Carmelite friars (in Spain) preferred to remain within the realm of the Spanish Empire, the Italian Carmelites, in reflecting more clearly the wishes of the Foundress, Teresa of Avila, looked beyond their own country in order to spread throughout the world.

In 1597, Pope Clement VIII, with the support of the King of France, Henry IV, obtained the city of Ferrara for the Papal States, which for three centuries, had been under the dominion of the d'Este family. The Duke (of Ferrara), Cesare, had decided to fight to defend the city, but when faced with excommunication and the threat of an interdict, as well as the French troops, he was forced to capitulate. He lost his territory to the Papal States

2 Its proper title in Rome is: 'San Giuseppe a Capo le Case.'

but was able to keep his freedom, the archives, the library and the family's art collection. Pope Clement VIII, happy about recuperating this territory, and in spite of his gout and the cost, moved his entire court to Ferrara in January of 1598 and remained there until the Holy Year.

Cardinal Deza had accompanied the Pope to this northern city. Gratian was left free and decided to sail to Naples where he resided until the month of October. On 14 January he wrote to his mother from Gaeta giving her news about their relatives: the children of Peter Godoy, who had married Jerome's paternal grandmother, Isabel de Hermosilla, it being Peter's second marriage.

> It was a pleasure to visit the Lady Isabella, the daughter of John of Godoy who is now in glory, and her sister, Olympia, a nun of the Bernardine community of St Catherine's. Isabella reminds me in appearance of Adriana [one of his sisters]. She has a son who is a Judge in this place, a very honourable and principled man. He it was who dealt with the Jewish merchant when he came here to sell his merchandise, and asked him if he would obtain my ransom. The whole town offered money for this purpose. It is quite amazing how pleased they were to see me.

In Naples, he told the Brother, Francis of the Child Jesus, 'I was in a district known as "The Spaniards", where I challenged what was going on there. With my own eyes I saw the shameful way the local people offend the Infant Jesus and his holy Mother Mary. I felt so afflicted and upset that if I could I would have returned to Tunis with my heavy chains so as not to put up with the daily blasphemies committed by those who manage to enter through the door of baptism; were the Moors baptized they would not behave like this.'

In Naples he attended to the needs of the Spanish soldiers, which is what he had done before in Lisbon. And, as in Lisbon, he opened a house for repentant prostitutes. When he was visiting a hospital for incurables, with the Marchioness del Valle, a Spanish lady had told him: 'If there were a house for reformed Spanish prostitutes in Naples, it would bear much fruit and many sins would be avoided in this city.'

He strove to open such a house with a Jesuit, Inigo de Mendoza, the son of Alvaro de Mendoza, a Spaniard, who lived in the largest castle in Naples. They rented a house in the Spanish Quarter, next to St Anne's Church. Using some of the money he had from his ransom he bought beds, tables and other furniture for the house. The project was beset with difficulties but, thanks to the help of the Counts de Lemos, who were the Viceroys, it proved to be a success. After this, he returned to Rome.

Jerome arrived back in Rome in October, where he hoped to gain entry to the Pontifical Court. It would soon be 1600, a Holy Year. On 19 May 1599, with the Bull *Annus Domini placabilis*, the twelfth jubilee of Pope Clement VIII was convoked. The Pontiff declared it to be a time of 'true penance and spiritual rejoicing'.

In 1599 Gratian published in Rome a book entitled: *Treatise on the Jubilee for the Holy Year*; it was written in Italian and especially for pilgrims. He also concluded another book: *Life of Mother Teresa* and again a study entitled: *Treatise on the Rule of Carmel*, that dealt with perfection and the spirit with which the Rule should be observed. The following year he wrote a book on the souls in purgatory. Prior to all these he had published a *Summary on the Virtues of the Glorious St Joseph, Husband of the Blessed Virgin Mary* in 1597. In 1600 Teresa's *Interior Castle* and *Way of Perfection* were published in Italian; and perhaps also her other writings.

Jerome wrote to his youngest sister, Juliana, a nun in Seville: 'Let us glorify the Lord, for here, during this Holy Year, all is going well for us [Carmelites?]. Every day new groups [of pilgrims] come from all over Italy and France, which is good to see. I have done what I can to help with all sorts of books and leaflets and booklets, both in Italian and Spanish.'

On 11 June 1600, he received a Brief from the Pope commissioning him to go to Africa to 'preach to the captives about indulgences, to cure their wounds with the medicine of the sacraments, to negotiate for their freedom and to tell them about pardon, jubilee and reconciliation, as graces of the Holy Year.'

He wrote to reassure his mother, Joanna, that 'although it might sound dangerous for my well-being, in truth it isn't, because the Moors are very happy to welcome anyone who comes to negotiate the ransom of Christians; it doesn't bother them that we go there to preach and hear confessions.' He asked for prayers from the Discalced Carmelite nuns in Spain. 'My spirit is so weak and my prayer so lukewarm that I must turn to your Reverences to buy some of that oil so that my lamp may always be burning brightly on earth where there is need of so much light.'

He left Rome in the month of July, 'just when the summer's heat was at its peak.' He passed through Sienna, Florence, Pisa... In Livorno he got on one of the papal vessels that took him to Genoa. Everywhere he went (throughout Italy) he took letters from the families of Christians who were captives and noted the condition for their ransom. He went to Florence, 'because the Mayor of Florence had requested the Mayor of Rome to tell him that he wanted to give twelve thousand gold coins to ransom some Florentine gentlemen and that he [Jerome] should collect alms from the Grand Duchess. I arrived [in Florence] on horseback. My clothes and books had come by sea: the city officials had agreed to pay for this. I suffered a great deal from the sun and was really tired. However, the Mayor of Florence was not there nor did the Grand Duchess give me anything.'

On 1 August, he found himself in Genoa, ready to set sail for Algiers, his first port of call. After disembarking at Algiers, 'we went to Fez, Morocco, Tetuan and those other parts of North Africa close to Spain, because Mount Carmel was more to the east.' He did not know that area well. Mount Carmel is located in Galilee, known for being the place where the prophet Elijah fled from Queen Jezabel and where the same prophet slew the prophets of Baal. There, in the 13th century some hermits began to lead a contemplative life, 'which is where our Order began'.

He carried with him a Patent from the General of the Carmelite Order that would allow him to rebuild the monastery on Mount Carmel. He confided to his sister, Mary of St Joseph, 'I thought of dying in that place, if God does not take away from me a constant desire to walk from Algiers to Heaven.' He also had faculties to dress and live as he liked, either as a Discalced or Calced Carmelite.

Jerome had got a surprise while waiting to embark in Genoa. The Papal Brief that authorized him to undertake this missionary enterprise also authorized two Capuchins. Reaching Genoa on 21 September, the two friars were not the least enthusiastic at the thought of travelling with this Carmelite. Unlike the Carmelite they had brought a safe-conduct document from the Great Turk which allowed them to roam around Algiers.

The Capuchins behaved badly towards him, whom they didn't trust because he had been expelled from his Order. 'They were right,' Jerome confessed humbly to Cardinal Frederick Borromeo, 'as I was such a bad person. My life has been so full of scandal. In the eyes of my own Order I am too lax, and were I to be readmitted it would be to them a cause of shame. However, sometimes bad and disreputable people (as I am) have a gift for dealing with such bad people as the Turks.'

In Rome, the Capuchins had told several Cardinals and even the Pope that Jerome did not want to go to Africa. The latter wrote that the Pope 'gave them four hundred gold coins but gave nothing to me, other than the few alms his Holiness had to give me when he knew I was going; I felt his lack of support keenly.'

Jerome wrote to the Cardinals of Propaganda Fide to tell them: 'One thing I can swear: that I never tried to procure or obtain this commission before his most illustrious Cardinal, Santa Severina, on behalf of his Holiness, recommended me for it. As soon as I was given to understand that it was his [the Pope's] wish that I should accept it, I did so readily. Never in my life have I done anything with greater willingness.'

On 31 August, the Pope dispatched another Brief meant only for Jerome, to allow him to go freely where ever he chose (in Africa). As the Capuchins had a safe-conduct document from the Great Turk for Algiers, Bona, Susa, Bizerta, Tunis and Tripoli, Jerome kept the western part of North Africa for himself: i.e. Fez, Morocco and Tetuan.

Gratian had to change his plan for the journey. To get to Morocco it was better to go through Spain and get on a boat in Seville. This is what he told Juliana, his sister, who was a Carmelite nun in Seville. He wrote to his mother, Joanna, that he would pass through Madrid in order to obtain his pass for Africa, 'from Martin de Arriaga or some other Minister who knows something about Morocco.'

He also told his mother how Cardinal Deza, his Patron, was close to death in Rome. 'If I should be in his house when he dies, or if I have to look for another Cardinal to employ me (which I do not really want to do) or if I have to enter a Priory, and this in Italy, they [Cardinals from Propaganda Fidei?] would not be happy'.

However, a mission on behalf of the Pope led him to Morocco. He had to pass through Madrid to find his letter of safe-passage. His mother was very happy to be able to see her son again and embrace him after an absence of eight years.

Chapter Twenty-Six

An Honourable Mission in Africa

In November 1600, Jerome Gratian once again walked on Spanish soil. He did not leave us with any kind of description of his journey, which was strange for someone who usually went into great detail. He had disembarked in eastern Spain, since he had to visit the priories of Consuegra and Cuerva before going to Toledo. In Cuerva he preached on the feast of the Immaculate Conception in a public church and they gave him some 'very delicious sardines and eggs, which is what I always ate.'

Reaching Toledo on 9 December, he went to the priory of the Discalced Carmelites and the following day, Sunday, he preached at the Sunday morning Mass to the nuns of St Clement's and, in the evening, to the nuns of Santa Fe. 'Some were very happy to see me but the Provincial and others were much less enthusiastic until they let go of their misgivings and we all became good friends.'

It was December, a cold month in Toledo. Gratian admitted that 'it was not strange that the Provincial, who was Alonso of Jesus and Mary, and some of the friars suddenly felt a shiver down their spines and to have goose pimples when the heinous prodigal son suddenly walked through the door of the Priory. Afterwards they became good friends.'

Changes had occurred in the Discalced Carmelite Order. Months before, at the General Chapter celebrated in Toledo on 7 September Fr Francis of the Mother of God replaced Fr Elias as the General, and implemented once more Doria's corrosive ideas and methods.

In Toledo, Jerome visited Archbishop Bernard de Sandoval y Rojas, an old companion from his student days in Alcala. They discussed matters at great length; 'We spoke about many things which seemed to me to be of great service to God.'

He also visited his family in Madrid: his mother, brothers and sisters. 'The Lord has given us a wonderful Christmas with the arrival of your brother, the Master, we are all so happy about this,' wrote Joanna on Christmas Day to her daughter, Juliana, in Seville Carmelite convent. 'He is well, thanks be to God. He has spent the last couple of days with your Discalced Carmelite friars as he did not want to be away from them for Christmas Eve. They got on really well and they enjoyed his company.'

Jerome added a postscript to the letter his mother sent to his sister: 'I am very busy preparing sermons. I wish I could write you a proper letter, but I am grateful to be well and God will help me; I am getting on well with everyone, with the lay people as well as with the Discalced and Calced friars.' His dealings with the Calced Carmelites continued to flourish, but with the Discalced, after the initial reaction, the old issues resurfaced.

He busied himself at the court of Madrid with the principal matter that had brought him there: to obtain a safe-passage document from the King, Philip III – Philip II had died in 1598. He also kept himself busy with preaching. In the convent of the Discalced Reales he spoke with the Empress, Maria of Austria, the daughter of Charles V and wife of Maximilian II, who was keen to know about his captivity. He also preached to Queen Margaret of Austria's ladies-in-waiting, 'some of whom had a fear of God but did not have anyone to help them find what their wounded hearts desired.' However, he avoided the Queen, as she knew from the Countess de Fuensalida that he had a relic of Teresa's finger; and he feared that because the Queen had a great devotion to Teresa, she would ask for it. 'Here in this Court we go about preaching and chatting. There is much talk about prayer and spirituality but not much practice,' he wrote to his sister, Mary of St Joseph in Consuegra.

Although it did not make sense, the Court moved to Valladolid; this was at the behest of the Duke of Lerma, a close friend of King Philip III. The Duke sought to distance the King from the influence of the old Empress, now confined to the convent of the Discalced Reales. She was the aunt and grandmother (*sic*) of King Philip III, who had seen how the Empire, so extolled by her father Charles V, collapsed and how, his brother, Philip II, had been in the pockets of his favoured friends.

On 11 January 1601, Philip III headed off to Valladolid. Madrid was devastated when the Court moved; Valladolid had to improvise a welcome as tumultuous as it was costly. Four days later the Queen followed. In the following days and months the city gate of Guadarrama, impassable in the winter, became a busy place with carriages belonging to the ministers, secretaries and advisors to the Queen.

Gratian arrived in Valladolid, by mule, at the beginning of March. He sought to find accommodation at his brother Thomas' place, who was

Secretary to the King. Thomas was still in Madrid with his sickly wife, Laurencia and with their tired and elderly mother, Joanna. Jerome knocked on the door of the Discalced Carmelites, but was given a cool reception, he recounted later. Next he went to the Calced Carmelites, their priory located at the city gate called 'del Campo', where he was given a warm welcome. 'When I arrived they greeted me with open arms and gave me a very good and comfortable cell with an alcove.'

Jerome Gratian wore a habit that looked Discalced, but by now he himself did not know what it was, having in his lifetime changed, as Anastasius said: 'more clothes than a salesman'. When he was expelled from the Order he exchanged his patched and dirty sackcloth habit for the cassock and mantle of a university academic. He walked to Rome wearing the habit of a hermit with a large hat and tonsure of a friar. At the time he was abducted by the Turks he was wearing a black sackcloth habit without a capuche that looked like the habit of the Discalced Augustinians. The Turks removed all his clothes leaving him with only his birthday suit. Afterwards he wore a threadbare sackcloth garment and a small blue bonnet and worn out sandals on his feet. In Tunis he wore a linen garment made of red and blue coloured strips of cloth. A little later he was all in white with a small scapular; on his feet he wore boots with leather strappings in order to support the irons and on his head a round hat like those worn by Jewish men. On being ransomed, he re-entered the Christian world with a habit of white wool and a grey capuche like those the galley slaves wore, with a large sun hat and a cross around his neck like those worn by ransomed captives. On his travels to Rome he wore a black-and-white striped mantel that he had brought from North Africa. In Rome he put on a garment dyed black and a soutane dyed the same colour, like a priest freed from the land of the Turks. Finally, he put on the habit of the Calced Carmelites. It really was as Anastasius said: 'I changed clothes more often than a salesman.'

When Gratian finally arrived in Spain, he put on the habit of the Discalced. The Protector of the Carmelite Order, Cardinal Pinelli, had given him permission to wear whatever habit he wanted and had instructed the Discalced Carmelite priories to welcome him. They were not happy on either count and so, while they did welcome him warmly into their houses, they quietly sent two friars to Rome to get Cardinal Pinelli to revoke the permission he gave to Jerome and, at the same time to command that he be refused admittance in to their priories.

'The Master', as he was known within his family, was in Valladolid when the notification from Rome arrived, dated 1 January (counteracting Pinelli). However, by the time he received this new blow he was in the city of Pisuerga. He was angry due to 'the ease with which these Fathers obtained edicts from Rome based on false information.'

On 22 March, the General of the Discalced Carmelite Order, Francis of the Mother of God, sent Jerome a courteous letter from Pastrana in which he stated: 'Given the past, it would seem only right that, since your Paternity now has a different habit, those of us who wear this one commend you to God, and that we should talk about you with love and due respect. As for the rest, each one should only attend to his own Order and his own business.' Which was tantamount to saying: stick to the Calced Carmelites and leave us in peace.

However, it was they, the Discalced Carmelites, who did not leave him in peace, as noted in the General's conclusion. 'I find it very irksome that the Father Prior of Valladolid did not give you the courtesy you deserve, and I will tell him.'

In fact the Prior of Valladolid came with another Discalced Carmelite to see Gratian in the Calced Carmelite priory. There they presented him with eight grave charges against him. The first was a threat: to reveal, publicly, the old accusations that led to him being expelled. Jerome responded that 'it is not good that the Discalced Carmelites who profess perfection (which is the summit of charity) should do wrong and discredit one of their brothers.'

Secondly, they accused him of wearing a Discalced Carmelite habit without permission, having been deprived of this habit and expelled from the Order by a sentence, later confirmed by an Apostolic Brief; of having worn a Calced Carmelite habit in Rome and on his journeys but here wearing a Discalced Carmelite habit with the intention of insulting and belittling them. The last charge came with a hint of menace rather than an accusation: What has he to do with the Court? Why doesn't he go to Africa?

The Nuncio, Dominic Ginasio, Archbishop of Manfredonio, was also involved in this matter. Once again, Jerome had to use his gifts to neutralize this new offensive from the Discalced Carmelites. He wrote to the Nuncio to say that he had received 'Sentences and ignominious letters accusing me of outrageous things', and also he wrote to the General of the Order: 'I cannot believe that the General is so duplicitous that he writes to me of peace while ordering them [the friars in Spain] to make war.' He defended himself with the only weapon he had: the pen.

> If they say that I had come to Spain and put on their habit in order to mock them, I myself swear that it was not like that, but rather, in order to make peace and bolster the Order's good name, and to let it be known that, with the death of some of those who persecuted me, the things of the past have all been forgotten, and that it was wrong of them to provoke me and impugn my intentions in public. I have the strength to suffer and endure in silence any affront and the courage to defend myself. They should realize that having spent five years in Rome, I have friends there to help me.
>
> If they say they were afraid of me and for this reason they wanted to expel me from Spain, please tell them that the better way is through friendship rather than through upsetting me; and also tell them to get a written commitment from secular guarantors that if the Moors were to take me they would pay my ransom, once this piece of paper has been written then I will leave for Africa.
>
> Regarding what pertains to my character, tell them that God knows each one of us; and they must believe this. Mother Teresa of Jesus, as everyone knows and your Reverence knows, had a different opinion of me. And tell them that there is plenty of evidence that all the key people involved believe the opposite of what my accusers are saying. And that when they [his accusers] talk about 'the entire Order of the Discalced Carmelites', tell them that you know what it is like with friars. It only takes a few, particularly when they are Superiors, who, when they want something, for some particular reason they usually refer to 'the entire Order'. And finally they should ask those Discalced friars and nuns who are holier than I am what they think about me.
>
> Why don't you come one day to the Discalced Carmelite nuns and ask them what scandals I had committed with them since arriving in Valladolid? The friars in this place complained to the Prior and to the Nuncio that I had caused scandal, and they have written to Rome about this. Please tell them to leave the nuns in peace and not make them the talk of the town.

In the end, it did not come to anything. However, these episodes tell us that the doors of the Discalced Carmelite Order were definitively closed to him.

Jerome could not nor did not want to delay his departure for Morocco, although the Discalced Carmelite friars complained that he remained a long time in the Court. The Duke of Lerma, the King's favourite, entertained 'some detestable ideas about me.' What were these 'detestable ideas'? Had the Discalced won him over to their cause: to evict him from the Court? Rather, it seems they wanted to present him with a bishopric and send him off to South America. This was done to Fr Martin Ignacio de Loyola, a Discalced Franciscan, who was consecrated bishop before being sent to Mexico; because 'they cannot really carry out conversions properly unless they act in the same way as the apostles who were empowered to ordain priests amongst those whom they converted.'

Gratian, fearing that they would make him a bishop, could not wait to go to North Africa. However, 'every time I wanted to start on my journey there was a setback,' he shared with the Nuns in Consuegra. In the end he decided to go without saying anything, even without saying goodbye to his old mother, Joanna; it cost him a great deal to leave her like this. However, when, finally, he got permission to go to Morocco, he had to turn back when he caught a fever. He believed that this illness was providential so that he was able to be with his mother at the time of her death: 'I wanted to be present more than anything else in the world.'

Thomas Gratian lived in Valladolid with his family and his mother in a house next door to a convent of Discalced Bernardine Nuns. On 4 October, the feast of St Francis of Asissi, Thomas' six-year-old daughter Anita died. The night before the little girl had said to her mother, Laurencia, 'Mama, I am very sorry that I did not confess yesterday, now that I am going to die.' Her mother told her, 'If you would want, Father Master is here and he will hear your confession?' The child responded, 'Can he, Mama?' 'Yes,' she replied. 'Then call him; I shall tell him some bad things.' Her uncle, Jerome, heard her confession which was 'very much to my edification, as if she were twenty years old.'

Joanna, who was very close to death, asked her son, Jerome, 'Has the little one been to confession?' He, not wishing to reply, exclaimed: 'Jesus!' Joanna said: 'She belongs to God, let her go to God.' Two days later, on Saturday 6 October, a day when Joanna would normally have received Communion, she died at about one o'clock in the afternoon. Every night, since she fell ill, Jerome looked after her. 'I did not leave her side for three nights, even if they had been one hundred it wouldn't have tired me.' Shortly before she died he gave her the Carmelite habit 'like a nun with all the privileges'. At the moment of her death he closed the eyes of his mother.

Joanna was clothed in the Carmelite habit and buried in the convent of the Discalced Bernardines in Valladolid, in front of the choir grille, where she had usually knelt. Alongside her are the burial places of her grandchildren, Margaret and Anita, who preceded her in death. In his inspired eulogy Jerome referred to that verse from the Book of Proverbs, 31.28: *Surrexerunt filii eius et beatissimam predicaverunt* (her children will rise up and proclaim her blessed).

At the end of October Gratian finally left Valladolid for Africa. On 7 November he wrote to the Carmelite nuns in Consuegra from Gibraltar, telling them that he would cross over that same day or perhaps the next day. 'It takes three or four hours as the channel is no more than fifteen miles wide. Every day they transport wheat from here to the other side.' He asked the nuns to pray, as he felt in need of their prayers.

He went from Gibraltar to Ceuta, a port conquered by the Portuguese in 1415 and at that time under the Spanish crown. 'Thanks be to God, I have arrived safely in Africa, having crossed over the channel in good time.' He showed his credentials from the King to the Marquis of Villarreal, the Governor of Ceuta. The latter issued him with a safe-passage document from the Mayor of Tetuan, a city located some seven miles away, where the Mayor made 'profit out of the captives and renegades of that city.'

Tetuan, sacked and destroyed by the Portuguese in 1437, was rebuilt by Sidi Ali al-Mandari, a native of Granada, at the end of the 15th century. He led a group of Andalucians who settled within the ruins of the town with permission from the Sultan of Fez. Built out of nothing it was to become a typical Andalucian town. The Arab poets called it 'the white dove'. It was also called 'the daughter of Granada' or 'the little Jerusalem', situated in the valley of the Martil river, nestling among the Dersa and Gorgues mountains, and ten miles from the nearest beach.

The Mayor of Tetuan, Mumen ben Abdelquirin El Mesuar, 'who is very close to their King and professes to be half Arab and a holy man,' when he saw Gratian's letters from the King and Bulls from the Pope, believed 'I had more authority than I actually had.' He thought that between us we could bring about peace between the Sheriffs of Morroco and Fez and the King of

Spain that had been destroyed by the involvement of the English.

Jerome explained that he was a nobody, but the Mayor told him: 'A thin thread, of little value, is one that mends. I also say to you, with reference to Morocco and Spain: when two lions are next to each other and one bites the other, if it does not manage to kill it, it would be better to have left it alone.'

The Mayor wrote to the Sheriff of Morocco and told him about Jerome's visit and how he carried with him letters from his King and Bulls from the Pope in order to bring about peace. Our man did not want to disappoint the Mayor. He had come simply to bring spiritual support to the Christian captives and to console them with indulgences for the jubilee year. However, to the Mayor of Tetuan the letters from the King and the Bulls from the Pope sounded like a peace treaty. 'As I saw the fruit that could come from peaceful dialogue, I did not want to disappoint and spoke about this to the Marquis of Villareal in Ceuta, as well as to the Duke of Medina Sidonia in Sanlucar and to the Governor of Castille in St Juan del Puerto. They all saw this as providential and wrote to the King and to the Duke of Lerma about it. I preached a retreat in Ceuto while waiting for a reply.'

Jerome did not remain long in Tetuan. He was not even able to venture further into Morocco in order to meet the Sheriff. He returned to Ceuta 'with orders to make peace between our King and the Sheriff.' He crossed the Straights of Gibraltar and went to Puerto de Santa Maria and San Juan del Puerto where he spoke with the Duke of Medina Sidonia and with the Governor of Castile. The townsfolk of Sanlucar begged him to preach a Lenten retreat. However, he returned to Ceuta because his commission was for Africa. There he noticed that there had been no response to his initiatives for peace by either side. He remarked laconically: 'It hasn't worked.'

In Ceuta rumours were running wild that two hundred English ships were coming to attack them; also, that countless Moors would arrive by land. Jerome shared this with his sister, Adriana, a Jeronomite nun in Madrid: 'Such is my life here, living with all these lively rumours, advising and helping these peoples' souls. It is such a pity to see them suffering from hunger and the little encouragment they are getting from these rumours.'

When the Lent of 1602 had ended Jerome returned to Spain. He was in a hurry, not even stopping in Seville, to greet his sister, Juliana. He met King Philip II and the Duke of Lerma in Aranjuez, where he informed them of his diplomatic efforts. 'However, they wanted me to return to Morocco. I was to go to my Priory in Toledo to await their orders.'

When there was no response from the King, Jerome went to Madrid, where he resided in the Calced Carmelite Priory, 'where they welcomed me with much pleasure and kindness. I am reviewing my papers to see what I can publish.' He wrote to Rome, to the Congregation of Propaganda Fide, and gave them an account of his mission to Africa.

> I went to Africa in fulfillment of what His Holiness and Your Illustrious Lords had ordered me to do. I left behind a deposit of money for the ransoming of captives, and arranged to meet Moorish, Jewish and Christian merchants so that they could ransom those who are most in danger of losing their faith. I returned to collect the money that was used to ransom people, of which there was an abundance in Spain. I reported to the King that I saw some signs that the Moors from Africa were joining together with the English should the latter come to these shores, and I also spoke about a peace treaty between the Sheriff and the King… This is all I managed to do in those parts of Africa. If it seems to Your Illustrious Lords that I should go to Ethiopia, where there are innumerable gentile souls who could be baptized if there were ministers and those that are baptized who lack any doctrine, I would need to be commissioned by His Holiness…

Jerome would spend the next couple of years mostly in Madrid and Valladolid, wearing his Calced Carmelite habit, preaching a lot, publishing his book, *Lampara Encendida* (*The Burning Lamp*), and endeavouring to promote the beatification of Teresa of Avila, whose cause had lain dormant for some time. His preaching must have been fervent as, during the Lent of 1603, while preaching to some nuns in Madrid, he had swung his arms so much that 'my left arm began to hurt. The pain has never gone away, in fact it has increased, and my hand is numb so I can't write.'

In April he found himself in Valladolid. On his way to Avila, he completed some formalities for Teresa's canonization 'but I have not had much success.' He did not find what he had been looking for. In sharing his disappointment with the Carmelite nuns in Consuegra, he told them: 'If I don't give 200 reales to Rome the report [on Teresa] will not be presented to the [Vatican] Rota. This canonization of Mother Teresa is like the entrance of Christ into Jerusalem: *Benedictus qui venit…*, but nobody invited Him to eat that night.'

Gratian kept among his papers an undated letter, written most probably about this time, from Fr Philip of Jesus, a Discalced Carmelite friar, who had been elected Provincial, Definitor and Prior many times. Fr Philip reproached Jerome in no uncertain terms for meddling in Teresa's canonization:

> To what purpose and with what authority is your Paternity involved in the deliberations for the canonization of our holy Mother? Why have you got involved in them, since it is your Paternity alone and the erroneous process you are following that has hindered her canonization. Is your Paternity bearing a grudge? How dare you appear with all these fabrications before these good people, who know you very well; and before our nuns and friars, and again even before the people of this town, where they know every detail of your life and the reasons why you are in the state you are in now.

Jerome's life was never short of put downs! The Discalced Carmelites continued to oppress him... On 28 October 1603, his sister-in-law died, Laurencia de Zurita, the wife of Thomas Gratian. She had a talent for music, and could play the harp while singing verses from Homer, Ovid and Virgil, and the psalms of David. She was also a good Latinist, and has left us letters and verses in Latin. Andrew del Marmol, in his biography of Jerome Gratian, pointed out her very deep humility, 'She never spoke with other women as if she were wiser but rather as one among equals, neither for this (her erudition) did she see herself above others. She was very prudent, honest and modest, and rarely wore jewelry, many people spoke highly of her so that she was known as "the perfect wife". If anyone wants to find out more about this gifted lady they can read a book about famous women written by Moya. She died a holy death, in the odour of sanctity; her body seemed transparent and was buried in the Carthusian monastery in Aniago, located close to the town of Pisuerga where her son, Fr Diego, was professed.'

Lope de Vega, in his *Laurel de Apollo*, dedicated a specially written eulogy for her to Thomas and Diego Gratian:

> That gentle genius, the famous
> Dona Laurencia de Zurita,
> Admired by all the world,
> Her gifts being so profound...

> Laurencia was her name.
> She was blessed with much erudition and
> the gentleness of virtue,
> adding to her gifts
> that endure forever.
> Thomas, who was her noble spouse,
> The scribe and secretary
> of Apollo, the great Philip,
> Now also in immortal repose.

Thomas Gratian married again the following year, 1604, to Isabel de Berruguete, daughter of the Lord de la Ventosa. On 30 May 1605 their son was baptized in the parish of San Lorenzo in Valladolid.

In October 1603, a French expedition, led by John de Quintanaduenas, Lord of Brittany, arrived in Spain to bring some Discalced Carmelite nuns to France. He, having a Spanish father and French mother, played a fundamental role in the establishment of the Teresian Carmel in France. In 1582 he had known the Seville Carmel and its Prioress, Mary of St Joseph; he also knew Fr Gratian. Since that time he had been attracted by the spirit of the Teresian Reform and put all his efforts into getting the nuns to make foundations in France. However, years passed without his desires being fulfilled. Doria had always seemed reticent to go beyond the frontiers of Spain, and the political tensions between France and Spain were not appeased until the signing of the peace treaty of Vervins in 1598. That year, John of Brittany was ordained priest and translated the works of Teresa of Avila into French, which were rapidly disseminated.

Jean's translation inspired others. Having read the *Life* of St Teresa, Madame Acarie attracted a circle of friends who could be called the élite of the religious world in Paris, which included the young Pierre Berulle, who would later become Cardinal. John of Brittany, who also joined Madame Acarie's circle, was keen to meet the man who translated Teresa's works. St Francis de Sales also attended the meetings some time in 1602.

John of Brittany had arrived in Spain ready to take back with him some nuns who had been companions of Teresa of Avila, the foremost of all being Mary of St Joseph. He brought with him letters from France, including a Papal Bull, to persuade a reticent Discalced Carmelite Order to give permission for a group of nuns, who were 'living images of the holy Mother.'

John met with initial disappointment; Mary of St Joseph, whom he had hoped would lead the group, had died in Cuerva. He could not believe this, and suspected that the Discalced Carmelite friars had hidden her. So he visited Cuerva to confirm for himself the death of Teresa's faithful friend.

Prior to her death she had been secretly removed from her convent in Lisbon by order of the Discalced Carmelite General, Alonso of Jesus & Mary, for reasons unknown to this day. A boat had been made ready for her at the foot of the escarpment where the convent of St Albert was located, and took her to Aldea Gallega. Then she together with Sr Blanca of Jesus rode on horseback to Castile, accompanied by two friars. On 7 September 1603 they reached Talavera de la Reina, where she and Sr Blanca were separated: the latter was led to Seville and Mary of St Joseph to Cuerva where she was welcomed coldly and contemptuously by the Prioress. Faced with such contempt, she did what she believed was the best thing to do, she died.

Mary of St Joseph died on 19 October, at nine o'clock at night; she was fifty-five years old and had been in exile in that convent for just nine days. She had wanted to go to France, even taking French lessons in Lisbon. She was the inheritor of Teresa's charism. In fact the Saint remarked, 'If I could get my wish, after my death they would elect her as Foundress.' Persecuted and vilified, Mary was buried in an obscure little place near Toledo.

Her friend, Anne of Jesus, who also inherited Teresa's charism, was more fortunate. Exiled to Salamanca, where she had been taken some time before from Madrid, she became head of a group of nuns who later made foundations in France and Belgium. During her years in Belgium she encountered the third person of the triumvirate who had inherited the charism of Teresa's Reform, Jerome Gratian.

With the death of Mary of St Joseph, all that was left for Jerome Gratian and Anne of Jesus was exile. However, it turned out to be a fruitful exile, when the world saw the breadth and grandeur of the Teresian Reform and the missionary expansion that Teresa had wanted.

In 1604, Cardinal Frederick Borromeo invited Jerome to his Milan diocese. The Carmelite friar replied from Toledo on 20 September: 'I am already sixty years old. I am tired and have a lot of work to do. It seems to me that my sermons and confessions are bearing fruit. I am also writing books that will be published in my own country, Spain, whose language and ways

I understand, and where I am bearing fruit and *adimplebam ministerium meum.*[1] If in Milan I could do more, *paratus sum et ad mortem ire…*'[2]

On 19 November Jerome arrived in Valencia, ready to take a boat that would take him to Milan and then on to Rome, where he would tell the Pope about all he had been doing. The Patriarch, St Juan de Ribera, Archbishop of Valencia, encouraged him to return to the Discalced Carmelites, 'who have great need of members.' Jerome told him that the Pope had put him in the Calced Carmelite habit and in it he had prospered, 'without any more misfortunes that I would have had with them [the Discalced].'

He resided in the Carmelite priory in Valencia. Shortly after his arrival he shared his first impressions with the nuns in Conseguera 'They [the Calced] gave me a very good cell, and treated me with the utmost courtesy and love, because they greatly esteem that I come from Castile and I repay their kindness by my sermons,' and added, 'these friars have a great affection for me.'

Valencia was a healthy town, the climate mild, and there was fresh fish and lots of good fruit. 'I am enjoying good health in this place, because the climate is very temperate. Right now it is December but it feels like May in the springtime.' What was meant to have been a stopover and a transitory residence turned out to be permanent. He lived on the eastern coast of Spain for the space of more than two years, preaching and publishing his books. He even offered the nuns a small lesson in gastronomy:

> This Advent, the fresh fish has given me new life. I am very spoilt, as the nuns send me sardines and other stuff that is fresh. The people of Valencia think nothing of eating fresh eels, which are abundant and cost just half a real a pound, or delicious oranges, lemons and sweet citrus fruits which grow abundantly in our garden. What the [Valencian] nuns send are guavas, garnished with citron or lemon or I don't know what, very sweet smelling, all contained in some very highly polished glass dishes, so that now I have an abundance of this delicacy…

In January 1605, shortly after the Epiphany, he went to Alicante where he prepared to sail to Italy. However, the inclement weather and the thought of spending Lent at sea kept him in Alicante. He liked the city and its

1 Where I can fulfil my ministry.

2 I am prepared to go till I die.

inhabitants. 'It is a city where the people are very courteous,' he wrote. After Lent, during which he preached on the theme of 'The twelve mysteries of the Passion', he travelled to Murcia, a region he didn't much like, describing it as 'a morbid land'. He wrote to the nuns in Consuegra: 'In Murcia they don't know either God or the devil, only silkworms. Everyone, be they servants or lords, spend their time cultivating them.' This phenomenon inspired him to preach a sermon in which he drew out lessons to be learned from silkworms, which he considered 'a doctrine about the end times'. He asked the nuns in a letter, 'Do you wish to be silkworms?'

He returned to Valencia where the Patriarch appointed him Visitator to the Discalced Augustinian Nuns. These were founded by the Archbishop, with the norms and spirit of Teresa of Avila. At the time the Discalced Carmelite friars did not want to be responsible for these nuns because the Patriarch wanted the nuns to be subject to the local bishop. Jerome complained that the Augustinian Nuns and other Orders benefitted from his services and teaching but not the Discalced Carmelite nuns, who belonged to Teresa's own Order. He had been forbidden in the Doria days from visiting them: they had been in Valencia since 1588, during the time of Doria. 'I have never seen them nor has anyone seen them or had anything to do with them.'

It was not like this with the Calced Carmelite nuns, who had two convents in Valencia: one, the Incarnation, with sixty nuns, and the other, St Anne's, with thirty. Jerome praised the nuns in both: 'May God be praised at how devout, how prayerful and spiritual these nuns of Mother Teresa of Jesus are! They are the most reformed nuns in Valencia, who love to engage in discourse about the Spirit.'

The Jesuits called Jerome Gratian as a witness for the beatification of their founder, Ignatius of Loyola. The tribunal was presided over by the Archbishop, John de Ribera. When Gratian was asked if he had been disciplined by any tribunal and why; and if, afterwards, his honour had been restored – because disgraced persons were not allowed to be witnesses – he replied, 'Yes, I have been disciplined by a Discalced Carmelite Tribunal for wanting to defend the good government of my Order. However, in order to prove that I am fit to give evidence at such an august process without any trace of calumny, look at the Brief that Pope Clement VIII gave me, in which he describes my person and with which he sent me to Africa to preach apostolically. There is also a handwritten document that Mother Teresa of Jesus has left me.'

The document from St Teresa is none other than the vow of obedience she made in 1575 in the hermitage of Ecija, when on her way to make a foundation in Seville. Jerome took it with him everywhere, but never showed it to anyone. He thought that now it would be a service to God to show it in order to support himself, 'so that false testimonies and insults from friars would never invalidate my evidence.' The saintly Archbishop (John de Ribera) held that letter from Teresa in his hands, he kissed it repeatedly like a relic and asked Jerome to give him a translation of the text.

'Obedience disrupts all our plans.' Jerome had received an order from the (Calced Carmelite) Provincial of Aragon, Fr John de Heredia, in 1607, to go to Pamplona and preach a Lenten retreat. He felt he had no choice but to obey this awkward command, and set out on the journey. He later wrote, 'As I had to live with these Fathers, and being an outsider to their Order, I had to keep them happy and go on an eighty-mile journey. … For the sake of these friars, God never lets me rest as long as I shall live nor does He let me remain where I want to be.'

He had to overcome a temptation: the Marquis de Guadalest, Philip Folch de Cardona y Borja, had been appointed Ambassador to Belgium by Philip III and asked Jerome to go with him, saying that he would not leave Valencia without him. Our Carmelite told him: 'As the Bishop of Pamplona himself has requested this retreat I can't refuse. When Lent is over I shall continue to do whatever my Superiors tell me, as I can leave the Province only in obedience to the Pope, the Nuncio or my General. I do whatever I am asked.'

The Marquis de Guadalest managed to get the Nuncio to write a Brief ordering Gratian to accompany him on his trip to Belgium. Having given him his word, our man joined the Marquis' retinue at the end of May when it passed through Pamplona on its way to France. The Marquis' wife, Isabel de Bas y Cardona, and their children also joined the party.

Chapter Twenty-Seven

The Sun Sets in Belgium

I have the author Eduardo Marquina's permission to use the title of his play, *The Sun Sets in Belgium*, and a couple of lines that apply to Jerome Gratian:

> I did not want to leave the world
> Without first putting my pike in Belgium.

Jerome arrived in Brussels in July 1607, putting his pike in a land convulsed by religious struggles. He had thought long and hard and then in the end decided to go to Belgium, motivated by 'a desire to die for Christ.' Being no longer involved with the Moors, 'I wanted to try my luck between the Heretics and Lutherans.' He had not yet put into practice the scholastic theology he had learnt in Alcala, 'where one was taught to defend the faith using the art of Apologetics against the Heretics,' and, 'I did not want God to ask me for an account of that talent, if I hadn't used it before the end of my life.' He felt it was Teresa of Jesus, herself, who motivated him from heaven.

The missionary spirit of the Discalced Carmelites abounded not only in France but had also reached Brussels, where, in the same year as his arrival, 1607, Anne of Jesus had just begun to make a foundation. 'However, they [Anne and her nuns] were very much on their own and without anyone to help them.' Jerome rememberd the vow St Teresa made in 1575: how the Lord 'took us both by the hand and ordered us to be of one mind in the government of her Discalced Carmelite Nuns.' It was Teresa, 'who when she was on this earth said it cost her a year of prayer to take me from the world and into the Order, and now she is in heaven her prayers are even more powerful. It is she, as I know in the depth of my soul, who "must have arranged my departure."'

Jerome chose to come because in Brussels he could have both his and Teresa's books printed. 'If I have my books printed in Spanish, Latin and French as I hope, they will be of greater benefit to Christendom than if they were printed there [Spain] only in Spanish, taking into account also the lack of equipment there. I have found there are merchants here in Brussels who will print them at their own expense.'

Jerome counted on his Portuguese friend, Prince Cardinal Albert. Since they had last met several years previously, this Cardinal Archduke, Albert of Austria and Viceroy of Portugal, had become Governor of the Netherlands in the name of the Spanish Crown in 1595. In September 1598, King Philip II, conceded the sovereignty of the Netherlands to his daughter, Isabel Clara Eugenie, shortly before he died. He had arranged her marriage to the Archduke Albert, who then had to renounce his title of Cardinal.

View of Brussels in the 16th century from a contemporary engraving.
The Royal Library, Brussels.

Jerome recalled that he had served the Archduke in Lisbon for five years, 'where I had felt competent in many of the tasks given me in the service of God, given that we had an affinity with each other. I hope in God that I shall find many new opportunities in Belgium, like a mine to be explored in God's service; I shall be spoilt for choice.'

Jerome also found support from Philip III's Ambassador,[1] the Marquis de Guadalest, who had replaced the intransigent John de Ibarra. This intransigent man had insisted that the King of Spain could not negotiate with the rebels of the United Provinces 'without ruining his reputation and honour.' Following the arrival of the new Ambassador, the King agreed to a twelve-year truce which he signed on 12 April 1609, thus ending a long struggle that had lasted forty years. In fact, with the Twelve Year Truce the seventeen Northern Provinces (the Netherlands), seceded from Spain, to become independent under a Protestant banner, bordering as they did the Provinces of the south, which had Brussels as their capital under a Catholic banner (Belgium).

Jerome's friends tried to dissuade him from going to Belgium; at his age of sixty-plus, he should be seeking peace and quiet; he would die there in that very cold country, and the works he had begun here (Spain) would end… However, he responded: 'The more people dissuade me from taking this journey, the more I am inclined to get up and go.' He suspected that Belgium would be his last journey, the twilight of his life, where the sun would set.

'Gratian went to Belgium knowing he would die there…,' Donazar wrote bluntly. 'He was quite simply a mediaeval man living in the past, an old-school Spaniard who was out of place, a flawless poem that ends in sadness, like all that is pure and chivalrous.' Donazar is, however, too trenchant: 'His [Jerome's] life and what he did in Belgium is devoid of historical interest.'

I would say that Jerome Gratian is a Don Quixote who went to Belgium, in the twilight of his life, ready to do battle with his pen against the windmills of the heretics. Titles such as: *The Ten Lamentations*, *The Deceitful Leviathan*, *Blindness and Confusion in Babylon*, *The Catholic Soldier*, *The Thunderbolts of Heresy*, and *Apologia Against The 'Perfect Ones'*, suggests to me someone with a combatative spirit, somewho who was ready to challenge the Protestant Reformation. His time in Belgium, which was to end there, enabled him to complete a work he had begun to write in Spain: *The Pilgrimage of Anastasius*. This book spills over into sixteen dialogues consisting of 'all his works, the scandals, his captivity and his shipwrecks, the foundations of the Discalced Carmelites, the books he wrote, and, finally his spirit, the revelations about him and his dealings with the mother, Teresa of Jesus and other Discalced Carmelite nuns.'

1 King Philip II having died in 1598.

In this book, written principally for his family, he pours out his life, which is like a long pilgrimage. It was the best legacy he could have left them, but which they were not to read until after his death. Written with such deep sensitivity and indifference towards himself, he praises his bitterest enemies and treats them with consummate charity.

Nicholas Anthony, in his *Bibliotheca Hispana Nova*, cites four hundred and forty-five published or unpublished works by Jerome Gratian. However, we know that there are even more.

To reach Belgium Jerome had to cross through France. As he wrote to his sister, Mary of St Joseph, 'It was a pleasant journey and my health was good.' In Bordeaux, his port of arrival, he did not encounter many Lutherans but on the road to Paris he was upset to see 'destroyed churches, Catholics who had no one to look after them and many heretics in other places.' However, his spirits were lifted in Paris when Henry IV welcomed the Marquis de Guadalest's retinue, 'We recognized in the King and Queen a very great desire to strengthen the Catholic faith.'

In Paris Gratian saw for himself the great devotion to Teresa and her nuns. 'All her books, that of the *Life*, the *Interior Castle*, the *Way of Perfection* and the book [biography] by Doctor Ribera have been printed in French and now they are being published in Flemish. They are read with such fervour and profit, the like of which I could never have imagined. People here, who have read Doctor Ribera's book, know me by name, as if I were in Spain. I trust in God that this will bear fruit, especially when my books are published in French, as the doctrine in them, being devout and spiritual, is very appropriate for those who are Catholics.' Jerome gave talks to the nuns in the Carmelite convent in Paris, where Anne of St Bartholomew, who had been Teresa's Secretary and Nurse, was the Prioress. 'The credit and esteem in which they are held is great as is the fruit of their labours.'

There had also been Discalced Carmelite nuns in Brussels from January 1607; Anne of Jesus had arrived with a group of nuns at the invitation of the Duchess, Isabel Clara Eugenie. So there were Discalced Carmelite nuns in France and now in Belgium. 'I am amazed at the speed with which these foundations are being made,' wrote Gratian. However, the nun's spiritual directors were secular priests, 'who, though holy, did not understand the Order very well.' For this reason Gratian believed that God, through the intercession of St Teresa, had arranged that he should be there at that particular time.

The General of the Carmelites had asked him to found Reformed Calced Carmelite priories in Belgium. However, he felt hesitant 'not wanting to upset our Discalced Carmelite friars in Spain.' In Brussels he was given a home with the Calced Carmelites. 'I find myself content and alone in a cell in the garden, where I spend my day until meal times… I busy myself as much as I can with prayer to prepare for my death.' He hung a portrait of Teresa on the wall of his cell, which he had commissioned a Belgium artist to paint. He spoke to her. She inspired him. In his prayers he asked her to intercede for him. He had copies of this portrait printed and sent to Spain.

In his letters, Jerome kept repeating that the end of his life was close. During the autumn of 1610 while in Antwerp he suffered from a fever that almost took him to the grave. On the seventh day two doctors said that his illness was terminal; 'For another seven days I was not given anything to eat except crushed bezoar stones [found in the stomach of goats] with hyacinth preserve.' However, he recovered, although remained quite thin due to digestive problems. I don't know if his recovery was due to the bizarre medication which perhaps came from the New World, sent to him by his sister in Seville. He told her: 'I would like to be absolutely sure about the bezoar stones you sent me. They tell me that the one in the shape of an egg is made from a mixture of the stone and compressed grass, whereas the one with bumps they tell me is fake and the big round one is very good. They also tell me about the special qualities in herbal oil [from a tree in Colombia] that no one knows about here.'

In sum, these were original healing methods! In his *Mystical Theology*, Jerome reveals the origin of the bezoar stone. 'The best medicine against all poison is the bezoar stone, that is born in the belly of goats in the New World, for the goats become ill, in fact poisoned, by the grass they have eaten.' My dictionary tells us that bezoar is a calcium stone that you normally find in the stomach or in the urinary tracts of some quadrupeds, and that it was considered to be an antidote and medicinal.

However, Jerome with undying faith busied himself also 'in acts of preparation to pass over to the next life, of which, if God be served, I will write something.' He began to write *El Arte de Bien Morir* (*The Art of Dying Well*). It was his last work, published just months before he died.

He was now in a hurry to publish his works. He wrote to the Carmel of Consuegra: 'Now I have much to do here to get my works published. I have

Jhs maria

Paresceralea V. R.ª cosa muy nueva esta nueva
Pues sepa que ha muchos años que esta tracada de Dios
y dela santa m.e Theresa de Jhus que como tan ami-
ga de que se ayudasen almas especial m.te de las mas
necessitadas ha mouido esta jornada En la qual
espero en Dios hemos de acabar con trabajos desta vida
y caminar a gozar de la otra. Bien cierto puede
estar que no me oluidare de encomendarla al S.or
y lo otro que no se oluidara de mi que aunque
no lleuase otro consuelo desta vida sino acabarla
en parte donde no me glorie el acudir a las mis
hijas las descalças con los mandatos y descomunio-
nes que aca han procurado mis p.es descalços regu-
llas de mi. El sea glorificado por todo y le
de aquella gra. y sp.u que desseo. De Pamplona 29 de Mayo 1607

Fr. Geron.mo Gracian
de la m.e de Dios

Remitome en las razones que me han mouido al
p. [illegible] la m.e [illegible]

[illegible] oy el Marques de
Guadalupe y su muger que
va Imbaxador a flandes y ten-
go mas comodidad de escriuir
mas largo por el camino

A letter from Jerome with his signature.

already published the enlarged *Diluciario añadido* (*A Further Explanation*), and the fuller *Lampara* (*The Light*) and the *San Jose*, and I am getting published the *San Buenaventura*, having made careful corrections, adding a note about the three ways and all the things that conspire to block one's journey to perfection. I believe it should bear much fruit, and not less the treatise on the *Vida del Alma e Imitacion de Cristo* (*The Life of the Soul and Imitation of Christ*) where the spirit of the holy Teresa is to be found in one book. Then I will give you the *Disciplina regular.* If *Flos Carmeli* should be published I will adapt it so that it will be of benefit.'

His book, *Vida del alma* (*The Life of the soul*), published by Jean Mommarte in Brussels in 1609, was criticized by a Capuchin priest. Jerome thanked him for his objections and replied to the criticisms with cogent arguments and in a way that was clearly humble. At the end he wrote: 'You are very welcome Father to amend and correct this book if you are not happy with it, which I did not write to be polemical but rather for the good of souls and the glory of God. To err is human.'

He had more than two hundred pages of his works published, 'that all told will cost three silver coins per book; God has given and continues to give money for it all.'

The *Life* of St Teresa was printed in Latin, following the announcement of her beatification. This book had already been translated into Italian, French and Flemish. Jerome wrote 'now it is being translated into English. The Saint while alive had such great zeal for the conversion of souls (I do not know if her children follow her example) and continues to do this after her death.' He called her 'the Foundress of the Discalced Carmelite friars and nuns', because they (the Discalced Carmelite friars) had written to him from Rome 'that our Discalced Carmelites from Spain do not want us to call mother Teresa Foundress of the Friars, but rather, Fr John of the Cross as Founder.'

Gratian recounted: 'This book, which is short, has been sent all over Germany and England and Poland, where, in Cracow, it will be translated and printed in Polish. It will also go to Moscow and by way of Portugal to the West Indies and to the East Indies via Seville, so that our holy Mother will be read in every language throughout the world, by heretics and Catholics alike. Even though it cost me fifty silver coins to print, I consider it money well spent.'

Jerome preached to the Discalced Carmelite nuns in Brussels and to the Spanish soldiers in Antwerp but he did not appear in other convents and churches because of the difficulty of the language barrier.

In December 1608 he received news from a Calced Carmelite in Rome that Pope Paul V had appointed him 'for an expedition to Persia with the title of Bishop of Armenia.' There was no doubt that this was true, only it never materialized. A Fr Thomas of Jesus, a Discalced Carmelite who had been professed in Valladolid in 1587 by Gratian himself, was in Rome. After a profound experience of the solitary and eremitical life under the leadership of Doria, who was responsible for the first Desert, Bolarque, Thomas felt called to the missionary life. He went to Rome and convinced the Pope about a new missionary Congregation, called the Congregation of St Paul: Thomas would be its first Vicar General. His idea for a mission consisted of ten priests and two brothers from the Discalced Carmelites in Italy. 'He had already made arrangements with Pope Paul V,' recounted Anastasius, 'for me [Gratian] to be sent there with the title of Bishop of Armenia, for the conversion of Persia.'

However, as Jerome put it, 'the idea of Persia went cold.' The said missionary Congregation did not last long and Thomas of Jesus returned to the sheepfold of the Discalced Carmelites in Italy. There he began to write about the missions and, in 1610, turned up in Brussels, where he founded a priory of Discalced Carmelites. At least it was on record that Jerome was recommended to be Bishop of Armenia, even though he was not consecrated!

In Brussels he lived, as he wrote to his friend Peter Cerezo in Seville, 'in a manner that appears, to some at least, to be contrary to my profession as a Discalced Carmelite.' Thomas of Jesus invited him to join the Discalced Carmelites of the Italian Congregation (in Brussels). At first he was unsure what to do but eventually he declined. 'I replied in writing to Fr Thomas, having consulted with Mother Prioress here about this and with other friends, and after praying a great deal to God that in all my transactions I would do what his Holiness asked me and not what I wanted to do. Even if that involved changing habits, I would wait to know how negotiations were going [between the Spanish and Italian OCD Congregations]. I knew that the Discalced Carmelites from Italy were so divided from those in Spain, that, if I were to join the Italians, I would have to give up my links to the Discalced in Spain and would never see them again.'

There were other decisive reasons: 'To tell you the truth, it did not seem right that the Italian Discalced Carmelites had made new Constitutions, new vows and new ceremonials. You would be shocked if you knew how much time Teresa of Jesus and I spent on them.' He would also have to renounce Spain and the customs of the Order into which he had been professed.

There were many Discalced Carmelites in Spain who liked him, but there was no written contact from those in authority; neither from the General nor anyone close to him. If he had put on the habit of the Calced, it was out of obedience to Pope Clement VIII, but with the same apostolic obedience he would happily have changed it, with the assurance that it would be God's will. However, he also felt attached to the Discalced Carmelites in Spain. If those in Italy had made new Constitutions, those in Spain had mutilated the primitive 1581 Constitutions of Alcala, which were the embodiment of Teresa's Reform.

Jerome lived his final years uncertain about what to do and at a distance from both the Italian and Spanish Discalced Carmelites. In the end he died with the Calced Carmelites, who had taken him in and treated him with the greatest kindness. 'I live like a hermit, in a cell in the garden of this Calced Carmelite Priory in Brussels. The friars being Flemish they are for me like embroidered wall hangings.'

He heard rumours from Spain of never-ending gossip and intrigue. 'They wrote to me from there to say that every day there are new stories about me; one, that I was dead; another that the heretics had tried to kill me with their arrows; another that the Pope had sent for me to come to Rome, etc. I am sick of all this wagging of tongues. May God give me hearts that will follow Him and open mine more to Him.'

For the most part he limited his correspondence to his family. He wrote to Adriana, a nun in Madrid, Juliana, in the Seville Carmel and, while she lived, to Mary of St Joseph, in Consuegra Carmel, who died on 7 May 1611, aged 48. Her Prioress wrote a very detailed account of her life and particularly her last illness and death saying, 'She suffered greatly but with such great patience, just as she had shown throughout her trials and for those of Father Master [Gratian]. Never, at the time nor afterwards, did we hear a single complaint nor a word of self pity. She remained serene in spite of all the legal cases and Sentences [against her brother] that became known to her.'

Gratian sent his family boxes of the books he had published in Antwerp. Some of them were lost and some intercepted by the Inquisition, which was concerned and suspicious of books that came from that country. He gave Juliana Teresa's finger as an inheritance: he had always carried it around his neck. On 20 October 1609 he wrote to her saying that he would not let go of the relic before his death: 'While I live I will not be separated from it. If God calls me soon, as I desire and think, for though I am healthy I am very old and tired, this finger I will leave to your convent because, as your Reverence quite rightly says, it deserves it.'

On one occasion he visited Mons de Hainaut, 50 kilometers from Brussels, where Anne of Jesus had founded a convent of Discalced Carmelite nuns in 1608. Word went round that he had a relic of Teresa's finger. 'There was a huge crowd of people,' Gratian wrote to his sister, Juliana; there were 'as many nuns as friars, who had come for me to touch their heads with the finger and dip it into jars of water. I was amazed when they then brought the water to the sick for them to drink it. As these lands belong to heretics who curse the relics of the saints but who were incredulous when they saw what the relic of the Mother did, I would not dare to upset her.'

When he had been in Rome, Cardinal Cesar Baronio asked for the relic of St Teresa for Pope Clement VIII, but he replied: 'The Pope has many relics; he can leave me my finger.' When the Pope heard what Jerome had said he laughed.

In March 1610 Jerome wrote to his sister, Juliana, that it would be the convent of the Discalced Carmelite nuns in Seville who would inherit the finger. 'I would not want them to have only this but also my body. The other day I was thinking where I might go to die. I found that there was no better place than Seville; being a hot place it is good for bones.' However, shortly afterwards he changed his mind. The nuns in Consuegra were upset, so he wrote to them: 'It is enough for my daughters in Consuegra to have my body and papers, leave the finger with the nuns in Seville.'

When Jerome Gratian died the finger that was due to go to the Discalced Carmelite nuns in Seville never got there, for the Calced friars in Brussels kept it. It was placed inside a round glass reliquary on top of an enamelled golden pedestal. Following a Papal Brief, it was then given to the Princes, Albert and Isabel Clara Eugenia, who deposited it with the Discalced Carmelite nuns in Brussels. So it was Anne of Jesus, as Prioress, who finally received the longed-for relic.

Jerome had his differences with Anne of Jesus. While she clearly preferred to see the Spanish Discalced Carmelite friars arrive in Belgium, he preferred the friars from Italy. 'Here we are fighting over matters with the Discalced Carmelite nuns,' Jerome wrote to Consuegra in July 1609. 'Teresa worked many miracles and would like these to help achieve perfection in many souls, but the angry lion has hold of these foolish nuns, causing a lot of difficulties, because Mother Anne, who is very insistent on getting her own way, continues to await the Discalced Carmelite friars from Spain to govern them. However, I see that no one is coming, that they are making many mistakes and are wasting their time. May God remedy this. Amen.'

The friars came from Italy, much to the regret of those (nuns) from Spain, bringing with them peace, and later glory. In October 1611, Anne of St Bartholomew left Paris for the town of Mons, near Brussels, where she was Prioress of the new convent. A year later, they made a foundation in Antwerp, where, during Advent, Gratian preached to them as well as to Spanish soldiers. He told his sister Juliana about this: 'The Prioress of the convent is Anne of St Bartholomew, a companion of Mother, whom they took from France for this foundation, and who has the same sincerity and simplicity as when we went about together with Mother. The people of this country adore her Spanishness. I seem to be back in the times when the Discalced Carmelites first began.'

Jerome encouraged Anne to write about her mystical experiences and her Carmelite life. When he returned to Antwerp, in the Lent of 1613, he edited Anne of St Bartholomew's words and put them into the form of a dialogue. It is the work known as *Diálogos sobre su espiritu* (*Dialogues on her Spirit*). At the end of this short book, more the length of an exercise book, Jerome explained the reason for this work:

> I, Father Jerome of the Mother of God, declare that ... my intention for writing was that at a particular time and in some soul these words may be of profit. If the glorious Saint Hildegard, Saint Isabel Escomaugense, Saint Matilde, Saint Brigit, Saint Catherine of Siena, the Blessed Joanne of the Cross and Mother Teresa of Jesus and many others did not speak or write or make known their revelations, we would not have the fruit they produced.

It was Jerome who asked Teresa of Jesus to write the *Interior Castle*; the original of this substantial work has been kept in the Seville Carmel. Now he did the same with Anne of St Bartholomew, asking her to put her spirit and revelations into writing. As he said, he did this once again so that it might be of benefit to someone. I think that in order to do justice to Jerome's efforts, Anne of St Bartholomew should have written more discreetly in her 'Defence of Teresa's Inheritance'.

Written in 1621, seven years after our Carmelite's death and thirty years after those lamentable events that led to his expulsion, and with the passing of time, she should have been fairer in what she wrote of this man who had lived in Antwerp at the same time as her. True, she described him as one of the most outstanding friars of his time, but she wrote that St Teresa said something regrettable the year she died, that 'it seemed that this Father, being Provincial, did not do many things that she [Teresa] would have wished.' Anne also praised Nicholas Doria as 'the dearest to our Mother.'

Anne of Jesus

Anne of St Bartholomew

Anne of St Bartholomew said of Mary of St Joseph, Prioress of Lisbon, and Mary of the Nativity, Prioress of Madrid, that 'the Provincial, meaning Doria, acted so gently, that he only removed them from office, and did not punish them further.' And about Jerome Gratian, 'that he was in a Priory for a whole year without going out and without preaching; but he did not want to accept this, but rather preferred to leave the Order. However, things went so bad, that before arriving in Rome he was taken captive, where he endured more trials, but the Order helped as much as it could to rescue him.'

Anne of St Bartholomew had many revelations that were recalled in her books, one of which Jerome had encouraged her to write about. She has been beatified by the Church. However, as an historian, I am sorry to say that she should be disqualified. She too had sought exile and lived in the same country, Belgium, as Anne of Jesus and Jerome Gratian. She was able to hear first-hand from Anne of Jesus about what happened to the nuns who defended the Constitution that Teresa had given them and about the conflict over the *Consulta* and Jerome's expulsion. This is what can happen with old age!

In Belgium, by publishing and distributing Teresa's books, Jerome continued to promote the figure of his holy Mother. He prepared the formal declaration for the process of the Saint's beatification, following the format that arrived from Italy... He was able to smile, being profoundly happy, when he learned that she had been beatified by Pope Paul V in Rome on 24 April 1614. He could say, like the old Simeon: 'At last, Lord, you can let your servant go in peace.'

He baptized a Turk at Pentecost, 18 May; the Archduke and his wife, Isabel Clair Eugenie, offered him this man who would work for him. He was called Mahamet and was robust and strong. When he was baptized he took the name of Jerome of the Mother of God. 'I am catechizing him in order to be ready to baptize him at Easter.'

The Archduke and his wife laughed at the things Jerome recounted about the Turk. Isabel Clair Eugenie asked him if the Turk knew what to do to serve him. Our man replied to the Princess: 'Prepare and starch collars. However, he will know how to be a good Christian, as he has taken to it very well.'

Mahamet had fled from a knight with whom he had been in Naples for five years. He had come to the Netherlands together with an Ambassador of the Great Turk in order to obtain ships with which to fight against Christians. And even though he was made a prisoner he never wanted to be a Christian. However, he converted once he began working for Gratian. It was possibly the last conversion he made in his long life.

Six days before Jerome died, he wrote to his sister, Juliana in Seville. It is the last letter of his that we possess. He hoped that she would distribute the books he had sent her and that the money made would help her and could be used as alms for the convent. He also hoped that 'other houses of Discalced

Carmelite nuns and friars would enjoy his teaching, though they do not have to pay for it. They have never been more in my heart than now. I would want to be buried with them, but no one ever writes to me. And knowing that my bad and lax soul has lived in a body like mine, a dunghill is enough for me. I quietly go to God, who knows my intention was to serve them.'

His love for his Discalced Carmelite Order remained until the end of his life. 'I would like to die among them,' he remarked, but 'no one ever writes to me.' It was a love that was not reciprocated.

On 20 September 1614, a Saturday, Jerome, accompanied by a lay brother, visited a house in Aloste about five miles from Brussels; a visit that was 'a matter of charity and for the common good'. It was dark by the time he returned to Brussels and the city gates were already closed, so they had to spend the night in a house in the suburbs, called St John. People from Valencia have an adage: 'To sleep under the moon of Valencia', in other words, spending the night sleeping out in the open. Who knows, maybe this also happened to him in Valencia as he spent a long time there. However, the climate in Brussels was much colder and, though it was late summer, it was not good to sleep out in the open.

The two friars found a coach-driver to take them to a house in the suburbs. At two in the morning, Jerome felt he was close to death. He was able to get up in order to be sick, but did not feel any better. He spent the night on the floor with a blanket around him. At dawn he asked the coachman to let the Carmelite Priory know (where he was). However, the coachman, who had no idea about the different Orders of friars, saw a Dominican who, because it was a Sunday and the feast of St Matthew, was on his way to preach in a small village. He asked the Dominican to come quickly to the house where he would find a very sick friar from his Order.

Jerome welcomed the Dominican like an angel from heaven and made his confession to him in Latin and the friar then left to go to where he had to preach. In the meantime, the coachman had arrived at the Dominican Priory where he told them about a sick man. One of the friars, who knew Gratian, put on his white cape and made his way there. First, however, he called into the nearby Ambassador's residence, to give the disturbing news.

The next day, Sunday, a friend of Jerome's arrived and told him: 'Father, there are obvious signs that you are dying. You should put yourself at rights with God. Do you have any concerns?' Jerome replied: 'I confessed this morning and I do not have anything on my conscience that I need to worry about.'

They brought him Communion from the nearby parish and gave him the last rites. He made an act of faith, asked for pardon and forgave all. He recited the *Te Deum* and many 'Glory be's' which was among his favourite prayers. Those near him heard him say a phrase in Latin that a Bishop muttered to St Augustine when the Bishop had asked God to lengthen his (Augustine's) life: '*Si nunquam, bene; si aliquando, quare non modo?*' (If I never have to die, good; but if I have to one day, why not now?)

Jerome asked the Dominican friar to search in his habit and take out his two *matresas* (a French word to indicate ladies who are served by young gentlemen). The friar found two pictures, one of the Virgin Mary the other of Teresa of Jesus, together with Teresa's finger that Jerome always carried with him. The house filled up with visitors: the Provincial of the Calced Carmelites with a Doctor and Pharmacist, the Prior of the Discalced Carmelites, Thomas of Jesus, the Spanish Ambassador, Marquis de Guadalest,...

By three in the afternoon the Doctor of the Royal Highnesses, Prince Albert of Austria and Isabel Clara Eugenie, arrived and announced that he would die within a couple of hours. Those with him did not dare move him because he was in such pain. However, Jerome indicated that he wanted to die in his priory. Six men, gripping the corners of a blanket, lifted him up and placed him in a covered wagon equipped with a mattress. He was taken to the Carmelite Priory in Brussels, where he arrived almost lifeless, without uttering a word. He died peacefully shortly afterwards. It was 6 p.m. on Sunday 21 September 1614, the feast of St Matthew: he was sixty-nine years old.

The following day, the Provincial of the Carmelites, Fr Hernando of St Victor, presided at the funeral Mass. A Spanish Dominican, preacher to the Prince and Princess, gave the panegyric. Jerome Gratian was buried with the habit of the Calced Carmelites, in a tomb in front of the altar in the Priory's Chapter room.

The news of his death reached Spain. While the Discalced Carmelite priories gave this scant attention, it was different with the Calced Carmelites. By order of the General, a solemn funeral Mass was to be said for him in all the priories 'as if he had been the Provincial.'

In a house in Madrid, a Fr Andrew de Lezama preached at the special funeral Mass. He had known Jerome and considered him a saint. In his sermon he said this of the deceased: 'He was once in the presence of Pope Clement VIII, of happy memory, who allowing him to speak of his enemies, he, Fr Jerome Gratian, said they were saints and that he alone was a bad man and a sinner. He said this with such great humility and submissiveness that the same Pontiff said to some Cardinals who were present: "This man is truly a saint." I am not saying that he was canonized or beatified by these words, but I would like to say two things: first, that the one who said these words is the one who canonizes and beatifies on this earth; and second, that when he canonizes or beatifies, he says no more than he said.'

After Jerome's death his family wanted to open a process for his beatification but the Discalced Carmelite Order threatened to open up files in the archives. Notwithstanding this threat, in 1619, five years after his death, there appeared a treatise by the scholar, Andrew del Marmol, entitled *Excelencias, vida y trabajos del padre fray Gerónimo Gracián de la Madre de Dios Carmelita.*[2] Laurence of the Holy Mother, one of Jerome's younger brothers and a Discalced Carmelite friar, who was Prior of Evora, made known that the scarcity of facts in Andrew de Marmol's biography was due to a respect and regard for the Discalced Carmelite Order.

Laurence died in 1645, at the age of seventy-five, having spent his final years in the Priory of Criptana. He was the last bastion of the family who experienced within the Discalced Carmelite Order the ominous silence that developed around the figure of Jerome Gratian. Twenty-five years after Jerome's death, Laurence complained about how ignorant the friars were concerning events in the past in which his brother was involved. 'Almost all those who knew him from the beginning have died and this year, 1639, as more than fifty years have passed, what remains of the Religious of those times? In the world today people continue to believe Jerome's opponents [that he was incorrigible and did not want to accept the smallest penance], either that or they just ignore him.'

This is the story of someone they tried to destroy, and who, over the course of years, has been forgotten. The official history of the Discalced Carmelites was careful to separate Teresa from Jerome and, indeed, this is the way it has remained till our own days. Alonso of Jesus & Mary, the General of the Discalced Carmelites in 1607, in his work *Doctrina de religiosos*, published in Madrid a year after Jerome's death, denied emphatically that Teresa was the Foundress of the Discalced Carmelite friars, but rather Fr John of the Cross; only the nuns acknowledged her with this title. The Order later yielded when she was canonized. Where her books were entitled 'Foundress

2 The sublime life and works of Fr Jerome Gratian of the Mother of God, a Carmelite.

of the Discalced Carmelite nuns,' in the Priories of the friars, they had to add, 'and of the Discalced Carmelite friars.'

However, the official Chronicle saw to it that Jerome Gratian continued to be ostracized. Four hundred years have passed since that injustice, but just before the Holy Year of 2000 the Discalced Carmelite Order has asked forgiveness: 'The Definitory judges that the moment has arrived to make a declaration in seeking justice for a most important Religious in the plan of the Teresian Refoundation.'

Let us praise God for this. In Heaven Teresa of Jesus will have celebrated with Jerome Gratian of the Mother of God, who died wearing the Calced Carmelite habit in the Carmelite Priory of Brussels.

Seville, 21 September 2006
Feast of St Matthew
392nd *anniversry of the death of Fr Jerome Gratian*

The Dantisco Family Tree

I Grandparents

DANTISCO Johann (1485–1548)

Maternal Grandfather. Born Danzig, Germany (today Gdansk in Poland) of a Germany middle-class family, son of Johann Flashbinder von Höfen a merchant and Christine Schulze. Ambassador for the King of Poland to the Court of Charles V. Was in Valladolid with Isabel Delgada, unmarried, two children. Was consecrated Bishop of Chelmno (Culm in German) in 1530 and later named bishop of Warmia in 1537.

DELGADA Isabel

Maternal Grandmother. Though single she had two children with the Polish Ambassador, Dantisco. Later married Michael Navarro Azpilicueta, brother of Martín Navarro Azpilicueta, a doctor famous for his Thesis.

TORRES Peter

Paternal Grandfather, son of Diego Garcia, armourer of the Catholic Monarchs. Died young in Medina del Campo, shortly after 1525, having taken the King's side in the battle against the *Comuneros*. Inherited the nobility of his father. Took over the role of armourer from his father. Married in 1498 in Medina del Campo to Isabel de Hermosilla.

HERMOSILLA Isabel

Paternal Grandmother, daughter of Peter de Monzon, the official 'money changer' in the Court of the King, married Agnes Rodriguez. The Monzon family lived in the Santiago Street, Valladolid. Isabel de Hermosilla remarried to Francis Xerez de Godoy, son of a nobleman who had died in 1566. He was responsible for the weaponry. The wedding took place in Medina del Campo.

II Parents

DE ALDERETE Diego (1499–1586)

Emperor Charles V's Secretary and Translator to King Philip II. Studied in Paris and Louvain. Belonged to a group who followed Erasmus in the Court of Charles V. 'Multilingual and translator by profession,' is known for his translations of Plutarch, Thucydides, Xenophon, etc. which were published in 1533. Married Joanna Dantisco, with whom he had twenty children, of whom we know the names of sixteen.

DANTISCO Joanna (1527–1601)

Illegitimate daughter of Johann Dantisco, Polish Ambassador for the King of Poland, and the Spanish woman Isabel Delgada. Married Diego, had twenty children. Great friend of Teresa of Avila.

III Dantisco's Brothers and Sisters

1 **Joanna**

Died very young.

2 **Anthony** (1541–6th March 1576)

Educated by his father in the study of Latin and Greek literature, had lessons with the scholar Bustos in Valladolid, with Alvar Gomez in Toledo and studied at the University of Alcala. Entered into service with the king in 1565, but was not officially named secretary to Philip II until the 1st January 1571, with an annual salary of one hundred thousand maravedies. He was the first installer and classifier of the library in the Escorial. Died unmarried aged thirty-five, and so poor that the King, Philip II ordered his jeweller, Hernando de Briviesca, to take care of the funeral expenses. There is an important collection of Anthony's letters kept in the Academy of History in Madrid. At his death St Teresa exclaimed, 'I have lost an angel given to me by God for my salvation'.

3 **Lucas** (1543 – 8th July 1587)

Baptized on 23rd October 1543 in the parish of St James, Valladolid.

His parents had wanted him to become a priest. He studied canon law in Alcala. However, his vocation was not very strong and he married in Toledo on 17th October 1576 to Joanna Carrillo a lady of noble birth in the parish of St Martin in Madrid. Lived in Madrid where he worked as a lawyer. Wrote a book entitled, *Galateo español.* The day after his brother Anthony died, 7th May 1576, he was asked by Philip II to continue his brother's work of 'listing and cataloguing the books of the San Lorenzo el Real Monastery'.

4 **Jerome** (Valladolid 6th June 1545 – Brussels 21st September 1614)
He is the subject of this book.

5 **Adriana** (1546 – 3rd Feb. 1631)
Nun in the Conception Convent, Jeronomites, Madrid. Professed aged twenty-nine with the name Adriana of the Holy Spirit on 18th May 1574. Died aged eighty-six.

6 **Alonso** (Born Valladolid 1551 – …)
Baptized 1st February 1551 in the parish of St James. Died as a child.

7 **Justina** (1552 – 1599)
Baptized in St Gines on 6th October 1552. Educated in the Colegio for noble ladies, Toledo. She took over the role of her mother in looking after the house and her siblings. Married Peter Zapata del Mármol, Secretary to the King's Council and the King's chamber.

8 **Francesca**
Died in infancy.

9 **Thomas** (1558 – 1615)
Baptized on 13th March 1558. Was secretary of Languages to King Philip II. He inherited a mastery over languages, excelling in historical languages and the liberal arts. He was secretary of languages for Philip II. He wrote a treatise on the art of writing letters. Translated the *Ordinances made by the French Kings on the rule of life, and the salaries of the gentlemen of arms.* He had a passion for books. Cervantes mentions him in 'The Song of Caliope' in *La Galatea* and in the *Viaje del Parnaso.* Was censor of the book *El peregrino en su patria*, by Lope de Vega, for which he received

praise and the friendship of the latter. Married Laurencia de Zurita, a highly educated lady in Latin, calligraphy and music. When Laurencia died in 1603, Thomas soon remarried, in 1604, to Isabel de Berruguete, daughter of the Lord of la Ventosa. Their first child was baptized the following year on 30th May 1605 in St Lawrence parish, Valladolid. Their son, also named Thomas, entered the Jesuit Order, with whom he ministered in Bogota, Colombia.

10 **Joanna (1560–...)**

Baptized 24th June 1560. In July 1576 she began to study at the College for Noble Ladies, Toledo, founded by the Archbishop Silicio. Here she met St Teresa who called her 'very pretty'. Married an alderman from Segovia but died before the marriage was one year old.

11. **Maria** (1563–May 1611)

Was received into the Order by St Teresa in Valladolid on 5th May 1578 with the name *Maria of St Joseph*. Professed on 10th May 1579. Nine years later, May 1588, she left Valladolid to join the community in Madrid. In 1590 she exercised the role of sub-prioress. She went to Consuegra as a foundress (1597), where she was prioress for six years: from 1597 to 1601 and from 1604 to 1608. She died aged forty-eight, having spent thirty-two years in the Order. She frequently wrote to her brother, Jerome, who kept the letters, and we still have them today.

12 **Louis** (1564–1596)

Studied in Alcala, in the College of Ss Philip and James. Secretary to the wife of the Viceroy of Sicily. Married Agnes de Barrionuevo. Marmol described him as 'a clever young man from a good background'. Died from a stroke aged 32.

13 **Peter** (1565–1599)

Entered the Order in Pastrana in January 1588 with his younger brother, Lorenzo. Left after eleven months, without taking vows, due to ill health. Was later ordained a priest (1591). Jerome could not preach at his first Mass, as he was imprisoned in St Hermenegildo priory, Madrid. Rector of the Latina hospital in Madrid. Mary of

St Joseph, his sister, in a biographical note wrote, 'While treating the plague victims in the Latin Hospital in Madrid in 1599, he contracted the plague and died in the said hospital, where he was Rector, being 34 years old.'

14 **Isabel** (1569 – 13th November 1640)
Was admitted aged just seven into the Carmelite convent in Toledo. Teresa called her 'my beautiful one' and professed her with the name *St Joseph of Jesus* on 29th September 1584. After two years she left for the foundation in Cuerva, where she was sub-prioress on various occasions. She was blind for eighteen years. With admirable patience she endured what was being done to her brother; 'I see the way they are treating my well-known brother (Jerome) with the utmost contempt'. She died aged seventy-one.

15 **Lawrence** (1570 – 2nd December 1645)
Discalced Carmelite. With Ambrose Morales, was chronicler for Philip II, began studying in Puente del Arzobispo. In 1583 entered the College of Ss Philip and James, also called of the King, in Alcala University. He obtained an outstanding degree in Arts. Entered the Order in Pastrana on 16th January 1588, shortly after his brother, Peter. He was professed with the name *Lawrence of the Mother of God*. After his novitiate, already an ordained priest, he read Arts in Cogollado, and was novice director in Daimiel and, subsequently, lecturer in Theology at Manzanares and Baeza (1599), in Alcala (1604), Rector in Coimbra (1611), Prior of Evora (1613), Lecturer in moral theology in Ocanna until 1623 when he was elected Prior of Almodóvar. They thought to make him provincial but, he was forced to rest in the priory in Criptana, where he died.

16 **Juliana** (1574 – 28th August 1621)
Discalced Carmelite nun, who took the name *Juliana of the Mother of God*. Entered aged just eight with the nuns in Seville. Made her religious profession on 25th December 1590, aged sixteen. At twenty-four she was made Director of Novices, and Prioress when thrity-four. She died aged 47.

Bibliography

Abbreviations

ABC	Archivum Bibliographicum Carmelitanum
BRAE	Journal of the Spanish Royal Academy
BRAH	Journal of the Royal Academy of History
Carm	Carmelus
CT	Thomist Science
CD	City of God
EphCarm	Ephemerides Carmeliticae
EtudCarm	Etudes Carmelitaines
HS	Sacred Spain
MHCT	Monumenta Historica Carmeli Teresiani (Roma)
MteCarm	El Monte Carmelo (Burgos)
RABM	Review of Archives, Bibliographies and Museums
RevEspTeol	Spanish Theological Review
RevEsp	Revista de Espiritualidad
RevSJCruz	Review of St John of the Cross
RHisp	Review Hispanique
RevTeolMist	Mystical Theological Review

Various Authors, *En torno a Dantisco*, Cervantes Institute, Warsaw 2001.

ABELLÁN, JOSÉ LUIS, *El erasmismo español*, Madrid 1982.

ALBERTO DE LA VIRGEN DEL CARMEN, *Historia de la Reforma Teresiana (1562-1962)*, Madrid 1968.

ALONSO FERNÁNDEZ, MARÍA DEL PUERTO, *Ana de Jesús, profeta de ayer y hoy*, RevEsp 63 (2004) 251-299.

ÁLVAREZ, SIMEÓN, *Orientación bibliográfica sobre Jerónimo Gracián*, MteCarm 91 (1983) 620-625.

ÁLVAREZ, TOMÁS, *Jerónimo Gracián, pionero de las Misiones Teresianas*, MteCarm 110 (2002), nº 1-3.

— *Alderete y Dantisco: padre y abuelo de Gracián. El drama de dos Humanists of the XVI century*, MteCarm 91 (1983) 383-432.

— *Apéndice documental: carteo entre Diego Gracián y Juan Dantisco*, MteCarm 91 (1983) 433-450.

— *Tres retratos autobiográficos por Gracián, su padre y su abuelo*, MteCarm 91 (1983) 499-575.

— *Poema "de vita sua " de Juan Dantisco*, MteCarm 91 (1983) 499- 575.

— *"Cartas a Juan Dantisco" La colección "H 154" de Upsala*, MteCarm 91 (1983) 610-619.

— *En torno a Santa Teresa y los orígenes de los Carmelitas Descalzos*, MteCarm 95 (1987) 559-570.

— *"Glanes ": Apuntes de Gracián sobre Santa Teresa*, MteCarm 96 (1988) 369-383.
— *Las "Constituciones" de Santa Teresa*, Mt. Carm 86 (1978) 97- 117.
— *El carisma teresiano: desde las Constituciones de Santa Teresa hasta las "Declaraciones para las*
Carmelitas Descalzas", MteCarm 86 (1978) 331-352.
— *Reviven las Constituciones de Santa Teresa entre Doria, San Juan de Ribera y Gracián*, Mt. Carm 88 (1980) 67-86.
— *Jirones del drama familiar: más sobre los abuelos y padres de Jerónimo Gracián*, Mt. Carm 103 (1995) 111-123.
— Nota sobre "Adiciones y Escolias" de Gracián a "La vida" de la Santa por Ribera, Mt. Carm 112 (2004) 277-281.
— *El "voto de obediencia" de Santa Teresa y sus tres relatos autógrafos*, EphCarm 15 (1964) 155-176.
ANA DE JESÚS, *Escritos y documentos*. Edited by Antonio Fortes & Restituto Palmero. Burgos 1966.
ANNE OF St BARTHOLOMEW, BTA., *Beata Ana de San Bartolomé. Obras completas*, Ed. By Julián Urkiza. Burgos 1999.
ANGELO OF THE BLESSED TRINITY, D. *Teutonio de Braganza, Arzobispo de Évora y los Carmelitas Descalzos*. Evocaciones de hace IV siglos, Mt.Carm 34 (1930) 339-351.
ANTOLÍN, FORTUNATO, *Observaciones sobre las constituciones de las carmelitas descalzas promulgadas en Alcalá de Henares en 1581*, EphCarm 24 (1973) 291-374.
— *Noticias sobre el Capítulo O.C.D. de abril 1587, en Valladolid*, MteCarm 96 (1987) 609-614.
— *En torno a las Constituciones de las Carmelitas Descalzas*, MteCarm 98 (1990) 105-110.
ASTIGARRAGA, JUAN LUIS, *Las cartas de Santa Teresa a Jerónimo Gracián*, EphCarm 29 (1978) 103-118.
— *Expulsión del P. Gracián. Documentos de un Proceso 1587–1601*, Teresianum, Roma 2004.
— *Últimos días y muerte de Santa Teresa*, EphCarm 33 (1982) I-II,7-69.
— *Páginas de María de San José (Salazar)*, EphCarm 29 (1978) 494-495.
ÁVILA, JULIÁN DE, *Vida de Santa Teresa de Jesús, por el maestro —, primer capellán de la Santa*. Edited, annotated and added to by Vicente de la Fuente. Madrid 1881.
AXER, JERZY, *Juan Dantisco y sus relaciones con España*, Internet.
BATAILLON, MARCEL, *Erasmo y España*, Madrid 1966.
BEAUVAIS, F. DE, *La vie de M. de Brétigny, preste fondateur des carmélites de sainte Thérèse en France*
et aux Pays-Bas, París 1947.
BELTRÁN, GABRIEL, *Jerónimo Gracián, fundador de los conventos de Úbeda y Jaén*. RevSJCruz 22 (1998/II) 163-290.
— *Un condiscípulo de Gracián: Juan de Jesús Roca en el Libro de Protocolo del Colegio de Baeza* (1582-1585), MteCarm 91 (1983) 259-309.
— *Elecciones hechas en los primeros Capítulos de la Reforma Teresiana* (1581-1622 y1634), MteCarm 74 (1966) 241-278.
— *El Carmen y San José de Toledo: notas para la historia de ambas comunidades (1568-1573)*, MteCarm 101 (1994) 157-169.
— *San Juan de la Cruz: defi nidor y consiliario general en Segovia (1588-1591)*, MteCarm 104 (1996) 425-465.
— *Capítulo General de Cremona: presencia del Carmelo Teresiano (5-13 de junio, 1593)*, MteCarm 105 (1997) 515-522.
BELTRÁN DE HEREDIA, V. OP., *El licenciado Juan Calvo de Padilla y su proceso inquisitorial*, CT 42 (1930) 168-198.
— *Los alumbrados de la diócesis de Jaén. III. El maestro Gaspar Lucas y las beatas de Jaén*, RevEspTeol 9 (1949) 445-488.

BENGOECHEA, ISMAEL, *"Centellas de fuego de herejía "; memorial inédito del P. Gracián,* EphCarm 31 (1980) 245-260;

— *En torno a la «Rehabilitación» del Padre Jerónimo Gracián de la Madre de Dios. Una página de historia carmelitana contemporánea,* RevSJCruz 17 (1996/I) 1-170.

— *Decor Carmeli: el Carmelo en Andalucía,* Córdoba 2002;

— *Nota aclaratoria sobre la «rehabilitación» del P. Jerónimo Gracián,* RevSJCruz 20 (1997/II) 225-375.

— *"Tratado de las Cifras": nuevo inédito del Padre Jerónimo Gracián,* MteCarm 104 (1996) 291-311.

BERTOLDO-IGNACIO DE SANTA ANA, *Vida de la Venerable Madre Ana de Jesús, coadjutora de Santa Teresa en la Reforma del Carmelo y Fundadora de la Orden en Francia y en Bélgica,* Burgos 1901.

BOHMER, EDUARDO, *Alphonsi Valdesii litterae XL ineditae,* en "Homenaje a Menéndez y Pelayo", t. I, Madrid 1899.

BONILLA Y SAN MARTÍN, ADOLFO, *Clarorum hispaniensum epistolae ineditae,* RHisp 8 (1901) 181-308.

BOSSCHE, LOUIS VAN DEN, *Vénérable Anne de Jesus (1545-1621),* Desclée de Brouwer 1958.

CÁCERES WÜRSIG, INGRID, *Breve historia de la secretaría de interpretación de lenguas,* Universidad Europea de Madrid. Internet.

CAEIRO, FRANCISCO, *O Archiduque Alberto de Austria, Vice-rei e Inquisidor Mor de Portugal, Cardeal Legado do Papas, Governador e despois Soberano dos Paixes Baixos,* Lisboa, Neogravura, 1961.

CARMELO DE LA CRUZ (PÉREZ MILLA), *Gracián y Sega frente a frente,* MteCarm 72 (1964) 365-422.

— *Un manuscrito inédito del P. Gracián. Scholias y addiciones al libro de la Vida de la Madre Teresa de Jesús,* MteCarm 68 (1960) 86-156.

— *"Lamentación lamentable". En torno a una obra del P. Gracián.* MteCarm 68 (1960) 514-52.

CANO NAVAS, MARÍA LUISA, *El convento de San José del Carmen de Sevilla. Las Teresas,* Sevilla 1984.

CORTIJO OCAÑA, ADELAIDA Y CORTIJO OCAÑA, ANTONIO, *Vida de la madre Catalina de Cardona por fray Juan de la Miseria: un texto hagiográfi co desconocido del siglo XVI* (Bancroft Library, UCB, Fernan Núñez Collection, vol. 143) "Dicenda. Cuadernos de Filología Hispánica" 21 (2003) 21-34.

CRISÓGONO DE JESÚS SACRAMENTADO, *Santa Teresa de Jesús. Su vida y su doctrina,* Barcelona 1936.

— *Vida de San Juan de la Cruz,* BAC, Madrid 1991.

— *La escuela mística carmelitana,* Madrid-Ávila 1930.

CUARTERO Y HUERTA, BALTASAR, *Historia de la Cartuja de Santa María de las Cuevas, de Sevilla, y de su fi lial de Cazalla de la Sierra,* Madrid 1950, tomo I.

DAVID DO CORAÇAO DE JESÚS, OCD, *A Reforma Teresiana em Portugal,* Lisboa 1962.

General Definitory, OCD, *Offical Declaration of Fr Jerome of the Mother of God, OCD rehabilitation* (251-254), RevSJCruz 26 (2000/II) 133-291.

DENEUVILLE, D., *Santa Teresa de Jesús y la mujer,* Barcelona 1966. *Documenta primigenia de la serie Monumenta Historica Carmeli Teresiani* (=MHCT). Volumen I (1560-1577) y volumen II (1578-1581), Roma 1973; Volumen III (1582-1589), Roma 1977.

DONÁZAR ZAMORA, ANSELMO, *Principio y fin de una Reforma. Una revolución religiosa en tiempos de Felipe II. La Reforma del Carmen y sus hombres*, Ediciones Guadalupe, Bogotá (Colombia) 1968.

— *Meditaciones teresianas (grandeza y miseria de una santa española)*, Barcelona 1957.

— *El libro "Principio y fin de una Reforma"*, MteCarm 79 (197 1) 387-400.

EDUARDO DE SANTA TERESA, *(Introducción al) Libro de Recreaciones de la Venerable Madre María de S. José*, MteCarm 10 (1909) 9-17.

EFRÉN DE LA MADRE DE DIOS - O. STEGGINK, *Tiempo y vida de Santa Teresa de Jesús*, BAC, Madrid 1996, 3ª ed.

ENRIQUE DEL SAGRADO CORAZÓN, *Santa Teresa de Jesús y la Inquisición española; estudio introductivo*, RevEsp 24 (1965) 337-342.

EZQUERRO, MILAGROS, *Diego Gracián de Alderete*, tesis doctoral leída en la Universidad de Toulouse, 1976. (Copia en Biblioteca Nacional).

FERNÁNDEZ DE MENDIOLA, DOMINGO A., *Opción misional de la Congregación italiana siguiendo el espíritu de Sta. Teresa y la llamada de los Papas*. Internet.

FLORENCIO DEL NIÑO JESÚS, *La Orden de Santa Teresa y la fundación de la Propaganda Fide y las misiones carmelitanas*, Madrid 1923.

— *Fr Francisco el Indigno, apóstol del Congo*, Madrid-Cuenca 1924.

— *La beata Ana de San Bartolomé, compañera y secretaria de santa Teresa de Jesús*, Madrid 1948.

— *Los Carmelitas Descalzos y la Sagrada Congregación de Propaganda Fide*, MteCarm 25 (1921) 100-102, 212- 219.

FONTÁN, ANTONIO Y AXER, JERZY, *Españoles y polacos en la Corte de Carlos V. Cartas del embajador Juan Dantisco*, Alianza Editorial, Madrid 1994.

FORTES RODRÍGUEZ, ANTONIO MARÍA, *El P. Jerónimo Gracián y su producción literaria*, ABC 15 (1973) 175-303.

— *Doctrina espiritual del P. Jerónimo Gracián de la Madre de Dios, amigo y director de Santa Teresa de Jesús*, MteCarm 71 (1963) 485-520 y 72 (1964) 197-221.

— *Edición de las constituciones femeninas del ciclo teresiano. 1607*, MteCarm 104 (1996) 171-181.

— *"Flores del Monte Carmelo", un opúsculo inédito del P. Gracián*, MteCarm 91 (1983) 603-609.

— *"Pedro de Bérulle y las Carmelitas Descalzas de Francia": Anotaciones*, MteCarm 103 (1995) 401-438.

FRANCISCO DE SANTA MARÍA PULGAR, *Reforma de los Descalzos de Nuestra Señora del Carmen de la Primitiva Observancia*. 7 vol. Madrid 1644-1739.

FUENTE, VICENTE DE LA, *Historia Eclesiástica de España*, Madrid 1873- 1875.

Fuentes históricas sobre la muerte y el cuerpo de Santa Teresa de Jesús (1582-1596), Ed. preparada por JUAN LUIS ASTIGARRAGA, EULOGIO PACHO, OTILIO RODRÍGUEZ, MHCT 6, Roma 1982.

GABRIEL DE LA CRUZ, *Elecciones hechas en los primeros capítulos de la reforma teresiana (1581-1622 y 1634)*, MteCarm 74 (1966) 241- 278.

GARCÍA MERCADAL, J., *Viajes de extranjeros por España y Portugal*, Madrid 1952.

GARRIDO, PABLO MARÍA, O.CARM., *Catálogo de Carmelitas antiguos que pasaron a la Descalcez (1568-1593)*, Carm 45 (1998) 90-134.

— *Noticias bio-bibliográficas sobre el Padre Jerónimo Gracián de la Madre de Dios*, Carm 41 (1994) 88-125.

— *Nuevos datos bio-bibliográficos sobre el P. Jerónimo Gracián*, Carm 42 (1995) 237-266;

— *Interpretaciones erróneas de algunos textos teresianos*, MteCarm 105 (1997) 485-498.
GÓMEZ CENTURIÓN, JOSÉ, *Relaciones biográfi cas inéditas de Santa Teresa de Jesús: con autógrafos*
de autenticidad en documentación indubitada, Madrid 1916. (pp. 309-312)
GOYAN, G., *Jérome Gratien de la Mere de Dieu et Dominique de J. M. aux origines de la propagande*, EtudCarm 18 (1933) 23-50.
GRACIÁN, JERÓNIMO, *Historia de las fundaciones de los carmelitas descalzos*, MHCT 3, p. 533-694.
— *Diálogos del tránsito de la M. Teresa de Jesús*, Roma 1982.
— *Escolias a la Vida de Santa Teresa de Jesús compuesta por el P. Ribera*. (Introducción y notas del P. Astigarraga). EphCarm 32 (1981) 343-430.
— *Peregrinación de Anastasio*, ed. preparada por Juan Luis Astigarraga, Roma 2001.
— *Diez lamentaciones del miserable estado de los ateístas de nuestros tiempos*, ed. Otger Steggink, Madrid 1959.
— *Obras*, ed. Silverio de Santa Teresa, Burgos 1932-33.
— *Cartas*, ed. preparada por Juan Luis Astigarraga, Roma 1989.
GRACIÁN DANTISCO, LUCAS, *Galateo español*, Estudio preliminar de Margherita Morreale, CSIC,
Madrid 1968.
GRANADA, FRAY LUIS DE, *Historia de Sor María de la Visitación y Sermón de las caídas públicas*, Estudio preliminar de Álvaro Huelga, Barcelona 1962.
GRAZIANO DELLA CROCE, *Patrimonio espiritual de la Congregación de S. Elías O.C.D. en su primer*
siglo de historia, MteCarm 70 (1962) 203-246.
GRAZIANO DI SANTA TERESA, *Lettere inedite del P. Gerolamo Graziano*, EphCarm 3 (1949) 549-93.
GREGOIRE DE SAINT JOSEPH, *El P. Gracián de la Madre de Dios, carmelita Descalzo, y sus Jueces*, Burgos, MteCarm 1904.
HILARIO DE SAN JOSÉ, *Espiritualidad avilina y espiritualidad carmelitana*, MteCarm 72 (1964) 337-364.
HERRÁIZ, M., *Sólo Dios basta: claves para la espiritualidad teresiana*, Madrid 2000.
HERRERA CASADO, ANTONIO, *La princesa de Éboli*, Guadalajara 2000.
HUERGA, ÁLVARO, *Fray Luis de Granada*, BAC, Madrid 1988.
— *La vida seudomística y proceso inquisitorial de sor María de la Visitación*, HS 12 (1959) 35-110.
— *El proceso inquisitorial de "la monja de Lisboa" y fray Luis de Granada*, HS 12 (1959) 333-356.
HUESA LOPE, GONZALO, *La mano de Santa Teresa de Jesús*, Ronda 1996.
IZQUIERDO, MONTSERRAT, *Teresa de Jesús. Con los pies descalzos*, Madrid 2006.
JAN KIENIEWICZ, *Dantisco, diálogo y futuro de las relaciones hispano-polacas*, "Estudios Hispánicos", Wroclaw 1997, vol. VI, pp. 29- 40.
JAVIERRE, JOSÉ MARÍA, *Teresa de Jesús*, ed. Sígueme, Salamanca 1983.
— *Juan de la Cruz, un caso límite*, ed. Sígueme, Salamanca 1992.
JERÓNIMO DE SAN JOSÉ, OCD, *Historia del Carmen Descalzo*, Madrid 1637.
JOSÉ DE SAN JUAN DE LA CRUZ, *Apuntes bio-bibliográficos: R. M. María de San José*, MteCarm 7 (1906) 466-468.
JOSÉ LUIS DE JESÚS MARÍA, *Fin y régimen de la Reforma Teresiana (1568–1591). Santa Teresa, San Juan de la Cruz y primeras Constituciones*, MteCarm 72 (1964) 303-334; 73 (1965) 3-47.
KAMEN, HENRY, *El gran duque de Alba, soldado de la España imperial*, Madrid 2005.
LANUZA, MIGUEL, *Vida de la sierva de Dios Francisca del Stmo. Sacramento, carmelita descalza, del Convento de Pamplona*, Zaragoza 1659.

LARRACOECHEA, HIPÓLITO (DE LA SAGRADA FAMILIA), *Le conflict Doria Gratien, Etude histórico juridique*, EtudCarm 15 (1946) 196- 273.
— *Hacia la independencia jurídica del Carmelo teresiano. Actuación del Padre Nicolás Doria (1582-1586)*, EphCarm 18 (1967) 314- 347.
— *La Consulta. Estudio históricojurídico*, MteCarm 77 (1969) 153- 189, 341-368.
— *El Capítulo de Alcalá*, MteCarm 79 (1971) 27-76.
— *Erección de la reforma teresiana en Provincia independiente*, MteCarm 81 (1973) 59-120.
— *Los procesos de beatificación y canonización de Santa Teresa*, MteCarm 78 (1970) 85-130).
— *La misión de los primitivos Carmelitas en el Congo*, MteCarm 75 (1967) 392-404.
— *Principio y fin de una Reforma*, 76 (1968) 308-318.
LEONOR DE LA MISERICORDIA, *Relación de la vida de la venerable Catalina de Cristo*, Monte Carmelo, Burgos 1995.
LLAMAS MARTÍNEZ, ENRIQUE, *Santa Teresa de Jesús y la Inquisición española*, Madrid, CSIC, 1972.
— *Jerónimo Gracián Dantisco en la Universidad de Alcalá (1560- 1572)*, EphCarm 26 (1975) 176-212.
— *Jerónimo Gracián de la Madre de Dios, escritor místico, compañero y confesor de Santa Teresa. Su familia y su ascendencia genealógica*, RevEsp 136 (1975) 379-395.
— *Pedro Gracián Torres Alderete, hermano del P. Jerónimo Gracián, autor espiritual*, RevEsp 136 (1975) 396-407.
— *El P. Jerónimo Gracián de la Madre de Dios y su ascendencia genealógica*, MteCarm 102 (1994) 61-86.
— *Talante humano de Juan Dantisco (1485-1584), abuelo del P. Jerónimo Gracián*, MteCarm 103 (1995) 25-44.
— *Talante humano, cultural y religioso de Felipe II, a través del "Diurnal" del secretario Antonio Gracián Dantisco*, CD 216 (2003) 991-1024.
— *La Beata Ana de San Bartolomé (1549-1626), secretaria de Sta. Teresa, alma mística y eminente*
escritor, RevTeolMist 642 (nov-dic 2005).
— Una rareza bibliográfi ca: edición española de poemas religiosos del humanista polaco Juan Dantisco (1571-1576), MteCarm 106 (1998) 275-291.
— Un apologista tardío del Padre Gracián: el P. Antonio de los Reyes y sus "Vindicias" (1810-1811), MteCarm 91 (1983) 577-599.
— *Antonio Gracián Dantisco y la Biblioteca de El Escorial en su primera etapa (1571-1576)*, CD 208 (1995) 277-317, CCX (1997) 5-40.
LUIS DE LEÓN, *Obras completas castellanas*, Madrid 1951.
MANERO SOROLLA, Mª PILAR, *La peregrinación autobiográfica de Anastasio-Jerónimo (Gracián de*
la Madre de Dios), Revista de Literatura 2001 Vol. 630 Núm. 125, pp. 21-37.
— *Exilios y destierros en la vida y en la obra de María de Salazar*, Madrid, Castalia, 1988, pp. 51-59.
— *El exilio europeo de un carmelita descalzo (en el IV centenario de la expulsión del Carmen de Jerónimo Gracián)*, Departamento de Filología Española III (F. CC. Información) Universidad Complutense de Madrid, 1996.
MANRIQUE, ÁNGEL, La V. M. *Ana de Jesús, discípula y compañera de la S. M. Teresa de Jesús y principal aumento de su orden. Fundadora de Francia y Flandes*, Bruselas 1632.
MARAÑÓN, GREGORIO, *Antonio Pérez*, Madrid, 2002.
— *Españoles fuera de España*, Madrid 1961.
MARÍA DE SAN JOSÉ (SALAZAR), *Escritos espirituales*, Roma 1979.
MARIE DE St JOSEPH, *Le Père Gratien dans le développement de la Réforme Thérèsienne*,

Éditions du Carmel, Tarascon, II, 1962.
MÁRMOL, ANDREW DEL, *Excelencias, vida y trabajos del padre fray Gerónimo Gracián de la Madre*
de Dios Carmelita, Valladolid 1619. (According to the opinion of Nicholas Antonio, Andrew del Marmol was the only Editor of the work and Fr Christiopher Márquez, O.C., the effective author of the first part; the second was written by Fr himself; Mármol joined the two parts and edited them).
MAROTO, DANIEL DE PABLO, OCD, *María de San José (Salazar), heredera del espíritu de Santa Teresa y escritora de espiritualidad*, RevEsp 63 (2004) 213-250.
MARTÍN, TARSICIO, *Un apologista tardío del Padre Gracián: el P. Antonio de los Reyes y sus "Vindicias" (1810-1811)*, MteCarm 91 (1983) 577-599.
MARTÍNEZ, ISMAEL, O.CARM., *Los carmelitas. Historia de la Orden del Carmen. VI. Figuras del Carmelo*, BAC, Madrid 1996.
MATÍAS DEL NIÑO JESÚS, OCD, *El V. Hº Fr Juan de la Miseria, sus restos y sus escritos*, MteCarm 46 (1945) 36-43.
— *Documentos primitivos del Carmen Descalzo. El Discurso del Capítulo de Alcalá de 1581*, MteCarm 71 (1963) 255-269.
MEJÍA, RAFAEL, *Las fundaciones de las Carmelitas Descalzas en España y Portugal (1562-1995)*, Burgos 1998.
MENÉNDEZ PELAYO, MARCELINO, *Historia de los Heterodoxos Españoles*, BAC t. II, Madrid 1967.
MIR, MIGUEL, *Santa Teresa de Jesús. Su vida, su espíritu, sus fundaciones*, Madrid 1912, 2 vols.
MONTALVA, EFRÉN J.M., *La herencia teresiana*, Madrid 1975.
— *Santa Teresa por dentro*, Madrid 1973.
MORIONES, ILDEFONSO, *El Carmelo teresiano, páginas de su historia*, Vitoria 1978.
— *El P. Doria y el Carisma Teresiano* (edición privada), Roma 1994.
— *Jerôme Gracien de la Mère de Dieu*, en "Carmel" nº 104, junio 2002.
— *Rehabilitación pontificia del P. Jerónimo Gracián en 1595*, MteCarm 103 (1995) 453-491.
— *Las "Vindicias de la inocencia del Padre Gracián ": Testamento de Antonio de los Reyes*, MteCarm 106 (1998) 475-533.
— *Ana de Jesús y la herencia teresiana. ¿Humanismo cristiano o rigor primitivo?*, Teresianum, Roma, 1968.
— *Humor y espiritualidad en la Escuela Teresiana Primitiva*, Burgos 1982.
— *Un precursor del Doctorado Teresiano: Jerónimo Gracián de la Madre de Dios*, MteCarm 78 (1970) 131-142.
— *Bartolomé de Jesús, expulso (1588) y olvidado*, MteCarm 103 (1995) 579-584.
— *Antonio de los Reyes y la memoria histórica del Carmelo Teresiano*, MteCarm 104 (1996) 515-587.
— *A propósito del Capítulo de 1588*, MteCarm 105 (1997) 523-528.
MORUJÂO, ISABEL, *María de San José (Salazar) ocd, fundadora del primer Carmelo descalzo femenino*
en Portugal, RevEsp 63 (2004) 177- 211.
MUÑOZ JIMÉNEZ, JOSÉ MIGUEL, *El real convento de Carmelitas Descalzas de Santa Teresa de Madrid*, MteCarm 95 (1987) 495-505.
MURO, GASPAR, *Vida de la princesa de Éboli*, Madrid 1877.
NICOLÁS ANTONIO, *Hieronimus Gracián a Matre Dei*, en "Biblioteca Hispana Nova", vol I (pp. 567a-585b), Madrid 1783.
NOVALÍN, JOSÉ LUIS G., *El inquisidor general Fernando de Valdés (1483–1568). Su vida y su obra*, Oviedo 1968, 2 v.
ORCIBAL, JEAN, *La rencontre du Carmel thérésien avec les mystiques du Nord*, París 1959.

PACHO, ALBERTO, *La cautividad en Berbería. Dos cautivos: Miguel de Cervantes y Jerónimo Gracián*,
MteCarm 91 (1983) 361-382.
— *El P. Doria y la llegada del Carmelo Teresiano a Italia*, MteCarm 93 (1985) 163-169.
PACHO, EULOGIO, *Jerónimo Gracián de la Madre de Dios. Vida y obras*, MteCarm 91 (1983) 259-309.
— *Jerónimo Gracián, preceptista. Tratado de ortografía española*, MteCarm 91 (1987) 331-354.
— *Jerónimo Gracián de la Madre de Dios. ¿ Otra rehabilitación?*, MteCarm 109 (2001) 145-151.
PANEDAS, PABLO, *Agustinas descalzas 400 años (1597–1997)*, Valencia 1998.
PAZ Y MELIÁ, ANTONIO, *El embajador polaco Juan Dantisco en la corte de Carlos V (1524–1527)*, BRAE XI (1924) 54-69; 305-320; 427- 444; 586-600 y XII (1925) 73-93.
— *Otro erasmista español: Diego Gracián de Alderete, Secretario de Carlos V. Su correspondencia.*
Su Speravi, RABM t. V (190 1) 27-36, 125-139, 608-625.
PEDRA, JOSÉ ALBERTO, *Jerónimo Gracián de la Madre de Dios OCD: o herdeiro exilado*, Curitiba, 2003.
PIÑERO RAMÍREZ, PEDRO M., *La Sevilla imposible de Santa Teresa*,
Sevilla 1982.
Regla primitiva y Constituciones de las monjas Descalças de la Orden de Nuestra Señora la Virgen María del Monte Carmelo, Salamanca 1581.
Regla primitiva y Constituciones de la Provincia de los frayles Descalzos de la Orden de Nuestra Señora
la Virgen María del Monte Carmelo. Written and ordered with Apostolic authority, at the Provincial Chapter that took place in St Cyril College, part of the University of Alcalá de Henares, on 5th March, in 1581. Printed in Salamanca, by Peter Lasso. Year 1582.
Regula et Constitutiones fratrum Carmelitarum primitivae observantiae qui Discalciati nuncupantur, editae in Capitulo Provinciali Compluti celebrato, auctoritate Apostolica Sanctissimi domininostri Gregorij XIII, Divina provide(n)tia PP. Die quarto Martij, anno D(omi)ni 1581. Impresso en Alcalá, en casa de Hernán Ramírez. Año 1585.
RENAULT, EMMANUEL, *Ste Therése d'Avila et l'experience mystique*, París 1998.
RIBER, LORENZO, *Diego Gracián de Alderete, su familia y la Madre Teresa de Jesús*, BRAE XXXIV (1954) 225-255.
RIBERA, FRANCISCO DE, SI, *La Vida de la Madre Teresa de Jesús, fundadora de las Descalças y Descalços, compuesta por el Doctor F. de R., de la Compañía de Jesús, y repartida en cinco libros*, Salamanca 1590. (New edition, expanded with an introduction, copious notes and appendices by Fr Jaime Pons, Barcelona 1908).
ROBRES, ANDRÉS, F., *La Peregrinación de Anastasio de fray Jerónimo Gracián: misticismo... y memorialismo autojustifi cativo*, en "Actas de la VI Reunión Científica de la Fundación Española de Historia Moderna", Alcalá de Henares, 5-7 de Junio de 2000.
ROBRES LLUCH, RAMÓN, *San Juan de Ribera, Patriarca de Antioquia, Arzobispo y Virrey de Valencia, 1532–1611*, Barcelona 1960.
RODRÍGUEZ, OTILIO, *Leyenda áurea teresiana*, Madrid 1970.
— *Gracián, el amigo lejano*, MteCarm 88 (1980) 619-623.
— *Mariología del V. P. Jerónimo (Gracián) de la Madre de Dios, OCD*,
MteCarm 49 (1945) 369-388.
— *El testamento teresiano*, MteCarm 78 (1970) 11-83.
RODRÍGUEZ CARRETERO, MIGUEL, *Epytome de los Carmelitas de Andalucía y Murcia*, Primera edición del ms. original 18.118 de la Bibl. Nac. de Madrid, preparada por el P. Ismael Martínez Carretero, Sevilla 2000.

ROS, CARLOS, *Los Arzobispos de Sevilla. Luces y sombras en la sede hispalense*, Sevilla 1986.
ROSALES, LUIS, *Jerónimo Gracián de la Madre de Dios. Crónica de cautiverio y de misión*, Madrid 1942.
RUIZ, ALFONSO, *La correspondencia de Gracían con Santa Teresa vista desde el epistolario teresiano*,
MteCarm 91 (1983) 311-360.
— *Anécdotas teresianas*, Burgos 1981.
SAGGI, LUDOVICO, *Le origini dei Carmelitani Scalzi (1567–1593)*, Roma 1986.
SAN JUAN DE PIEDRAS ALBAS Y DE BENAVIDES, BERNARDINO DE MELGAR Y ABRÉU, MARQUÉS DE, *Fray Jerónimo Gracián de la Madre de Dios: insigne coautor de la reforma de Santa Teresa de Jesus / discurso leído ante la Real Academia de la Historia por el excmo. señor Marqués de San Juan de Piedras Albas en su recepción pública; y contestación del excmo. señor D. Juan Pérez de Guzmán y Gallo el día 30 de junio de 1918*, Madrid 1918.
SÁNCHEZ CANTÓN, FRANCISCO JAVIER, *Doña Leonor de Mascareñas y fray Juan de la Miseria*, Madrid 1918.
SANTA ANA, BELCHIOR DE, *Chronica dos Carmelitas Descalços do Reyno de Portugal*, Lisboa 1657, tomo I.
SÉROUET, PIERRE, *Jean de Brétigny (1556–1634). Aux origines du Carmel de France, de Bélgique et du Congo*, Lovaina 1974.
SILVERIO DE SANTA TERESA, O.C.D., *Historia del Carmen Descalzo en España, Portugal y América*,
Burgos 1935-1937. 15 vols.. — Vida de Santa Teresa de Jesús, Burgos 1935-1937, 5 v.
— *Procesos de beatificación y canonización de Santa Teresa de Jesús*, Burgos 1934-1935, 3 v.
— *Un comentario a las Siete Palabras, por el P. Jerónimo Gracián*, MteCarm 20 (1917) 173-175, 208-212, 229-232; 21 (1917) 105- 110.
— *Un libro de Santa Teresa de Jesús con notas del P. Gracián*, MteCarm 21 (1917) 242-246, 337-341.
SIMEÓN DE LA S.FAMILIA, *Panorama storico-bibliografico degli autori spirituali teresiani*. Roma 1972.
— *Prima Instructio Novitiarum Carmeli Teresiani - Opus hucusque ignotum M. Mariae a S. Joseph (Salazar)*, EphCarm XV (1964) 130-154.
SMET, JOAQUÍN, O.CARM., *Los carmelitas. Historia de la Orden del Carmenj Los orígenes. En busca*
de la identidad. II. Las reformas. En busca de la autenticidad. III, Las reformas. Personas, literatura, arte, BAC, Madrid 1987-1991.
STEGGINK, OTGER, O. CARM., *La reforma del Carmelo español, la visita canónica del general Rubeo*
y su encuentro con Santa Teresa (1566–1567), Roma 1965.
TERESA DE JESÚS, SANTA, *Obras completas*, ed. Efrén de la Madre de Dios, Madrid, BAC, 1974.
TOMÁS SANCHÍS, DIONISIO DE, *Jerónimo Gracián por tierras de Valencia, Alicante y Murcia*, MteCarm 91 (1983) 481-497.
TORRES SÁNCHEZ, CONCEPCIÓN, *Ana de Jesús. Cartas (1590–1621). Religiosidad y vida cotidiana*
en la clausura femenina del Siglo de Oro, Ediciones Universidad, Salamanca 1995.
— *Ana de Jesús (1545-1621)*, Ediciones del Orto, Madrid 1999.
URKIZA, JULEN, *Comienzos del Carmelo Teresiano francés. Búsqueda de candidatas (1604)*, Burgos 2004.
— *La Beata Ana de San Bartolomé y la transmisión del espíritu teresiano*, MteCarm 84 (1976) 105-110.